Moxon

Mechanick Exercises

ISBN: 978-1-948837-94-1

This classic reprint was produced from digital files in the archive.org digital collection, which may be found at http://www.archive.org. Omissions and/or errors in this book are due to either the physical condition of the original book or due to the scanning process. Cover design by Jon Townsend.

This edition of Moxon' **Mechanick Exercises** was originally published in 1703 (London).

Townsends
PO Box 415, Pierceton, IN 46562
www.Townsends.us

Mechanick Exercises:

OR THE

DOCTRINE

OF

HANDY-WORKS.

Applied to the Arts of { Smithing, Joinery, Carpentry, Turning, Bricklayery }

To which is added

Mechanick Dyalling: Shewing how to draw a true Sun-Dyal on any given Plane, however Scituated; only with the help of a ſtraight *Ruler* and a pair of *Compaſſes*, and without any *Arithmetical Calculation.*

The Third Edition.

By JOSEPH MOXON, *Fellow of the Royal Society, and Hydrographer to the late King* Charles.

LONDON:

Printed for *Dan. Midwinter* and *Tho. Leigh*, at the *Roſe and Crown* in St. *Paul's-Church-Yard.* 1703.

PREFACE.

I See no more *Reason*, why the *Sordidness* of *some Workmen*, *should be the cause of contempt upon* Manual Operations, *than that the excellent Invention of a* Mill *should be dispis'd, because a blind Horse draws in it. And tho' the* Mechanicks *be, by some, accounted Ignoble and Scandalous? yet it is very well known, that many Gentlemen in this Nation, of good Rank and high Quality, are conversant in* Handy-Works: *And other Nations exceed us in numbers of such. How pleasant and healthey this their Diversion is, their Minds and Bodies find; and how Harmless and Honest, all sober men may judge?*

That Geometry, Astronomy, Perspective, Musick, Navigation, Architecture, *&c. are excellent Sciences, all that know but their very Names will confess: Yet to what purpose would* Geometry *serve, were it not to contrive Rules for* Handy-Works? *Or how could* Astronomy *be known to any perfection, but by Instruments made by Hand?*

PREFACE.

What Perspective *should we have to delight our Sight? What* Musick *to ravish our Ears? What* Navigation *to Guard and Enrich our Country? Or what* Architecture *to defend us from the Inconveniencies of different Weather, without* Manual Operations? *Or how waste and useless would many of the Productions of this and other Counties be, were it not for* Manufactures.

To dive into the Original of the Mechanicks *is impossible, therefore I shall not offer at it; only I shall say, it is Rational to think, that the* Mechanicks *began with* Man, *he being the only Creature that Nature has imposed most Necessity upon to use it, endow'd with greatest Reason to contrive it, and adapted with properest Members (as Instruments) to perform it.*

Nor is it easie to find by any Authority, what part of the Mechanicks *was first Practised by* Man; *therefore I shall wave that too, and only consider, that if we our selves were the first Men, what Branch of the* Mechanicks *we should first Need, and have recourse to.*

I have considered, and Answer, That without the Invention of Smithing *primarily, most other* Mechanick *Invention would*

would be at a ſtand: The Inſtruments, or Tools, that are uſed in them, being either made of Iron, or ſome other matter, form'd by the help of Iron. But pray take Notice, that by Iron, I alſo mean Steel, it being originally Iron.

Nor would I have you underſtand, that when I name the Mechanicks, *I mean that rough and Barbarous ſort of working which is uſed by the Natives of* America, *and ſome other ſuch Places; for, though they did indeed make Houſes, Canoes, Earthen Pots, Bows, Arrows,* &c. *without the help of Iron, becauſe they had then none amongſt them: Yet ſince Iron is now known to them, they leave of their old way of working without it, and betake themſelves to the uſe of it. Nor are, at this day, (though now they have in part the uſe of Iron) their* Machines *made by good and ready Rules of* Art; *for they know neither of* Rule, Square, *or* Compaſs; *and what they do, is done by Tedious Working, and he that has the beſt Eye at Gueſſing, works beſt upon the* Straight, Square *or* Circle, *&c.*

The Lord Bacon, *in his* Natural Hiſtory, *reckons that* Philoſophy *would be improv'd, improv'd, by having the Secrets of all Trades lye open; not only because much* Experimental Philosophy, *is Coucht amongst them; but also that the* Trades *themselves might, by a* Philosopher, *be improv'd. Besides, I find, that one* Trade *may borrow many Eminent Helps in* Work *of another* Trade.

Hitherto I cannot learn that any hath undertaken this Task, though I could have wisht it had been performed by an abler hand then mine; yet, since it is not, I have vetured upon it.

I thought to have given these Exercises, *the Title of* The Doctrine of Handy-Crafts; *but when I better considered the true meaning of the Word* Handy-Crafts, *I found the* Doctrine *would not bear it; because* Hand-Craft *signifies* Cunning, *or* Sleight, *or* Craft *of the Hand, which cannot be taught by Words, but is only gained by* Practise *and* Exercise; *therefore I shall not undertake, that with the bare reading of these* Exercises, *any shall be able to perform these* Handy-Works; *but I may safely tell you, that these are the* Rules *that every one that will endeavour to perform them*

them muſt follow; and that by the true obſerving them, he may, according to his ſtock of Ingenuity and Diligence, ſooner or later, inure his hand to the Cunning or Craft of working like a Handy-Craft, and conſequently be able to perform them in time.

For the Reaſon aforeſaid I intend to begin with Smithing, which comprehends not only the Black-Smith's Trade, but takes in all Trades which uſe either Forge or File, from the Anchor-Smith, to the Watch-Maker; they all working by the ſame Rules, tho' not with equal exactneſs, and all uſing the ſame Tools, tho' of ſeveral Sizes from thoſe the common Black-Smith uſes, and that according to the various purpoſes they are applied to: And in order to it, I ſhall firſt ſhew you how to ſet up a Forge, and what Tools you muſt uſe in the Black-Smith's work; then the Rules, and ſeveral Circumſtances of Forging, till your Work come to the File: Then of the ſeveral Sorts of Iron that are commonly uſed; and what ſort is fitteſt for each purpoſe. Afterwards of Filing in general, and the Rules to be obſerved in it, in the making of

PREFACE.

Jacks, Hinges, Screws, Clocks, Watches, *&c.* *In which Examples, you will find all other Sorts of* Forging *or* Filing *work whatsoever comprehended. And lastly, as a close to* Smithing, *I shall Exercise upon* Steel, *and its several Sorts, and how to Order and Temper it for its several Uses; and what Sort is fittest for each particular purpose; as which is fittest for* Edge-Tools, *which for* Springs, *which for* Punches, *&c.*

Some perhaps would have thought it more Proper, to have introduced these Exercises *with a more Curious, and less Vulgar Art, than that of* Smithing; *but I am not of their Opinion; for* Smithing *is in all parts, as curious a* Handy-Craft, *as any is: Besides, it is a great Introduction to most other* Handy-Works, *as* Joynery, Turning, *&c. they (with the* Smith) *working upon the* Sraight, Square, *or* Circle, *though with different* Tools, *upon different* Matter; *and they all having dependance upon the* Smith's Trade, *and not the* Smith *upon them.*

Joseph Moxon.

Page.1.

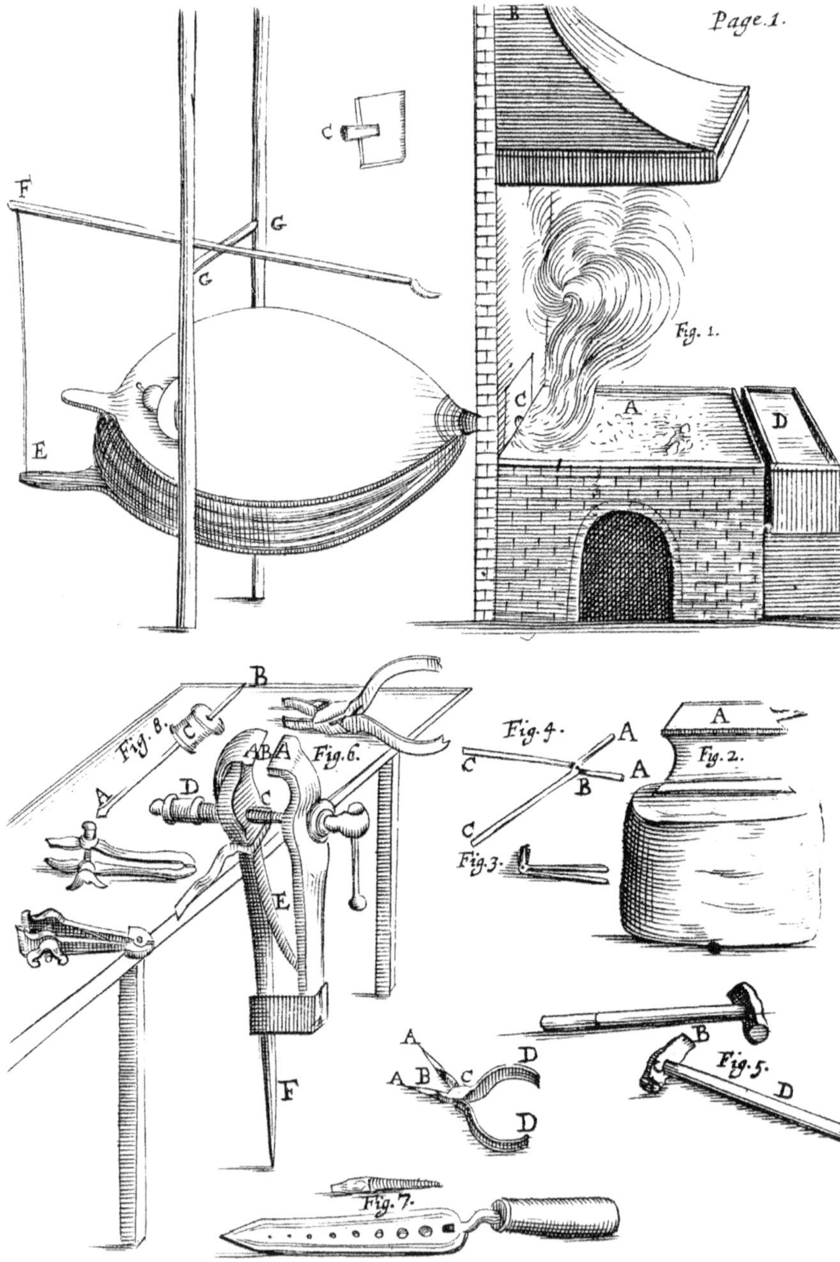

MECHANICK EXERCISES:

OR,

The Doctrine of *Handy-Works*.

Of SMITHING *in General.*

Definition.

SMITHING *is an Art-Manual, by which an irregular Lump (or ſeveral Lumps) of Iron, is wrought into an intended Shape.*

This Definition, needs no Explanation; therefore I ſhall proceed to give you an Account of the Tools a Smith uſes; not but that (they being ſo common) I ſuppoſe you do already know them; but partly becauſe they may require ſome precaution in ſetting them up fitteſt to your uſe; and partly becauſe it behoves you to know the Names, Smiths call the ſeveral parts of them by; that when I name them in Smith's Language (as I ſhall oft have occaſion to do in theſe *Exerciſes*) you may the eaſier underſtand them, as you read them.

Of ſetting up a Smith's Forge.

THE *Hearth*, or Fire-place of the *Forge* marked A. (in Plate 1.) is to be built up from your floor with Brick about two foot and an half, or ſometimes two foot nine Inches high, according to the purpoſe you deſign your *Forge* for; for if your *Forge* be intended for heavy work, your *Hearth* muſt lie lower than it need be for light work, for eaſineſs of management, and ſo broad as you think convenient: It may be built with hollow Arches underneath, to ſet ſeveral things out of the way. The Back of the *Forge* is built upright to the top of the Ceiling, and incloſed over the Fire-place with a *Hovel*, which ends in a *Chimney* to carry away the Smoak, as B. In the back of the *Forge* againſt the Fire-place, is fixed a thick Iron Plate, and a taper Pipe in it about five Inches long, called a *Tewel*, or (as ſome call it) a *Tewel-Iron* marked *, which Pipe comes through the Back of the *Forge*, as at C. Into this taper Pipe or *Tewel* is placed the Noſe, or Pipe of the *Bellows*. The Office of this *Tewel*, is only to preſerve the Pipe of the Bellows, and the back of the *Forge* about the Fire-place from burning. Right againſt the Back is placed at about twenty Inches, or two foot diſtance, the *Trough*, and reaches commonly through the whole breadth of the *Forge*, and is as broad and deep as you think good, as at D. The *Bellows* is placed behind the Back of the *Forge*, and hath as aforeſaid, its Pipe fitted into the Pipe of the *Tewel*, and hath one of its Boards fixed ſo that it move not upwards or downwards. At the Ear of the upper Bellows board is faſtened a *Rope*, or ſometimes a *Thong* of Leather, or an Iron *Chain* or *Rod*, as E; which reaches up to the *Rocker*, and is faſtened there to the farther end of the Handle, as at F. This *Handle* is faſtened a croſs a *Rock-ſtaff*, which moves between two Cheeks upon the *Center-pins*, in two Sockets, as at G. So that by drawing down this Handle, the moving Board of the *Bellows* riſes, and by a conſiderable weight ſet on the top of its upper Board ſinks down again, and by this Agitation performs the Office of a pair of *Bellows*.

Of

Of the Anvil.

THE ſhape of a Black Smith's *Anvil* I have inſerted in this Figure, though it is ſometimes made with a *Pike*, or *Bickern*, or *Beak-iron*, at one end of it, whoſe uſe I ſhall ſhew you when I come to round hollow work. Its *Face* muſt be very flat and ſmooth, without Flaws, and ſo hard that *a File will not touch it* (as Smiths ſay, when a File will not cut, or race it.) The upper Plain A. is called the *Face*; it is commonly ſet upon a wooden *Block*, that it may ſtand very ſteady and ſolid, and about two foot high from the floor, or ſometimes higher, according to the ſtature of the Perſon that is to work at it.

Of the Tongs.

THere are two ſorts of *Tongs* uſed by Smiths; the one the *Straight-noſed Tongs*, uſed when the work is ſhort, and ſomewhat flat, and generally for all Plate Iron. The other *Crooked-nos'd Tongs*, to be uſed for the forging ſmall Bars, or ſuch thicker work, as will be held within the Returns of their *Chaps*. The *Chaps* are placed near the Joint, becauſe, that conſidering the length of the *Handles*, they hold the Iron faſter than they would do, were they placed farther from the Joint, as in the Fig. 3. 4. A the *Chaps*, B the *Joint*, CC the *Handles*.

Of the Hammer, *and the* Sledge.

THere are ſeveral ſorts of *Hammers* uſed by Black-Smiths; as firſt the *Hand-hammer*, which is ſometimes bigger, or leſs, according to the Strength of the Work-man; but it is a *Hammer* of ſuch weight, that it may be weilded, or governed, with one hand at the *Anvil*. Secondly, the *Up-hand Sledge*, uſed by under-Workmen, when the Work is not of the largeſt, yet requires help to batter, or *draw it out*; they uſe it with both their hands before them, and ſeldom lift their *Hammer* higher than their head. Thirdly, the *About Sledge* is the biggeſt *Hammer* of all, and is alſo uſed by under-Workmen, for the battering, or *drawing out* of the largeſt Work; and then they hold the farther end of the *Handle* in both their Hands, and ſwinging the *Sledge* above their Heads, they at Arms end let fall as heavy a Blow as they can upon the Work. There is alſo another *Hammer* uſed by them, which they call a *Rivetting-hammer*. This is the ſmalleſt *Hammer* of all, and very rarely uſed at the *Forge*, unleſs your Work prove very ſmall; but upon cold Iron it is uſed for rivetting, or ſetting ſtraight, or crooking ſmall work. In Fig. 5. A the *Face*, B the *Pen*, C the *Eye*, D the *Handle*.

Of the Vice.

THE *Vice* muſt be ſet up very firmly that it ſhake not, and ſtand upright with its *Chaps*, parallel or range with your *Work-bench*; becauſe ſquare filing, is a great piece of good Workmanſhip in a Smith; and ſhould the Vice not ſtand upright, and range with the Work-bench, the *Chaps* pinching upon two ſquare ſides, would make the top ſide of your work either lean towards you, or from you; and conſequently you filing (as a good Workman ought to do) upon the flat, or Horizontal Plain of your work, would take off more of that Angle, or Edge, which riſes higher than the Plain, and leſs off that Edge, that lies lower than the Plain; ſo that one Angle being higher, or lower, than the other, your work inſtead of being filed *Square*, would be filed *Square-wiſe*, when you ſhall have filed all its flat ſides, and that more or leſs, according to the leaning of the *Chaps* of your *Vice*. AA the *Face*, hath its two

two ends in a ſtraight Line with the middle of its *Face*, or *Plain*. B the *Chaps* muſt be cut with a Baſtard Cut, and very well tempered; C the *Screw Pin*, cut with a ſquare ſtrong Worm. D the *Nut*, or *Screw Box*, hath alſo a ſquare *Worm*, and is brazed into the round *Box*. E the *Spring* muſt be made of good Steel, and very well temper'd: Where note that the wider the two ends of the *Spring* ſtand aſunder, the wider it throws the *Chaps* of the *Vice* open. F the *Foot* muſt be ſtraight, and therefore will be the ſtronger to bear good heavy blows upon the work ſcrewed in the *Chaps* of the *Vice*, that it neither bow, or tremble.

Of the Hand-Vice.

OF the *Hand-Vice* are two Sorts, one is called the *Broad Chapt Hand-Vice*, the other the *Square Nos'd Hand-Vice*. The Office of the *Hand-Vice*, is to hold ſmall work in, that may require often turning about; it is held in the left hand, and each part of your work turned upwards ſucceſſively, that you have occaſion to file with your right. The *Square-nos'd Hand-Vice* is ſeldom uſed, but for filing ſmall Globulous Work, as the Heads of Pins that round off towards the Edges, *&c.* And that becauſe the *Chaps* do not ſtand ſhouldering in the way, but that the flat of the *File* may the better come at the Edges. Their *Chaps* muſt be cut as the *Vice* aforeſaid, and well tempered.

Of the Plyers.

PLyers are of two Sorts, *Flat Nos'd*, and *Round Nos'd*. Their Office is to hold, and faſten upon all ſmall work, and to fit it in its place. The *Round Nos'd Plyers* are uſed for turning, or bowing Wyer, or ſmall Plate, into a circular Form. The *Chaps* of the *Flat Nos'd Plyes*, muſt alſo be cut and temper'd, as the *Chaps* of the *Vice.* A the *Noſe*, B the *Chaps*, C the *Joint*, DD the *Handles.*

Of the Drill, *and* Drill-Bow.

DRills are uſed for the making ſuch Holes as *Punches* will not conveniently ſerve for; as a piece of work that hath already its Shape, and muſt have an hole, or more, made in it. Here the force of a *Punch*, will ſet your work out of order and ſhape, becauſe it will both batter the Surface of the Iron, and ſtretch its Sides out: The ſhank of a Key alſo, or ſome ſuch long Hole, the *Punch* cannot ſtrike, becauſe the Shank is not forged with ſubſtance ſufficient; but the *Drill*, tho' your work be filed and poliſh'd, never batters or ſtretches it,but cuts a true round Hole, juſt in the point you firſt place it. You muſt have ſeveral Sizes of *Drills*, according as your work may require. The ſhape in Fig. 8. is enough to ſhew the Faſhion of it; but it muſt be made of good Steel, and well temper'd. A the *Point*, AB the *Shank*, C the *Drill-barrel*: Where note, that the bigger the *Drill-barrel* is, the eaſier it runs about, but leſs ſwift.

And as you muſt be provided with ſeveral *Drills*, ſo you may ſometimes require more than one *Drill-bow*, or at leaſt, ſeveral *Drill-ſtrings*; the ſtrongeſt Strings for the largeſt *Drills*, and the ſmalleſt *Strings* for the ſmalleſt *Drills*: But you muſt remember, that whether you uſe a ſmall or ſtrong *String*, you keep your *Drill-Bow* ſtraining your String pretty ſtiff, or elſe your String will not carry your Barrel briskly about. But your String and Bow, muſt both be accommodated to the Size of your *Drill*; and if both, or either, be too ſtrong, they will break, or bend your *Drill*; or if too weak, they will not carry about the Barrel, as aforeſaid. The

The *Drill-Plate*, or *Breast-Plate*, is only a piece of flat Iron, fixt upon a flat Board, which Iron hath an hole punched a little way into it, to set the blunt end of the Shank of the *Drill* in, when you drill a hole: Workmen instead of it, many times use the *Hammer*, into which they prick a hole a little way on the side of it, and so set the *Hammer* against their Breast.

Of the Screw-Plate, *and its* Taps.

THE *Screw-Plate* is a Plate of Steel well temper'd, with several holes in it, each less than other, and in those *Holes* are *Threds* grooved inwards; into which *Grooves*, fit the respective *Taps* that belong to them. The *Taps* that belong to them, are commonly made tapering towards the Point, as Fig. 7. shews. But these tapering *Taps*, will not serve for some sorts of works, as I shall shew in its proper place.

These are the most Essential Tools used in the Black-Smith's Trade; but some accidental work, may require some accidental Tools, which, as they may fall in, I shall give you an account of in convenient place.

Of Forging *in general.*

I Think it needless to tell you how to make your Fire, or blow it, because they are both but Labourers work; nor how little, or big, it need to be, for your own reason will, by the Size of your work, teach you that; only let me tell you the Phrase Smiths use for[make the Fire] is, *Blow up the Fire*, or sometimes, *Blow up the Coals.*

When it is burning with the Iron in it, you must, with the *Slice*, clap the Coals upon the out-side close together, to keep the heat in the body of the Fire; and as oft as you find the Fire begin to break out, clap them close again, and with the *Waſher* dipt in Water, wet the out-ſide of the Fire to damp the out-ſide, as well to ſave Coals, as to ſtrike the force of the Fire into the in-ſide, that your work may heat the ſooner. But you ought oft to draw your work a little way out of the Fire, to ſee how it *takes its Heat*, and quickly thruſt it in again, if it be not hot enough: For each purpoſe your work is deſigned to, ought to have a proper *Heat* ſuitable to that purpoſe, as I ſhall ſhew you in the ſeveral *Heats* of Iron: For if it be too cold, it will not *feel the weight of the Hammer* (as Smiths ſay, when it will not batter under the *Hammer)* and if it be too hot, it will *Red-ſear*, that is, break, or crack under the *Hammer*, while it is working between hot and cold.

Of the ſeveral Heats *Smiths take of their Iron.*

THere are ſeveral degrees of *Heats* Smiths take of their Iron, each according to the purpoſe of their work. As firſt, a *Blood-red Heat*. Secondly, a *White Flame Heat*. Thirdly, a *Sparkling*, or *Welding Heat*.

The *Blood-red Heat* is uſed when Iron hath already its form and ſize, as ſometimes ſquare Bars, and Iron Plates, *&c.* have, but may want a little Hammering to ſmooth it. Uſe then the Face of your *Hand-hammer*, and with light flat Blows, hammer down the irregular Riſings into the Body of your Iron, till it be ſmooth enough for the File. And note, that it behoves a good Workman, to hammer his Work as true as he can; for one quarter of an hour ſpent at the *Forge*, may ſave him an hours work at the *Vice*.

The *Flame*, or *White Heat*, is uſed when your Iron hath not its Form or Size, but muſt be forged into both; and then you muſt take a piece of Iron thick enough, and with the *Pen* of your *Ham-*

Hammer, (or ſometimes, according to the ſize of your work, uſe two or three pair of hands with *Sledges* to) batter it out; or, as Workmen call it, to *draw it out*; till it comes to its breadth, and pretty near its ſhape; and ſo by ſeveral *Heats*, if your work require them, frame it into Form and Size; then with the Face of your *Hand-hammer*, ſmooth your work from the Dents the *Pen* made, as you did with a *Blood-red Heat*.

A *Sparkling*, or *Welding-heat*, is only uſed when you *double up* your Iron (as Smiths call it) to make it thick enough for your purpoſe, and ſo *weld*, or work in the *doubling* into one another, and make it become one entire lump; or it is uſed when you join ſeveral Bars of Iron together to make them thick enough for your purpoſe, and work them into one Bar; or elſe it is uſed when you are to join, or *weld* two pieces of Iron together end to end, to make them long enough; but, in this caſe, you muſt be very quick at the *Forge*; for when your two ends are throughout of a good *Heat*, and that the inſide of the Iron be almoſt ready to Run, as well as the outſide, you muſt very haſtily ſnatch them both out of the Fire together, and (after you have with the Edge of your *Hammer* ſcraped off ſuch Scales or Dirt as may hinder their incorporating) with your utmoſt diligence clap your left hand-piece, upon your right hand-piece, and with all ſpeed (leſt you loſe ſome part of your good Heat) fall to Hammering them together, and work them ſoundly into one another: and this, if your Bars be large, will require another, or ſomtimes two or three pair of Hands beſides your own to do: but if it be not throughly *welded* at the firſt *Heat*, you muſt reiterate your *Heats* ſo oft, till they be throughly *welded*; then with a *Flame-heat* (as

before

before) ſhape it, and afterwards ſmooth it with a *Blood-red Heat*. To make your Iron come the ſooner to a *Welding-heat*, you muſt now and then with your *Hearth-ſtaff* ſtir up the Fire, and throw up thoſe Cinders the Iron may have run upon; for they will never burn well, but ſpoil the reſt of the Coals; and take a little white Sand between your Finger and your Thumb, and throw upon the heating Iron, then with your Slice, quickly clap the outſide of your Fire down again; and with your *Waſher* dipt in Water, damp the outſide of the Fire to keep the Heat in.

But you muſt take ſpecial Care that your Iron *burn* not in the Fire, that is, that it do not *run* or melt; for then your Iron will be ſo brittle, that it will not endure Forging without breaking, and ſo hard, that a *File* will not touch it.

Some Smiths uſe to ſtrew a little white Sand upon the *Face* of the *Anvil* alſo, when they are to hammer upon a *Welding-heat*; for they ſay it makes the Iron *weld*, or incorporate the better.

If through Miſtake, or ill management, your Iron be too thin, or too narrow towards one of the ends; then if you have ſubſtance enough (and yet not too long) you may *up-ſet* it, that is, take a *Flame-heat*, and ſet the heated end upright upon the *Anvil*, and hammer upon the cold end, till the heated end be beat, or *up-ſet*, into the Body of your Work. But if it be a long piece of Work, aud you fear its length may wrong the middle, you muſt hold it in your left hand, and lay it flat on the *Anvil*; but ſo as the heated end intended to be *up-ſet*, may lie a little over the further ſide of the *Anvil*, aud then with your *Hand-hammer* in your right hand, beat upon the heated end of your work, minding that every ſtroak you take, you hold your work ſtiff

ſtiff againſt the *Face* of the *Hammer*. Afterwards ſmooth it again with a *Blood-red Heat*.

If you are to Forge a *Shoulder* on one, or each ſide of your work, lay the Shank of your Iron at the place where your *Shoulder* muſt be on the edge of your *Anvil* (that edge which is moſt convenient to your hand) that if more *Shoulders* be to be made, turn them all ſucceſſively, and hammer your Iron ſo, as that the Shank of the Iron that lies on the flat of the *Anvil*, feel as well the weight of your Blows, as the *Shoulder* at the edge of the *Anvil*; for ſhould you lay your blows on the edge of the *Anvil* only, it would inſtead of flatting the Shank to make the *Shoulder*, cut your work through.

Your Work will ſometimes require to have holes punched in it at the Forge, you muſt then make a Steel *Punch* to the ſize and ſhape of the hole you are to ſtrike, and harden the point of it without tempering, becauſe the heat of the Iron will ſoften it faſt enough, and ſometimes too faſt, but then you muſt re-harden it; then taking a *Blood-heat* of your Iron, or if it be very large, almoſt a *Flame-heat*; lay it upon your *Anvil*, and with your left hand, place the point of the *Punch* where the hole muſt be, and with the *Hand-hammer* in your right hand punch the hole; or if your work be heavy, you may hold it in your left hand, and with your Punch fixed at the end of a *Hoop-ſtick*, or ſome ſuch Wood, hold the ſtick in your right hand, and place the point of your *Punch* on the work where the hole muſt be, and let another Man ſtrike, till your Punch come pretty near the bottom of your work; which when it does, the ſides of your work round about the hole, will riſe from the Face of the *Anvil*, and your Punch will print a bunching mark upon the hole of a *Bolſter*, that is, a thick a thick Iron with a hole in it, and placing your Punch, as before, ſtrike it through. But you muſt note, that as oft as you ſee your Punch heat, or change Colour, you take it out of the hole, and pop it into Water to re-harden it, or elſe it will batter in the hole you intend to ſtrike, and not only ſpoil it ſelf, but the Work too, by running aſide in the Work. Having punched it through on the one ſide, turn the other ſide of your work, and with your Hammer ſet it flat and ſtraight, and with a *Blood-heat* punch it through on the other ſide alſo; ſo ſhall that hole be fit for the *File*, or ſquare bore, if the curioſity of your purpoſed Work cannot allow it to paſs without filing. When your Work is Forged, do not quench it in water to cool it, but throw it down upon the *Floor*, or *Hearth*, to cool of it ſelf; for the quenching it in water will harden it; as I ſhall ſhortly ſhew you, when I come to the Tempering of Steel.

Of Brazing *and* Soldering.

YOU may have occaſion ſometimes to *Braze* or *Solder* a piece of work; but it is uſed by Smiths only, when their work is ſo thin, or ſmall, that it will not endure *Welding*. To do this, take ſmall pieces of Braſs, and lay them on the place that muſt be brazed, and ſtrew a little Glaſs beaten to powder on it to make it run the ſooner, and give it a *Heat* in the *Forge*, till (by ſometimes drawing it a little way out of the Fire) you ſee the Braſs run. But if your work be ſo ſmall, or thin, that you may fear the Iron will run as ſoon as the Braſs, and ſo you loſe your work in the Fire, then you muſt make a *Loam* of three parts Clay, and one part Horſe-dung, and after they are wrought and mingled very well together in your hands, wrap your work with the Braſs, and a little beaten Glaſs upon

the

the place to be brazed close in the *Loam*, and laying it a while upon the *Hearth* of the *Forge* to dry, put the lump into the Fire, and blow the *Bellows* to it, till you perceive it have a full *Heat*, that is, till the Lump look like a well burnt Coal of Fire; then take it out of the Fire, and let it cool: Afterwards break it up, and take out your Work.

Thus much of Forging in general. It remains now, that you know what sorts of Iron are fittest for the several Uses, you may have occasion to apply them.

Of several Sorts of Iron, *and their proper Uses.*

IT is not my purpose, in this place, to tell you how Iron is made, I shall defer that till I come to treat of Mettals, and their Refinings. Let it at present satisfie those that know it not, that Iron is, by a violent Fire, melted out of hard Stones, called *Iron-Stones*; of these *Iron-Stones*, many Countries have great plenty. But because it wastes such great quantities of Wood to draw the Iron from them, it will not, in many Places, quit cost to use them. In most parts of *England*, we have abundance of these *Iron-Stones*; but our *English* Iron, is generally a course sort of Iron, hard and brittle, fit for Fire-bars, and other such course Uses; unless it be about the Forrest of *Dean*, and some few places more, where the Iron proves very good.

Swedish Iron is of all Sorts, the best we use in *England*. It is a fine tough sort of Iron, will best endure the Hammer, and is softest to file; and therefore most coveted by Workmen, to work upon.

Spanish Iron, would be as good as *Swedish* Iron, were it not subject to *Red-sear*, (as Workmen phrase it) that is to crack betwixt hot and cold. Therefore when it falls under your hands, you

must

muſt tend it more earneſtly at the Forge. But tho' it be good, tough, ſoft Iron, yet for many Uſes, Workmen will refuſe it, becauſe it is ſo ill, and un-evenly wrought in the Bars, that it coſts them a great deal of labour to ſmooth it; but it is good for all great works that require *welding*, as the bodies of Anvils, Sledges, large Bell-clappers, large Peſtles for Mortars, & all thick ſtrong Bars, *&c.* But it is particularly choſen by *Anchor-Smiths*, becauſe it abides the Heat better than other Iron, and when it is well wrought, is tougheſt.

There is ſome Iron comes from *Holland* (tho' in no great quantity) but is made in *Germany*. This Iron is called *Dort Squares*, only becauſe it comes to us from thence, and is wrought into ſquare Bars three quarters of an Inch ſquare. It is a bad, courſe Iron, and only fit for ſlight Uſes, as Window-Bars, Brewers-Bars, Fire-Bars, *&c.*

There is another ſort of Iron uſed for making of *Wyer*, which of all Sorts is the ſofteſt and tougheſt: But this Sort is not peculiar to any Country, but is indifferently made where any Iron is made, though of the worſt ſort; for it is the firſt Iron that runs from the *Stone* when it is melting, and is only preſerved or the making of *Wyer*.

By what hath been ſaid, you may ſee that the ſofteſt and tougheſt Iron is the beſt: Therefore when you chuſe Iron, chuſe ſuch as bows ofteneſt before it break, which is an Argument of toughneſs; and ſee it break ſound within, be grey of Colour like broken Lead, and free from ſuch gliſtering Specks you ſee in broken *Antimony*, no flaws or diviſions in it; for theſe are Arguments that it is ſound, and well wrought at the Mill.

Of

Of Filing *in General.*

THE ſeveral ſorts of Files that are in common uſe are the *Square*, the *Flat*, the *three Square*, the *half Round*, the *Round*, the *Thin File*, *&c.* All theſe ſhapes you muſt have of ſeveral *Sizes*, and of ſeveral *Cuts*. You muſt have them of ſeveral ſizes, as well becauſe you may have ſeveral ſizes of work, as for that it ſometimes falls out that one piece of work may have many parts in it joined and fitted to one another, ſome of them great, and others ſmall; And you muſt have them of ſeveral *Cuts*, becauſe the *Rough-tooth'd File* cuts faſter than the *Baſtard-tooth'd File*, the *Fine-tooth'd File* faſter than the *Smooth-tooth'd File*.

The *Rough* or *Courſe-tooth'd File* (which if it be large, is called a *Rubber*) is to take off the unevenneſs of your work which the *Hammer* made in the Forging; the *Baſtard-tooth'd file* is to take out of your work, the deep cuts, or file-ſtrokes, the *Rough-file* made; the *Fine-tooth'd file* is to take out the cuts, or file-ſtrokes, the *Baſtard-file* made; and the *Smooth-file* is to take out thoſe cuts, or file-ſtrokes, that the *Fine file* made.

Thus you ſee how the *Files* of ſeveral *Cuts* ſucceed one another, till your Work is ſo ſmooth as it can be filed. You may make it yet ſmoother with *Emerick*, *Tripoli*, *&c.* But of that in its proper place, becauſe it ſuits not with this Section of *Filing*.

You muſt take care when you uſe the *Rough File*, that you go very lightly over thoſe dents the *Hammer* made in your work, unleſs your work be forged ſomewhat of the ſtrongeſt, for the dents being irregularities in your work, if you ſhould file away as much in them, as you do off the Eminencies or Riſings, your work (whether it be ſtraight or circular) would be as irregular, as it was before you filed it: And when

when you file upon the Prominent, or rising Parts of your Work, with your *course cut File*, you must also take care that you file them not more away than you need, for you may easily be deceived; because the *course File* cuts deep, and makes deep scratches in the Work; and before you can take out those deep scratches with your finer cut Files, those places where the Risings were when your work was forged, may become dents to your Hammer dents; therefore file not those Risings quite so low, as the dents the Hammer made, but only so low as that the scratches the *Rough-file* makes may lie as low, or deep in your work, as your Hammer dents do; for then, when you come with your smoother Cut Files, after your *Rough-file*, the scratches of your *Rough-file*, and your Hammer-strokes, or dents, may both come out together. But to do this with greater certainty, hold your File so, that you may keep so much of the length of your File as you can to rub, range, (or, as near range as you can) upon the length of your work; for so shall the File enter upon the second Rising on your work, before it goes off the first, and will slip over, and not touch the dent or hollow between the two Risings, till your Risings are brought into a straight line with your hollow dent. But of this more shall be said when I come to the Practice of Filing, upon several particular sorts of work.

If it be a square Bar, (or such like) you are to file upon, all its Angles, or Edges, must be left very sharp and straight. Therefore your *Vice* being well set up, according to foregoing Directions, you must in your filing athwart over the *Chaps* of the *Vice*, be sure to carry both your hands you hold the *file* in, truly Horizontal, or flat over the Work; for should you let either of your hands mount, the other would dip, and the edge of that Square it dips upon would be taken off; and should you let your hand move never so little circularly, both the Edges you file upon would be taken off, and the Middle of your intended Flat would be left with a Rising on it. But this Hand-craft, you must attain to by Practice; for it is the great Curiosity in Filing.

If it be a round Piece, or Rod of Iron, you are to file upon, what you were forbid upon Square Work, you must perform on the Round for you must dip your Handle-hand, and mount your end-hand a little, and laying pritting near the end of your File to the Work, file circularly upon the Work, by mounting your Handle-hand by degrees, and dipping your End-hand, in such manner, as when the Middle of your File comes about the top of your Work, your File may be flat upon it, and as you continue your stroaks forwards, still keep your hands moving circularly till you have finished your full Stroak, that is, a Stroak the whole length of the File. By this manner of Circular filing, you keep your Piece, or Rod round; but should you file flat upon the top of your work, so many times as you shall remove, or turn your work in the *Vice*, so many Flats, or Squares, you would have in your work; which is contrary to your purpose.

When you thrust your *File* forwards, lean heavy upon it, because the *Teeth* of the *File* are made to cut forwards; but when you draw your *File* back, to recover another thrust, lift, or bear the File lightly just above the work; for it cuts not coming back.

Thus much of FILING in General.

Of the making of Hinges, Locks, Keys, Screws, and Nuts, Small and Great.

Of Hinges.

IN *Fig.* 1. A the *Tail*, B the *Croſs*, C D D D D E the *Joint*, D D D D the *Pin-hole*. When the *Joint* at C on the *Tail*, is pind in the *Joint* at E in the *Croſs*, the whole *Hinge* is called a *Croſs-Garnet*.

Hinges, if they be ſmall (as for Cup-board doors; *Boxes*, *&c.*) are cut out of cold Plate Iron with the (*a*) *Cold-Chiſſel*, but you mark the out-lines of your intended *Hinge*, as *Fig.* 1. the *Croſs-Garnet*, either with Chalk, or elſe raſe upon the Plate with the corner of the *Cold-Chiſſel*, or any other hardned Steel that will ſcratch a bright ſtroke upon the Plate; and then laying the Plate flat upon the *Anvil*, if the Plate be large, or upon the (*b*) *Stake*, if the Plate be ſmall, take the *Cold-Chiſſel* in your left hand, and ſet the edge of it upon that Mark, or Raſe, and with the *Hand-hammer* in your right hand, ſtrike upon the head of the *Cold-Chiſſel*, till you cut, or rather punch the edge of the *Cold-Chiſſel*, almoſt thro' the Plate in that Place, I ſay, almoſt through, becauſe, ſhould you ſtrike it quite through, the edge of the *Cold-Chiſſel* would be in danger of battering, or elſe breaking; for the *Face* of the *Anvil* is hardned Steel, and a light blow upon its *Face* would wrong the edge of the *Cold-Chiſſel*; beſides, it ſometimes happens, that the *Anvil*, or *Stake*, is not all over ſo hard as it ſhould be, and then the *Cold-Chiſſel* would cut the *Face* of the *Anvil*, or *Stake*, and conſequently ſpoil it: Therefore when the edge of the *Cold-Chiſſel* comes pretty near the bot-

Plate 2.

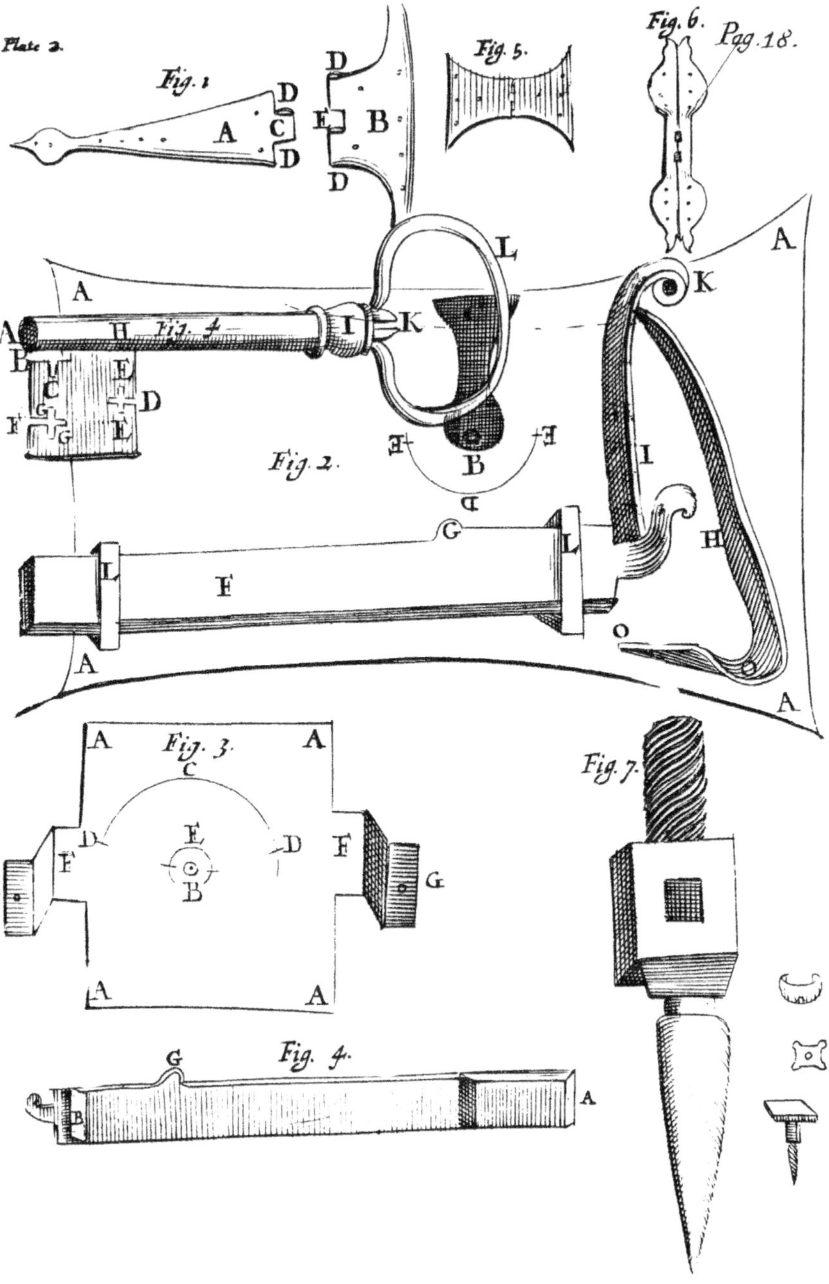

Pag. 18.

bottom of the Plate, you muſt lay but light blows upon the *Cold-Chiſſel*; and yet you muſt ſtrike the edge of the *Cold-Chiſſel* ſo near through the bottom of the Plate, that you may break the remaining ſubſtance aſunder with your Fingers, or with a pair of *Plyers*, or ſometimes by pinching the Plate in the *Vice*, with the Cut place cloſe to the Superficies of the *Chaps* of the *Vice*; and then with your Fingers and Thumb, or your whole hand, wriggle it quite aſunder. But having cut one breadth of the *Cold-Chiſſel*, remove the edge of it forward in the Raſe, and cut another breadth, and ſo move it ſucceſſively, till your whole intended ſhape be cut out of the Plate.

When you cut out an *Hinge*, you muſt leave on the length of the Plate A B in this Figure, Plate enough to lap over for the *Joints*, I mean, to *Turn*, or *Double* about a round Pin, ſo big as you intend the Pin of your *Hinge* ſhall be, and alſo Plate enough to *Weld* upon the inſide of the *Hinge* below the *Pin-hole* of the *Joint*, that the *Joint* may be ſtrong.

The ſize, or diameter of the *Pin-hole*, ought to be about twice the thickneſs of the Plate you make the *Hinge* of, therefore lay a wyre of ſuch a diameter towards the end B, in this Figure on

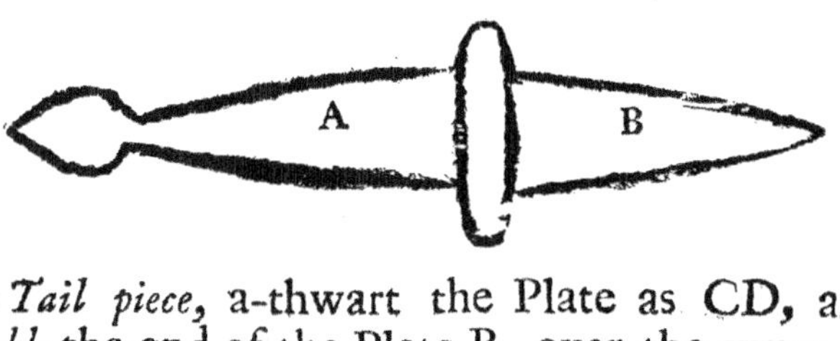

the *Tail piece*, a-thwart the Plate as CD, and *Double* the end of the Plate B, over the wyre to lap over it, and reach as far as it can upon the end A; then *hammer* the Plate that is lap'd over the wyre cloſe to the wyre, to make the *Pin-hole* round; but if your Plate be thick, it will require the taking of an *Heat* to make the *hammer* the cloſer to the wyre, and conſequently make the *Pin-hole* the rounder: Your work may alſo ſometimes require to be Screwed into the *Vice*, with the doubled end upwards, and the bottom ſide of the wyre cloſe againſt the *Chaps* of the *Vice*, and then to *hammer* upon the very top of the *Pin-hole* to round it at the end alſo. When you have made the *Pin-hole* round in the inſide, take the *Pin* CD out of the *Pin-hole*, and put the *Joint-end* of the *Hinge* into the Fire to make a *Welding-heat*; which when it hath, ſnatch it quickly out of the Fire, and *hammer*, or *weld*, the end B upon the *Tail-piece* A till they be incorporate together. But you muſt have a care that you *hammer* not upon the Plate of the *Pin-hole*, leſt you ſtop it up, or batter it; when it is well Welded, you muſt again put in the *Pin* CD, and if it will not well go into the *Pin-hole*, (becauſe you may perhaps have *hammer'd* either upon it, or too near it, and ſo have ſomewhat cloſed it) you muſt force it in with your *hammer*; and if it require, take a *Blood-heat*, or a *Flame-heat*, of the *Joint* end) and then force the *Pin* into the *Pin-hole*, till you find the *Pin-hole* is again round within, and that the *Pin*, or Wyre, turn evenly about within it.

Afterwards with a *Punch* of hardned Steel (as you were taught *Page* 11. 12.) *Punch* the *Nail-holes* in the Plate; or if your Plate be very thin, you may *punch* them with a (*c*) cold *Punch*. After all, *ſmooth* it as well as you can with your *Hand-hammer*; take a *Blood-red-heat*, if your work require it, if not, *ſmooth* it cold; ſo will the *Tail-piece* be fit for the *File*. *Double*, and *Weld* the *Croſs-piece*, as you did the *Tail-piece*.

Having *forg'd* your *Hinge* fit for the *File*, you muſt proceed to make the *Joint*, by cutting a Notch in the Middle of the *Pin-hole* between D D in Plate 2. on the *Croſs*, as at E, and you muſt cut down the Ends of the *Pin-hole* on the *Tail-*

Tail-piece, as at D D, till the *Joint* at C fit exactly into the Notch in the *Cross*, and that when the *Pin* is put into the *Pin-hole* D D on the *Cross*, the *Pin-hole* in the *Tail-piece* may alſo receive the *Pin*; then by holding the *Tail-piece* in one Hand, and the *Croſs* in the other, double the *Tail* and *Croſs* towards one another, to try if they move evenly and ſmoothly without ſhaking on the *Pin*; which if they do, the *Joint* is made; if they do not, you muſt examine where the Fault is, and taking the *Pin* out, mend the Fault in the *Joint*.

Then *File* down all the Irregularities the *Cold-Chiſſel* made on the Edges of your Work, and (if the Curioſity of Work require it) *file* alſo the outer Flat of your Work. But tho' *Smiths* that make Quantities of *Hinges*, do *brighten* them, (as they call it) yet they ſeldom *file* them, but *Grinde* them on a Grindſtone till they become *bright*, &c.

Having finiſhed the *Joint*, put the *Pin* in again; but take care it be a little longer than the Depth of the *Joint*, becauſe you muſt batter the Ends of the *Pin* over the outer Edges of the *Pin-hole*, that the *Pin* may not drop out when either Edge of the *Croſs* is turned upwards.

The chiefeſt Curioſity in the making theſe, and, indeed, all other *Hinges* is, 1. That the *Pin-hole* be exactly round, and not too wide for the *Pin*. 2. That the *Joints* are let exactly into one another, that they have no play between them, leſt they ſhake upwards or downwards, nor yet are forced too hard into one another, leſt when they are nailed on the Door, the *Joint* be in Danger of Breaking. 3. That the *Croſs*, and the *Tail* lie on the Under-ſide exactly flat, for ſhould they warp out of flat when they are nailed on, the Nails would draw the *Joint* a-wry, and not only make it move hard, and unevenly, but by oft Opening and Shutting break the *Joint*. 4. If your Work be intended to be curious, the true *Square-filing* the Upper-ſide, as you were taught *Page* 15, 16, 17. is a great Ornament.

(*a*) Smiths call all *Chiſſels* they uſe upon cold Iron, *Cold-Chiſſels.*

(*b*) The *Stake* is a ſmall *Anvil*, which either ſtands upon a broad Iron Foot, or Baſis, on the *Work-Bench*, to remove as Occaſion offers; or elſe it hath a ſtrong Iron *Spike* at the Bottom, which Iron *Spike* is let into ſome certain Place of the *Work-Bench* not to be removed. Its Office is to ſet ſmall cold Work ſtraight upon, or to Cut or Punch upon with the *Cold-Chiſſel*, or *Cold-Punch.*

(*c*) *Smiths* call all *Punches* they uſe upon cold Iron, *Cold-Punches.*

If the *Hinge* you are to make be large, and Plate-Iron is not ſtrong enough for it, you muſt *Forge* it out of Flat Bar-Iron, as you were taught from *Page* 7 to *Page* 12.

The manner of working *Duſtails*, *Fig.* 5. and *Side-hinges*, *Fig.* 6. &c. is (the ſhape conſidered) in all reſpects the ſame I have here ſhewed you in *Croſs-Garnets*; but in theſe (or others) you may (if your Work require Curioſity) inſtead of *Doubling* for the *Joint*, *Forge* the *Round* for the *Joint* of full Iron, and afterwards *Drill* a Hole through it, for the *Pin-hole*; and by curious *Filing*, work them ſo true into one another, that both ſides of the *Hinge* ſhall ſeem but one Piece; as I ſhall ſhew more at large, when I come to the making of Compaſſes, and other Joints for Mathematical Inſtruments

Of Locks *and* Keys.

AS there are *Locks* for ſeveral Purpoſes, as *Street-door Locks*, called *Stock-Locks*; *Chamber-door Locks*, called *Spring-Locks*; *Cupboard-Locks*, *Cheſt-Locks*, *Trunk-Locks*, *Pad-Locks*, &c. So are there ſeveral Inventions in *Locks*, I mean, in the

the Making and Contriving their *Wards*, or *Guards*. But the Contrivances being almost innumerable, according to the various Fancies of Men, shall be referred to another Time to discourse; and I shall now shew you the Working of a *Spring-Lock*, which when you know how to do, your Fancy may play with Inventions, as you best like.

In *Fig*. 2. A A A A the *Main-plate*, B C the *Key-hole*. E D E the *Top-hook*, E E *Cross-wards*, F the *Bolt*, G the *Bolt-Toe*, or *Bolt-Nab*. H the *Draw-back Spring*, I the *Tumbler*, K the *Pin* of the *Tumbler*, L L the *Staples*.

In *Fig*. 3. A A A A the *Cover-Plate*, B the *Pin*, B C D the *Main-ward*, D D *Cross-wards*, E the *Step-ward* or *Dap-ward*.

In *Fig*. 4. A the *Pin-hole*, B the *Step*, or *Dap-ward*, C the *Hook-ward*, D the *Middle*, or *Main Cross-ward*, E E the *Cross-ward*, F the *Main-ward*, G G *Cross-ward*, H the *Shank*, I the *Pot*, or *Bread*, K the *Bow-ward*, L the *Bow*, B C D E E F G G the *Bit*.

First, Cut out of an Iron Plate with a *Cold-Chissel*, the Size and Shape of the *Main-Plate*, as you were taught to cut the *Cross* and *Tail-piece* of the *Cross-Garnet*; then consider what Depth you intend the *Bit* of the *Key* shall have, and set that Depth off on the *Main-Plate*, by leaving about half an Inch of Plate between the Bottom of the *Key-hole*, and the Lower Edge of the *Main-Plate*, as at C (or more or less, according to the Size of the *Lock*.) Then measure with a Pair of *Compasses* between the Bottom of the *Bit*, and the *Centre* of your *Key* (or your intended *Key*) and set that distance off from C to B, near the Middle between the two Ends of the *Main-Plate*, and with the (*a*) *Prick-punch*, make there a Mark to set one *Foot* of your *Compasses* in, then opening your *Compasses* to the Middle of the *Bit* of your intended *Key*, as to D, deſcribe the Arch E D E for the true Place the *Top-hoop* muſt ſtand on.

Then cut one other Piece of Plate as A A A A in *Fig.* 3. for a *Cover-plate,* with two Pieces one on each ſide, long enough to make *Studs* of to turn downwards, and then outward again as F F, G G, that the *Cover-plate* may ſtand off the *Main-plate,* the Breadth of the *Bit* of the *Key;* and at the two End of theſe *Studs* Punch holes, as G G, to *Rivet* the *Cover-plate* into the *Main-plate.* In the Middle of this Plate make the *Centre,* as at B, then open your *Compaſſes* to three Quarters the Length of the *Bit,* and half the Diameter of the *Shank* of the *Key,* and placing one *Foot* in the Point B, deſcribe with the other *Foot* the Arch D C D for the true Place of the *Main-ward,* then ſet your *Compaſſes* to a little more than half the Diameter of the *Shank,* and place one *Foot* (as before) in the *Centre* B, and with the other *Foot* deſcribe the ſmall Arch E, for the true Place the *Step-ward,* or (as ſome call it) the *Dap-ward* muſt ſtand: So have you the true Places of the *Wards,* for an ordinary *Spring-Lock;* you may (if the Depth of your *Bit* will bear it) put more *Wards* in your Plates. But you muſt note, that the more *Wards* you put in, the weaker you make your *Key;* becauſe that to every *Ward* on the Plates, you muſt make a Slit, or *Ward* in the *Bit* of the *Key;* and the more *Wards* you make, the weaker the Iron of the *Bit* will be; and then if the *Bolt* ſhoot not eaſily backwards, or forwards, the *Bit* may be in Danger of Breaking.

Having marked on your Plates the Places of all your *Wards,* you muſt take thin Plate, and with *Hammering* and *Filing* make them both (*b*) *Hammer-hard,* and of equal Thickneſs all the way. Then *file* one Edge very ſtraight, by laying a *ſtraight Ruler* juſt within the Edge of it, and drawing, or racing with a Point of hardned Steel, a bright Line by the ſide of the *Ruler; File* away the

the Edge of the Plate to that Line, then draw (as before) another ſtraight Line Parallel to the firſt ſtraight Line, or which is all one, Parallel to the filed Edge, juſt of the Breadth you intend the *Wards* ſhall be, and file as before, only, you muſt leave two, or ſometimes three *Studs* upon this Plate, one near each End, and the other in the Middle, to *Rivet* into the *Main-plate*, to keep the *Ward* fixt in its Place. Therefore you muſt take care when you elect this thin Piece of Plate, that it be broad enough for the *Ward*, and theſe Studs too. Then laying the Plate a-thwart the *Pike* of the *Bickern*, hold your Hand even with the *Face* of the *Bickern*, and *hammer* this Plate down ſomewhat by the ſide of the *Pike*, and by Degrees you may (with care taken) bring it unto a circular Form, juſt of the Size of that Circle you deſcribed on the *Main-plate*; which when you have done, you muſt apply this *Ward* to the Circle you deſcribed on the *Main-plate*; ſetting it in the Poſition you intend it ſhall be fixed, and marking with a Steel Point where the *Studs* ſtand upon that Circle, in thoſe marks *Punch* holes to *Rivet* the *Studs* to. Work ſo by all the other *Wards*.

If you have a *Pin* to the *Lock*, *Punch* a Hole through the *Centre* on the *Cover-plate*, ſomewhat ſmaller than the Wyre you are to make your *Pin* of, becauſe you may then *file* one End of the *Pin* away to a *Shank*, which muſt fit the ſmaller Hole on the Plate, and the whole Thickneſs of the *Pin* will be a *Sholder*, which will keep the *Pin* ſteddy in the *Centre-hole* of the Plate, when the *Pin* is *rivetted* into the Plate. But becauſe there is ſome Skill to be uſed in *Rivetting*, I ſhall, before I proceed any farther, teach you

The manner of Rivetting.

RIvetting is to batter the Edges of a *Shank* over a Plate, or other Iron, the *Shank* is let into, ſo as the Plate, or other Iron, may be clinched cloſe, and fixed between the Battering at the End of the *Shank* and the *Sholder*. So that

When you *Rivet* a *Pin* into a Hole, your *Pin* muſt have a *Sholder* to it thicker than the Hole is wide, that the *Sholder* ſlip not through the Hole, as well as the *Shank*; but the *Shank* of the *Pin* muſt be exactly of the Size of the Hole the *Shank* muſt be *Rivetted* into, and ſomewhat longer than the Plate is thick; *file* the End of the *Shank* flat, ſo ſhall the Edges of the End, the eaſilier batter over the Plate; then put your *Shank* into the Hole, wherein it is to be *Rivetted*, but be ſure you force the *Shank* cloſe up to the *Sholder*; then turn the Top of this *Sholder* downwards (Plate and all) upon your *Stake*, but lay it ſo, as that the *Sholder* lie ſolid, and the *Shank*, at the ſame time, ſtand directly upright, and with your left Hand, keep your Work bearing hard upon the Flat, or *Face* of the *Stake*. Then holding your *Hammer* in your Right-hand, hold the Edge of the *Face* of it Dripping a-ſlope from the Right-hand outwards, and lay pretty light Blows upon the Edge of the End of the *Shank*, turning with your Left-hand your Work round to the *Face* of the *Hammer*, till you have battered the Edges of the *Shank* quite round about; but this is ſeldom done, with once turning your Work about; therefore you may thus work it round again and again, till you find it is pretty well *Rivetted*; then lay heavier Blows upon it ſometimes with the *Face*, ſometimes with the *Pen* of the *Hammer*, till the End of the *Shank* is battered effectually over the Plate.

One main Conſideration in *Rivetting* is, that the *Pin* you *rivet* in, ſtand upright to the Plate, or or other Iron you *rivet* it upon; for if it do not ſtand upright, you will be forced to ſet it upright, after it is *rivetted*, either in the *Vice*, or with your *Plyers*, or with your *Hammer*, and that may, if your Plate be thin, bow it, or if it be thick, break the Shank, or elſe the *Sholder* of your *Rivet*, and ſo you loſe your Labour, and ſometimes ſpoil your Work.

Another Conſideration is, that when you *rivet* a *Pin* to any Plate, and you fear it may afterwards twiſt about by ſome force that may be offered it, you muſt, to provide againſt this Danger, *file* the *Shank* you intend to *Rivet*, either Square, or Triangular, and make the Hole in the Plate you *rivet* it into, of the ſame Size and Form, and then *rivet* in the *Shank*, as before. There are two ways to make your Hole, Square or Triangular, one is by *filing* it into theſe Forms, when it is firſt Punched round; the other by making a *Punch* of Steel, of the Size and Shape of the *Shank* you are to *rivet*, and punching that *Punch* into the Plate, make the ſame Form.

Now to return where I left off. The *Pins* and *Shanks* of theſe *Wards* muſt be made of a long Square Form, becauſe, (the Plates of the *Wards* being thin) ſhould you make them no broader than the Plate is thick, the *Studs*, or *Shanks* would be too weak to hold the *Wards*, therefore you muſt make the *Rivetting-ſhank* three or four times, or ſometimes more, as broad as the Plate is thick, and then *rivet* them in, as you were taught juſt now.

Then place the *Cover-plate* upon the *Main-plate*, ſo as the *Centre* of the *Cover-plate*, may ſtand directly over and againſt the *Centre* of the *Main-plate*, and make marks through the Hole G G, of the *Studs* of the *Cover-Plate* upon the *Main-plate*, and on thoſe Marks Punch holes, and fit two *Pins* into them, to faſten the *Cover-plate* on to the

the *Main-plate*, but you muſt not yet *rivet* them down, till the *Key-hole* be made, becauſe this *Cover-plate* would then ſtop the Progreſs of the *File* through the *Main-plate*, when you *file* the *Key-hole*. When you have placed the *Cover-plate* upon the *Main-plate*, and fitted it on with *Pins*, ſo, as you may take it off, and put it on again, as your Work may require, you muſt *Punch* the *Key-hole*, or rather drill two Holes cloſe by one another, if the *Key-hole* falls near the *Wards*, becauſe *Punching* may be apt to ſet the *Wards* out of Form, and with ſmall *Files*, file the two Holes into one another, to make the Hole big enough to come at it with bigger *Files*, and then file your *Key-hole* to your intended Size and Shape.

The *Key-hole* being finiſhed, forge your *Key*, as you were taught, *Page* 7. and if your *Key* is to have a *Pin-hole*, drill the Hole in the Middle of the End of the *Shank*, then file the *Wards*, or Slits in the *Bit* with thin *Files*; yet ſometimes Smiths *Punch*, or cut them with a *Cold-Chiſſel*, at the ſame Diſtances from the Middle of the *Pin-hole* in the End of the *Shank* (which is the ſame *Centre*, which was made before, in the *Main-plate* on the *Cover-plate*) which you placed the *Wards* at, from the *Centre* of the *Main* and *Cover-plate*. But before you file theſe *Wards* too deep into the *Bit* of the *Key*, make Trials, by putting the *Bit* into the *Key-hole*, whether the *Wards* in the *Bit*, will agree with the *Wards* on the Plates, which if they do, you may boldly cut them to the Depth of the *Wards* on the Plate; if not, you muſt alter your Courſe till they do; but you muſt take great Care in Cutting the *Wards* down ſtraight, and ſquare to the Sides of the *Bit*; for if they be not cut down ſtraight, the *Wards* on the Plates, will not fall in with the *Wards* in the *Bit* of the *Key*; and if they be not Square to the Sides of the *Bit*, the *Bit* will not only be weaker than it need be, but it will

ſhew

ſhew unhandſomely, and like a Botch to the Eye.

The *Croſs* and *Hock-wards* is made, or, at leaſt, entred at the *Forge*, when the Iron hath a *Blood*, or almoſt a *Flame Heat*, yet ſometimes Smiths do it on cold Iron, with a thin *Chiſſel*, as you was taught *Page* 11. 12. But you muſt take care that your *Chiſſel* be neither too thick, or too broad, for this Punching of *Wards* is only to give the thin *Files* Entrance to the Work; which Entrance when you have, you may eaſily file your *Croſs*, or *Hook-wards*, wider or deeper, as your Work may require; but if your *Chiſſel* be too broad, or too thick, it will make the *Wards* in the *Bit* too long, or too wide, and then (as I ſaid before) the *Bit* of your *Key* will prove weaker than it needs to be.

Having made the *Wards* on the Plate, and in the *Bit* of the *Key*, you muſt *Forge* the *Bolt* of a conſiderable Subſtance, Thick and Square at the End that ſhoots into the *Staple* in the Frame of the Door, that it may be ſtrong enough to guard the whole Door; but the reſt of the *Bolt* that lies between the two *Staples* on the *Main-plate*, may be made very thin inwards, that is, the Side that lies towards the *Main-plate*, which becauſe it cannot be ſeen when the *Bolt* is fixed upon the Plate, I have made a Figure of it, and turned the Inſide to View, as in *Fig.* 4. where you may ſee, that the End A, hath a conſiderable Subſtance of Iron to guard the whole Door, as aforeſaid, and B is a Square *Stud*, which doth as well keep the Outſide flat of the *Bolt* on the Range, as ſerve for a *Stud* for the *Spring* H in *Fig.* 2. to preſs hard againſt, and ſhoot the *Bolt* forwards: This *Bolt* muſt be wrought ſtraight on all its Sides, except the Topſide, which muſt be wrought ſtraight only as far as the *Sholder* G, called the *Toe*, or *Nab* of the *Bolt*, which riſes, as you ſee in the Figure, conſiderably high, above the Straight on the Top of the *Bolt*: The Office of this *Nab*, is to receive the Bottom of the *Bit* of the *Key*, when in turning it about, it ſhoots the *Bolt* backwards or forwards.

Having *forged* and *filed* the *Bolt*, you muſt fit the Hollow-ſide of it towards the *Main-plate*, at that Diſtance from the *Key-hole*, that when the *Key* is put into the *Key-hole*, and turned towards the *Bolt*, the Bottom of the *Bit* may fall almoſt to the Bottom of the *Nab*, and ſhoot the *Bolt* back ſo much, as it needs to enter the *Staple* in the *Door-frame*. And having found this true Place for the *Bolt*, you muſt with ſquare *Staples*, juſt fit to contain the *Bolt* with an eaſie Play, faſten theſe *Staples*, by *Rivetting* them with the *Bolt* within them, one near the *Bolt* end, the other near the *Nab* end, as at L L to the *Main-plate*.

Then *Punch* a pretty wide Hole in the *Main-plate*, as at K, to receive a ſtrong *Pin*, and *file* a *Sholder* to the *Shank* of the *Pin* that goes into the Plate. This *Pin* is called the *Pin of the Tumbler*; the *Tumbler* is marked I, which is a long Piece of *Iron*, with a round Hole at the Top to fit the *Pin* of the *Tumbler* into, that it may move upon it, as on a *Joint*, and it hath an *Hook* returning at the Lower End of it, to fall into the Breech of the *Bolt*, and by the *Spring* H forces the *Bolt* forwards, when it is ſhot back with the *Key*. This *Spring* is made of Steel, and afterwards temper'd (as I ſhall ſhew you in proper Place.) It is fixed at the Bottom of the *Main-plate*, by two ſmall Shanks proceeding from that Edge of the *Spring* that lies againſt the *Main-plate*, as at O O: Theſe Shanks are to be *rivetted* (as you were taught even now) on the other Side of the *Main-plate*.

All things being thus fitted, *punch* an Hole on each Corner of the *Main-plate* for *Nails* to enter, that muſt nail the *Lock* to the *Door*. Or if you intend to ſcrew your *Lock* on the *Door*, you muſt make wide Holes, big enough to receive the

Shank

Shank of the *Screw*. Last of all, *rivet* down your *Cover-plate* to the *Main-plate*, and *file* your *Key*, and *polish* it too, if you will; so shall the *Lock* and *Key* be finished.

(*a*) A *Prick-punch*, is a Piece of temper'd Steel, with a round Point at one End, to prick a round Mark in cold Iron.

(*b*) *Hammer-hard*, is when you harden Iron, or Steel, with much hammering on it.

The making of Screws *and* Nuts.

THE *Shank* of the *Screw* for Doors, and many other Purposes, must be *forged* square near the *Head*, because it must be let into a Square-hole, that it may not twist about when the *Nut* is turned about hard upon the *Screw-pin*. Therefore take a Square-bar, or Rod of Iron, as near the Size of the *Head* of the *Screw-pin* as you can, and taking a *Flame-heat* of it, lay so much of this Bar as you intend for the Length of the *Shank*, with one Square-side flat, upon the Hither-side of the *Anvil*, and *hammer* it down to your intended Thickness: But have a care you do not strike your Iron on this Side the Edge of the *Anvil*, lest you cut the Iron, as I told you *Page* 11. Thus, at once you will have two Sides of your *Shank forged*; the Under-side made by the *Anvil*, and the Upper-side beaten flat with the *Hammer*: The *Head* will be in the main Rod of Iron; then if your Iron grows cold, give it another *Heat*, and lay one of the unwrought Sides upon the Hither-side of the *Anvil*, just to the *Head*, and *hammer* that down, as before, so shall the two other Square-sides be made; then *hammer* down the Corners of so much of this *Shank*, as you intend for the *Screw-pin*, and round it, as near as you can, with the *Hammer*; set then the *Chissel* to the Thickness you intend the *Head* shall have, and strike it about half through, then turn the Sides successively, and cut each Side also half through, till it be quite cut off. If the *Sholder* be not square enough, hold it in your *Square-nos'd*

Tongs,

Tongs, and take another *Heat*, and with ſpeed (leſt your Work cool) ſcrew the *Shank* into the *Vice*, ſo as the *Sholder* may fall flat upon the *Chaps* of the *Vice*; then *hammer* upon the *Head*, and ſquare the *Sholder* on two Sides, do the like for ſquaring the other two Sides. This was, in part, taught you before, in *Page* 11. but becauſe the cutting this Iron Rod, or Bar, juſt above the *Sholder* makes the *Head*, and for that I did not mention it there, I thought fit (ſince the Purpoſe required it) to do it here: The *Forging* of the *Nuts* are taught before, *Page* 11. 12.

Having *forged* and *filed* your *Shank* ſquare, and the *Head* either Square or Round, as you intend it ſhall be, *file* alſo the *Screw-pin*, from the Riſings and dents left at the *Forge*; and *file* it a little Tapering towards the End, that it may enter the *Screw-plate*; the Rule how much it muſt be Tapering is this, conſider how deep the Inner *Grooves* of the *Screw-plate* lie in the outer *Threds*, and *file* the End of the *Screw-pin* ſo much ſmaller than the reſt of the *Screw-pin*, for the outer *Threds* of the *Screw-plate* muſt make the *Grooves* on the *Screw-pin*, and the *Grooves* in the *Screw-plate*, will make the *Threds* on the *Screw-pin*. Having fitted your ſelf with a Hole in your *Screw-plate* (that is, ſuch a Hole whoſe Diameter of the hollow *Grooves*, ſhall be equal to the Diameter of the *Screw-pin*, but not ſuch a Hole, whoſe Diameter of the outer *Threds*, ſhall be equal to the Diameter of the *Screw-pin*, for then the *Screw-plate* will indeed turn about the *Screw-pin*, but not cut any *Grooves*, or *Threds* in it) *ſcrew* the *Shank* with the *Head* downwards in the *Vice*, ſo as that the *Screw-pin* may ſtand directly upright, and take the *Handle* of the *Screw-plate* in your Right-hand, and lay that Hole flat upon the *Screw-pin*, and preſs it very hard down over it, and turn the *Screw-plate* evenly about with its *Handle* towards you, from the Right towards the Left-hand, ſo ſhall the outer

Threds

Threds of the *Screw-plate* cut *Grooves* into the *Screw-pin*, and the ſubſtance of the Iron on the *Screw-pin*, will fill up the *Grooves* of the *Screw-plate*, and be a *Thred* upon the *Screw-pin*. But take this for Caution, that, as I told you, you muſt not make your *Screw-pin* too ſmall, becauſe the *Screw-plate* will not cut it, ſo if you make it too big (if it do enter the *Screw-plate* where it is Taper) it will endanger the breaking it, or, if it do not break it, yet the *Screw-plate* will, after it gets a little below the Tapering, go no farther, but work and wear off the *Thred* it made about the Tapering.

To fit the *Pin* therefore to a true ſize, I, in my Practiſe, uſe to try into what *hole* of the *Screw-plate*, the *Tap* or place of the *Tap*, (if it be a tapering *Tap*,) I make the *Nut* with, will juſt ſlide through; (*Threads* and all;) (which generally in moſt *Screw-plates* is the *hole* next above that to be uſed) for then turning my *Pin* about in that *hole*, if the *Pin* be irregularly *filed*, or but a little too big on any part of it, the *Threds* of that *Hole* will cut ſmall marks upon the *Pin*, on the irregular places, or where it is too big; ſo that afterwards *filing* thoſe Marks juſt off, I do at once *file* my *Pin* truly round, and ſmall enough to fit the *H le* I make my *Screw-pin* with.

As the *Hole* of the *Screw plate* muſt be fitted to the *Screw-pin*, ſo muſt the *Screw-tap* that makes the *Screw* in the *Nut*, be fitted to the round *hole* of the *Nut*; but that *Tap* muſt be of the ſame ſize of your *Screw-pin* too, which you may try by the ſame *hole* of the *Screw-plate* you made the *Screw-pin* with. *Screw* the *Nut* in the *Vice* directly flat, that the *hole* may ſtand upright, and put the *Screw-tap* upright in the *hole*; then if your *Screw-tap* have an *handle*, turn it by the *handle* hard round in the *Hole*, ſo will the *Screw-tap* work it ſelf into the *Hole*, and make *Grooves* in it to fit the *Threds* of the *Screw-pin*. But if the *Screw-tap* have no *handle*, then it hath its upper end filed to a long ſquare, to fit into an hollow ſquare, made near the *handle* of the *Screw-plate*; but that long ſquare hole, over the long ſquare on the top of the *Tap*, and then by turning about the *Screw-plate*, you will alſo turn about the *Tap* in the *hole*, and make *Grooves* and *Threds* in the *Nut*.

But though ſmall *Screws* are made with *Screw-plates*, yet great *Screws*, ſuch as are for *Vices*, *Hot-Preſſes*, *Printing-Preſſes*, &c. are not made with *Screw-plates*, but muſt be cut out of the main Iron, with heavy blows upon a *Cold-Chiſſel*. The manner of making them, is as follows.

The Rules and manner of Cutting Worms *upon great* Screws.

THE *Threds* of *Screws*, when they are bigger than can be made in *Screw-plates*, are call'd *Worms*. They conſiſt in length, breadth and depth; the length of a *Worm* begins at the one end of the *Spindle*, and ends at the other; the breadth of the *Worm*, is contain'd between any two *Grooves* on the *Spindle*, viz. The upper and under *Groove* of the *Worm*, in every part of the *Spindle*; the depth of the *Worm*, is cut into the Diameter of the *Spindle*, viz. The depth, between the outſide of the *Worm*, and the bottom of the *Groove*.

The depth ought to be about the one ſeventh part of the Diameter, on each ſide the *Spindle:*

You ought to make the *Groove* wider than the *Worm* is broad, becauſe the *Worm* being cut out of the ſame intire piece with the *Spindle*, will be as ſtrong as the *Worm* in the *Nut*, tho' the *Worm* on the *Spindle* be ſmaller; for you cannot come at the *Worm* in the *Nut*, to cut it with *Files*, as you may the *Spindle*, and therefore you muſt either

Turn

Turn up a Rod of Iron, to twiſt round about the *Grooves* on the *Spindle*, and then take it off, and *Braze* it into the *Nut*, or elſe you muſt *Caſt* a *Nut* of *Braſs* upon the *Spindle*, which will neither way be ſo ſtrong as the *Worm* cut out of the whole Iron, by ſo much as *Braſs* is a weaker Mettal than Iron, and therefore it is that you ought to allow the *Worm* in the *Nut*, a greater breadth than the *Worm* on the *Spindle*, that the ſtrength of both may, as near as you can, be equaliz'd; for both being put to equal force, ought to have equal ſtrength. The *Worm* may very well be the one ſeventh part ſmaller than the *Groove* is wide, as aforeſaid.

Having conſider'd what breadth the *Worm* on the *Spindle* ſhall have, take a ſmall thin Plate of Braſs, or Iron, and *file* a ſquare notch at the end of it, juſt ſo wide, and ſo deep, as your *Worm* is to be broad and deep, and *file* the ſides of the Plate that this notch ſtands between, juſt to the width of the *Groove*. This Plate, muſt be a *Gage* to *file* your *Worm* and *Groove* to equal breadth by; then draw a ſtraight and upright Line the whole length of the *Spindle*; divide from this line the Circumference of the whole *Spindle* into eight equal Parts, and through thoſe Diviſions, draw ſeven Lines more parallel to the firſt Line; then open your *Compaſſes* juſt to the breadth of one *Worm*, and one *Groove*, and ſet off that diſtance as oft as you can, from the one end of the Spindle to the other, (but I ſhould firſt have told you, that the end of your Spindle muſt be ſquare to the outſide) and with a *Prick-Punch*, make a mark to every ſetting off on that line: Do the like to all the other ſtraight upright Lines. Note, that you may chuſe one of theſe eight upright Lines for the firſt, and make the next towards your left Hand, the ſecond (but then the firſt muſt ſtand towards you) and the next that, the third, and ſo on. And the top mark of every one of theſe upright ſtraight Lines, ſhall be call'd the firſt Mark, the next under that the ſecond Mark, the third, the third Mark, and ſo downwards in Order and Number.

Having marked one of theſe eight Lines at the top of the *Spindle*, to begin the winding of the *Worm* at, with a Black-lead Pencil, draw a line from that Mark to the ſecond Mark, on the next upright Line towards the left hand, from thence continue drawing on with your Pencil to the third Mark, on the third upright Line, draw on ſtill to the fourth Mark, on the fourth upright Line, and ſo onwards, till you have drawn over the eight ſtraight Lines, which when you have done, you muſt ſtill continue on, drawing downwards to each lower Mark on each ſucceſſive upright Line, till you have drawn your *Worm* from end to end: Then examine, as well as you can, by your Eye, whether the *Worm* you have carried on from Mark to Mark with the Black-led Pencil, do not break into Angles, which if it do any where, you muſt mend it in that place: Then with the edge of an *half-round File*, file a ſmall Line in the Black-lead Line, and be ſure that the Line you are *filing*, run exactly through all the Marks that the Black-lead Pencil ſhould have run through (if it did not, for want of good guidance of the Hand.) This ſmall Line is only for a guide to cut the *Groove* down by; for the making of a *Screw* is, indeed nothing elſe, but the cutting the *Groove* down, for then the *Worm* remains: But you muſt not *file* in this ſmall line, but leave it as a guide to lie on the middle of the *Worm* (as I ſaid before): Therefore to cut down the *Groove*, take a *Cold Chiſſel*, ſomewhat thinner than you intend the *Groove* ſhall be wide, *viz.* about the

the thickneſs of the breadth of the *Worm*, and, with heavy blows, cut out the *Groove* pretty near. The reaſon why you ſhould not offer to cut the *Grooves* to their full wedth at the firſt, is, becauſe your Hand may carry the *Cold-Chiſſel* ſomewhat awry, and ſhould yonr *Cold-Chiſſel* be as thick as the *Groove* is wide, you could not ſmooth the Irregularities out, without making the *Worm* narrower than you intended it: Then with a *Flat-file* open and ſmooth the *Groove*, *filing* in the middle between the two next fine Lines cut by the *half-round File*, till you have wrought the *Spindle* from end to end, ſo ſhall the *Worm* remain. But you muſt not expect, that though the *Groove* be cut, it is therefore finiſhed, for now you muſt begin to uſe the thin *Plate-Gage*, and try firſt, whether the *Worm* have equal breadth all the way. Secondly, whether the *Grove* have equal breadth all the way. And Thirdly, whether the *Groove* have equal depth all the way; and where ever you find the *Worm* too broad, you muſt *file* it thinner, and where the *Groove* is not deep enough, *file* it deeper; therefore in cutting down the *Groove* you may obſerve, that if, at firſt, you *file* the *Worm* never ſo little too narrow or the *Groove* never ſo little too deep, you ſhall have all the reſt of the *Worm* or *Groove* to *file* over again; becauſe the whole *Worm* muſt be brought to the breadth of the ſmalleſt part of it, and the whole *Groove* to the depth of the deepeſt place all the way, eſpecially if the *Nut* be to be *Caſt* in *Braſs* upon the *Spindle*; becauſe the Mettal running cloſe to the *Spindle* will bind on that place, and not come off it; but if the *Nut* be not to be *Caſt* in *Braſs*, but only hath a *Worm* brazed into it, this niceneſs is not ſo abſolutely neceſſary, becauſe that *Worm* is firſt *Turned up*, and bowed into the *Grooves* of the *Spindle*, and you may try that before it is

Braz'd in the *Nut*, and if it go not well about, you may mend, or botch it, either by ***Hammering*** or *Filing*, or both.

The manner of *Casting* the *Nut* upon the ***Spindle***, I shall shew when I come to the *Casting* of ***Mettals***; and the manner of *Brazing* hath been Taught already. *Num.* I. *fol.* 12, 13.

If your ***Spindle*** is to have three or four ***Worms*** winding about it, as ***Coining-Presses*** and ***Printing-Presses*** have, that they may not wear out too fast, you must divide the Circumference into three or four equal Parts, and having straight upright Lines, drawn as before, begin a ***Worm*** at each of those three, or four Divisions, on the Circumference, and considering the breadth of your ***Worm*** and width of your *Groove*, measure that width as oft as you can on all the upright Lines, and making Marks on those at each Setting off, draw as before, a Line from the end of the ***Spindle***, on the first upright Line to the Mark below it, which is the second Mark on the second upright Line, from thence to the third Mark, on the third upright Line, and so on to the other end of the *Spindle*. Having drawn the first ***Worm***, work the other *Worm* as this.

Thus much may at present suffice for ***great Screws***.

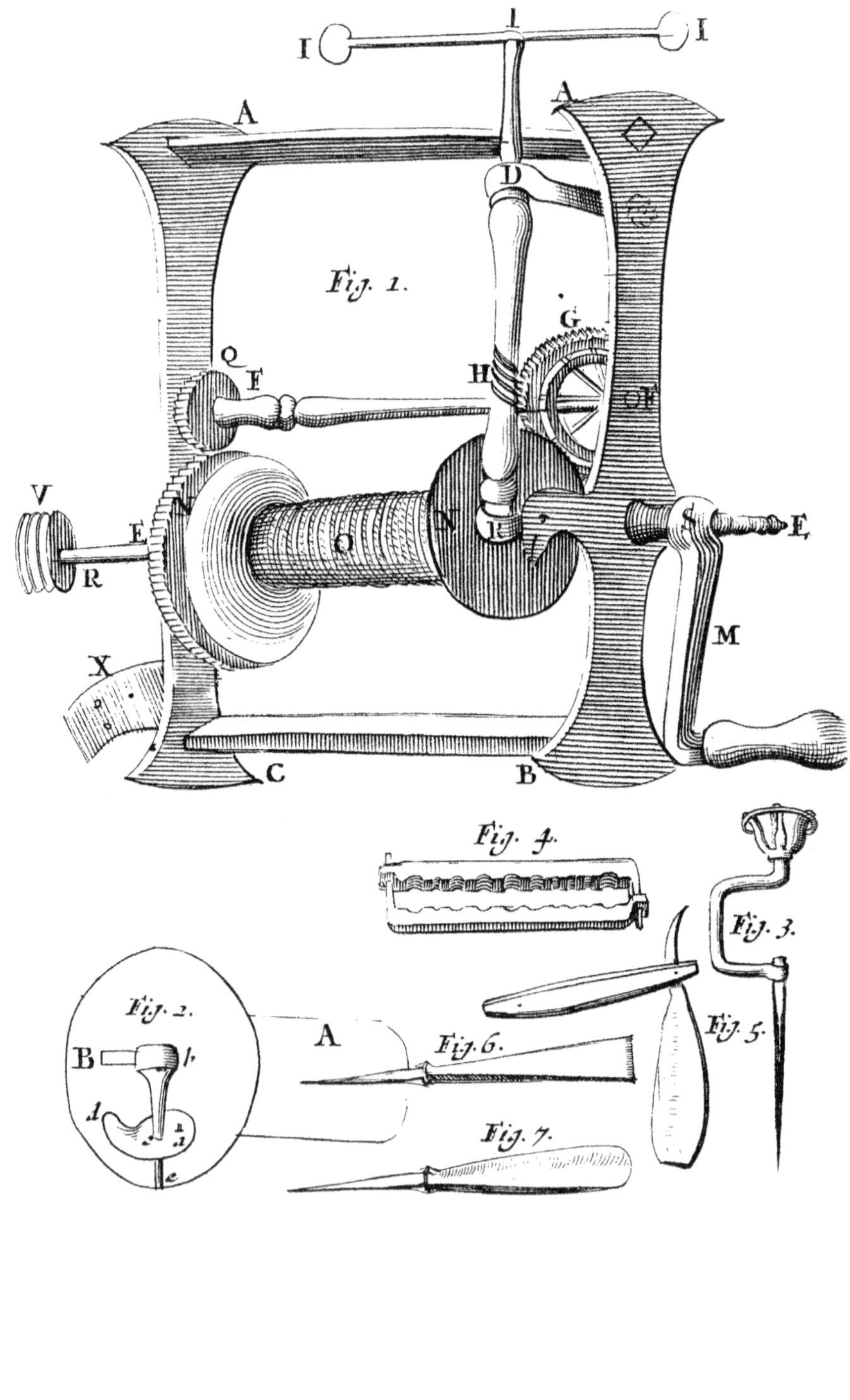
Fig. 1.
Fig. 2.
Fig. 3.
Fig. 4.
Fig. 5.
Fig. 6.
Fig. 7.

MECHANICK EXERCISES; OR, The Doctrine of *Handy-Works*

Viz. The making of Jacks and Bullet-Molds, the twisting of Iron, and Case-hardning it, with the use of some Tools *not treated of before: Also of the several sorts of* Steel, *the manner of Softning, Hardning and Tempering them.*

Of Jacks.

FIG. 1. is call'd a *Worm-Jack.* A B the *Fore-side*, A C the *Back-side*, A A the *Top-piece*, B C the *Bottom-piece*, altogether the *Jack-frame*, E E K the *Main-Spindle*, N O N the *Main-Wheel* and *Barrel*, O the *Barrel*, D the *Wind-up-piece*, fastned into the *Barrel*, F F the *Worm-wheel Spindle*, G the *Worm-wheel*, Q the *Worm-Nut*, H the *Worm*, R the *Stud* of the *Worm-Spindle*, D the *Worm-Loop*, L the *Wind-up-piece*, M the *Winch* or *Winder* or *Handle*, the Iron part is the *Winder*, the Wood the *Handle*, S the *Eye of the Winder*, I I the *Fly*, T the *Socket* of the *Fly*, V the *Struck-Wheel*, X the *Stayes* or *Back fastnings.*

First you are to Forge the *Jack-frame*, and on the left side of the *Foreside*, a Shank for the *Stud* of the *Worm-spindle*, as you are taught *Numb.* I. *fol.* 8, 9, 10, 11, 12. and then file it as you were taught *Numb.* I. *fol.* 14, 15, 16.

The *top* and *bottom Pieces* are let into ſquare holes at the ends of the *Fore* and *Backſide.* But you muſt Forge the *top* and *bottom Pieces* with two ſmall Squares towards the ends of them, and two round ends for *Screw-pins,* beyond thoſe ſquares. The ſmall ſquares are to be fitted into ſquare holes into the *Fore* and *Backſides,* and the round *Screw-pins* are to make *Screws* of, to which a ſquare *Nut* is to be fitted to draw the *top* and *bottom Pieces* cloſe and right up to the inſides of the *Fore* and *Backſides.* The manner of Filing of theſe Ends you were, in part, taught *Numb.* II. *fol.* 15, 16. and *Numb.* I. *fol.* 29. but another way is by trying your Work with an Inſtrument, call'd by Workmen, a *Square,* as you ſee deſcrib'd in this Figure.

Of the Square *and its Uſe.*

THE ſides ABC are call'd the *Outer-ſquare*; the ſides DEF the *Inner-ſquare.* Its Uſe is thus. If your Work, as in this Caſe, be an *Outer-ſquare,* you muſt uſe the *Inner-ſquare,* DEF to try it by; applying either the ſide ED or DF (but ſuppoſe the ſide ED) to one of the ſides of your Work, chuſe the flatteſt and trueſt wrought; if neither of the ſides be flat, make of them flat, as you were

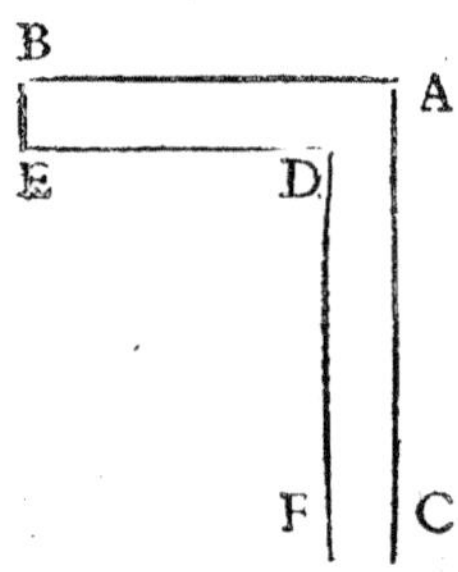

taught *Numb.* I. *fol.* 15, 16. if then you find the ſide DF of your *Square* lie all the way even upon the adjoining ſide of your Work, you may conclude thoſe ſides are Square; but if the adjoining ſide of your Work comply not all the way with the adjoining ſide of the *Square,* you muſt file away your Work where the *Square* rides upon it, till the whole ſide be wrought to comply with the

the adjoining ſide of the *Square*, that is, till both the ſides of your Work agree with both the ſides of the *Squares*, when they are appli'd to one another. Having tried two ſides Square, make a third ſide of your Work Square, by applying one of the ſides of the *Square* to one of thoſe ſides of your Work, that are already made ſquare, and as before, try the third untry'd ſide, and make that Square; and by the ſame Rule make the fourth ſide ſquare.

If the Work you are to file be an hollow ſquare, you muſt apply the outer Square A B C to it, and try how, when one ſide of the *Square*, is applied to one ſide of your Work, the other ſide of your Work agrees with the other ſide of the *Square*; which if it do, all is well: But if the *Square* and the Work comply not with one another, you muſt file the Work where it bears the *Square* off. But to return where I left.

Having made theſe two ends ſquare, you muſt fit the length of them to the thickneſs of the *Fore* and *Backſides* into which they are to enter, but ſo as the Squares be not full ſo long as to come quite thro' the *Fore* and *Backſides*, leſt when the *Nuts* are ſcrew'd on the *Screw-pins* that are at the ends of theſe Squares, they ſcrew full up to the Squares, and bear againſt the corners of them; which if they do, the *Nuts* will not draw the *Fore* and *Backſides* cloſe againſt the ſhoulder of the Squares, on the *top* and *bottom Pieces*, and then the whole *Jack Frame* will not ſtand faſt and firm together.

But before you fit this *Frame* thus together, you muſt conſider the Diameter of the *Main wheel*, that you may Pnuch round Holes in the *Fore* and *Backſides* to enter the *Main-ſpindle*. Therefore open your Compaſs to half the intended Diameter of the *Main-wheel*, and half a quarter, or an whole quarter of an Inch more for play, between

the

the Semi-diameter of the *main Wheel*, and the upper flat of the *bottom Piece*, and ſet that diſtance off from the upper flat of the *bottom Piece*, on the *Fore* and *Backſides*, and with a round Punch, ſomewhat ſmaller than the intended ſize of the *main Spindle*, Punch Holes at that ſetting off. Your Punch muſt be ſmaller than the *main Spindle*, becauſe the holes may perhaps not be ſo exactly round, or Punch'd ſo truly upright, or perfectly ſmooth as they ought to be; and ſhould you make the holes ſo wide at firſt as they need to be, you could not mend them, without making them wider. Theſe holes muſt be Punch'd at the *Fire* or *Forge* (as Smiths ſay, when they take an *Heat* of their Work to Punch it) becauſe the *Fore* and the *Backſides* are *too ſtrong* (as Smiths ſay) that is, too thick to Punch with the *Cold Punch*. The way of Punching them you were taught *Numb.* I. *fol.* 11, 12. Beſides a *Cold Punch* is commonly made flat at the bottom, and therefore does not prick an Hole, but cut an Hole (if the Iron be not too ſtrong) for that flat bottom, and the upright ſide about it, met in an Angle or Edge at the bottom, which Edge, by the force of the Hammer, cuts the Iron (if it be not too ſtrong) when it is laid upon a *Bolſter*, as it is deſcrib'd *Numb.* I. *fol.* 12. and ſhould you cut out ſo much Iron in the *Fore* and *Backſides*, as would entertain the *main Spindle* (it being thick) you will make the *Fore* and *Backſides* too wide; therefore as I ſaid, the Holes muſt be prickt in the *Fore* and *Backſides* at the *Fire* or *Forge*, which with a ſharp pointed *Punch* is ſooner done; nor does pricking diminiſh the ſubſtance or ſtrength of the Iron, but makes it ſwell out at the ſides, and retain both ſubſtance and ſtrength. The irregularity or ſwelling out that this Punching makes on the flats of the *Fore* and *Backſides*, you muſt Hammer down

again

again with almost a *Blood-red-heat*, I say, almost a *Blood-red-heat*; because, should you take too great an *Heat*, you may make the *Fore* and *Backsides* stretch, and so put the whole *Jack-frame* out of order.

Having punch'd the Holes for the *main Spindle*, you must Punch the Holes in the *Fore* and *Backsides* for the *Worm-wheel Spindle*, as you Punch the Holes for the *main Spindle*; but these must be small Holes, to entertain the small Ends or Pins of the *Worm-wheel Spindle*.

These Holes thus Punch'd, may perhaps not be exactly round or fit your size, nor will they be smooth enough within; therefore, with a [a] *Square-bore*, you must [b] open them wider to your size, and that opening them in the inside, will both round and smooth them.

You must also Punch a square hole towards the top of the *Foreside*, for the *Shank* of the *Worm-Loop*.

Then Forge and fit in your *Main-wheel Spindle*, and your *Worm-wheel Spindle*, which Spindles must both be exactly straight between the corners of their two ends (unless you like to have Moldings for Ornaments on them) and Forge a Square towards the ends of both the Spindles, to fit into a square hole in the middle of the *Cross* of their *Wheels*, and leave substance enough for a shoulder beyond the square, to stop the square hole in the *Cross* of the *Wheels* from sliding farther on the *Spindle*, and you must leave substance of Iron enough to Forge the *Nut* of the *Worm-wheel* near the other end. But in this, and indeed in all other Forging remember (as I told you *Numb.* I. *fol.* 9.) that it behoves you to *Hammer* or *Forge* your Work as true as you can, least it cost you great pains at the *Vice*.

Then

Then Forge the *Worm-ſpindle*, which is all the way round and ſtraight, unleſs you will have Moldings for Ornaments (as aforeſaid) upon the *Shank* of it: But you muſt be ſure to Forge ſubſtance enough for the *Worm* to be cut out of it.

The *Main* and *Worm-wheels* are Forg'd round and flat.

The manner of Forging theſe Wheels (which in Smith's Language is, *Turning up the Wheels*) is, firſt, to draw out a ſquare Rod (as you were taught *Numb.* I. *fol.* 9. among the ſeveral *Heats of Iron*) ſomewhat thicker than you intend your *Wheel* ſhall be; but it muſt be almoſt as thin on one ſide, as you intend the inner edge of the *Wheel* ſhall be, and the oppoſite to it above twice that thickneſs, for the outer edge of the *Wheel*: the reaſon you will find by and by. Having drawn from your ſquare Rod a convenient length, *viz.* almoſt three times the Diameter of your intended Wheel, you muſt take almoſt a *Flame-heat*, and Hammer all along the whole length upon the thick edge, ſo will you find the long Rod by this Hammering, turn by degrees rounder and rounder in, upon the thin edge, which you Hammer'd not upon, till it become a Circle, or pretty near a Circle. But you muſt make it ſomewhat more than a Circle, for the ends muſt lap over one another, that they may be *welded* upon one another.

Thus you may ſee the Reaſon for making the outer edge of the Rod thick, and the oppoſite Edge thin; for your Hammering upon the outer edge only, and not on the inner, makes the outer edge a great deal thinner, and at the ſame time makes the Wheel broader.

The

The Reaſon why I told you, you ſhould draw fourth the Rod to almoſt three times the Diameter of the Wheel, and not to the Geometrical proportion; is, becauſe that in Hammering upon it to make it round, the Rod will ſtretch ſo conſiderably, that it will be long enough to make a *Wheel* of your intended Diameter, and moſt commonly ſomewhat to ſpare. But to return.

Before you take a *welding Heat*, as by *Numb.* I. *fol.* 9, 10. you muſt flatten the two ends that are to be *welded* together, to a little more than half their thickneſs, that when they are lapt over one another, and *welded* together, they may be no thicker than the other part of the *Wheel*.

If the *Wheel* be not *turned up* ſo round, that with a little labour you may mend them at the *Vice*; you muſt with *Blood red Heats* Hammer them round upon the *Pike* or *Bickern* of the *Anvel*, holding with your *Tongs* the inner edge of the *Wheel* upon it, and Hammering upon the outer edge of the *Wheel*, till the *Wheel* be fit for the *Vice*: Their inſides muſt be divided into four equal Parts or four [c] *Dufftail* notches to be fil'd into them. The *Dufftail* notches are cut in the inner edge of the *Wheel*, ſomewhat more than a quarter of an Inch deep, and ſpreading ſomewhat wider towards the outer edge. The notches are to receive the four ends of a *Croſs* Forg'd ſomewhat thicker towards the ends than the thickneſs of the *Wheel*, and muſt be filed outer *Dufftails*, to let exactly into the inner *Dufftail* notches made in the inſide of the *Wheel*. They muſt be Forg'd thicker than the *Wheel*, becauſe they muſt batter over both the flat ſides of the *Wheel*, to keep the *Wheel* ſtrong and ſteady upon the *Croſs*; and ſometimes (for more ſecurity) they are *brazed* into the *Wheel* (yet that is but ſeldom) the middle of this *Croſs*

is

is made broad, that when the ſquare of the *Spindle*, it may have ſtrength enough to bear the violence offered at, as well in winding up the great weight, that keeps the *Wheels* in motion, as in the checking and turning the *Jack-winder* back, to ſet the *Jack* a going, when by the winding up, it may be ſubject to ſtand ſtill, or ſometimes, for want of weight, or elſe for want of Oiling or ſome other accident.

Theſe *Wheels* thus Forg'd and Filed flat, muſt be divided, the *main Wheel* commonly into 64 equal parts, and the *worm Wheel* into 32 equal parts; but theſe Numbers are not exactly obſerv'd by Smiths, for ſometimes they make them more and ſometimes leſs, either according to the ſize of their *Wheels*, or according as they intend their *Wheels* ſhall go, ſwifter or ſlower about (for the fewer the *Teeth* on a *Wheel* are, the ſooner a *Wheel* goes about and the more *Teeth* on a *Wheel*, the ſlower the *Wheel* goes about) or ſometimes as they have open'd their Compaſſes to divide them: For if by luck, they at firſt open their Compaſſes to ſuch a width, as will juſt meaſure out on a Circle, (which they deſcribe on the Center of the *Wheel* for that purpoſe) their intended number, than the *Wheel* ſhall have the intended Number of *Teeth*; if not, let it ſomewhat fall ſhort, or exceed that Number, they matter not, but make that Number of *Teeth* on the *Wheel*. And having thus divided the *Wheel*, they by the ſide of a ſtraight Ruler laid to the Center, and every diviſion markt on the *Wheel*, draw or ſcratch a ſtraight line from the outer limb of the *Wheels*, to the Circle, which Circle (I ſhould have told you before) is deſcrib'd at that diſtance from the outer Verge, they intend the *Teeth* ſhall be cut down to. This is indeed a rough way of working, but the Office of a *Jack* is well enough performed by this rough Work;

Work; and the uſual prizes ſuch, as will ſcarce pay Workmen for better, as they ſay.

Theſe *Wheels* thus divided, muſt be cut down into theſe Diviſions with a [d] *Jack-file*, the *Main-wheel* ſtraight thwart the outer Verge, (which to ſpeak Mathematically, makes an Angle of 90 degrees with the flat ſides of the *Wheel*,) and the *Worm-wheel* aſlope, making an Angle of about 115 degrees with its ſides, that is, an Angle of 25 degrees, with a line drawn ſtraight athwart the outer Edge of the *Wheel*, and that *Teeth* of the *Worm-wheel* may gather themſelves into the *Grooves* of the *Worm* in the *Worm-ſpindle*; the *Worm* on the *Worm-ſpindle* running about 65 degrees aſlope from this Axis, or Perpendicular of the *Worm-ſpindle*; the notches you make with the File muſt be ſo wide, as to contain about twice the thickneſs of of each *Tooth*: Therefore you may obſerve, that the Number of *Teeth* cannot be aſſign'd, becauſe the Sizes of all *Jack wheels* are not of equal Diameters, and the Sizes of the *Teeth* muſt be filed very ſquare and ſmooth, as the corners taken off, and rounded on both ſides towards the middle of the top or end of the *Tooth*, which much helps the *Teeth* to gather in upon the *Teeth* of the *Nut*, and the *Worm* on the *Worm-ſpindle*.

The *Teeth* of the *Wheels* being cut down, and the whole *Wheel* finiſh'd, they muſt be forc'd ſtiff and hard upon the ſquare of the *Spindle*, cloſe up to the Shoulder; which Square being made ſomewhat longer than the *Croſs* of the *Wheel* is thick, muſt with a *Cold-Chiſſel* be cut on the top of that Square, to make the Iron that comes through the Square hole of the *Wheel*, ſpread over the *Croſs* of the *Wheel*, and then that ſpreading muſt be battered with the *Pen* of the Hammer; that it may ſtand up ſtiff againſt the ſhoulder of the Square, on the other ſide of the *Wheel*; but in doing

doing this, you must be very careful that the *Spindle* stand exactly Perpendicular to the flat sides of your *Wheels*; for should the *Spindle* lean never so little to one, or the other side of the *Wheel*, the the *Wheel* when it is moving in the *Jack-frame* would not move perpendicular, but wabble towards the *Fore* or *Backsides* of the *Jack-frame*, and perhaps by this irregular motion, before a revolution of the *Wheel* be perform'd, it would go off from the length of the *Teeth* of the *Nut*.

Then file the *Spindle-pins* (which are the ends of the *Spindle*, that go into the Center-holes of the *Fore* and *Backsides* of the *Jack-frame*) exactly round and fit to their Center-holes, and place them into their proper Center-holes. Then try if the *Wheels* are exactly round on their outer edges, and that in turning about, their flat sides wabble not, but in a revolution keep Parallel to the *Fore* and *Backsides*. The way Smiths use to try them by is, to turn them about by the *Spindle*, and holding a piece of Chalk steddy to the outer Limb of the *Wheel*, not letting the Point of the Chalk slip forwards or backwards, or towards the right or left Hand, for then if the Chalk make a white stroke round the whole *Wheel*, and that white stroke lie exactly Parallel to the two outer Edges of the *Wheel*, the *Wheel* is not only round, but stands also true upon its *Spindle*, that is, Perpendicular to the *Spindle*, and the *Spindle* Perpendicular to the flat of it: But if the Chalk does not touch round the *Wheel*, you must file down so much of the outer Verge of the *Wheel*, where the Chalk does touch, as will bring down or equalize the Diameter of the *Wheel* in that place, to the Diameter of the *Wheel* in the place where it does not touch; so you may conclude the *Wheel* is round. If the Mark of the Chalk lie not exactly in the middle between the two edges of the

the *Wheel*, then it is not Perpendicular to the *Spindle*, and you muſt with the Hammer ſet it right, that is Perpendicular, by forcing the *Wheel* over from the ſide it leans too much to, or elſe by forcing the *Spindle*, which is all one; yet this is an help you ought not to rely upon but in caſe of neceſſity; rather be ſure your *Wheel* and *Spindle* ſtand Perpendicular to one another, before you faſten the *Wheel* upon the ſquare of the *Spindle*, for by this help the ſquare on the *Spindle* will be apt to looſen in the ſquare of the *Wheel*, and you will have your *Wheel* to new faſten upon the Square of the *Spindle* again.

As you try'd the *Wheels* with Chalk, ſo you muſt try the *Nut*, the *Worm* and the *Spindle*.

The upper part of the *Worm-ſpindle*, muſt be Fil'd truly round to fit into the *Worm-loop*, that it ſhake not in it, and yet go very eaſily about, without the leaſt ſtopping. At the upper end of this round on the *Worm Spindle*, you muſt file a ſquare to fit the ſquare hole of the *Fly* upon.

The *Shank* of the *Worm-loop* and the *Stud* of the *Worm-ſpindle*, muſt ſtand ſo far off the left ſide of the fore ſide, that the *Teeth* of the *Worm-wheel*, may fall full into the *Grooves* of the *Worm*; for ſo both being cut with the ſame ſlope, the ſlope *Teeth* of the *Worm-wheel* will gather into the ſlope *Grooves* of the *Spindle*, and preſſing upon the *Worm*, drive about the *Worm-ſpindle* and the *Fly*.

The *Fly* is made ſometimes with two, ſometimes with four Arms from the Center, and ſometimes the Arms are made longer, ſometimes ſhorter: The more Arms, and alſo the longer Arms, are to make the *Jack* go ſlower.

There is yet a ſmall matter more of Iron-work about the *Jack*, which is the *Tumbler*; but it lies in the farther end of the *Barrel*, and cannot well be describ'd without a particular Figure, which therefore I have inserted. As in *Fig.* 2. A the *Barrel*, B the *Main spindle* coming through the *Barrel*, [a] the Center of the *Tumbler* moving upon the *Center-pin*, which is fasten'd into an Iron-plate behind the *Barrel*. [b] The *Coller* upon the *Main-spindle*, from which proceeds a *Tongue*, which passes through a pretty wide hole at [c] in the *Tumbler*, as far as [e] [d] the *Catch of the Tumbler*. The *Tumbler* moves as aforesaid, upon the Center hole [a], but receives the *Tongue* through it at [c], and passes as far as [e]. This *Tongue* serves as a *Check* to the *Tumbler*, that it cannot tumble above an Angle of 20 degrees, from the Iron-plate it is fasten'd to; and that the width of its Center-hole, and the width of the *Tongue* passes through, and the motion of the *Coller* about the *Main-spindle* allows it; but were the Center-hole [a], and its *Center-pin* fit, and the Hole [c], and the *Tongue* that also passes through it also fit, and the *Coller* fixt, it could not move at all. But this play is enough for it, to do the purpose it is design'd for. The *Tumbler* is so plac'd behind the *Barrel*, that while the *Jack line* is winding up upon the *Barrel*, its round britch passes forwards by all the *Crosses* of the *Main-wheel*, and the *Point* or *Catch* [d], as then claps it self snug or close to the Iron-plate of the *Barrel*: But when the *Barrel* is turn'd to the contrary way, the weight of the *Catch* in half a revolution of the *Barrel* (let the *Tumbler* be posited where it will) makes it open and fall from the Iron-plate, and butt against one or other of the *Crosses* on the *Main-wheel*, and so thrusts the *Main wheel* about with the *Barrel*.

The *Eye* of the *Winch* or *Winder*, is forg'd as you were taught to forge the *Pin-hole* in the *Cross-garnet*, *Numb.* II. *fol.* 18. But that was to be a small round hole, and therefore you were direct-

ly

ly to lay a ſmall round piece of Iron or Wyre, where you intended the Pin hole ſhould be, and lap the other end of your Work over it; but this is to be a wide ſquare hole, therefore you muſt lay a ſquare piece of Iron of your ſize, where the *Eye* of the *Jack-winch* ſhall be and lap or double the other end over it, and Weld and Work as you were directed. The reſt of the *Winch* is but common *Forging* and *Filing* Work, which hath been ſufficiently taught already.

The Wood-work belonging to the *Jack*, is a *Barrel*, a *Spit-wheel* and a *Handing of the Winch*; which being *Turners* Work, I ſhall ſay nothing to, till I come to the Art of *Turning*. Only thoſe *Wheels* that have more than one *Groove* in them, are call'd Two, Three, *&c.* *Struck-wheels*, in Workmens corrupting Language; but I ſuppoſe, originally two *Stroak*, three *Stroak-wheels*, &c. from the number of *Grooves* that are in them.

The Excellencies of a good *Jack* are, 1. That the *Jack-frame* be Forg'd and Fil'd Square, and conveniently Strong, well ſet together, and will Screw cloſe and tight up. 2. That the *Wheels* be Perpendicularly, and ſtrongly fix'd on the Squares of the *Spindles*. 3. That the *Teeth* be evenly cut and well ſmooth'd, and that the *Teeth* of the *Worm-wheel* fall evenly into the *Groove* of the *Worm*. 4. That the *Spindle Pins* ſhake not between the *Fore* and *Backſides*, nor are too big, or too little for their Center holes.

[a] The *ſquare Bore*, is a ſquare Steel Point or Shank well Temper'd, fitted into a ſquare Socket in an Iron *Wimble*: It is deſcrib'd, *Fig.* 3. Its uſe is to open a Hole and make it truly round and ſmooth within; when you uſe it, you muſt ſet the Head againſt your

Breast, and put the Point of the *square Bore* into the Hole you punch'd or would open, and turning the Handle about, you with it turn about the Shank of the *square Bore*, whose Edges cut away the Irregularities of the Iron made in the Punching. But you must thrust or lean hard with your Breast against the Head of the *square Bore*, that it may cut the faster: And you must be sure to guide the *square Bore* truly straight forwards in the Hole, lest the Hole be wrought aslope in the Iron.

[b] To *open an Hole*, is in Smith's Language, to make the Hole wider.

[c] A *Duftail*, is a Figure made in the form of a Doves-tail, and is us'd by many other Handy-crafts, as well as Smiths, but most especially by Joyners, as I shall shew, when I come to *Joynery*.

[d] A *Jack-file*, is a broad File somewhat thin on both Edges, and stronger in the Middle.

The manner of making Molds *to Cast* Leaden-Bullets *in.*

I Insert the making of *Bullet molds*, because there is some sort of Work in them different from what hath yet been taught. The Handles, and the Heads are Forg'd as other Work, but the two concave Hemispheres, are first Punch'd with a round ended *Punch*, of the shape and almost of the size you intend the Bullet shall be. They must be Punch'd deep enough at the *Forge* with a *blood red heat*; then are the Edges of the Chaps Filed flat, first with a common File the common way, but afterwards with an using File as Workmen call it. The using File, is a long and broad File, exactly flat on both its cut sides, having a square Iron handle down out at one

one end with an hole in it; but the Handle is not to hold it by when you uſe it, but the hole in it to go over a pin you hang it upon, when you do not uſe it. When you uſe it, you muſt lay it flat upon the Work bench, with its Handle, from you, and you muſt take care that it lies ſolid and ſteady, leſt when you Work upon it, it ſlip from you; therefore you may ſtrike a Nail in at the hole in the Handle, a little way into the Work bench, that you may draw it again, when you have done with the *uſing File*, you may drive in a ſmall Tack on each ſide the *uſing File*, to keep it ſteddy or you may Tack down two ſmall thin boards on either ſide and rip them off again when you have done. Your *uſing File* lying thus ſtraight and ſteddy before you, lay the Chaps of one half of the *Mold* flat upon the hither end of the *uſing File*, and holding your two Thumbs, and your two Fore-fingers upon the Head of the *Mold*, thruſt your Work hard down from you the whole length of the *Uſing-file*, then draw your Work lightly back, and thruſt it again hard from you; retire theſe thruſts thus, till upon the Chaps of the *Mold*, you can ſee no irregularities, or the File-ſtroaks of the common File left, ſo may you be ſure that the Chaps of the *Mold* is truly flat. Do the like by the other half of the *Mold*.

Now you muſt try whether each of theſe concaves be an exact half-round; thus you may deſcribe an Arch a little more than a Semi-circle, juſt of the Diameter of the *Bullet*, upon the end of a thin piece of Braſs-latin, draw a ſtraight Line through the Center, and the Arch on both ſides it, for the limits of the Semi-circle; File very curiouſly all the Braſs away on the end, juſt to this Semi-circle, and juſt to the Diametral-line, on either side of the Semi-circle, so have you a convex Semi-circle: Put this convex Semi-circle into the Concave *Molds*, if it fits them so as the Convex reaches just the bottom of the *Molds*, when its Shoulder touches just the Chaps of the *Mold*, they are each a true concave Hemisphere. But if the Shoulder of the Convex (that is, a Diametral-line prolong'd) rides upon the Chaps of the Concave, and the bottom of the Convex touch not the bottom of the Concave, the Concave is Punch'd too deep, and must have its Chaps rubb'd upon the *Using-file* again, till it comply with the Convex. Then put into the two Concaves a round *Bullet*, that will just fill them both, and pinching the Heads of the *Mold* close together in a *Vice*, with the *Bullet* in it, drill an hole through both the handles of the *Joint*. The reason why the *Bullet* is put into the *Mold* is, because the Chaps of the two Halves should lie exactly upon one another, whilst the hole for the *Joint* is drilling. Then fit a Rivet-pin for this hole, and Rivet them together, but not so hard, but that the *Mold* may open and shut pretty easie, and yet go true. Then take the *Bullet* out, and File in each half of the Head, half a round hole directly against one another for the a *Gea*, which two half holes, when the *Mold* is shut, will make one round hole.

You may now try with Clay, or by casting a leaden *Bullet* in it, whether it be exactly round or no; for making a true round hole in a thin piece of Brass, just of the Circumference of the Chaps, you may try if the *Cast-bullet* will just pass thro', and also fill that hole when the *Bullet* is turn'd every way; which if it do, you may conclude the *Mold* is true. This thin piece of Brass, with a round hold in it, is call'd a *Sizer*.

But

But the inside wants cleansing, for hitherto it is only Punch'd. Therefore you must provide a [b] *Bullet-bore*, with which you may bore the inside of each half to clear it. Or if they be not quite deep enough Punch'd, you may bore them deeper. You may bore them severally, or together, by putting the *Bullet-bore* into the *Mold*, so as the *Shank* may come through the *Geat*.

In this Section you see, first the use of a *Using-file*, an Instrument of great use for a flat Filing; for by it you may make two pieces of Iron of somewhat considerable breadth, so true, that by laying the two flat sides upon each other, they shall draw up one another. It is much used by *Clock-makers*, *Watch-makers*, *Letter-mold-makers*, and indeed all others that frame Square-work on Iron, Steel or Brass. Secondly, the use of a *Bullet-bore*, which though it be seldom us'd, yet it may serve not only for *Bullet-molds*, but for other purposes; and by altering its shape into an Oblong, a Cone or Cilinder, you may bore these hollow Figures either for *Molds*, or some other accidental Uses.

[a] A *Geat*, is the hole through which the Metal runs into the *mold*. The Word is us'd by most *Founders*.

[b] The *Bullet-bore*, is a *Shank* of Steel, having a Steel *Globe* or *Bullet* at one end, just of your intended *Bullet* size. This Globular end must be Hatch'd with a fine cut, by a *File-cutter*, and Harden'd and Temper'd. The end of the *Shank*, this Globular Bore is fastned to, must be round and so small, that when the *Bullet-bore* is in the *mold*, the *Geat* will easily receive it. The other end of the *Shank* must be fitted into the square Socket of the *Wimble*, and have a Shoulder to it,

to ſtop the Socket from ſliding too far upon the *Shank*. From this Shoulder, the reſt of the *Shank* muſt run Tapering down, to the ſmall end the *Bullet-bore* is faſtned to. You muſt Work with it, as you were taught to Work with the *Square-bore*.

Of Twiſting of the Iron.

SQuare and flat Bars, ſometimes are by Smiths, *Twiſted* for Ornament. It is very eaſily done; for after the Bar is Square or flat Forg'd (and if the curioſity of your Work require it truly Fil'd) you muſt take a *Flame-heat*, or if your Work be ſmall, but *Blood-red heat*, and you may twiſt it about, as much or as little as you pleaſe, either with the *Tongs*, *Vice* or *Hand-vice*, &c.

Of Caſe-hardning.

C*Aſe-hardning* is ſometimes us'd by *File-cutters*, when they make courſe *Files* for Cheapneſs, and generally moſt *Raſps* have formerly been made of Iron and *Caſe-hardned*, becauſe it makes the outſide of them hard. It is us'd alſo by *Gun-ſmiths*, for Hardning their Barrels; and it is us'd for *Tobacco-boxes*, *Cod-piece-buttons*, *Heads* for *Walking-ſtaves*, &c. And in theſe Caſes, Workmen to ſet a greater value on them in the Buyers eſteem, call them *Steel-barrels*, *Steel-tobacco-boxes*, *Steel-buttons*, *Steel-heads*, &c. But Iron thus hardned takes a better Poliſh and keeps the Poliſh much longer and better, than if the Iron were not *Caſe hardned*. The manner of *Caſe-hardning* is thus, Take *Cow-horn* or *Hoof*, dry it thoroughly in an Oven, and then beat it to Powder, put about the ſame quantity of Bay-Salt to it, and mingle them together with ſtale Chamberly, or elſe White-wine-vinegar. Lay ſome of this mixture upon the Loam, made as you were taught

taught *Numb.* I. *fol.* 13. And cover your Iron all over with it; then wrap the Loam about all, and lay it upon the Hearth of the Forge to dry and harden: When it is dry and hard, put it into the Fire and blow up the Coals to it, till the whole Lump have just a *Blood-red-heat*, but no higher, lest the quality of your mixture burn away and leave the Iron as soft as at first. Then take it out and quench it: Or, instead of Loam, you may wrap it up in Plate Iron, so as the mixture may touch every part of your Work, and blow the Coals to it, as aforesaid.

Of several sorts of Steel in common use among Smiths.

THE difficulty of getting good Steel makes many Workmen (when by good hap they light on it) commend that Country-Steel for best, from whence that Steel came. Thus I have found some cry up *Flemish-steel*, others *Swedish*, *English*, *Spanish*, *Venice*, &c. But according to my Observation and common Consent of the most ingenious Workmen, each Country produces almost indifferently good and bad; yet each Country doth not equally produce such Steel, as is fit for every particular purpose, as I shall shew you by and by. But the several sorts of Steel, that are in general use here in *England*, are the *English*, the *Flemish*, the *Swedish*, the *Spanish* and the *Venice-steel*.

The *English-steel* is made in several places in *England*, as in *Yorkshire*, *Gloucestershire*, *Sussex*, the *Wild of Kent*, &c. But the best is made about the *Forrest of Dean*, it breaks Fiery, with somewhat a course Grain. But if it be well wrought and proves sound, it makes good Edge-tools, Files and Punches. It will work well at the Forge, and take a good Heat.

The

The *Flemiſh-ſteel* is made in *Germany*, in the Country of *Stiermark* and in the *Land of Luyck*: From thence brought to *Colen*, and is brought down the River *Rhine* to *Dort*, and other parts of *Holland* and *Flanders*, ſome in *Bars* and ſome in *Gads*, and is therefore by us call'd *Flemiſh-ſteel*, and ſometimes *Gad-ſteel*. It is a tough ſort of Steel, and the only Steel us'd for Watch-ſprings. It is alſo good for Punches; File-cutters alſo uſe it to make their Chiſſels of, with which they cnt their Files. It breaks with a fine Grain, works well at the Forge, and will take a welding Heat.

I cannot learn that any Steel comes from *Sweden*, but from *Dantzick* comes ſome which is call'd *Swediſh-ſteel*: It is much of the ſame Quality and Fineſs with *Flemiſh-ſteel*.

The *Spaniſh-ſteel* is made about *Biſcay*. It is a fine ſort of Steel, but ſome of it is very difficult to work at the Forge, becauſe it will not take a good Heat; and it ſometimes proves very unſound, as not being well *curried*, that is well wrought. It is too quick (as Workmen call it) that is, too brittle for Springs or Punches, but makes good fine Edg'd-tools.

Venice-ſteel is much like *Spaniſh ſteel*, but much finer, and Works ſomewhat better at the Forge. It is us'd for Razors, Chirurgion's Inſtruments, Gravers, *&c.* Becauſe it will come to a fine and thin Edge. Razor makers generally clap a ſmall Bar of *Venice-ſteel* between two ſmall Bars of *Flemiſh-ſteel*, and ſo Work or Weld them together, to ſtrengthen the back of the Razor, and keep it from cracking.

There

There is another ſort of Steel, of higher commendations than any of the forgoing ſorts. It is call'd *Damaſcus-ſteel*; 'tis very rare that any comes into *England* unwrought, but the *Turkiſh-Cymeters* are generally made of it. It is moſt difficult of any Steel to Work at the Forge, for you ſhall ſcarce be able to ſtrike upon a Blood-heat, but it will *Red-ſear*; inſomuch that theſe *Cymeters* are, by many Workmen, thought to be caſt Steel. But when it is wrought, it takes the fineſt and keeps the ſtrongeſt Edge of any other Steel. Workmen ſet almoſt an ineſtimable value upon it to make Punches, Cold-punches, *&c.* of. We cannot learn where it is made, and yet as I am inform'd, the Honourable Mr. *Boyl* hath been very careful and induſtrious in that enquiry; giving it in particular charge to ſome Travellers to *Damaſcus*, to bring home an Account of it: But when they came thither they heard of none made there, but were ſent about 50 Miles into the Country and then they were told about 50 Miles farther than that: So that no certain Account could be gain'd where it is made. *Kirman* towards the Ocean affords very fine Steel, of which they make Weapons highly priz'd; for a *Cymeter* of that Steel, will cut through an Helmet with an eaſie blow. *Geog. Rect. fol.* 279.

The Rule to know good Steel by.

BReak a little piece of the end of the Rod, and obſerve how it breaks; for good Steel breaks ſhort of all Gray, like froſt work Silver. But in the breaking of the bad you will find ſome veins of Iron ſhining and doubling in the Steel.

Of

Of Nealing of Steel.

HAving chose your Steel and forg'd it to your intended shape, if you are either to File Engrave or to Punch upon it, you ought to Neal it first, because it will make it softer and consequently work easier. The common way is to give it a *Blood-red-heat* in the Fire, then take it out, and let it cool of it self.

There are some pretenders to know how to make Steel as soft as Lead; but so oft as my Curiosity has prompted me to try their pretended Processes, so oft have they fail'd me; and not only me, but some others, careful Observers. But the way they most boast of, is the often heating the Iron or Steel in red-hot Lead, and letting it cool of it self with the Lead. I have many times try'd this without any other success, than that it does make Iron or Steel as soft as if it were well Neal'd the common way, but no softer: And could it be otherwise, the small Iron Ladles, that Letter-founders use to the casting of Printing Letters, would be very soft indeed; for their Iron Ladles are kept constantly Month after Month in melting Mettal, whereof the main Body is Lead, and when they cast small Letters, they keep their Mettal red-hot; and I have known them many times left in the Mettal and cool with it, as the Fire has gone out of it self; but yet the Iron Ladles have been no softer, than if they had been well Neal'd the common way. But perhaps these Pretenders mean the Iron or Steel shall be as soft as Lead, when the Iron or Steel is red-hot; if so, we may thank them for nothing.

But

But that which makes Steel a very ſmall matter ſofter than the common way of Nealing is, by covering Steel with a courſe Powder of Cow-Horns, or Hoofs, or Rams-Horns, and ſo incloſing it in a Loam: Then put the whole Lump into a Wooden Fire to heat red-hot and let it lie in the Fire till the Fire go out of it ſelf, and the Steel cool with the Fire.

Of Hardning and Tempering Steel.

ENnglish, *Flemiſh* and *Swediſh-ſteel*, muſt have a pretty high heat given them, and then ſuddenly quench in Water to make them very hard; but *Spaniſh* and *Venice-ſteel* will need but a Blood-red-heat, and then when they are quench'd in Water, will be very hard. If your Steel be too hard, that is to brittle, and it be an edg'd or pointed Inſtrument you make, the edge or point will be very ſubject to break; or if it be a Spring, it will not bow, but with the leaſt bending it will ſnap aſſunder: Therefore you muſt *let it down* (as Smiths ſay) that is, make it ſofter, by *tempering* it: The manner is thus, take a piece of Grin-ſtone or Whet-ſtone and rub hard upon your Work to take the black Scurf off it, and brighten it; then let it heat in the Fire, and as it grows hotter you will ſee the Colour change by degrees, coming to a light goldiſh Colour, then to a dark goldiſh Colour, and at laſt to a blew Colour; chooſe which of theſe Colours your Work requires, and then quench it ſuddenly in Water. The light goldiſh Colour is for Files, Cold-chiſſels and Punches, that Punch into Iron and Steel: The dark goldiſh Colour for Punches to uſe on Braſs, and generally for moſt Edge-tools: The blew Colour gives the Temper to Springs in general, and is alſo us'd to Beautifie both Iron and Steel; but then Workmen ſome-

times

times grind *Indico* and *Sallad-oyl* together, and rub that mixture upon it, with a woollen Rag, while it is heating, and let it cool of it self.

There is another sort of *Hardning*, call'd *Hammer-hardning*, It is most us'd on Iron or Steel Plates, for *Dripping pans*, *Saws*, *Straight-Rulers*, &c. It is perform'd only, with well Hammering of the Plates, which both smooths them, and beats the Mettal firmer into its own Body, and somewhat hardens it.

The manner of Forging Steel, either for Edge-tools, Punches, Springs, *&c.* Is (the several shapes consider'd) the same with forging Iron: Only this general Rule observe, from an old *English* Verse us'd among Smiths, when they Forge Edge-tools,

He that will a good Edge win,
Must Forge thick and Grind thin.

Plate 5. Page . 63

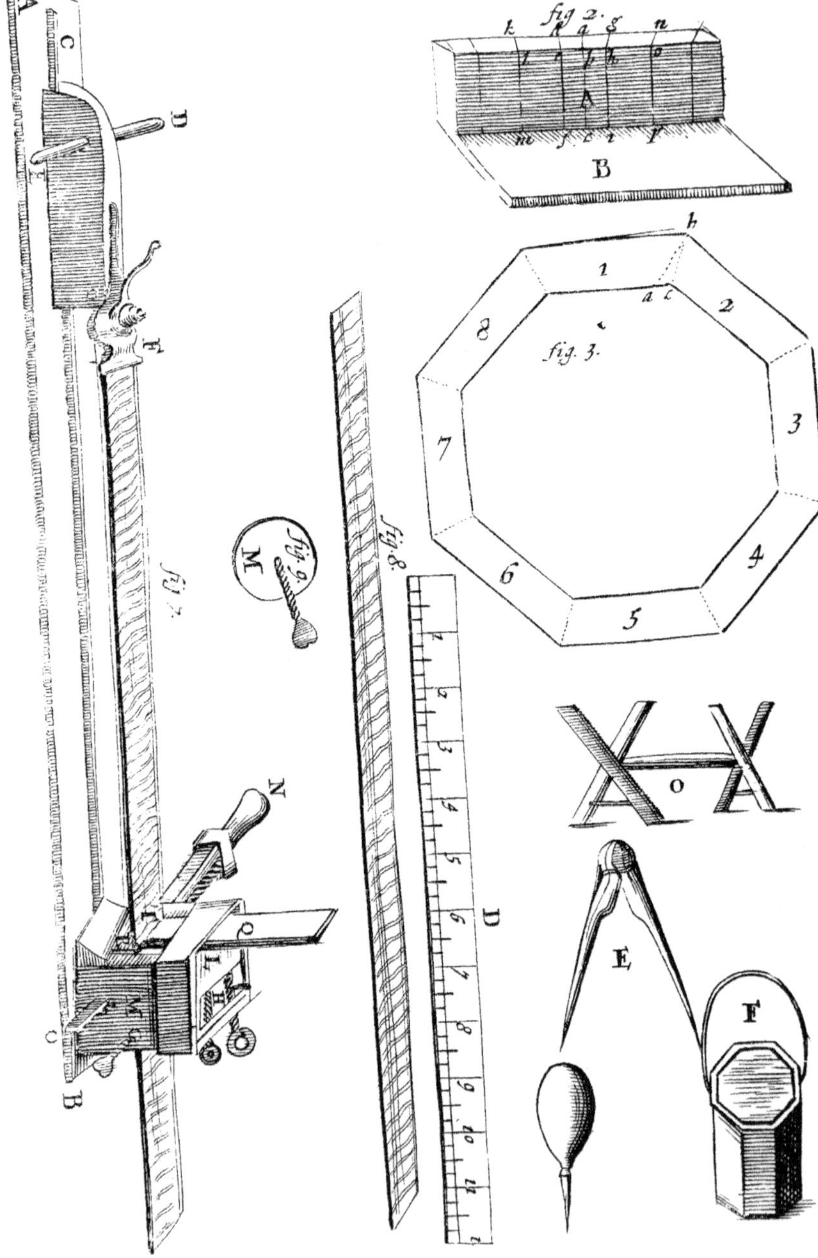

MECHANICK EXERCISES;

O R,

The Doctrine of *Handy-Works*

The Art of JOINERY.

Definition.

JOINERY, *is an Art Manual, whereby several Pieces of Wood are so fitted and join'd together by* Straight-line, Squares, Miters *or any* Bevel, *that they shall seem one intire Piece.*

Explanation.

By *Straight-Lines* I mean that which in Joyner's Language is call'd a Joint, That is, two Pieces of Wood are Shot (that is Plained,) or else they are Pared, that is, the irregularities that hinder the closing of the two Pieces are cut off with a Pairing-chissel. They are Shot or Pared (as I said) so exactly straight, that when they are set upon one another, light shall not be discern'd betwixt them. This they call Shooting of a Joint, or Paring to a Joint, because these two Pieces are with Glew commonly join'd together, either to make a Board broad enough for their purpose, or to [a] Clamp one piece of Wood to the end of another piece of Wood to keep it from Casting or Warping.

By

By *Squares*, I mean the making of Frames, either for Door-cases or such like, which is the Framing of two pieces of Wood athwart two other pieces of Wood, so as the four Angles of the Frame may comply with the *Square* marked D.

By *Miters* are meant the joining of two pieces of Wood, so as the Joint makes half a Square, and does comply with the *Miter-square* marked E.

By a *Bevel* is meant any other Angle: As Frames that may be made of *Pentagon*, *Hexagon*, *Octagon*, &c. Figures.

§ 1. *The Names of Joyners Tools describ'd, in Plate* IV.

A A Work-bench. *b* The Hook in it, to lay Boards or other [b] Stuff flat against, whilst they are [c] Trying or Plaining. *c* The Bench-Screw (on its hither side) to Screw Boards in, whilst the Edges of them are Plaining or [d] Shooting; and then the other edge of the Board is set upon a Pin or Pins (if the Board be so long as to reach the other Leg) put into the Holes marked *a a a a a* down the Legs of the Bench; which Pin or Pins may be removed into the higher or lower holes, as the breadth of the Board shall require: So then, the Bench-screw keeps the Board close to the edge of the Bench, and the Pins in the Legs keep it to its height, that it may stand steddy whilst the other edge is working upon: For in the Shooting of a Joint, if the Board keeps not its exact position, but shakes or trembles under the Plain, your Joint will very hardly be truly straight. *d* The Hold-fast, let pretty loose into round holes marked *b b b b b b*, in the Bench: Its Office is to keep the Work fast upon the Bench, whilst you either Saw, Tennant, Mor-

Mortess, or sometimes *Plain* upon it, *&c.* It performs this Office with the knock of an *Hammer*, or *Mallet*, upon the *head* of it; for the *Beak* of it being made crooked downwards, the end of the *Beak* falling upon the flat of the *Bench*, keeps the *head* of the *Hold-fast* above the flat of the *Bench*, and the *hole* in the *Bench* the *Shank* is let into being bored straight down, and wide enough to let the *Hold-fast* play a little, the *head* of the *Hold-fast* being knockt, the point of the *Beak* throws the *Shank* a-slope in the *hole* in the *Bench*, and presses its back-side hard against the edge of the *hole* on the upper Superficies of the *Bench*, and its fore-side hard against the oppersite side of the under Superficies of the *Bench*, and so by the point of the *Beak*, the *Shank* of the *Hold-fast* is wedged between the upper edge, and its oppersite edge of the round hole in the *Bench*. Sometimes a double *Screw* is fixed to the side of the *Bench*, as at g; or sometimes its farther *Cheek* is laid an edge upon the flat of the *Bench*, and fastned with an *Hold-fast*, or, sometimes, two on the *Bench*. *e* A *Mallet*.

§. 2. B B B B B B B *Plains* of several Sorts: as,

B 1. A *Fore Plain*. *a* The *Tote*. *b* The *Mouth*. *c* The *Wedge*. *d* The *Iron*. *e* The *Sole*. *f* The *Fore-end*. *g* The *Britch*. *f g h* The *Stock*. All together *A Plane*. It is called the *Fore Plane* because it is used before you come to work either with the *Smooth Plane*, or with the *Joynter*. The edge of its *Iron* is not ground upon the straight, as the *Smooth Plane*, and the *Joynter* are, but rises with a Convex-Arch in the middle of it; for its Office being to prepare the Stuff for either the *Smoothing Plane*, or the *Joynter*, Workmen set the edge of it [e] *Ranker* than the edge either of the *Smoothing Plane*, or the *Joynter*; and should the *Iron* of the *Plane* be ground to a straight edge, and it be ſet never ſo little R*anker* on one end of the edge than on the other, the *Ranker* end would (bearing as then upon a point) in working, dig Gutters on the Surface of the *Stuff*; but this *Iron* (being ground to a Convex-Arch) though it ſhould be ſet a little *Ranker* on one end of its edge than on the other, would not make Gutters on the Surface of the *Stuff*, but (at the moſt) little hollow dawks on the *Stuff*, and that more or leſs, according as the *Plane* is ground more or leſs Arching. Nor is it the Office of this *Plane* to ſmooth the *Stuff*, but only (as I ſaid) to prepare it, that is, to take off the irregular Riſings, whether on the ſides, or in the middle, and therefore it is ſet ſomewhat *Ranker*, that it may take the Irregularities the ſooner off the *Stuff*, that the *Smoothing Plane*, or the *Joynter*, may afterwards the eaſier work it *Try*. The manner of *Trying* ſhall be taught, when I come to Treat of the uſe of the *Rule*.

You muſt note, that as I told yon in *Smithing*, *Num.* I. *fol.* 14, 15, 16. it was the Office of the *courſe tooth'd File* to take off the prominent Irregularities the *Hammer* made in the *Forging*, &c. and that you were not to *file* them more away than you need, ſo the ſame Caution is to be given you in the uſing of this *fore Plane* in *Joynery*, for the reaſon there alledged in *Smithing*, whether, to avoid Repetition, I refer you; only with this Conſideration, that there *Iron*, or *Steel*, was the matter wrought upon, and there a *courſe File* the *Tool*; but now *Wood* is the matter, and a *Courſe*, or *Fore-Plane*, the *Tool*.

§. 3 Of *ſetting* the *Iron*.

WHen you *ſet* the *Iron* of the *Fore-Plane*, conſider the *Stuff* you are to work upon, *viz.* Whether it be *hard* or *ſoft*, or *Curling*, as *Joyners* call

call *Croſs grain'd Stuff*: If it be *hard* or *curling*, you muſt not *ſet* the *Iron* veay *rank*, becauſe a Man's ſtrength will not cut deep into hard *Wood*; and if it be not hard *Wood*, but *curling*, or *knotty*, and the *Iron Rank-ſet*, you may indeed work with it till you come to ſome *Knot*, or *Curl*, but then you may either tear your *Stuff*, or break the edge of your *Iron*; therefore you may perceive a reaſon to *ſet* the *Iron fine* for *curling*, and *knotty Stuff*.

But if you ask me how *rank* your *Iron* ought to be ſet? I anſwer, If your Wood be *ſoft*, and your *Stuff free*, and *frowy*, that is, evenly temper'd all the way, you may *ſet* the *Iron* to take a ſhaving off the thickneſs of an old coined Shilling, but ſcarce thicker; whereas, if your *Stuff* be *hard*, or *curling*, or *knotty*, you ſhall ſcarce be able to take a ſhaving off the thickneſs of an old Groat. Therefore you muſt examine the Temper of your *Stuff*, by eaſy Trials, how the *Plane* will work upon it, and *ſet* your *Iron* accordingly. And obſerve this as a General Rule, that the *Iron* of the *Fore-Plane* is, for the firſt working with it, to be *ſet* as *rank* as you can make good work with; and that for ſpeed ſake.

If your *Iron* be *ſet* too *rank*, knock with an *Hammer* upon the *Britch* of the *Stock*, and afterwards upon the *Wedge*; for this knocking upon the *Britch*, if you knock hard enough, 'twill raiſe the *Iron* a little, and *ſet* it *fine*; if you knock not hard enough, you muſt knock again, till the *Iron* do riſe; but if you knock too hard, it will raiſe the *Iron* ſo much, that its edge will riſe above the *Sole* into the *Mouth* of the *Stock*, and conſequently not touch the *Stuff*: Therefore you muſt knock ſoftly at firſt, till, by trials, you find the *Iron* riſes to a convenient *fineneſs*. But as this knocking on the *Britch* raiſes the *Iron*, ſo it alſo raiſes and looſens the *Wedge*; therefore (as aforeſaid) whenever

 you

you knock upon the *Britch*, you muſt alſo knock upon the *Wedge*, to ſoften the *Iron* again.

If you have raiſed the edge of the *Iron* too *fine*, you muſt knock ſoftly upon the head of the *Iron*, and then again upon the *Wedge*, and this you may ſometimes do ſeveral times, till you fit your *Iron* to a convenient *fineneſs*.

When you have occaſion to take your *Iron* out of the *Stock* to *rub* it, that is, to *whet* it, you may knock pretty ſmart Blows upon the *Stock*, between the *Mouth* and the *Fore-end*, to looſen the *Wedge*, and conſequently the *Iron*.

Theſe ways of *ſetting*, are uſed to all other *Planes*, as well as *Fore-planes*.

In the uſing of this, and indeed, all other *Planes*, you muſt begin at the hinder end of the *Stuff*, the Grain of the Wood lying along the length of the *Bench*, and Plane forward, till you come to the fore-end, unleſs the *Stuff* proves *Croſs-grain'd*, in any part of its length; for then you muſt turn your *Stuff* to Plane it the contrary way, ſo far as it runs *Croſs-grain'd*, and in Planeing, you muſt, at once, lean pretty hard upon the *Plane*, and alſo thruſt it very hard forwards, not letting the *Plane* totter to, or from you-wards, till you have made a Stroak the whole length of the *Stuff*. And this ſometimes, if your *Stuff* be long, will require your making two or three ſteps forwards, e'er you come to the fore-end of the *Stuff*: But if it do, you muſt come back, and begin again at the farther end, by the ſide of the laſt plan'd Stroak, and ſo continue your ſeveral lays of Planeing, till the whole upſide of the *Stuff* be planed.

And if the *Stuff* be broad you are to Plane upon, and it *warp* a little with the *Grain*, or be any ways crooked in the breadth, you muſt then turn the *Grain* athwart the *Work-bench*, and Plane upon the

Plate. (4) Page. 6

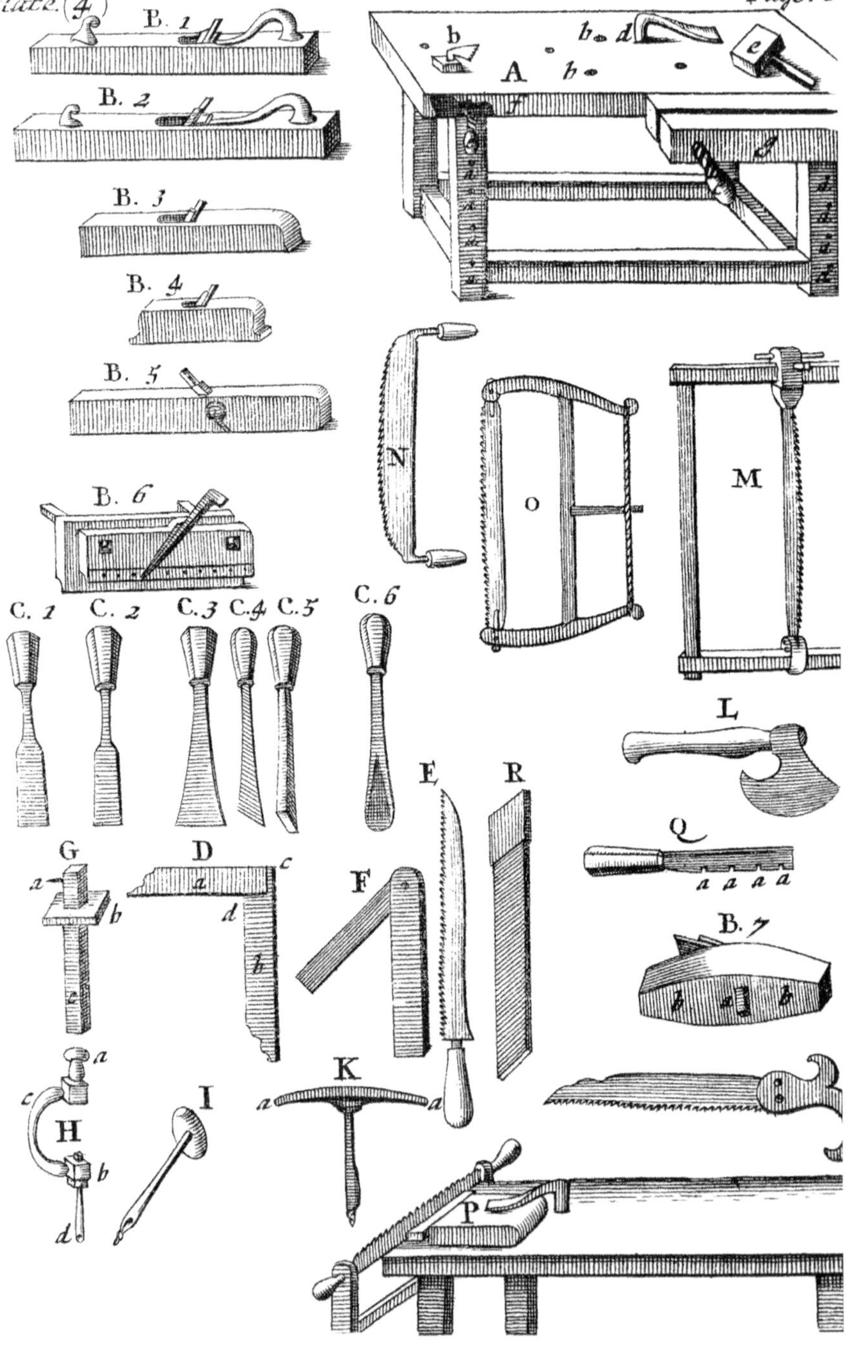

the *Cross-grain*. For, if your work be hollow in the middle, you must Plane both the Bearing sides thinner, till they come to a *Try* with the middle. Then turn the other side of your work, and working still *Cross-grain'd*, work away the middle, till it come *Try* with the two sides.

This way of *Cross-grain'd* working, is, by Workmen, called *Traversing*.

Thus have you, in general, the use of all the other *Planes*: But the use of those Planes, that are designed for other particular purposes, I shall shew, as they come in Order.

§. 4. Of the *Joynter*. B. 2.

THe *Joynter* is made somewhat longer than the *Fore-plane*, and hath its *Sole* perfectly straight from end to end. Its Office is to follow the *Fore-plane*, and to *shoot* an edge perfectly straight, and not only an edge, but also a Board of any thickness; especially when a *Joynt* is to be *shot*. Therefore the Hand must be carried along the whole length, with an equal bearing weight, and so exactly even, and upright to the edges of the Board, that neither side of the *Plane* encline either inward or outwards, but that the whole breadth be exactly square on both its sides; supposing its sides straight: so will two edges of two Boards, when thus *shot*, lie so exactly flat and square upon one another, that light will not be discerned betwixt them. But yet it is counted a piece of good Workmanship in a *Joyner*, to have the Craft of bearing his Hand so curiously even, the whole length of a long Board; and yet it is but a sleight to those, Practice hath inur'd the Hand to. The *Joynter* is also used to *Try* Tables with, (large or small) or other such broad Work; and then *Joyners* work, as well upon the *Traverse* with it, as with the Grain of the

Wood, and alſo Angularly, or Corner-wiſe, that they may be the more aſſur'd of the flatneſs of their Work.

Its *Iron* muſt be *ſet* very *fine*, ſo fine, that when you wink with one Eye, and ſet that end the ſtraight ſide of the *Iron* is next to the other Eye, there appears a little above an hairs breadth of the edge above the Superficies of the *ſole* of the *Plane*, and the length of the edge muſt lie perfectly ſtraight with the flat breadth of the *ſole* of the *Plane*: For the *Iron* being then well wedg'd up, and you working with the *Plane* thus *ſet*, have the greater aſſurance that the *Iron* cannot run too deep into the *Stuff*, and conſequently you have the leſs danger that the *Joynt* is wrought out of ſtraight.

§. 5. The Uſe of the *Strike-block*.

THe *Strike-block* marked B 3. is a *Plane* ſhorter than the *Joynter*, having its *ſole* made exactly flat, and ſtraight, and is uſed for the *ſhooting* of a ſhort *Joynt*; becauſe it is more handy than the long *Joynter*. It is alſo uſed for the framing, and fitting the Joynts of *Miters* and *Bevels*; but then it is uſed in a different manner from other *Planes*: For if the *Miter* and *Bevel* you are to fit be ſmall, you muſt hold it very ſteddy in your left hand, with the *ſole* of it upwards, and its fore-end towards your right hand: and you muſt hold your work in your right hand very ſteddy: Then apply the ſawn *Miter*, or ſawn *Bevel* at the end of your *Stuff*, to the fore-end of the *Strike-block*, and ſo thruſt it hard and upright forwards, till it paſs over the edge of the *Iron*, ſo ſhall the edge of the *Iron*, with ſeveral of theſe thruſts continued, cut, or plane off your *ſtuff* the roughneſs that the *Teeth* of your Saw made: But if your work be ſo big that you cannot well weild

it

it in your right hand, you muſt ſet the end of your work in the *Bench-ſcrew*, and Plane upon it with a *ſmoothing Plane.*

§. 6. *The Uſe of the* Smoothing-Plane.

THe *Smoothing-plane* marked B 4. muſt have its *Iron ſet* very *fine*, becauſe its Office is to ſmoothen the work from thoſe Irregularities the *Fore-plane* made.

§. 7. *The Uſe of the* Rabbet-Plane.

THe *Rabbet-plane* marked B 5. is to cut part of the upper edge of a Board, or other *Stuff*, ſtraight, that is, ſquare down into the Board, that the edge of another Board alſo cut down in the ſame manner, may fit and join into the Square of the firſt Board thus cut away: And when two Boards are thus *lapped* on the edges over one another; this *lapping* over is called *Rabbetting.*

The *Rabbet-plane* is alſo ſometimes uſed to ſtrike a *Facia* in a piece of *Molding*; as ſhall be ſhewed in its proper place.

The ſides of the *Iron* are not incloſed in the *Stock* of this *Plane*, as the fore-going *Planes* are, but the *Iron* is full as broad as the *ſtock* is thick, that the very Angles of the edge of the *Iron* may not be born off the *Stuff*, to hinder the ſtraight and ſquare cutting it down: Nor doth it deliver its ſhaving at a *Mouth* on the top of the *Stock* as the other *Planes* do: But it hath its *Mouth* on the ſides of the *Plane*, and delivers its ſhavings there. Its *Iron* is commonly about an Inch broad.

§. 8. *The Uſe of the* Plow.

THe *Plow* marked B 6. is a narrow *Rabbet-plane*, with ſome Additions to it: *viz.* two ſquare *Staves*, marked *a a* (yet ſome of them have the upper edges of them rounded off for the better compliance with the Hand.) These *Staves* are let stiff through two square Mortesses in the *Stock*, marked *b b*. They are about seven or eight Inches long, and stand straight and square on the farther side of the *Stock*; and these two *Staves* have shoulders on the hither side of the *Stock*, reaching down to the wooden *sole* of the *Plane*, (for there is also an *Iron sole* belonging to the *Plow*.) To the bottom of these two Shoulders is, Rivitted with Iron Rivets, a *Fence* (as Workmen call it) which comes close under the *Wooden sole*, and its depth reaches below the *Iron sole* about half an Inch: Because the *Iron* of the Plow is very narrow, and the sides of it towards the bottom are not to be inclosed in the *Stock*, for the same reason that was given in the *Rabbet-plane*; therefore upon the *Stock* is let in, and strongly nailed, an Iron Plate of the thickness of the Plow-Iron, for Wood of that breadth will not be strong enough to endure the force the lower end of the Plow-Iron is put to: This Iron-Plate is almost of the same thickness that the breadth of a Plow-Iron is. Joyners have several *Plows*, for several widths of *Grooves*.

The Office of the *Plow* is, to plow a narrow square *Groove* on the edge of a Board; which is thus perform'd. The Board is set an edge with one end in the *Bench-screw*, and its other edge upon a Pin, or Pins, put into a Hole, or Holes in the Leg, or Legs of the Bench, such an Hole, or Holes, as will, most conveniently for height, fit the breadth of the Board: Then the *Fence* of the *Plow* is set to that Distance off the Iron-Plate of the Plow, that you intend the *Groove* shall lie off the edge of the Board: As if you would have the *Groove* lie half an Inch off the Board, then the two *staves* must, with the *Mallet*, be knocked

through

through the Morteſſes in the *Stock*, till the *Fence* ſtands half an Inch off the Iron-Plate; and if the *Staves* are fitted ſtiff enough in the Morteſs of the *Stock*, it will keep at that Diſtance whilſt you Plow the *Groove*: For the *Fence* (lying lower than the *Iron* of the *Plane*) when you ſet the *Iron* of the *Plow* upon the edge of the Board, will lie flat againſt the farther edge of the Board, and ſo keep the *Iron* of the *Plow* all the length of the Board at the ſame Diſtance, from the edge of the Board that the *Iron* of the *Plow* hath from the *Fence*. Therefore your *Plow* being thus fitted, plow the *Groove* as you work with other *Planes*, only as you laid hold on the *Stock* of other *Planes* when you uſe them, now you muſt lay hold of the two *ſtaves* and their *ſhoulders*, and ſo thruſt your Plow forwards, till your *Groove* be made to your depth.

If the *Staves* go not ſtiff enough in the Morteſs of the Stock, you muſt ſtiffen them, by knocking a little wooden Wedge between the Staves and their Morteſſes.

§. 9. *Of* Molding-Planes.

THere are ſeveral other *Planes* in uſe amongſt Joyners, called *Molding-planes*; as, the *Round*, the *Hollow*, the *Ogee*, the *Snipes-bill*, the *Rabbet-plane*, the *Grooving-plane*, &c. And of theſe they have ſeveral ſorts, *viz.* from half a quarter of an Inch, to an Inch and a half. They are uſed as other *Planes* are. In the Planeing of Stuff, you muſt uſe *Planes* whoſe *Irons* have different Mountings; and that according to the hardneſs, or ſoftneſs of the Wood, you are to work upon: For if the Wood be hard, the *Iron* muſt ſtand more upright than it need do, if the Wood be ſoft: For ſoft Wood, as *Deal*, *Pear-tree*, *Maple*, &c. The *Iron* is ſet to make an Angle of 45 Degrees,

grees, with the *Sole* of the *Plane*: But if it be very hard Wood you are to Plane upon, as *Box*, *Ebony*, *Lignum Vitæ*, &c. It is ſet to 80 Degrees, and ſometimes quite upright: So that theſe hard Woods, are, indeed, more properly ſaid to be Scraped, than Planed.

But before you come to uſe your *Planes*, you muſt know how to grind, and whet them, for they are not ſo fitted when they are bought, but every Workman accomodates them to this purpoſe, as if it be an hard Wood he is to work on, he grinds his *Baſil* to a more obtuſe Angle, than he would do for ſoft Wood.

The *Baſil*, or Angle, an Iron is ground to, to work on ſoft Wood is about 12 Degrees, and for hard Wood about 18, or 20 Degrees. Where note, That the more acute, or thinner the *Baſil* is, the better and ſmoother the *Iron* cuts; and the more obtuſe and thicker, the ſtronger the Edge is to work upon hard Work.

§. 10. *Of Grinding and Whetting the Iron, and other* Edge-Tools.

WHen you grind your *Iron*, place your two Thumbs under the *Iron*, and your Fingers of both Hauds upon the *Iron*, and ſo clap down your *Iron* to the Stone, holding it to that Angle with the Stone you intend the *Baſil* ſhall have: Keep the *Iron* in this Poſture, without either mounting, or ſinking its ends all the while the *Stone* is turning about; and when you lift the *Iron* off the *Stone*, to ſee if it be ground to your Mind; if it be not, you muſt be ſure you place the *Iron* again in the ſame Poſition on the *Stone* it had before; for elſe you will make a double *Baſil* on your *Iron*: But if it be true ſet on the *Stone*, and ſteddily kept to that Poſition, your *Baſil* will be *Hollow*, and the ſmaller your *Grind-*

ſtone

stone is, the hollower it will be. You may know when it is well Ground, by the evenneſs, and entireneſs of the Edge all the way.

Having ground your *Iron*, you muſt ſmoothen the edge finer with a good *Whet-ſtone*. Thus, hold the edge of your *Iron* upwards in your left Hand, and your *Whet-ſtone* in your right, and having firſt ſpit upon your Stone to wet it, apply it to the *Baſil* of your *Iron*, in ſuch a Poſition, that it may bear upon the whole breadth of the *Baſil*; and ſo working the *Stone* over the *Baſil*, you will quickly wear the courſer grating of the *Grind-ſtone* off the edge on that ſide: Then turn the flat ſide of the *Iron*, and apply the *Stone* flat to it, till you have worn off the courſe gratings of the *Grind-ſtone*, on that ſide too.

Joiners often grind their *Irons* upon a flat *Grind-ſtone* alſo: And then they hold the *Iron* alſo in their Hands, in the ſame Poſture as if it were to be ground on the *Round Grind-ſtone*: Yet then inſtead of keeping the *Iron* on one place of the *Stone*, they thruſt it hard ſtraight forwards, almoſt the length of the *Stone*, and draw it lightlier ſtraight back again, keeping it all the while at the ſame Angle with the Superficies of the *Stone*; and then ſmoothen its edge with the *Whet-ſtone*, as if it had been ground upon the round *Grind-ſtone*. And this they do ſo often, till they have rubbed the hollowneſs of the *Baſil* to a flat, and then they grind it again upon the round *Grind-ſtone*.

This Order and Manner of *Setting*, *Grinding* and *Smoothing* a *Baſil* and *Edge*, is alſo uſed in all other *Edge-tools Joiners* uſe.

§. 10.

§. 10. Of Chissels of several Sorts. And first of Formers.

FOrmers marked C 1. C 3. are of several sizes. They are called *Formers*, because they are used before the *paring Chissel*, even as the *fore Plane* is used before the *smoothing Plane*. The *Stuff* you are to work upon being first scribed, (as I shall shew in its proper place) you must set the edge of the *Former*, a little without the scribed Stroak. with its *Basil* outwards, that it may break, and shoulder off the Chips from your Work, as the Edge cuts it. And you must bear the *Helve* of the *Former* a little inwards over the *Stuff*, that the *Former* do not at first cut straight down, but a little outwards: For, should you venture to cut straight down at the first, you might with a negligent, or unluckly knock with the *Mallet*, drive the edge of the *Former* under the work. and so cut, before you are aware, more off the under side than the upper side of your Work, and so (perchance) spoil it. Therefore you may make several Cuttings, to cut it straight down by little and little, till your Work is made ready for the *paring Chissel*. When it is used, the *Helve* of it is knockt upon with a *Mallet*, to drive the edge into the *Stuff*.

§. 11. Of the Paring-Chissel.

THe *Paring-Chissel* marked C 2. must have a very fine and smooth edge: Its Office is to follow the *Former*, and to *pare* off, and *smoothen*, the Irregularities the *Former* made.

It is not knockt upon with the *Mallet*, but the Blade is clasped upon the out-side of the hindermost Joints of the fore and little Fingers, by the clutched inside of the middle and third Fingers

Fingers of the right Hand, and so its edge being set upon the *scribed line*, and the top of the *Helve* placed against the hollow of the inside of the right shoulder, with pressing the shoulder hard upon the *Helve*, the edge cuts and pares away the Irregularities.

This way of handling, may seem a Preposterous Posture to manage an Iron Tool in, and yet the reason of the Original Contriver of this Posture is to be approved; For, should Workmen hold the *Blade* of the *Paring-Chissel* in their whole Hand, they must either hold their Hand pretty near the *Helve*, where they cannot well manage the *Tool*, or they must hold it pretty near the edge, where the outside of the Fingers will hide the *scribed line* they are to *pare* in. But this Posture, all Workmen are at first taught, and Practice doth so inure them to it, that if they would, they could not well leave it.

§. 12. *Of the* Skew-Former.

THE *Skew-Former* marked C 4. is seldom used by Joiners, but for cleansing acute Angles, with its acute Angle on its edge, where the Angles of other *Chissels* will not so well come.

§. 13. *Of the* Mortess-Chissel.

THE *Mortess-Chissel* marked C 5. is a narrow *Chissel*, but hath its *Blade* much thicker, and consequently stronger (that it may endure the heavier blows with the *Mallet*) than other *Chissels* have, so that in grinding it to an edge, it is ground to a very broad *Basil* as you may see in the Figure. Its Office is to cut deep square holes, called *Mortesses*, in a piece of Wood. Joiners use them of several Breadths according as the Breadths of their *Mortesses* may require.

§. 14.

§. 14. *Of the* Gouge.

THe *Gouge* marked C 6. Is a *Chiſſel* having a round edge, for the cutting ſuch Wood as is to be Rounded; or Hollowed.

Theſe ſeveral ſorts of *Chiſſels* Joiners have of ſeveral Sizes, that they may be accommodated to do ſeveral Sizes of Work.

p
m
n
Plate 6.
l
r
s
c
b
g
f
h

MECHANICK EXERCISES;

O R,

The Doctrine of *Handy-Works*

Continued in the Art of JOINERY.

§. 15: *Of the* Square, *and its Use.*

THE *Square*, marked D, is two adjunct Sides of a Geometrical Square. *a* The *Handle*. *b* The *Tongue*. *c* The *Outer Square*. *d* The *Inner Square*. For Joiner's use, it is made of two pieces of Wood, the one about an Inch thick, and the other about a quarter of an Inch thick: These two pieces are severally shot exactly straight, and have each of their Sides parallel to each of their own Sides. The thick Piece (called the Handle) hath a Mortess in it, as long within a quarter of an Inch, as the thin piece (called the Tongue) is broad, and stifly so wide, as to contain the thickness of the Tongue. The Tongue is fastned into the Mortess of the Handle with Glew and wooden Pins, so as the two outer sides (and then consequently the two inner sides) may stand at right Angles with one another.

The Reason why the Handle is so much thicker than the Tongue, is, because the Handle should on either side become a Fence to the Tongue. And

And the reaſon why the Tongue hath not its whole breadth let into the end of the Handle is, becauſe they may with leſs care ſtrike a line by the ſide of a thin than a thick piece: For if inſtead of holding the Hand upright when they ſtrike a Line, they ſhould hold it never ſo little inwards, the ſhank of a Pricker falling againſt the top edge of the Handle, would throw the Point of a Pricker farther out than a thin Piece would : To avoid which Inconvenience, the Tongue is left about half an Inch out of the end of the Handle.

Another Reaſon is, That if with often ſtriking the Pricker againſt the Tongue it becomes ragged, or uneven, they can with leſs trouble Plane it again when the Stuff is all the way of an equal ſtrength, than they can, if Croſs-grain'd Shoulders be added to any part of it.

Its uſe is for the ſtriking of Lines ſquare either to other Lines, or to ſtraight ſides, and to try the ſquareneſs of their Work by; As if they would ſtrike a Line ſquare to a ſide they have already ſhot: They apply the inſide of the Handle cloſe to the ſide ſhot, and lay the Tongue flat upon the Work, than by the outerſide of the Tongue, they draw with a Pricker a ſtraight Line : This is called *Striking, or drawing of a Square.* Or, if they would Try the ſquareneſs of a Piece of Stuff ſhot on two adjoining ſides, they apply the inſides of the Handle and Tongue to the outſides of the Stuff, and if the outſides of the Stuff do all the way agree in Line with the inſides of the Square, it is true Square. Or if they would try the inward ſquareneſs of Work, they apply the two outſides of the Square to the inſides of the Work.

§. 16.

§. 16. *The manner of* Plaining *and* Trying *a piece of Stuff-ſquare.*

WE will take, for Example, a Piece of Stuff called a Quarter, which is commonly two Inches thick, four Inches broad, and ſeven Foot long. To plane this Square, lay one of its broad Sides upon the Bench, with one of its ends ſhov'd pretty hard into the Teeth of the Bench-hook, that it may lie the ſteddier. Then with the Fore-Plane, as you were taught, § 2. *Numb.* 2. Plane off the roughneſs the Saw made at the Pit, and work that ſide of the Quarter as ſtreight in its length and breadth as you can with the Fore-Plane; which you may give a pretty good gueſs at, if the edge of the Iron have born all the way upon the Work, yet you may try by taking up your Work, and applying one end of it to one Eye, whilſt you wink with the other, and obſerve if any Hollow, or Dawks be in the length; if not, you may conclude it pretty true: For the Work thus held, the Eye will diſcern pretty nearly. Or, for more certainty, you may apply the edge of the two-foot Rule, or rather a Rule ſnot the full length of the Quarter to your Work, and if it agree all the way with the Rule, you may conclude it is ſtraight in length. But if you find it not ſtraight, you muſt ſtill with the Fore-Plane work off thoſe Riſings that bear the edge of the Rule off any part of the Stuff: Then try if the Breadth be pretty ſtraight; if it be, (the Dawks the roughneſs the Fore-plane made excepted) the firſt office of the Fore-plane is perform'd: If it be not, you muſt ſtraighten the Breadth as you did the Length.

But tho' this Quarter be thus plained ſtraight in length and breadth, yet becauſe the Iron of the Fore-plane for its firſt working the Stuff is ſet

Rank, and therefore makes great Dawks in the Stuff, you muſt ſet the Iron of your Fore-plane finer, as you were taught, §. 3. *Numb.* 2. and with it then work down even almoſt to the bottom of thoſe Dawks: then try it again, as before, and if you find it try all the way, you may, with the Jointer, or Smoothing-plane, but rather with the Jointer, go over it again, to work out the irregularities of the fine Fore plane: For the Iron of the Fore-plane being ground to a Riſing in the middle, as has been ſhew'd, §. 2. *Numb.* 2. though it be very fine ſet, will yet leave ſome Dawks in the Stuff for the Jointer, or Smoothing-plane, to work out. Thus the firſt ſide of the Quarter will be finiſhed.

Having thus tryed one ſide of the Quarter ſtraight and flat, apply the inſide of the Handle to it, and if one of the adjoining ſides of the Quarter, comply alſo with the inſide of the Tongue all the way, you need only ſmooth that adjoining ſide: But if it do not ſo comply, that is, if it be not ſquare to the firſt ſide, which you will know by the riding of the inſide of the Tongue upon one of the Edges; or ſome other part between the Edges, you muſt, with the Fore-plane Rank-ſet, plain away that Stuff which bears off the inſide of the Tongue from complying all the way with it. But if the Riſings be great, you may, for quickneſs, hew away the Riſings with the Hatchet: but then you muſt have a care you let not the edge of your Hatchet cut too deep into the Stuff, leſt you either ſpoil your Stuff, by making it unſizeable, if it be already ſmall enough; or if it have ſubſtance enough, make your ſelf more labour to get out thoſe Hatchet-ſtroaks with the Plane than you need. Then take off the roughneſs the Hatchet made with the Fore-plane Rank-ſet, then fine ſet, and laſt

last of all with the Jointer, or Smoothing-plane: So is the second side also finished.

To work the third side, set the Oval of the Gage exactly to that width from the Gage, that you intend the Breadth of the Quarter (when wrought) shall have, which, in this our Example, is four Inches, but will be somewhat less, because working it true will diminish the Stuff: Therefore sliding the Oval on the Staff, measure on your Inch-Rule so much less than four Inches, as you think your Stuff diminishes in working: Measure, I say, between the Oval and the Tooth, your size: If, at the first proffer, your Oval stand too far from the Tooth, hold the Oval in your Hand, and knock the Tooth-end of your Staff upon the Work-bench, till it stand near enough: If the Oval stand too near, knock the other end of the Staff upon the Work-bench till it be fit. Then apply the flat of the Oval to the second wrought side of your Stuff, so as the Tooth may reach athwart the breadth of the Stuff upon the first side, and keeping the Oval close against the second side, press the Tooth so hard down, that by drawing the Gage in this posture all along the length of the Quarter, the Tooth may strike a Line. In like manner upon the side opposite to the first, *viz.* the fourth side, Gage another line opposite to the first gaged Line, and work your Stuff down to those two gaged Lines on the third side, either with Plaining along, or with Hewing, and afterwards Plaining, as you were taught to work the second side.

To work the fourth side, set the Tooth of the Gage to its exact distance from the Oval, *viz.* two Inches wanting so much as you think the Stuff diminish'd in working, and apply the flat of the Oval to each side of the first side, and Gage as before two Lines, one on the second, the other on the third wrought ſide. Work your Stuff then down on the fourth ſide to thoſe two Gage-lines, either with Plaining alone, or with Hewing, and afterwards Plaining, as you were taught to work the ſecond ſide

§. 17. *To* Frame *two* Quarters *Square into one another.*

YOU muſt take care in Morteſſing and Tennanting, that as near as you can equallize the ſtrength of the ſides of the Morteſs to the ſtrength of the Tenant. I do not mean that the Stuff ſhould be of an equal Subſtance, for that is not equalling ſtrength: But the equalling ſtrength muſt be conſidered with reſpect to the Quality, Poſition and Subſtance of the Stuff: As if you were to make a Tennant upon a piece of Fur, and a Morteſs to recieve it in a piece of Oak, and the Fur and Oak have both the ſame ſize: The Tennant therefore made upon this piece of Fur, muſt be conſiderably bigger than a Tennant need be made of Oak, becauſe Fur is much a weaker Wood than Oak, and therefore ought to have a greater Subſtance to equallize the ſtrength of Oak. And for Poſition, the ſhorter the Stuff that the Tennant is made on, the leſs Violence the Tennant is ſubject to. Beſides, it is eaſier to ſplit Wood with the Grain, than to break Wood croſs the Grain; and therefore the ſame Wood when poſited as a Tennant, is ſtronger than the ſame Wood of the ſame ſize when poſited as a Morteſs: for the injury a Morteſs is ſubject to, is ſpliting with the grain of the Wood, which, without good care, it will often do in working; but the force that muſt injure a Tennant, muſt offend it, croſs the Grain of the Wood, in which Poſition it will beſt indure Violence.

When

When two pieces of Wood, of the ſame quality and ſubſtance (as in this our Example) are elected to make on the one a Tennant, and in the other a Morteſs. If you make the Morteſs too wide, the ſides of the Morteſs will be weaker than the ſides that contain the Morteſs: And if one be weaker than the other, the weakeſt will give way to the ſtrongeſt, when an equal Violence is offer'd to both. Therefore you may ſee a neceſſity of equallizing the ſtrength of one to the other, as near as you can. But becauſe no Rule is extant to do it by, nor can (for many Conſiderations, I think,) be made, therefore this equallizing of ſtrength, muſt be referred to the Judgment of the Operator. Now to the Work.

The Morteſs to be made is in a Quarter four Inches broad. In this caſe Workmen make the Morteſs an Inch wide, ſo that an Inch and an half Stuff remains on either ſide it. Therefore your Stuff being ſquar'd, as was taught in the laſt Section, ſet the Oval of the Gage an Inch and an half off the Tooth, and gage with it, on either ſide your Stuff, a ſtraight line at that diſtance from the end you intend the Morteſs ſhall be, then open your Compaſſes to two Inches, and prick off that diſtance in one of the Lines, for the length of the Morteſs; then lay the inſide of the Handle of the Square to one ſide of the Stuff, and upon both the pricks ſucceſſively, and with your Pricker draw ſtraight Lines through them by the ſide of the Tongue, ſo ſhall the bounds of your Morteſs be ſtruck out on the Quarter. If your Morteſs go through the Quarter, draw the ſame Lines on the oppoſite ſide of the Quarter thus, Turn the Quarter, or its Edge, and apply the inſide of the Handle of the Square, to the ends of the former drawn Lines, and by the ſide of the Tongue draw two Lines on the edge of the Quarter; then turn the Quarter again with its other broad ſide upwards, and apply the inſide of the Handle of the Square to the ends of the laſt Lines drawn on the edge, and by the ſide of the Tongue, draw two Lines on this broad ſide alſo. Theſe two Lines (if your Quarter was truly ſquar'd) ſhall be exactly oppoſite to the two Lines drawn on the firſt broad ſide of the Quarter for the length of the Morteſs: And for the width of the Morteſs gage this ſide alſo, as you did the firſt; then for the Tennant, gage on that end of the Quarter you intend the Tennant ſhall be made, the ſame Lines you did for the Morteſs. And becauſe the Quarter is two Inches thick, prick from the end two Inches, and applying the inſide of the Handle of the Square to the ſide of the Quarter, and the Tongue to that Prick, draw by the ſide of the Tongue a Line through that ſide the Quarter; then turn the other ſides of the Quarter ſucceſſively, and draw Lines athwart each ſide the Quarter, as you were taught to draw the oppoſite Lines for the Mortreſs.

Then place the edge of the Inch-Morteſs-Chiſſel with its Baſil from you, and the Helve bearing a little towards you, within one half quarter of an Inch of one end of the ſtruck Morteſs, and with your Mallet knock hard upon it, till you find the Baſil of the Chiſſel will no longer force the Chips out of the Morteſs; then remove the Chiſſel to the other end of the Morteſs, and work, as with the firſt end, till the Chips will void no longer: Then work away the Stuff between the two Ends, and begin again at one of the Ends, and then at the other, and work deeper into the Morteſs, then again between both; and ſo work deeper by degrees, till you have wrought the Mor-

Mortefs through, or (if not through) to the intended Depth; then with the Mortefs-chiffel work nearer the drawn Lines at the ends of the Mortefs, (for before you were directed to work but within half a quarter of an Inch of the drawn Lines,) by laying light blows on it, till you have made it fit to pare fmooth with a narrow Paring-chiffel, and then pare the ends, as you were taught to work with the Paring-chiffel: Then with the broad Paring-chiffel, pare the fides of the Mortefs juft to the ftruck Lines; fo is the Mortefs finifhed.

To work the Tennant, lay the other Quarter on edge upon your Work-bench, and faften it with the *Holdfaft*, as you were taught Sect. I. Then with the Tennant, faw a little without the Struck-line towards the end: You muft not Saw juft upon the Struck-line, becaufe the Saw cuts rough: Befides, you muft leave fome Stuff to pare away fmooth to the Struck-line, that the *Stile* (that is, the upright Quarter) may make a clofe Joint with the *Rail* (that is) the lower Quarter; Saw therefore right down with the Tennant-Saw, juft almoft to the gaged Lines for the thicknefs of the Tennant, and have a care to keep the Blade of the Saw exactly upright. Then turn the oppofite Side of the Quarter upwards, and work as you were taught to work the firft Side.

Then with the Paring-chiffel, pare the Work clofe to the gaged Lines for the Tennant. Then try how it fits the Mortefs: If it be not pared enough away, you muft pare it where it bears, that is, fticks. But if you fhould chance to have made it too little, you have fpoiled your Work: Therefore you may fee how neceffary it is, not to make the Mortefs too wide at firft, or the Tennant too narrow.

Then with the Piercer pierce two holes through the Sides, or Cheeks of the Mortefs, about half an

Inch off either end one. Then knock the Tennant ſtiff into the Morteſs, and ſet it upright, by applying the Angle of the outer Square, to the Angle the two Quarters make, and with your Pricker, prick round about the inſides of the Pierced holes upon the Tennant. Then take the Tennant out again, and Pierce two holes with the ſame Bit, about the thickneſs of a Shilling above the Pricked holes on the Tennant, that is, nearer the Sholder of the Tennant, that the Pins you are to drive in, may draw the Sholder of the Tennant the cloſer to the flat ſide of the Quarter the Morteſs is made in. Then with the Paring-chiſſel make two Pins ſomewhat Tapering, full big enough, and ſetting the two Quarters again ſquare, as before, drive the Pins ſtiff into the Pierced holes.

If you make another Square, as you did this; and make alſo a Tennant on each Un-tennanted end of the Stiles, and another Morteſs on the top and bottom Rails, you may put them together, and make ſquare Frames of them.

§. 18. *Of the* Miter Square. *And its Uſe.*

THe Miter Square marked E, hath (as the Square) an Handle marked *a*, one Inch thick, and three Inches broad, and a Tongue marked *b*, of about the ſame breadth: The Handle and the Tongue (as the Square) have both their Sides parallel to their own Sides. The Handle (as the Square) hath in the middle of its narroweſt Side a Morteſs in it, of an equal depth, the whole length of the Handle: Into this Morteſs is fitted one end of the Tongue, but the end of the Handle is firſt Bereld off to make an Angle of 45 Degrees with its inſide. This Tongue is (as the Square) Pin'd and Glewed into the Morteſe of the Handle.

It

It is used for striking a Miter-line, as the Square is to strike a Square-line, by applying the inside of the Handle to the outside of the Quarter, or Batten, you are to work upon; and then by striking a Line by the side of the Tongue: For that Line shall be a Miter-line. And if upon two Battens you strike two such Lines, and Saw and Pare them just off in the Lines, when the flats of those two sawn ends are applied to one another, the ont and inside of the Battens, will form themselves into the Figure of a Square.

Thus Picture Frames, and looking Glass-frames, are commonly made, as by a more full Example you may see in the next Section.

§. 19. *Of the* Bevil.

AS the Square is made to strike an Angle of 90 Degrees, and the Miter an Angle of 45 Degrees, so the Bevil (marked F) having its Tongue movable upon a Center, may be set to strike Angles of any greater, or lesser numbers of Degrees, according as you open the Tongue wider from, or shut it closer to the Handle. It is used as the Square, and the Miter, and will perform the Offices of them both, though it be not purposely made for either; but for the striking such Bevil-lines, as one part of your work must be cnt away to, to make it join with another part of your Work: For Example,

We will propose to make a Frame for a Picture, Looking-glass, *&c.* containing eight straight Sides; You may quickly perceive that all the ends of these eight Sides must be cut to Bevils, and what Bevils they must be, you will find if you describe upon a smooth flat Board, a Circle of any bigness, but the larger the better: Divide this Circle into eight equal Parts, and from every point draw a Line to the Center: Draw also straight Lines from

from every point to its next Point: Then lay the inſide of the Handle of your Bevil exactly upon any one of theſe ſtraight Lines, ſo as the Angle made by the inſide of the Handle, and the inſide of the Tongue, lie exactly at the very Angle made by this ſtraight Line, and the Semi-Diametral Line proceeding from the Center, and move the Tongue nearer, or farther off the Handle, till the inſide of the Tongue and the inſide of the Handle, lie exactly upon thoſe two Lines, ſo ſhall your Bevil be ſet.

Then having fitted your Pieces to your Scantling, ſtick your Pricker as near the outward Corner of your Pieces as your Stuff will bear, and apply the inſide of your Handle alſo to the outer ſides of your Pieces, and ſo as the inſide of the Tongue may be drawn home to the Pricker. For then Lines drawn on thoſe Pieces by the inſide of the Tongue, ſhall be the Lines the Pieces muſt be cut in, to make theſe eight Pieces join evenly together by the ſides of each others Bevil: Then with the Strike-block ſmooth the ends of the Bevils, as you were taught in the Section of the Strike-block.

If you have a Board on the back-ſide of this Frame, you may Glew the back-ſides of theſe Pieces, piece by piece to the Board; but firſt you muſt fit them to an exact Compliance of every Bevil with its Match, and when they are ſo fitted, drive two Nails cloſe to the outſide of every piece, but drive not the Nails deep into the Board, becauſe when the Frame is ſet, and Glewed, or otherwiſe faſtned, you muſt draw the Nails out again: For theſe Nails are only intended to ſerve for Fences to ſet, and fit each piece into its proper Place, before the whole Frame is faſtned together. And ſhould you not thus Fence them, though by your Eye you might judge you fitted the Bevils exactly,

exactly, yet one piece being never ſo little out of its due Poſition, would drive the next piece more out, and that the next, till at the laſt, the laſt piece would not join, but either be too ſhort, or too long, or ſtand too much out, or in, or elſe too open, or too cloſe on the out, or inſide.

But if you have no Board on the backſide, you muſt, when you Saw the Bevilling Angles upon the ſquare ends of pieces, not ſawn quite through the depth of one end of every piece, but about half way through the depth, or thickneſs, and then with your Chiſſel either ſplit, or elſe pare, the upper ſide of the ſquare end flat away to the Bevil, and ſo leave part of the ſquare end of your piece, to lap under the piece it is joined to. For Example,

In Fig. 3. Plate 5. *a b* is the ſquare end of the piece, and *b c* is the Bevil you work the piece to. Therefore you muſt work away ſo much of the thickneſs of the ſquare end, as is comprehended between *a* and *c*, ſo that you will ſee the Triangle *a b c*, is to be wrought away half way down the thickneſs of the Stuff, and ſo will the Triangle *a b c* be left for the other half thickneſs of the Stuff. But that end of the piece marked 1, which joins to the piece marked 2, muſt, upon its Bevil-ſtroak, be ſawn quite off, and its underſide muſt have the ſame Triangle wrought into it, juſt ſo fit as to receive the Triangle in piece 2, and juſt ſo deep, as that when the Triangle on piece 2, is fitted into the Triangle in piece 1, the Superficies of both the pieces may be even with one another. And thus you may lap the ends of every piece into one another.

Theſe Triangles at the ends of the pieces you may Glew into one another, but if you think Glewing alone not ſtrong enough, you may Pierce an hole near the inner edge of the Frame, becauſe the Triangle hath there moſt Subſtance of Stuff;

and afterwards Pin it, as you are taught to Pin the Rail and Stile together in Sect. 17.

This way of Lapping over, is ſometimes uſed alſo for ſquare Miters, or other Angular Frames.

§. 20: *Of the* Miter-Box.

THere is another way uſed by Joiners that make many Frames, to ſave themſelves the labour of Drawing, or ſtriking out of Squares, Miters, and ſeveral Bevils upon their Stuff: And this is with a Tool called a *Miter-Box*, deſcribed in Plate 5. Fig. 2. It is compoſed of two pieces of Wood, of an Inch thick each, as A the upright piece, B the bottom piece. The Upright piece is nailed upright, faſt upon the bottom piece. And this upright piece hath on its upper ſide the Miter Lines ſtruck with the Miter Square, as *d e*, on the left hand, and *g h* on the right hand: On theſe two Miter Lines the edge of the Saw is ſet, and a kerf made ſtraight down the upright piece, as from *d e* on the left hand to *f*, and from *g h* on the right hand to *i*. In like manner any other Bevil is ſtruck upon the upper ſide of the upright piece with the Bevil, as *k l* on the left hand, and *n o* on the right. On theſe two Bevil Lines the edge of the Saw is ſet, and a kerf made ſtraight down the upright piece, as from *k* to *l m*, and from *g h* to *i*. You may make as many Bevils as you pleaſe on the upright piece of the Miter Box; Bevils to join Frames of either five, ſix, ſeven, eight Sides, *&c.* and the manner to make them to any number of Sides, was in part taught in the laſt Section. For as there you were directed to divide the Circle into eight equal Parts, becauſe eight was the number of Sides, we propoſed to make that Frame conſiſt of; So, if for any number of Sides you divide the Circle into the ſame equal parts, and work as you were there directed, you may find what Be-

vil

vil the pieces muſt have that make a Frame that conſiſts of any number of Sides.

So alſo for Sawing of any Batten, or other ſmall pieces ſquare: Strike at the Point *a*, on the upper ſide of the upright piece a line ſtraight athwart it, to *b*, and Saw ſtraight down the upper piece, to *c*.

The manner how theſe Kerfs are ſawn ſtraight down with greateſt certainty is, thus, Apply the inſide of the Handle of the ſquare to the upper ſide of the upright piece, ſo as the Tongue lie cloſe to that end of the Miter, Bevil, or ſquare Line ſtruck through the upper ſide of the Miter-Box, and with the Pricker ſtrike a Line cloſe by the ſide of the Tongue, through that ſide of the upright piece; Turn the Tongue to the other ſide of the upright piece, and apply the inſide of the Handle of the ſquare to the other end of the Miter, Bevil, or Square Line, and with the Pricker ſtrike alſo a Line cloſe by the ſide of the Tongue through that ſide the upright piece. Theſe two Lines ſtruck on either *ſide* of the upright piece, ſhall be a Line on each ſide in which the edge of the Saw muſt run, to ſaw it ſtraight down.

§. 21. *Of the* Gage.

THe *Gage* marked G (in *Plate* 4) The *Oval b* is fitted ſtiff upon the *Staff c*, that it may be ſet nearer or farther from the *Tooth a*. Its Office is to *Gage* a Line parallel to any ſtraight ſide. It is uſed for *Gaging* Tennants, and for *Gaging* Stuff to an equal thickneſs.

When you uſe it, you muſt ſet the *Oval* to the intended Diſtance from the *Tooth*: If the Oval ſtand too near the Tooth, Hold the Oval in your right hand, and knock the hinder end of the Staff upon the Work-bench, till it remove to its juſt Diſtance from the Tooth: If it ſtand too far off the

Tooth,

Tooth, knock the fore end of the Staff (*viz.* the Tooth end) till it remove to its juſt Diſtance from the Tooth: If the Oval ſlide not ſtiff enough upon the Staff, you may ſtiffen it by ſtriking a wooden Wedge between the Morteſs and the Staff: So may you apply the ſide of the Oval next the Tooth, to the ſide of any Table, or any other ſtraight ſide, with the Tooth Gage a Line parallel (or of equal Diſtance) all the way from that ſide.

§. 22. *Of the* Piercer.

THe *Piercer* H, in *Plate* 4, hath *a* the *Head*, *b* the *Pad*, *c* the *Stock*, *d* the *Bitt*. Its Office is ſo well known, that I need ſay little to it. Only, you muſt take care to keep the Bitt ſtraight to the hole you pierce, leſt you deform the hole, or break the Bitt.

You ought to be provided with Bitts of ſeveral ſizes, fitted into ſo many Padds.

§. 23. *Of the* Gimblet.

THe *Gimblet* is marked I, in *Plate* 4. It hath a Worm at the end of its Bitt. Its Office is to make a round hole in thoſe places of your work where the *Stock* of the Piercer by reaſon of its own Sholder, or a Sholder, or Butting out upon the work will not turn about. Its Handle is held in a clutched hand, and its Bitt twiſted ſtiff into your work. You muſt have them of ſeveral ſizes.

§. 24. *Of the* Augre.

THe *Augre* marked K in *Plate* 4, hath *a a* the Handle, *b* the *Bitt*. Its Office is to make great round holes. When you uſe it, the Stuff you work upon is commonly laid low under you, that you may the eaſier uſe your ſtrength upon it: For in twiſting the Bitt about by the force of both your Hands,

Hands, on each end of the Handle one, it cuts great Chips out of the Stuff. You muſt bear your ſtrength Perpendicularly ſtraight to the end of the Bitt; as with the Piercer.

§. 25. *Of the* Hatchet.

THe *Hatchet* marked L, in *Plate* 4. Its uſe is ſo well known (even to the moſt un-intelligent) that I need not uſe many Words on it, yet thus much I will ſay, Its uſe is to Hew the Irregularities off ſuch pieces of Stuff which may be ſooner Hewn than Sawn.

When the Edge is downwards, and the Handle towards you, the right *ſide* of its Edge muſt be Ground to a Bevil, ſo as to make an Angle of about 12 Degrees with the left *ſide* of it: And afterwards ſet with the Whetſtone, as the Irons of Planes, *&c.*

§. 26. *The Uſe of the* Saw *in general.*

IN my former *Exerciſes*, I did not teach you how to chuſe the Tools a Smith was to uſe; Becauſe it is a Smith's Office to make them: And becauſe in thoſe *Exerciſes* I treated of making Iron-work, and Steel-work in general, and the making and excellency of ſome Tools in particular, which might ſerve as a general Notion for the Knowledge of all Smith's Workmanſhip, eſpecially to thoſe that ſhould concern themſelves with Smithing: But to thoſe that ſhall concern themſelves with Joinery, and not with Smithing; It will be neceſſary that I teach them how to chuſe their Tools that are made by Smiths, that they may uſe them with more eaſe and delight, and make both quicker and nearer Work with them.

All ſorts of Saws, for Joiner's Uſe, are to be ſold in moſt Iron-monger's Shops, but eſpecially in *Foſter-lane*, *London*: Chuſe thoſe that are made

of

of Steel, (for ſome are made of Iron) for Steel of it ſelf is harder and ſtronger than Iron: You may know the Steel-*Saws* from Iron-*Saws* thus, The Steel-*Saws* are generally ground bright and ſmooth, and are (the thickneſs of the Blade conſidered) ſtronger than Iron-*Saws* : But the Iron-*Saws* are only Hammer-hardned, and therefore if they could be ſo hard, yet they cannot be ſo ſmooth, as if the Irregularities of the Hammer were well taken off with the Grindſtone: See it be free from flaws, and very well Hammered, and ſmoothly Ground, (that is, evenly Ground,) you may know if it be well Hammered by the ſtiff bending of it, and if it be well Ground, (that is, evenly Ground,) it will not bend in one part of it more than in another; for if it do, it is a ſign that part were it bends moſt is, either too much Ground away, or too thin Forged in that place: But if it bend into a regular bow all the way, and be ſtiff, the Blade is good: It cannot be too ſtiff, becauſe they are but Hammer-hardned, and therefore often bow when they fall under unskilful Hands, but never break, unleſs they have been often bowed in that place. The Edge whereon the Teeth are, is always made thicker than the Back, becauſe the Back follows the Edge, and if the Edge ſhould not make a pretty wide Kerf, if the Back do not ſtrike in the Kerf, yet by never ſo little irregular bearing, or twiſting of the Hand awry, it might ſo ſtop, as to bow the *Saw*; and (as I ſaid before) with often bowing it will break at laſt. When Workmen light of a good Blade thus qualified, they matter not much whether the Teeth be ſharp or deep, or ſet to their mind: For to make them ſo, is a Task they take to themſelves: And thus they perform it: They wedge the Blade of the *Saw* hard into the *Whetting-Block*, marked P, in *Plate* 4. with the Handle towards

wards their left Hand, and the end of the *Saw* to the right, then with a three-square File they begin at the left hand end, leaning harder upon the side of the File on the right Hand, than on that side to the left Hand; so that they File the upper-side of the Tooth of the Saw a-slope towards the right Hand, and the underside of the Tooth a little a-slope towards the left, or, almost down-right. Having filed one Tooth thus, all the rest must be so filed. Then with the *Saw-wrest*, marked O, in *Plate* 4. they *set* the Teeth of the Saw: That is, they put one of the Notches marked *a a a* of the *Wrest* between the first two Teeth on the Blade of the *Saw*, and then turn the Handle Horizontally a little about upon the Notch towards the end of the *Saw*; and that at once turns the first Tooth somewhat towards you, and the second Tooth from you: Then skipping two Teeth, they again put one of the Notches of the *Wrest* between the third and fourth Teeth on the Blade of the *Saw*, and then (as before) turn the Handle a little about upon the Notch towards the end of the *Saw*, and that turns the third Tooth somewhat towards you, and the fourth somewhat from you: Thus you must skip two Teeth at a time, and turn the *Wrest* till all the Teeth of the *Saw* are *set*. This *Setting* of the Teeth of the *Saw* (as Workmen call it) is to make the Kerf wide enough for the Back to follow the Edge: And is Set *Ranker* for soft, course, cheap Stuff, than for hard, fine, and costly Stuff: For the *Ranker* the Tooth is set, the more Stuff is wasted in the Kerf: And besides, if the Stuff be hard it will require greater Labour to tear away a great deal of hard Stuff, than it will do to tear away but a little of the same Stuff.

The *Pit Saw*, is Set so Rank for course Stuff, as to make a Kerf of almost a quarter of an Inch, but for fine and costly Stuff they set it finer to save

Stuff. The *Whip-Saw* is set somewhat finer than the *Pit-Saw*; the *Hand-Saw*, and the *Compass-Saw*, finer than the *Whip-Saw*; but the *Tennant-Saw*, *Frame-Saw*, and the *Bow-Saw*, &c. are set fine, and have their Teeth but very little turned over the Sides of their Blades: So that a Kerf made by them, is seldom above half a half quarter of an Inch.

The reason why the Teeth are filed to an Angle, pointing towards the end of the *Saw*, and not towards the Handle of the *Saw*, or directly straight between the Handle and end of the *Saw*, is, Because the *Saw* is designed to cut only in its Progress forwards; Man having in that Activity more strength to rid, and Command of his Hands to guide his Work, than he can have in drawing back his *Saw*, and therefore when he draws back his *Saw*, the Work-man bears it lightly off the unsawn *Stuff*; which is an ease to his Labour, and enables him the longer to continue his several Progressions of the *Saw*.

Master-Workmen, when they direct any of their Underlins to saw such a piece of Stuff, have several Phrases for the sawing of it: They seldom say *Saw that piece of Stuff*; But *Draw the Saw through it*; *Give that piece of Stuff a Kerf*; *Lay a Kerf in that piece of Stuff*; and sometimes, (but most unproperly,) *Cut*, or *Slit that piece of Stuff*: For the Saw cannot properly be said to cut, or slit the Stuff; but it rather breaks, or tears away such parts of the Stuff from the whole, as the points of the Teeth prick into, and these parts it so tears away are proportionable to the fineness, or rankness of the setting of the Teeth.

The Excellency of Sawing is, to keep the Kerf exactly in the Line marked out to be sawn, without wriggling on either, or both sides; And straight through the Stuff, as Work-men call it; that

that is, in a Geometrical Term, perpendicular through the upper and under ſide, if your Work require it, as moſt Work does: But if your Work be to be Sawn upon a Bevil, as ſome Work ſometimes is, then you are to obſerve that Bevil all the length of the Stuff, *&c.*

§. 27. *The Uſe of the* Pit-Saw, *marked* M, in Plate 4.

THe *Pit-Saw* is not only uſed by thoſe Workmen that make ſawing Timber and Boards their whole Buſineſs, but is alſo for ſmall matters uſed by Joiners, when what they have to do, may perhaps be as ſoon done at home, as they can carry or ſend it to the Sawyers. The manner of their working is both alike, for if it be a Board they would ſlit off a piece of Timber, or if they would take any Square, Quarter, or Batten, *&c.* off, they firſt ſet off their Scantlin: For Example, If it be an Inch (or more, or leſs) they would take off a piece of Stuff, they open the Points of their Compaſſes to an Inch Meaſure on their Rule, and ſo much more as they reckon the Kerf of the *Saw* will make, and from on ſide of their Stuff they ſet off at either end of the Stuff, the Diſtance of the points of their Compaſſes; at this Diſtance therefore they make with the points of their Compaſſes a prick at either end of the Stuff; Then with Chalk they whiten a Line, by rubbing the Chalk pretty hard upon it; Then one holds the Line at one end upon the prick made there, and the other ſtrains the Line pretty ſtiff upon the prick at the other end; then whilſt the Line is thus ſtrain'd, one of them between his Finger and Thumb draws the middle of the Line directly upright, to a convenient height (that it may ſpring hard enough down) and then lets it go again, ſo that it ſwiftly applies to its firſt Poſition, and ſtrikes ſo ſtrongly againſt the Stuff, that the Duſt, or Attoms of the Chalk that were rubbed into the Line, ſhake out of it, and remain upon the Stuff. And thus alſo they mark the under ſide of their Stuff: This is called *Lining of the Stuff*: And the Stuff cut into thoſe Lines ſhall be called *Inch-Stuff*, becauſe the Compaſſes that prickt the Stuff, were opened wider by the width of the Kerf than an Inch Meaſure upon the Rule: But had the Compaſſes been opened but an Inch exactly, that piece Sawn off ſhould, in Workmen's Language, have been called *Inch-prickt*, thereby giving to underſtand that it is half the breadth of the Kerf thinner than an Inch: And thus they call all other Scantlins 2 *Inches*, 2½ *Inches*, 3 *Inches*, &c. *Sawn*, or *Pricked*.

When two Work-men are not at hand to hold the Line at both ends, he that Lines it, ſtrikes one point of his Compaſs, or ſometimes a Pricker, or a Nail aſlope towards that end into the prick ſet off, and putting the Nooſe at the end of his Line over his Compaſſes, *&c.* goes to the other end, and ſtrains his Line on that prick, and ſtrikes it as before.

The Stuff being thus lined is faſtned with wedges over the *Pit*, (if the Joiner be accommodated with a *Pit*) if he have none, he makes ſhift with two high Frames a little more than Man high in its ſtead, (called *great Truſſels*) with four Legs, theſe Legs ſtand ſpreading outwards, that they may ſtand the firmer: Over theſe two *Truſſels* the Stuff is laid, and firmly faſtned that it ſhake not. Its outer ſide from whence the Pricks were ſet off muſt be Perpendiculer, which you muſt try by a Plumb-line, for ſhould the top edge of that ſide, hang never ſo little over the bottom edge, or the bottom edge not lie ſo far out as the top edge, the Scantlin you ſaw off would not be of an equal thickneſs on the Top or Bottom: Be-

cauſe

cauſe the Saw is to work exactly Perpendicular. Then with the *Pit-Saw* they enter the one end of the Stuff, the *Top-man* at the Top, and the *Pit-man* under him: The *Top-man* obſerving to guide the *Saw* exactly in the Line: And withal drawing the *Saw* ſomewhat towards him when the *Saw* goes down; and the *Pit-man* drawing it with all his ſtrength Perpendicularly down; but not ſo low that the upper and lower Handles of the *Saw* ſink below both their Managements: Then bearing the Teeth of the *Saw* a little off the Stuff, the *Top-man* draws the *Saw* up again, and the *Pit-man* aſſiſts, or eaſes him in it, and thus they continue ſawing on till the *Saw* has run through the whole length upon the Stuff. But when the Kerf is made ſo long, that by the working of the *Saw* the pieces of Stuff on either ſide will ſhake againſt one another, and ſo more, or leſs, hinder the eaſie Progreſs of the *Saw*, they drive a Wedge ſo far in the Kerf as they dare do for fear of ſplitting the Stuff, and ſo provide the *Saw* freer and eaſier Paſſage through the Stuff: This Wedging they continue ſo oft as they find occaſion.

MECHANICK EXERCISES;

OR,

The Doctrine of *Handy-Works*

Continued in the Art of JOINERY.

§. 28. *The Use of the* Whip-Saw, *marked* N *in* *Plate* 4.

THE *Whip-Saw* is used by Joiners, to saw such greater pieces of Stuff that the *Hand-Saw* will not easily reach through; when they use it, the Stuff is laid upon the *Trussel*, marked O in *Plate* 5. in the Angles of it. Then two Men takes each an Handle of the *Saw*; He to whom the Teeth of the *Saw* points, drawing to him, and the other thrusting from him: And (as before) the *Saw* having run its length, is lifted gently over the Stuff to recover another stroak of the *Saw*.

§. 29. *The Use of the* Hand-Saw *marked* D, *the* Frame *or* Bow-Saw, *the* Tennant-Saw, *marked* O *in* Plate 4.

THese *Saws* are accommodated for a single Man's Use, and cut forward as the other *Saws* do. The Office of the Cheeks made to the *Frame-Saw* is, by the twisted Cord and Tongue in the middle, to draw the upper ends of the Cheeks closer together, that the lower end of the Cheeks may

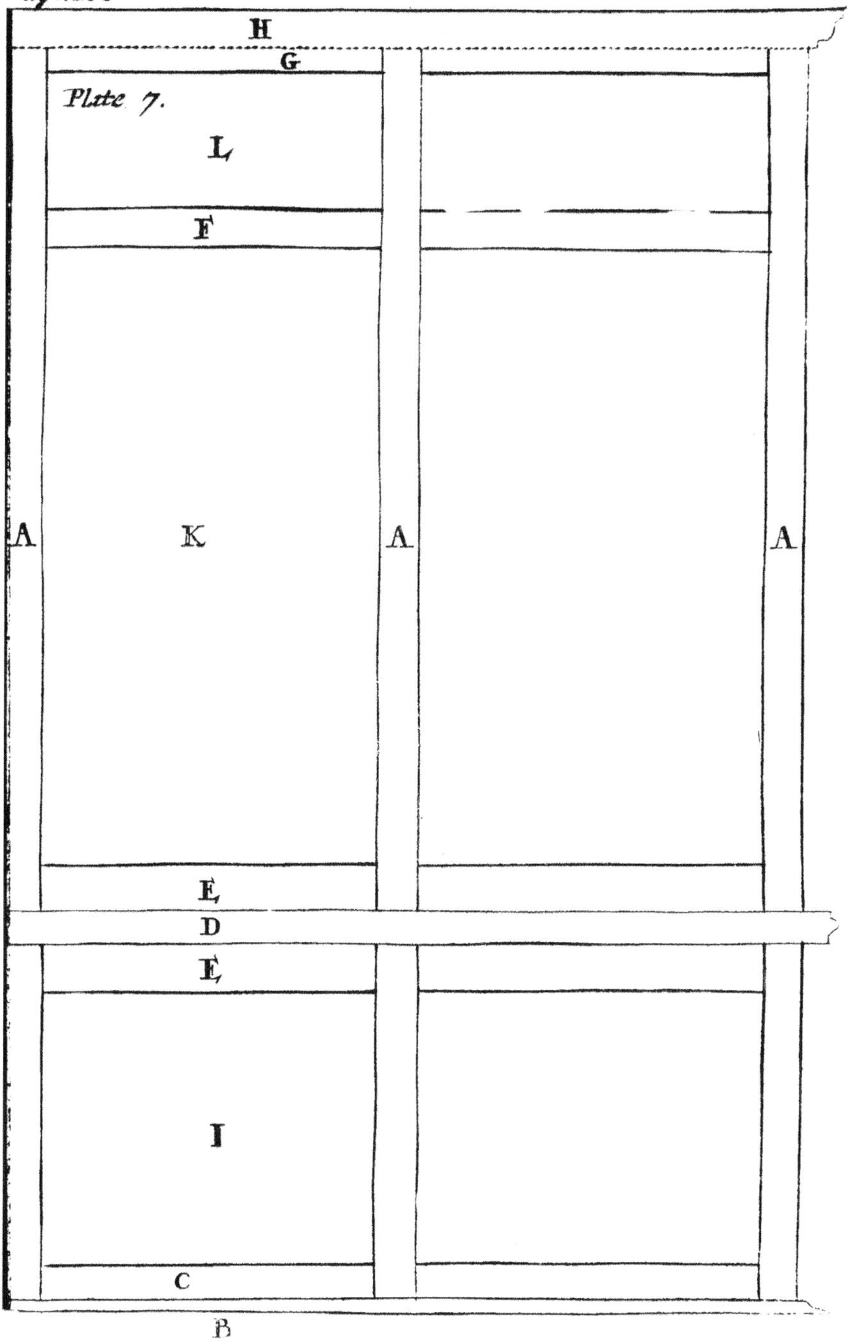
H
G
Plate 7.
L
F
A
K
A
A
E
D
E
I
C
B

may be drawn the wider asunder, and strain the Blade of the *Saw* the straighter. The *Tennant-Saw*, being thin, hath a Back to keep it from bending.

§. 30. *The Use of the* Compass-Saw, *marked* Q *in Plate* 4.

THe *Compass-Saw* should not have its Teeth *Set*, as other *Saws* have; but the edge of it should be made so broad, and the back so thin, that it may easily follow the broad edge, without having its Teeth *Set*; for if the Teeth be *Set*, the Blade must be thin, or else the Teeth will not bow over the Blade, and if it be thin, (considering the Blade is so narrow) it will not be strong enough to abide tough Work, but at never so little an irregular thrust, will bow, and at last break; yet for cheapness, they are many times made so thin that the Teeth require a setting. Its Office is to cut a round, or any other Compass kerf; and therefore the edge must be made broad, and the back thin, that the Back may have a wide kerf to turn in.

§. 31. *Of the* Rule *marked* D *in Plate* 5.

THe use of the *Rule* is to measure Feet, Inches, and parts of Inches, which for that Purpose, are marked upon the flat and smooth sides of the *Rule*, and numbred with Inches, and hath every Inch divided into two halfs, and every half into two quarters, and every quarter into two half-quarters; so that every Inch is divided into eight equal parts; And these Inches are numbred from one end of the *Rule* to the other; which commonly is in all 24 Inches: Which is a Two-Foot *Rule*.

They have commonly both Board and Timber-measure, *&c.* marked upon them, for the finding both the superficial and solid Content of Board or

Timber: The uſe of which Lines and Tables havin been often taught by others, and being more Mathematical than Mechanical, is unproper for me to meddle with in this Place: But rather to refer to thoſe Books.

But the manual Uſe of it is, either to meaſure length with it, or to draw a ſtraight Line by the ſide of it, or to Try the ſtraightneſs or flatneſs of their Work with. They Try their Work by applying one of its Edges to the flat of the wrought ſide of their Work, and bring their Eye as cloſe as they can, to ſee if they can ſee light between the edge of the *Rule* and their Work: If they cannot, they conclude their Work is *Try*, and well wrought.

§. 32. *Of the* Compaſſes *marked* E *in* Plate 5.

aa THe *Joint*, *bb* the *Cheeks* of the Joint, *cc* the *Shanks*, *dd* the *Points*. Their Office is to deſcribe Circles, and ſet off Diſtances from their Rule, or any other Meaſure, to their Work.

§. 33. *Of the* Glew-pot *marked* F *in* Plate 5.

THe *Glew-pot* is commonly made of good thick Lead, that by its Subſtance it may retain a heat the longer, that the *Glew Chill* not (as Work-men ſay when it cools) when it is to be uſed.

§. 34. *Of* Chuſing *and* Boiling Glew.

THe cleareſt, drieſt, and moſt tranſparent Glew is the beſt: When you boil it, break it with your Hammer into ſmall pieces, and put it into a clean Skillet, or Pipkin, by no means greaſie, for that will ſpoil the Clammineſs of the Glew, put to it ſo much Water as is convenient to diſſolve the Glew, and to make it, when it is hot, about the thickneſs of the White of an Egg: The

The quantity of Water cannot be aſſigned, becauſe of the different Quality there is in Glew: Keep it ſtirring whilſt it is melting, and let it not ſtick to the ſides or bottom of the Veſſel: When it is well boiled, pour it into your Glew-pot to uſe, but let your Glew-pot be very clean. When it is cold, and you would heat it again in your Glew-pot, you muſt take great care that it burn not to the ſides or bottom of the Glew-pot, for that burning either turns to a thick hard skin, or elſe to a burnt Cinder-like Subſtance, which if it mingle with the Glew, will ſpoil it all; becauſe by its Subſtance it will bear the two Joints you are to Glew together, off each other.

When (with often heating) the Glew grows too thick, you may put more Water to it; but then you muſt make it very hot, leſt the Glew and Water do not wholly incorporate.

Some Joiners will (when their Glew is too thick, put Small-Beer into it, thinking it ſtrengthens it: I have tried it, and could never find it ſo, but think it makes the Glew weaker, eſpecially if the Small-Bear chance to be new, and its Yeſt not well ſettled from it, or ſo ſtale, that it be either Draggy, or any whit mingled with the Settlings of the Cask.

§. 35. *Of uſing the* Glew.

YOur Glew muſt be very warm, for then it is thinneſt, and as it chills, it thickens: With a ſmall Bruſh you muſt ſmear the Glew well upon the Joint of each piece you are to Glew together; And before you ſet them as they are to ſtand, you muſt joſtle them one upon the other, that the Glew may very well touch and take hold of the Wood; and that the Glew on each Joints may well incorporate. Then fit the two Joints as they muſt ſtand; And when you ſet them by to dry, let

let the one stand upright upon the other; For if they stand a-slope, the weight of the Stuff when it leans upon two extream Edges, may make one end of the Joint *Open.*

§. 36. *Of the* Waving Engine.

THe *Waving Engine* discribed in *Plate* 5. *Fig.* 7. Hath A B a long square Plank, of about seven Inches broad, five Foot long, and an Inch and half thick: All along the length of this Plank, on the middle between the two sides, runs a *Rabbet*, as part of it is seen at C: Upon this Rabbet rides a *Block* with a *Groove* in its under side: This *Block* is about three Inches square, and ten Inches long, having near the hinder end of it a wooden Handle going through it, of about one Inch Diameter, as D E: At the Fore-end of this *Block* is fastned a Vice, somewhat larger than a great Hand-Vice, as at F: The *Groove* in the *Block* is made fit to receive the Rabbet on the Plank.

At the farther end of the Plank is erected a spuare strong piece of Wood, about six Inches high, and five Inches square, as G. This square piece hath a square wide Mortess in it on the Top, as at H. Upon the top of this square piece is a strong square flat Iron Coller, somewhat loosly fitted on, having two Male Screws fitted into two Female Screws, to screw against that part of the wooden Piece un-mortessed at the Top, marked L, that it may draw the Iron Coller hard against the Iron marked Q, and keep it stiff against the fore-side of the un-mortessed Piece, marked L, when the piece Q, is set to its convenient heighth; and on the other side the square wooden Piece is fitted another Iron screw, having to the end of its shank fastned a round Iron Plate which lies within the hollow of this wooden piece, and therefore cannot in Draft be seen in its proper place;

place; But I have deſcribed it a part, as at M. (Fig. 9.) Its Nut is placed at M, on the wooden Piece. On the farther ſide of the wooden Piece is fitted a wooden Screw called a *Knob*, as at N. Through the farther and hither ſide of the ſquare wooden Piece is fitted a flat Piece of Iron, about three quarters of an Inch broad, and one quarter of an Inch thick, ſtanding on edge upon the Plank; but its upper edge is filed round: (the reaſon you will find by and by:) Its hither end comes through the wooden Piece, as at O, and its farther end on the oppoſite ſide of the wooden Piece.

Upright in the hollow ſquare of the wooden Piece ſtands an *Iron*, as at Q, whoſe lower end is cut into the form of the Molding you intend your work ſhall have.

In the fore ſide of this wooden Piece is a ſquare hole, as at R, called the *Mouth*.

To this Engine belongs a thin flat piece of hard Wood, about an Inch and a quarter broad, and as long as the *Rabbet*: It is disjunct from the Engine, and in Fig. 8. is marked S S, called the *Rack*: It hath its under flat cut into thoſe faſhioned Waves you intend your Work ſhall have: The hollow of theſe Waves are made to comply with the round edge of flat Plate of Iron marked O (deſcribed before) for when one end of the Riglet you wave, is, with the Vice, ſcrewed to the plain ſide of the Rack, and the other end put through the Mouth of the wooden Piece, as at T T, ſo as the hollow of the Wave on the under ſide of the *Rack* may lie upon the round edge of the flat Iron Plate ſet on edge, as at O, and the Iron Q, is ſtrong fitted down upon the Reglet: Then if you lay hold of the Handles of the *Block* D E, and ſtrongly draw by them, the Rack and the Riglet will both together ſlide through the Mouth of the wooden Piece: And as the Rounds of the Rack

rid

rid over the round edge of the flat Iron, the Rack and Reglet will mount up to the Iron Q, and as the Rounds of the Waves on the under ſide of the Rack ſlides off the Iron on edge, the Rack and Reglet will ſink, and ſo in a Progreſſion (or more) the Riglet will on its upper ſide receive the Form of the ſeveral Waves on the under ſide of the Rack, and alſo the Form, or Molding, that is on the edge of the bottom of the Iron, and ſo at once the Riglet will be both molded and waved.

But before you draw the Rack through the Engine, you muſt conſider the Office of the Knob N, and the Office of the Iron Screw M; For by them the Rack is ſcrewed evenly under the Iron Q. And you muſt be careful that the Groove of the Block ſlip not off the Rabbet on the Plank: For by theſe Screws, and the Rabbet and Groove, your work will be evenly gaged all the way (as I ſaid before) under the edge of the Iron Q, and keep it from ſliding either to the right, or left Hand, as you draw it through the Engine.

§. 37. *Of* Wainſcoting *Rooms.*

AA A (in *Plate* 7.) The *Stiles.* B The *Baſe.* C The *Lower Rail.* D The *Sur-Baſe.* E E The *Middle Rail*, or *Rails.* F The *Frieſe Rail.* G The *Upper Rail.* H The *Cornice.* I The *Lying Pannel.* K The *Large Pannel.* L The *Frieſe Pannel.*

In Wainſcoting of Rooms there is, for the moſt part, but two heights of Pannels uſed; unleſs the Room to be Wainſcoting be above ten foot high, as ſome are eleven or twelve Foot high, and then three Heighths of Pannels are uſed: As I The *Lying Pannel*, above the *Baſe.* K The *Large Pannel* above the *Middle Rail*: And L The *Frieſe Pannel* above the *Frieſe Rail.*

The *Frieſe Rail* is to have the ſame breadth the *Margent* of the *Stile* hath; The *Middle Rail* hath com-

commonly two breadths of the *Margent* of the *Stile*, viz. one breadth above the *Sur-base*, and the other below the *Sur-base*. And the *Upper* and *Lower Rails* have also each the same breadth with the *Margent* of the *Stile*.

Those Moldings above the Prickt Line on the Top, as H, are called the *Cornice*.

Sometimes (and especially in low Rooms) there is no *Base* or *Sur-base* used, and then the *Middle* and *Lower Rail* need not be so broad: For the *Middle Rail* need not be above a third part more than the *Margent* of the *Rail*: and the *Lower Rail* you may make of what breadth you see convenient: They are commonly about three Inches and an half, or four Inches broad, yet this is no Rule: For sometimes Workmen make only a flat Plinth serve.

You may (if you will) adorn the outer edges of the *Stiles* and *Rails* with a small *Molding*: And you may (if you will) Bevil away the outer edges of the *Pannels*, and leave a Table in the middle of the Pannel.

An Explanation of Terms *used among Joiners*

WHen I first began to Print these Exercises, I marked some Terms in *Joinery* with *superiour Letters* (as Printers call them) thus [a] [b] [c] &c. intending, at the latter end of these Exercises, to have explained the Terms those Letters referr'd to: But upon consideration that those Terms might often be used in this Discourse, when the Superiour Letter was out of sight, and perhaps its Position (where) forgotten; I have changed my Mind, and left out the Superiour Letters beyond fol. 66. and instead of those References give you this Alphabetical Table of Terms, by which you may always more readily find the Explanation, though you often meet with the Term.

A

A.

Architrave. See Plate 6. *l.* is the *Architrave Molding.*

Augre § 24. Plate 4. fig. K.

B.

Base. See Plate 6. *b.* And Plate 7. B.

Bead. See Plate 6. *a.*

Bed-molding. See Plate 6. *d.*

Basil. The *Basil* is an Angle the edge of a Tool is ground away to. See fol. 71.

Batten. Is a Scantling of Stuff either two, three or four Inches broad; and is seldom above an Inch thick: and the length unlimmitted.

Beak. The end of the Hold-fast. See fol. 60, 61.

Bench-screw. See Plate 4. A *g.* and fol. 60.

Bevil. Any sloping Angle that is not a square, is called a Bevil. See fol. 60. 85. § 19. and Plate 4. F.

Bitt. See § 22.

Bow saw. Plate 4. O.

C.

Capital. See Plate 6. *g.*

Cast. Stuff is said to Cast, or Warp, when by its own Droughth or Moisture, or the Droughth or Moisture of the Air, or other Accident, it alters its flatness and straightness.

Clamp. When a piece of Board is fitted with the Grain to the end of another piece of Board cross the Grain the first Board is *Clampt.* Thus the ends of Tables are commonly *Clampt* to preserve them from warping.

Compass-saw. See fol. 9. and Plate 4. fig. R.

Cornice. See Plate 6. *q.* and Plate 7. H.

Cross-grain'd-stuff. Stuff is Cross-grain'd when a *Bough* or some *Branch* shoots out on that part of the

the Trunk of the Tree; For the *Bough* or *Branch* ſhooting forwards, the Grain of that branch ſhoots forwards alſo, and ſo runs a-croſs the Grain of the Trunk; and if they be well grown together, it will ſcarce be perceived in ſome ſtuff, but in working; yet in Deal-boards, thoſe Boughs or Branches are Knots, and eaſily perceiv'd, and if it grew up young with the Trunk, then inſtead of a Knot you will find a Curling in the *Stuff* when it is wrought.

Curling-ſtuff. If the Bough or Branch that ſhoots out of the Trunk of a Tree be large, and the ſtuff in that place ſawn ſomewhat a-ſlope, when that ſtuff comes under the Plane you will find a Turning about or Curling on that place upon the ſtuff; and in a ſtraight progreſs of the Plane the Iron will cut with, and ſuddenly *a-croſs* the Grain, and that more or leſs as the Bough grew in the Youth of the Tree, or grew more or leſs upright, or elſe ſloping to the Trunk, or was ſawn ſo. Such ſtuff therefore is called *Curling-ſtuff.*

D.

Door-caſe. Is the Fram'd work about the Door.

Double-Screw. See fol. 60. Plate 4. fig. *g.* on the Work-bench A.

F.

Facia. See Plate 6. *b.*

Fence. See § 8. Uſe of the Plow, and Plate 4. fig. B 6.

Fine-ſet. The Irons of Planes are ſet Fine, or Rank. They are ſet Fine, when they ſtand ſo ſhallow below the ſole of the Plane, that in working they take off a thin ſhaving. See § 3.

Flat Frieſe. See Plate 6. *p.*

Fore-Plane. See § 2. and Plate 4. B 1.

Former. See § 10. and Plate 4. C 1. C 3.

Frame,

Frame. See fol. 59, 60.
Frame Saw. See § 28. and Plate 4. O.
Free-stuff. See §. 3.
Friese. See Plate 6. *p.*
Friese Pannel. See Plate 7. L.
Friese Rail. See Plate 7. F.
Frowy stuff. See § 3.

G.

Gage. See § 21. and Plate 4. G.
Gimblet. See § 23. and Plate 4. I.
Gouge. See § 14. C 6.
Groove. See fol. 69.

H.

Hammer-hard. See Numb. I. fol. 58.
Handle. See § 15. and Plate 4. D *a.*
Hard Stuff. See § 3.
Hatchet. See § 25. Plate 4. L.
Head. See § 22. Plate 4. H *a.*
Hold-fast. See § 1. Plate 4. H *d.*
Hook. See § 1. Plate 4. A *b.*
Husk. See Plate 6. *n.*

I.

Inner-square. See § 15. and Plate 4. D *d.*
Joint. See fol. 59.
Jointer. See § 4. and Plate 4. B 2.
Iron. See § 2. and Plate 4. B 1 *d.*

K.

Kerf. The Sawn-away slit between two pieces of stuff is called a Kerf. See fol. 95.
Knob. See § 36. fol. 104. and Plate 5. fig. 7. N.
Knot. See Plate 6. *o.*

L.

Large Pannel. See Plate 7. K.

Lying

Lying Pannel. See Plate 7. I.

Lower Rail. See Plate 7. H.

M.

Margent. See Plate 7. at A A A the flat breadth of the Stiles besides the Moldings, is called the Margent of the Stiles.

Middle Rail. See Plate 7. E E.

Miter. See fol. 64.

Miter Box. See § 20. and Plate 5. fig. 1.

Miter ſquare. See § 18. and Plate 4. E.

Moldings. The ſeveral wrought-work made with Planes on Wood, is called *Moldings.* See Plate *6.*

Molding Planes. See § *9.*

Morteſs. Is a ſquare hole cut in a piece of ſtuff, to entertain a Tennant fit to it. See § 17.

Morteſs Chiſſel. See § 13. and Plate 4. C 5.

Mouth. See § 2. B 7. *a* The Mouth.

O.

Ogee. See Plate *6. c.*

Oval. See § 21. and Plate 4. G. *b.*

Outer Square. See § 15. and Plate 4. D *c.*

P.

Pad. See § 22. and Plate 4. H *b.*

Pannel. In Plate 7. I K L are Pannels, but diſtinguiſhed by their Poſitions.

Pare. The ſmooth cutting with the Paring-Chiſſel is called *Paring.*

Paring-Chiſſel. See § 11. and Plate 4. C 2.

Plaiſter. See Plate 6. *f.*

Peircer. See § 22. and Plate 4. H.

Pit-man The Saywer that works in the Pit, is called the Pit-man.

Pit-Saw. The Pit-ſaw is a great Saw fitted into a ſquare Frame; as in Plate 4. M is a Pit-ſaw.

Planchier. In Plate 6. between *d* and *e* is the Planchier.

Plinth. See Plate 6.

Plow. See § 8. and Plate 4. B 6.

Pricker. Is vulgarly called an Awl: Yet for Joiners Uſe it hath moſt commonly a ſquare blade, which enters the Wood better than a round blade will; becauſe the ſquare Angle in turning it about breaks the Grain, and ſo the Wood is in leſs danger of ſplitting.

R.

R*abbet.* See § 7.

Rabbet Plane. See § 7. and Plate 4. B 5.

Rack. See Plate 5. fig. 8. Read § 36.

Rail. See Plate 7. A A A.

Rank. The Iron of a Plane is ſaid to be *ſet Rank*, when its edge ſtands ſo flat below the Sole of the Plane, that in working it will take off a thick ſhaving. See § 3.

Rank-ſet. See Rank.

Range. The ſide of any Work that runs ſtraight, without breaking into Angles, is ſaid to *run Range*: Thus the Rails and Pannels of one ſtraight ſide of Wainſcoting is ſaid to *run Range.*

Return. The ſide that falls away from the foreſide of any Straight or Rank-work, is called the *Return.*

Riglet. Is a flat thin ſquare piece of Wood. Thus the pieces that are intended to make the Frames for ſmall Pictures, *&c.* before they are Molded are called *Riglets.*

S.

Saw-wreſt. See § 26. fol. 97. and Plate 4. O.

Scantlin. The ſize that your ſtuff is intended to be cut to.

Scribe.

Scribe. When Joiners are to fit a ſide of a piece of Stuff againſt the ſide of ſome other piece of Stuff, and the ſide of the piece of Stuff they are to fit to is not regular; To make theſe two pieces of Stuff join cloſe together all the way, they Scribe it, (as they phraſe it,) thus; They lay the piece of Stuff they intend to Scribe cloſe againſt the other piece of Stuff they intend to Scribe to, and open their Compaſſes to the wideſt Diſtance, theſe two pieces of Stuff bear off each other: Then (the Compaſſes moving ſtiff in their Joint) they bear the point of one of the ſhanks againſt the ſide they intend to Scribe to, and with the point of the other ſhank they draw a Line upon the Stuff to be Scribed; and then the points of the Compaſſes remaining unremov'd, and your Hand carried even along by the ſide of the piece to be Scribed to, that Line Scribed upon the piece intended to be Scribed, ſhall be parallel to the irregular ſide intended to be Scribed to: And if you work away your Stuff exactly to that Line, when theſe two pieces are put together, they ſhall ſeem a Joint.

Shoot a Joint. See fol. 63.

Skew-former. See § 12. and Plate 4. C 4.

Smoothing Plane. See § 6. and Plate 4. B 4.

Sole. See Plate 4. B 7. *b a b.* The under ſide of a Plane is called the *Sole.*

Square. See § 15. and Plate 4. D.

Staff. See § 21. and Plate 4. G *c.*

Staves. See § 8. and Plate 4. B 6. *a a.*

Stile. The upright Pieces AA in Pl. 7. are *Stiles.*

Stock. See § 22. and Plate 4. H *c.*

Stops. In Plate 6. *k k* are *Stops.*

Stuff. The Wood that Joiners work upon they call in general *Stuff.*

Sur-baſe. In Plate 7. D is the *Sur-baſe.*

Swelling-Frieſe. In Plate 6. *r* is the *Swelling-frieſe.*

H 2 T.

T.

Table. In Plate 6. *f* is the *Table.*

Taper. All ſorts of Stuff or Work that is ſmaller at one end than at the other, and diminiſhes gradually from the biggeſt end, is ſaid to be *Taper.*

Tennant. Is a ſquare end fitted into a Morteſs. See § 17.

Tennant-Saw. In Plate 4. O. would be a Tennant-ſaw, were the flat of the Blade turned where the edge there ſtands.

Tongue. See § 16. and Plate 4. D *b.*

Tooth. See § 21. and Plate 4. G *a.*

Top-man. Of the two Sawyers, the uppermoſt is called the *Top-man.*

Tote. See § 2. and Plate 4. B 1 *a.*

Traverſe. See fol. 69.

Truſſel. See fol. 100. and Plate 5. Fig. 3.

Try. See § 13.

V.

Vaws-Cornice. See Plate 6. *e.*

Upper Cornice. See Plate 6. *t.*

W.

Warp. The ſame that *Caſt* is.

Waving Engine. See § 46. and Plate 5.

Wedge. See § 2. and Plate 4. B 1. *c.*

Whetting-Block. See Plate 4. P.

Whip-Saw. See Plate 4. N.

Wreſt. See § 26. and Plate 4. Q.

Thus much of Joinery. The next Exerciſes will be of *Carpentry.*

MECHANICK EXERCISES;

OR,

The Doctrine of *Handy-Works*

Applied to the ART of *House-Carpentry.*

BEING now come to exercise upon the *Carpenters* Trade, it may be expected, by some, that I should insist upon *Architecture*, it being so absolutely necessary for Builders to be acquainted with: But my Answer to them is, that there are so many Books of *Architecture* extant, and in them the Rules so well, so copiously, and so compleatly handled, that it is needless for me to say any thing of that Science: Nor do I think any Man that should, can do more than Collect out of their Books, and perhaps deliver their Meanings in his own Words. Besides, *Architecture* is a Mathematical Science, and therefore different from my present Undertakings, which are (as by my Title) Mechanick Exercises: yet because Books of Architecture are as necessary for a Builder to understand, as the use of Tools; and lest some Builders should not know how to enquire for them, I shall at the latter end of *Carpentry* give you the Names of some Authors, especially such as are Printed in the *English* Tongue.

Some may perhaps also think it had been more proper for me in these Exercises to have introduced *Carpentry* before *Joinery*, because Necessity, (the Mother of Invention) did doubtless compel our Fore-fathers in the beginning to uſe the conveniency of the firſt, rather than the extravagancy of the laſt. I confeſs, I conſidered it my ſelf, and had in my own Reaſon been perſuaded to it. but that I alſo conſidered that the Rules they both work by are upon the matter in the ſame, in *Sawing*, *Morteſſing*, *Tenanting*, *Scribing*, *Paring*, *Plaining*, *Moulding*, &c. and likewiſe the Tools they work with the ſame, though ſome of them ſomewhat ſtronger for Carpenter's Uſe than they need be for Joiner's; becauſe Joiners work more curiouſly, and obſerve the Rules more exactly than Carpenters need do. And therefore I ſay it was, that I began with Joinery before Carpentry; for he that knows how to work curiouſly, may, when he liſts, work ſlightly; when as they that are taught to work more roughly, do with greater difficulty perform the curious and nice work. Thus we ſee Joiners Work their Tables exactly flat and ſmooth, and ſhoot their Joint ſo true, that the whole Table ſhews all one piece: But the Floors Carpenters lay are alſo by Rule of Carpentry to be laid flat and true, and ſhall yet be well enough laid, though not ſo exactly flat and ſmooth as a Table.

Yet though the Rules Joiners and Carpenters work by are ſo near the ſame, and the Tools they work with, and Stuff they work upon, the ſame; yet there are many Requiſites proper to a Carpenter, (eſpecially a Maſter Carpenter) that a Joiner need take little notice of, which, after I have deſcribed the Carpenters Tools that are not expreſt among the Joiners, I ſhall ſpeak to.

§ 1. *Of ſeveral Tools uſed in Carpentry, that are not uſed in Joinery. And firſt of the* Ax.

THe *Ax* marked *A* in *Plate* 8. is (as you ſee) different from what the Joiners Hatchet is, both

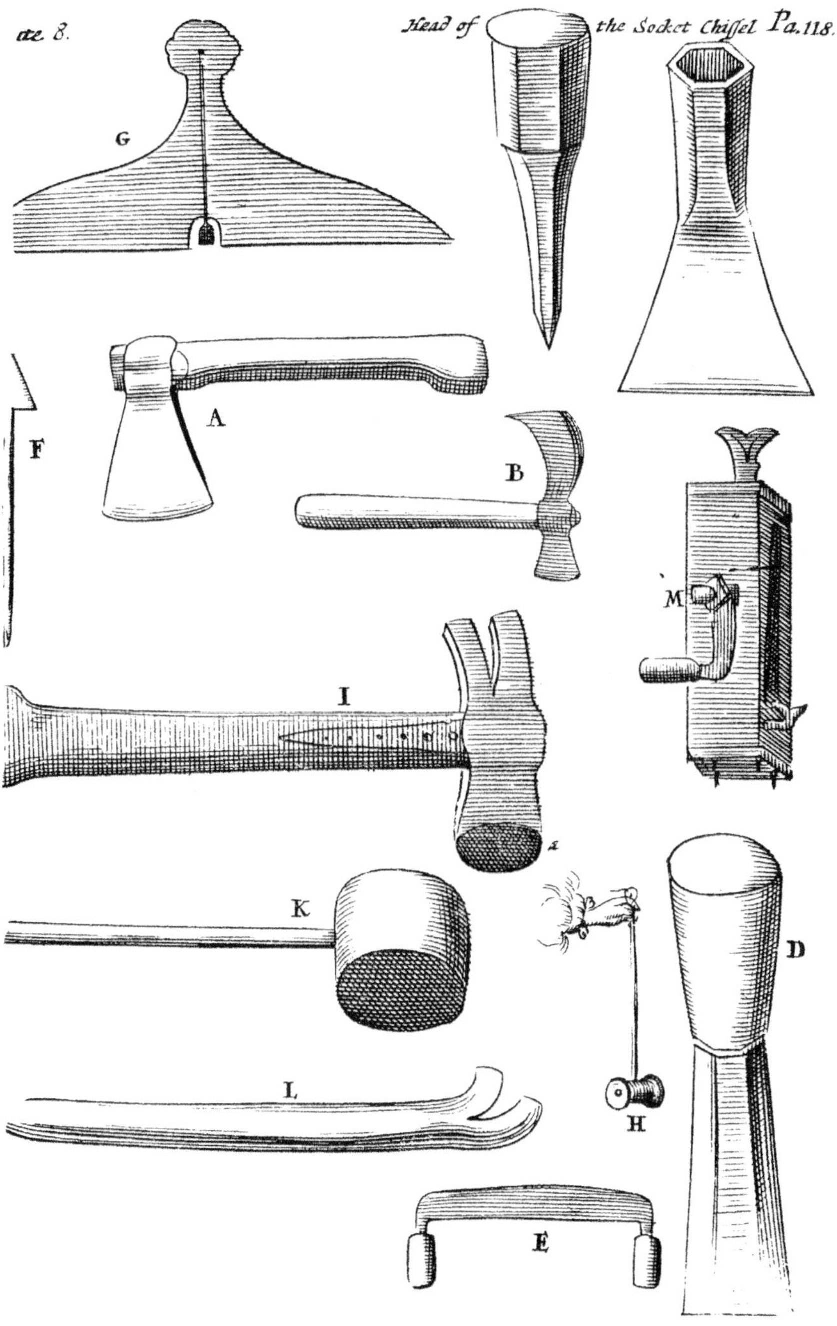
ate 8.
Head of the Socket Chissel
Pa. 118.
G
A
F
B
M
I
a
K
D
L
H
E

both in Size and Form ; theirs being a light Hatchet, with a Basil edge on its left side, because it is to be used with one hand, and therefore hath a short Handle: But the Carpenter's *Ax* being to hew great Stuff, is made much deeper and heavier, and its edge tapering into the middle of its Blade. It hath a long Handle, because it is used with both their Hands, to square or bevil their Timbers.

When they use the Ax, the Timber hath commonly some Bauk or Log laid under it near each end, that the edge of the Ax may be in less danger of striking into the ground, when they hew near the bottom of the Timber. And they commonly stand on that side the Timber they hew upon.

§ 2. *Of the* Adz, *and its use.*

THe *Adz* marked *B* in *Plate* 8. hath its Blade made thin, and somewhat arching. As the Ax hath its edge parallel to its Handle, so the *Adz* hath its edge athwart the Handle, and is ground to a Basil on its inside to its outer edge: Wherefore when it is blunt they cannot well grind it, unless they take its Helve out of its Eye.

Its general Use is to take thin Chips off Timber or Boards, and to take off those Irregularities that the Ax by reason of its Form cannot well come at; and that a Plane (though rank set) will not make riddance enough with.

It is most used for the taking off the Irregularities on the framed Work of a Floor, when it is framed and pin'd together, and laid on its place; for that lying flat under them, the edge of the Ax being parallel to its Handle (as aforesaid) cannot come at the Irregularities to take them off; but the *Adz* having its edge athwart the Handle will. Again, upon some Posts framed upright, and range with other framed Work close to it, the edge of the Ax cannot come at the Irregularities for the reaſon aforeſaid, but the *Adz* will. And the like for the Irregularities of framed Work on a Ceiling, *&c.*

When they work upon the framed Work of a Floor, they take the end of the Handle in both their Hands, placing themſelves directly before the Irregularity, at a ſmall Diſtance, ſtradling a little with both their Legs, to prevent Danger from the edge of the *Adz*, and ſo by degrees hew off the Irregularity. But if they hew upon an Upright, they ſtand directly before it.

They ſometimes uſe the *Adz* upon ſmall thin Stuff, to make it thinner, (but this is many times when the Ax, or ſome other properer Tool, lies not at hand) and then they lay their Stuff upon the Floor, and hold one end of it down with the Ball of the Foot, if the Stuff be long enough; if not, with the ends of their Toes, and ſo hew it lightly away to their ſize, form, or both.

§ 3. *Of Carpenters* Chiſſels *in general.*

THough Carpenters for their finer Work uſe all the ſorts of *Chiſſels* deſcribed in the Art of Joinery yet are not thoſe ſorts of *Chiſſels* ſtrong enough for their rougher and more common Work, and therefore they alſo uſe a ſtronger ſort of *Chiſſels*; and diſtinguiſh them by the name of *Socket-Chiſſels*: For whereas thoſe *Chiſſels* Joiners uſe have their wooden Heads made hollow to receive the Iron Sprig above the Shoulder of the Shank, Carpenters have their Shank made with an *hollow Socket* at its Top, to receive a ſtrong wooden Sprig made to fit into the *Socket*, with a ſquare Shoulder above it, the thickneſs of the Iron of the *Socket*, or ſomewhat more; which makes it much more ſtrong, and able to endure the heavy blows of the *Mallet* they lay upon the head of the *Chiſſel.*

ſel. And the Shanks and Blades are made ſtronger for Carpenter's Uſe than they are for Joiners.

Of theſe *Socket-Chiſſels* they have of the ſeveral ſorts deſcribed in Joinery, though not all ſeverally diſtinguiſhed by their Names; for they call them *Half-Inch*, *Three-quarter-Inch Chiſſels*, *Inch and Half*, *Two-Inch*, to *Three-Inch Chiſſels*, according to the breadth of the Blade. But their Uſes are the ſame mentioned in Joinery, though the manner of uſing them be ſomewhat different too: For, as I told you in Joinery, the Joiners preſs the edge of the Blade into the Stuff, with the ſtrength of their Shoulders, but the Carpenters with the force of the blows of the Mallet. And the Joiners guide their *Chiſſels* differently from what the Carpenters do their *Socket-Chiſſels*; for the Joiners hold the Shank and Blade of their *Chiſſels*, as I deſcribed in Joinery, *Sect.* 11. but the Carpenters hold the Shank of their *Chiſſels* in their clutched left Hand, and beat upon the Head with the *Mallet* in the right. See the Figure of *Socket-Chiſſel* in *Plate* 8. C. with its Head *a* out of the Socket.

§ 4. *Of the* Ripping-Chiſſel, *and its Uſe.*

THE *Ripping-Chiſſel* deſcribed in *Plate* 8. D. is a *Socket-Chiſſel*, and is about an Inch broad, and hath a blunt Edge. Its Edge hath not a *Baſil*, as almoſt all other *Chiſſels* have, and thereſore would more properly be called a *Wedge* than a *Chiſſel* But moſt commonly Carpenters uſe an old caſt off *Chiſſel* for a *Ripping-Chiſſel.*

Its Office is not to cut Wood, as others do, but to *rip* or *tear* two pieces of Wood faſtned together from one another, by entering the blunt Edge of it between the two pieces, and then knocking hard with the Mallet upon the head of the Handle, till you drive the thicker part of it between the two pieces, and ſo force the power that holds them

them together (be it Nails, or otherwiſe) to let go their hold: For its blunt Edge ſhould be made of Steel, and well tempered, ſo that if you knock with ſtrong blows of the Mallet the *Chiſſels* Edge upon a Nail (though of ſome conſiderable Subſtance) it may cut or brake it ſhort aſunder. If you cannot, at once, placing the *Ripping-Chiſſel*, part the two pieces, you muſt uſe two *Ripping-Chiſſels*, placing the ſecond at the remoteſt entrance in the breach, and driving that home, will both open the breach wider, and looſen the firſt *Ripping-Chiſſel*, ſo that you may take it again, and place it farther in the breach: And ſo you muſt continue edging farther and farther, till you have ſeparated your intended pieces.

It is ſometimes uſed when Carpenters have committed Error in their Work, and muſt undo what they did, to mend it. But it is generally uſed in all Alterations, and old Work.

§ 5. *Of the* Draw-knife, *and its Uſe.*

THe *Draw-knife* deſcribed *Plate* 8. E. is ſeldom uſed about Houſe-building, but for the making of ſome ſorts of Houſhold-ſtuff; as the Legs of Crickets, the Rounds of Ladders, the Rails to lay Cheeſe or Bacon on, *&c.*

When they uſe it, they ſet one end of their Work againſt their Breaſt, and the other end againſt their Work-bench, or ſome hollow Angle that may keep it from ſlipping, and ſo preſſing the Work a little hard with their Breaſt againſt the Bench, to keep it ſteddy in its Poſition, they with the Handles of the *Draw knife* in both their Hands, enter the edge of the *Draw-knife* into the Work, and draw Chips almoſt the length of their Work, and ſo ſmoothen it quickly.

§ 6. *Of* Hook-Pins, *and their uſe.*

THe Hook-Pin is deſcribed *Plate* 8. F. *a* the *Pin*, *b* the *Hook*, *c* the *Head*. Its Office is to pin the Frame of a Floor, or Frame of a Roof together, whilſt it is framing, or whilſt it is fitting into its Poſition. They have many of theſe *Hook-Pins* to drive into the ſeveral Angles of the Frame. Theſe drive into the Pin-holes through the Morteſſes and Tennants, and being made Taper, do with a Hammer ſtriking on the bottom of it knock it out again; or they moſt commonly ſtrike under the Hook, and ſo knock it out. Then if the Frame lie in its place, they pin it up with wooden Pins.

§ 7. *Of the* Level, *and its uſe.*

THe *Level* deſcribed in *Plate* 8. G. *a a* the *Level*, *b* the *Plumbet*, *c* the *Plumb-line*, *d d* the *Perpendicular* mark'd from the top to the bottom of the Board. The *Level* is from two to ten Foot long, that it may reach over a conſiderable length of the Work. If the *Plumb-line* hang juſt upon the *Perpendicular d d*, when the *Level* is ſet flat down upon the Work, the Work is *Level*: But if it hang on either ſide the *Perpendicular*, the Floor, or Work, muſt be raiſed on that ſide, till the *Plumb-line* hang exactly upon the *Perpendicular*.

§ 8. *Of the* Plumb-line, *and its uſe.*

THe *Plumb-line* is deſcribed in *Plate* 8. H. *a* the *Line-Rowl*, *b* the *Line*. It is uſed to try the upright ſtanding of Poſts, or other Work that is to ſtand Perpendicular to the Ground Plot; and then they draw off ſo much Line as is neceſſary, and faſten the reſt of the Line there, upon the *Line-Rowl* with a Slip-knot, that no more Line turn off. They hold the end of the Line between

their

their Finger and Thumb half the Diameter of the *Line-Rowl* off one corner of the Poſt, or Work; and if the *Line* and Corner of the Poſt be parallel to each other, the Poſt is upright: But if the Poſt be not parallel to the *Line*, but its bottom ſtands more than half the Diameter of the *Line-Rowl* from the *Line*, the Poſt hangs ſo much over the bottom of the Poſt on that ſide the *Line* bears off, and muſt be forced backwards till the ſide of the Poſt and the *Line* become parallel to each other: But if the bottom of the Corner of the Poſt ſtands out from the top of the *Line*, the Poſt muſt be forced forwards to comply with the *Line*.

§ 9. *Of the* Hammer, *and its Uſe.*

THe *Hammer* is deſcribed in *Plate* 8. I. *a* the *Face*, *b* the *Claw*, *c c* the *Pen* at the return ſides of the *Claw*. This Tool was forgot to be deſcribed in *Joinery*, though they uſe *Hammers* too, and therefore I bring it in here. Its chief Uſe is for driving Nails into Work, and drawing Nails out of Work.

There is required a pretty skill in driving a Nail; for if (when you ſet the point of a Nail) you be not curious in obſerving to ſtrike the flat face of the *Hammer* perpendicularly down upon the perpendicular of the Shank, the Nail (unleſs it have good entrance) will ſtart aſide, or bow, or break; and then you will be forced to draw it out again with the *Claw* of the *Hammer*. Therefore you may ſee a reaſon when you buy a *Hammer*, to chuſe one with a true flat *Face*.

A little trick is ſometimes uſed among ſome (that would be thought cunning Carpenters) privately to touch the Head of the Nail with a little Ear-wax, and then lay a Wager with a Stranger to the Trick, that he ſhall not drive that Nail up to the Head with ſo many blows. The ſtranger

ſtranger thinks he ſhall aſſuredly win, but does aſſuredly loſe; for the *Hammer* no ſooner touches the Head of the Nail, but inſtead of entring the Wood it flies away, notwithſtanding his utmoſt care in ſtriking it down-right.

§ 10. *Of the* Commander, *and its Uſe.*

THE *Commander* is deſcribed in *Plate* 8. K. It is indeed but a very great wooden *Mallet*, with an Handle about three foot long, to uſe in both the Hands.

It is uſed to knock on the Corners of Framed Work, to ſet them into their poſition. It is alſo uſed to drive ſmall wooden Piles into the ground, *&c.* or where greater Engines may be ſpared.

§ 11. *Of the* Crow, *and its Uſe.*

THE *Crow* is deſcribed in *Plate* 8. L. *a* the *Shank*, *b b* the *Claws*, *c* the *Pike-end.* It is uſed as a *Lever* to lift up the ends of great heavy Timber, when either a Bauk, or a Rowler, is to be laid under it; and then they thruſt the *Claws* between the Ground and the Timber, and laying a Bauk, or ſome ſuch Stuff behind the *Crow*, they draw the other end of the Shank backwards, and ſo raiſe the Timber.

§ 12. *Of the* Drug, *and its Uſe.*

THE *Drug* deſcribed in *Plate* 9. A. is made ſomewhat like a low narrow Carr. It is uſed for the carriage of Timber, and then is drawn by the Handle *a a*, by two or more Men, according as the weight of the Timber may require.

There are alſo ſome Engines uſed in Carpentry, for the management of their heavy Timber, and hard Labour, *viz.* the *Jack*, the *Crab*, to which belongs Pullies and Tackle, *&c.* Wedges, Rowlers, great Screws, *&c.* But I ſhall give you an account

account of them when I come to the explanation of Terms at the latter end of *Carpentry*.

§ 13. *Of the* Ten-foot Rod, *and thereby to measure and describe the* Ground-plot.

WE ſhall begin therefore to meaſure the *Ground-plot*, to which Carpenters uſe a *Ten-foot Rod* for Expedition, which is a Rod about an Inch ſquare, and ten foot long; being divided into ten equal parts, each part containing one foot, and is divided into 24 equal parts, and their Sub-diviſions.

With this *Rod* they meaſure the length and breadth of the *Ground-plot* into Feet, and if there be odd Inches, they meaſure them with the *Two-foot Rule*. Their meaſure they note down upon a piece of paper, and having conſidered the ſituation of the Sides, *Eaſt*, *Weſt*, *North* and *South*, they draw on paper their ſeveral Sides accordingly, by a ſmall Scale, either elected, or elſe made for that purpoſe. They may elect their *Two-foot Rule* for ſome plots; for an Inch and an half may commodiouſly ſerve to ſet off one Foot on ſome ſmall *Ground-plots*, and then you have the Inches to that Foot actually divided by the Marks for the half quarters on the *Two-foot Rule*. But this large Scale will ſcare ſerve to deſcribe a *Ground-plot* above ten Foot in length, becauſe a ſmall ſheet of Paper is not above 15 or 16 Inches long, and therefore one ſheet of Paper will not contain it, if the *Ground-plot* be longer: Therefore if you make every half quarter of an Inch to be a Scale for two Inches, a ſheet of Paper will contain 20 Foot in length: And if you make every half quarter of an Inch to be a Scale for four Inches, a ſheet of Paper will contain 40 Foot. And thus by diminiſhing the Scale, the ſheet of Paper will contain a greater number of Feet.

But

But having either elected, or else made your Scale, you are to open your Compasses to the number of Feet on your Scale your *Ground-plot* hath in length, and then transfer that Distance to your paper, and to draw a straight Line between the two points, and mark that straight Line with *East*, *West*, *North* or *South*, according to the situation of that side of the *Ground-plot* it represents. Then again open your Compasses to the number of Feet on your Scale one of the adjoining Sides contains, and transfer that Distance also to your paper, and draw a Line between the two points, and note its situation of *East*, *West*, *North* or *South*, as before. Do the like by the other Sides; and if either a Quirk, or any Addition, be added to the Building, on any side of your *Ground-plot*, you must describe it also proportionably.

Then you are to consider what Apartments, or Partitions, to make on your *Ground-plot*, or second, or third Story, and to set them off from your Scale, beginning at your intended Front. As for Example, Suppose your *Ground-plot* be a Long-square, 50 Foot in length, and 20 Foot wide: This *Ground-plot* will contain in its length two good Rooms, and a Yard behind it 10 Foot long. If you will, you may divide the 40 Foot into two equal parts, so will each Room be 20 Foot square: Or you may make the Rooms next the Front deeper, or shallower, and leave the remainder for the Back-Room: As here the Front-Room is 25 Foot, and the Back-Room 15 Foot deep, and a setting off of 8 Foot broad and 10 Foot long taking out of the Yard, for a Buttery below Stairs (if you will) and Closets above Stairs over it. But what width and depth soever you intend your Rooms shall have, you must open your Compasses to that number of Feet on your Scale, and set off that Distance on the *East*, *West*, *North* or *South*,

Line,

Line, according to the Situation of that ſide it re-preſents on your *Ground-plot*. If you ſet it off the *Eaſt* Line, you muſt alſo ſet it off on the *Weſt*; if on the *North* Line, you muſt alſo ſet it off on the *South* Line: Becauſe between the two Settings off on the *Eaſt* and *Weſt* Lines, or *North* or *South* Lines, you muſt draw a ſtraight Line of the length of your intended Partition. And in this manner you muſt from every Partition draw a Line in its proper place on the Paper, by meaſuring the Diſtances each Partition muſt have from the outſide of the *Ground-plot*.

And thus you are alſo to deſcribe by your Scale your Front, and ſeveral ſides of the Carcaſe; allowing the *Principal Poſts*, *Enterduces*, *Quarterings*, *Braces*, *Gables*, *Doors*, *Windows*, and *Ornaments*, their ſeveral Sizes, and true Poſitions by the Scale: Each ſide upon a Paper by it ſelf: Unleſs we ſhall ſuppoſe our Maſter-Workman to underſtand *Perſpective*; for then he may, on a ſinggle piece of Paper, deſcribe the whole Building, as it ſhall appear to the Eye at any aſſigned Station.

§ 14. *Of* Foundations.

HAving drawn the *Draft*, the Maſter-Workman is firſt to cauſe the Cellars to be dug, if the Houſe ſhall have Cellars. And then to try the Ground, that it be all over of an equal firmneſs, that when the weight of the Building is ſet upon it, it may not ſink in any part. But if the Ground be hollow or weaker in any place, he ſtrengthens it, ſometimes by well ramming it down, and levelling it again with good dry Earth, Lime-Core, Rubbiſh, *&c.* or ſometimes with ramming in Stones, or ſometimes with well Planking it; or moſt ſecurely by driving in Piles. But driving in of Piles is ſeldom uſed for Timber Houſes,

Houſes, but for Stone, or Brick Houſes, and that but in few places of *England* neither, but where the Ground proves *Fenny*, or *Mooriſh*. Therefore a farther account ſhall be given of Foundations, when I come to exerciſe upon *Maſonry*, &c.

Then are the Celler-Walls to be brought up by a *Brick-layer* with *Brick*; for ſmall Houſes two Bricks thick, for bigger two and an half Bricks thick, or three or four Bricks thick, according to the bigneſs of the Houſe, and quality of the Ground, as I ſhall ſhew when I come to Exerciſe on *Bricklaying*.

But if the Houſe be deſigned to have no Cellars (as many Country-Houſes have not) yet for the better ſecuring the Foundation, and preſerving the Timber from rotting, Maſter-Workmen will cauſe three, or four, or five courſe of Bricks to be laid, to lay their *Ground-plates* upon that Foundation.

The Foundation being made good, the Maſter-Workman appoints his Under-Workmen their ſeveral *Scantlins*, for *Ground-plates*, *Principal Poſts*, *Poſts*, *Breſſummers*, *Girders*, *Trimmers*, *Joyſts*, &c. which they cut ſquare, and frame their Timbers to, as has been taught in the ſeveral Exerciſes upon Joinery, (whither I refer you) and there ſet them up, each in its proper place, according to the Draft.

The Draft of a Foundation I have deſcribed in *Plate* 10, according to a Scale of eight Foot in an Inch; where you have the Front A B 20 Foot long, the ſides A C and B D 50 Foot long. The Shop, or firſt Room, E E 25 Foot (as aforeſaid) deep. I make the firſt Room a Shop, becauſe I intend to deſcribe *Shop-windows*, *Stalls*, &c. though you may Build according to any other purpoſe: The *Kitching*, or *Back-Room* F F 15 Foot deep. A *Buttry* or *Cloſet*, taken out of the *Yard*, marked G,

10 Foot deep, and 8 Foot wide: H a *Setting off* in the *Yard*, 4 Foot ſquare for the *Houſe of Office.* I *Leaving way* in the Shop for a *Stair-Caſe* 6 Foot, and 11 Foot. K The *Yard.* L The *Sink-hole* 1 Foot ſquare. M *Leaving way* in the *Kitching* 6 Foot deep, and 4 Foot wide for the *Chimneys.*

I do not deliver this Draft of Partitions for the moſt Commodious for this Ground-plot, nor is the Houſe ſet out deſigned for any particular Inhabitant; which is one main purpoſe to be conſidered of the Maſter-Workman, before he make his Draft; for a Gentleman's Houſe muſt not be divided as a Shop-keeper's, nor all Shop-keepers Houſe a-like; for ſome Trades require a deeper, others may diſpence with a ſhallower Shop, and ſo an Inconvenience may ariſe in both. For if the Shop be ſhallow, the Front Rooms upwards ought to be ſhallow alſo: Becauſe by the ſtrict Rules of *Architecture*, all Partitions of Rooms ought to ſtand directly over one another: For if your Shop ſtands in an eminent Street, the Front Rooms are commonly more Airy than the Back Rooms; and always more Commodious for obſerving publick Paſſages in the Street, and in that reſpect it will be inconvenient to make the Front Rooms ſhallow: But if you have a fair Proſpect backwards of Gardens, Feilds, &c. (which ſeldom happens in Cities) then it may be convenient to make your Back-Rooms the larger for Entertainment, &c. But I ſhall run no farther into this Argument; for I ſhall leave the Maſter-Workman to conſult Books of *Architecture*, and more particularly the Builder, which, in this caſe, they ought all to do.

Plate 10

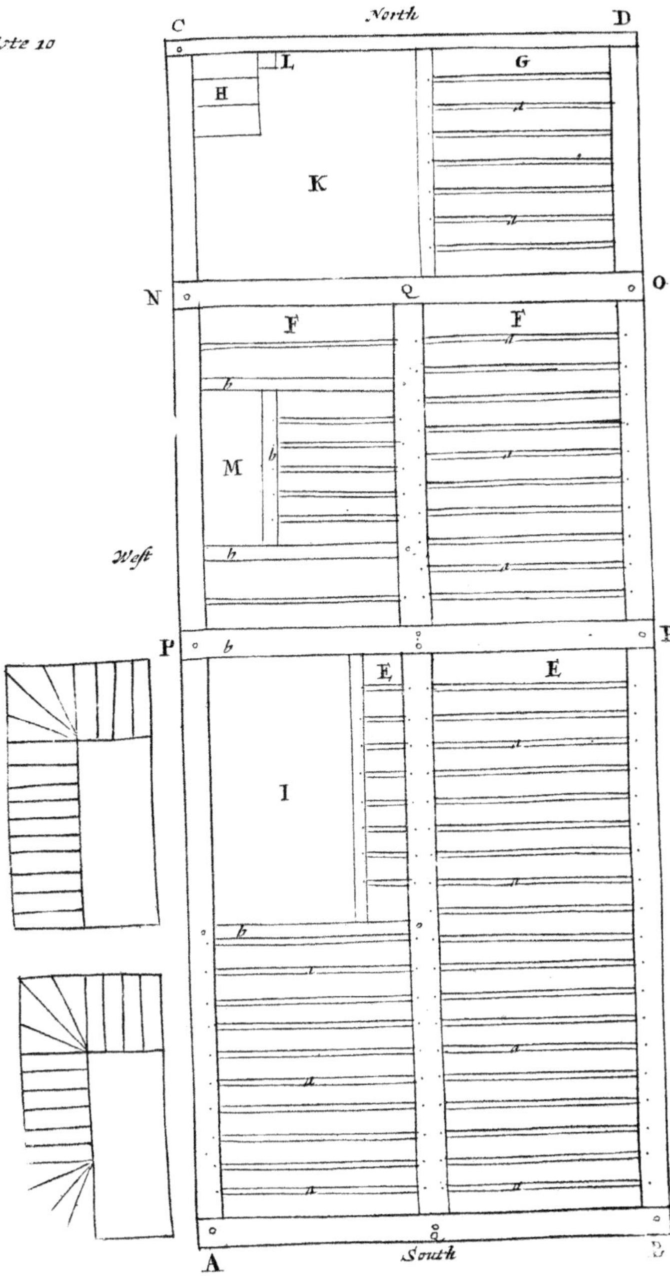

Plate 9.

Page.

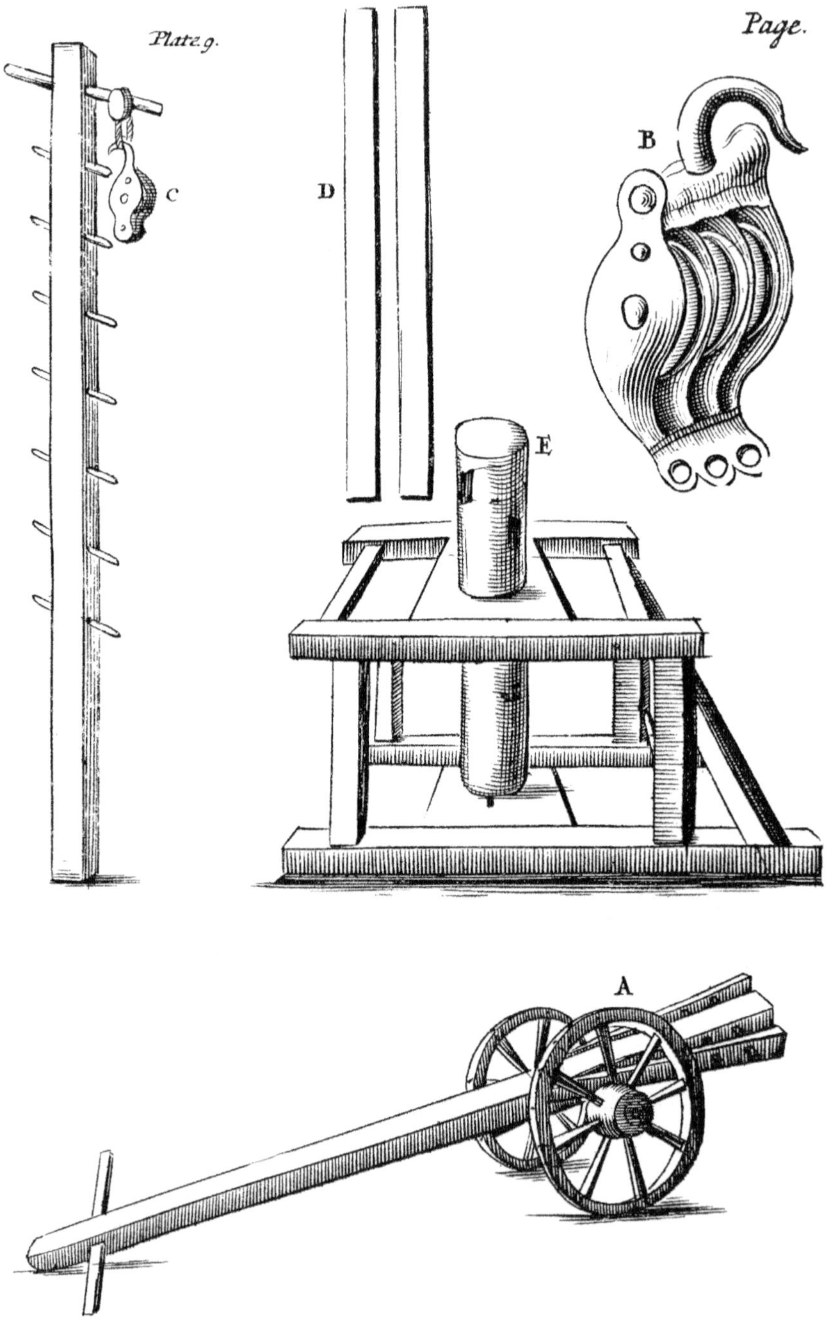

MECHANICK EXERCISES;

O R,

The Doctrine of *Handy-Works*

Continued in the ART of *House-Carpentry*.

A C, B D, C D, N O, *Ground-plates*, *Wall-plates*, *Bresummers*, *Lintels*, *the Thickness of the Wall.*
A B, *Also a Ground-plate*, *or Ground-sell.*
P P, *The Summer.*
Q Q Q, *Girders.*
I, *The Well-houle for the Stairs*, *and Stair-case.*
M, *Leaving a way for the Chimnies.*
b b, *Trimmers for the Chimny-way and Stair-case.*
a a a a, *Joysts.*

§ 15. *Of* Framing *for the* Floors.

THE four Plates, A B, A N, N O and B O, lying on the Foundation, are called *Ground-plates*. They are to be of good Oak, and for this size of Building about eight Inches broad, and six Inches deep. They are to be framed into one another with Tennants and Mortesses. The longer Ground-plates A N and B O are commonly tennanted into the Front and Rear Ground-plates A B and N O, and into these two side-Ground-plates are Mortesses made for the Tennants at the ends of the Joysts, to be fitted somewhat loosly in, at about ten Inches distance from one another, as in the Draft. These Ground-plates are to be bor d with an Inch and half *Augre*, and well pinned into

 one

one another with round Oaken Pins, made tapering towards the point, and so strong, that with the hard blows of a Mallet, they may drive stiff into the *Augre-hole*, and keep the Tennant firmly in the Mortess. The manner of making a Tennant and Mortess is taught in *Joinery*, p. 85. But because the Stuff *Carpenters* work upon, is generally heavy Timber, and consequently not so easily managed as the light Stuff Joiners work upon; therefore they do not at first pin their Tennants into their Mortesses with wooden Pins, lest they should lie out of square, or any other intended Position: But laying a *Block*, or some other piece of Timber, under the corner of the Frame-work to bear it hollow off the Foundation, or what ever else it lies upon, they drive *Hook-pins* (described in *Plate* 8. § 6.) into the four *Augre-holes* in the corners of the Ground-plates, and one by one fit the Plates either to a Square, or any other intended Position: And when it is so fitted, they draw out their *Hook-pins*, and drive in the wooden Pins (as aforesaid) and taking away the wooden *Blocks* one by one from under the corners of the Frame, they let it fall into its place.

But before they pin up the Frame of Ground-plates, they must fit in the *Summer* marked P P, and the *Girders* Q Q, and all the *Joysts* marked *a a a a*, &c and the *Trimmers* for the *Stair-case*, and *Chimny-way* marked *b b*, and the binding *Joysts* marked *c c*, for else you cannot get their Tennants into their respective Mortess-holes. But they do I say fit all these in, while the Frame of Ground-plates lies loose, and may, corner by corner, be opened to let the respective Tennants into their respective Mortesses, which when all is done, they Frame the *Raising-plates* just as the *Ground-plates* are Framed; and then Frame the Roof into the *Raising-plates* with *Beams*, *Joysts*, &c.

The

The *Summer* is in this Ground-plate placed at 25 Foot diſtance from the Front, and is to be of the ſame Scantlin the principal Plates are of, for Reaſons as ſhall be ſhewn hereafter: And the *Girders* are alſo to be of the ſame Scantlins the *Summers* and *Ground-plates* are of, though according to the nice Rules of *Architecture*, the *Back-Girder* need not be ſo ſtrong as the *Front-Girder*, becauſe it Bears but at 14 Foot length, and the *Front-Girder* Bears at 24 Foot length: Yet Carpenters (for uniformity) generally make them ſo, unleſs they build an Houſe by the Great, and are agreed for the Sum of Money, *&c.*

The *Joyſts* Bearing at 8 Foot (as here they do) are to be 7 Inches deep, and 3 Inches broad.

The *Trimmers* and *Trimming Joyſts* are 5 Inches broad and 7 Inches deep, and theſe *Joyſts*, *Trimmers* and *Trimming Joyſts*, are all to be pinned into their reſpective Morteſſes; and then its flatneſs try'd with the Level, as was taught § 7.

§ 16. *Of ſetting up the* Carcaſs.

THough the *Ground-plates*, *Girders*, &c. be part of the Carcaſs, yet I thought fit in the laſt Section they ſhould be laid, before I treated of the Superſtructure, which I ſhall now handle. The four Corner Poſts called the *Principal Poſts* marked A A, ſhould be each of one piece, ſo long as to reach up to the *Beam* of the *Roof*, or *Raiſing-plate*, and of the ſame Scantlin the *Ground-plates* are of, *viz.* 8 Inches broad, and 6 Inches thick, and ſet with one of its narroweſt ſides towards the Front. Its lower end is to be Tennanted, and let into a Morteſs made near the corner of the *Ground-plate* Frame; and its upper end hath alſo a Tennant on it, to fit into a Morteſs made in the Beam of the Roof, or *Raſing-piece.*

At the heighth of the firſt Story in this Principal Poſt, muſt be made two Morteſſes, one to receive the Tennant at the end of the Breſſummer that lies in the Front, and the other to entertain the Tennant at the end of the Breſſummer that lies in the Return-ſide.

Two ſuch Morteſſes muſt alſo be made in this Principal Poſt at the height of the ſecond Story, to receive the Tennant at the ends of the Breſſummers for that Story.

Though I have ſpoken ſingularly of one Principal Poſt, yet as you work this, you muſt work all four Principal Poſts; and then ſet them plumb upright, which you muſt try with a Plumb-line deſcribed in *Plate* 8 §. 8.

Having erected the Principal Poſts upright, you muſt enter the Tennants of the Breſſummers into their proper Morteſſes, and with a Nail or two (about a ſingle Ten or a double Ten) tack one end of a deal Board, or ſome other like piece of Stuff to the Breſſummer, and the other end to the Fram'd Work of the Floor, to keep the Principal Poſts upright, and in their places. Then ſet up the ſeveral Poſts between the Principal Poſts; but theſe Poſts muſt be Tennanted at each end, becauſe they are to be no longer than to reach from Story to Story, or from Entertiſe to Entertiſe, and are to be framed into the upper and under Breſſummer. If the Entertiſes be not long enough, they ſet up a Principal Poſt between two or three Lengths, to reach from the Ground-plate up to the Raiſing-plates.

It is to be remembred, that the Breſſummers and Girders are laid flat upon one of their broadeſt ſides, with their two narroweſt ſides Perpendicular to the Ground-plot; but the Joyſts are to be laid contrary: For they

are

are Framed ſo as to lie with one of their narroweſt ſides upwards, with their two broadeſt ſides Perpendicular to the Ground-plot. The reaſon is, becauſe the Stuff of the Breſſummers and Girders are leſs weakned by cutting the Morteſſes in them in this Poſition, than in the other Poſition; for as the Tennants for thoſe Morteſſes are cut between the top and bottom ſides, and the flat of the Tennants are no broader than the flat of the narroweſt ſide of the Joyſts; ſo the Morteſſes they are to fit into, need be no broader than the breadth of the Tennant, and the Tennants are not to be above an Inch thick, and conſequently the Morteſſes are to be made with an Inch Morteſs-Chiſſel, as was ſhewn in *Joinery*, p. 86. for great care muſt be taken that the Breſſummers and Girders be not weakned more than needs, leſt the whole Floor dance,

Theſe Tennants are cut through the two narroweſt ſides, rather than between the two broadeſt ſides, becauſe the Stuff of the Girders retains more ſtrength when leaſt of the Grain of the Stuff is cut: And the Tennants being made between the narroweſt ſides of the Joyces, requires their Morteſs-holes no longer than the breadth of that Tennant: And that Tennant being but an Inch thick, requires its Morteſs but an Inch wide to receive it; ſo that you Morteſs into the Girder no more than three Inches wide with the Grain of the Stuff, and one Inch broad contrary to the Grain of the Stuff. But ſhould the Tennant be cut between the two broad ſides of the Joyſts, the Morteſs would be three Inches long, and but one Inch broad, and conſequently, you muſt cut into the Girder three Inches croſs the Grain of the Stuff, which would weaken it more than cutting ſix Inches with the Grain, and one Inch croſs.

But it may be objected that the Tennants of the Joyſts being ſo ſmall, and bearing at an Inch thickneſs muſt needs be too weak.

Anſwer, Firſt, Though the Tennants be indeed but an Inch thick, and three Inches broad; yet the whole Bearing of the Joyces do not ſolely depend upon their Tennants; becauſe the Girders they are framed into, prove commonly ſomewhat Wainny upon their upper ſides, and the Joyſts are always ſcribed to project over that Waynnineſs, and ſo ſtrengthen their Bearing by ſo much as they project over the Roundneſs or Waynnineſs of the upper ſide of the Girder.

Secondly, The Floor is boarded with the length of the Boards athwart the Joyſts, and theſe Boards firmly railed down to the Joyſts, which alſo adds a great ſtrength to them.

Thirdly, The Joyſts are ſeldom made to Bear at above ten Foot in length, and ſhould by the Rule of good Workmanſhip, not lie above ten Inches aſunder at the moſt: So that this ſhort Bearing and cloſe diſcharging of one another, renders the whole Floor firm enough for all common Occupation. But if the Joyces do Bear at above ten Foot in length, it ought to be the care of the Maſter-workman to provide ſtronger Stuff for them, *viz.* Thicker and Broader. If not, they cut a Tusk on the upper ſide of the Tennant, and let that Tusk into the upper ſide of the Girders.

Having erected the Principal Poſt, and other Poſts, and fitted in the Breſſummers, Girders, Joyſts, *&c* upon the firſt Floor, they pin up all the Frame of Carcaſs-work. But though the Girders and Joyſts deſcribed for this firſt Floor, lie proper enough for it; yet for the ſecond Story, and in this particular Caſe, the Joyſts lie not proper for the ſecond Story; becauſe

in

in the ſecond Story we have deſcribed a *Balcony*.

Therefore in this Caſe you muſt frame the Front-Breſſummer about ſeven Inches lower into the Principal Poſts : Becauſe the Joyſts for the ſecond Floor are not to be Morteſſed into the Breſſummer to lie even at the top with it, but muſt lie upon the Breſſummer, and project over it ſo far as you deſign the *Balcony* to project beyond the Upright of the Front : And thus laying the Joyſts upon the Breſſummer renders them much ſtronger to bear the *Balcony*, than if Joyſts were Tennanted into the Front of the Breſſummer, and ſo project out into the Street from it.

But the Truth is, Though I have given you a Draft of the Joyſts lying athwart the Front and Rear for the firſt Floor, you may as well lay them Range with the two ſides on the firſt Floor. But then the Breſſummer that reaches from Front to Rear in the middle of the Floor muſt be ſtronger : And Girders muſt then be Tennanted into the Breſſummer, and the Ground-plates at ſuch a Diſtance, that the Joyſts may not Bear at above ten Foot in length. And the Tennants of the Joyſts muſt be Tennanted into the Girders, ſo that they will then lie Range with the two Sides.

But, a word more of the Breſſummer: I ſay (as before) the Breſſummer to Bear at ſo great Length muſt be ſtronger, though it ſhould be diſcharged at the Length of the Shop, (*viz*. at 25 Foot) with a Brick Wall, or a Foundation brought up of Brick. But if it ſhould have no Diſcharge of Brick-work, but Bear at the whole 40 Foot in Length, your Breſſummer muſt be yet conſiderably ſtronger than it need be, were it to Bear but 25 Foot in Length ; because the ſhorter all the Bearings of Timbers are, the firmer they Bear. But then the Fraiming Work will take up more Labour: And in many

many Cases it is cheaper to put in ſtronger Stuff for long Bearings, than to put a Girder between, to Diſcharge the Length of the Joyſts to be framed into the Girders.

But to make ſhort of this Argument, I ſhall give you the Scheme of Scantlins of Timber at ſeveral Bearings for *Summers, Girders, Joyſts, Rafters*, &c. as they are ſet down in the Act of Parlia. for the Re-building the City of *London*, after the late dreadful Fire: Which Scantlins were well conſulted by able Workmen before they were reduced into an Act.

Scantlins of Timber for the firſt Sorts of Houſes

		Foot	*Inches*		*Inches*
For the Floor	Summers under	15	12	and	8
	Wall-plates		7	and	5
For the Roof	Principal Rafters under	15 *Foot*	at foot--8 at top---5		6 Inch.
	Single Rafters		4	and	3 Inches.

	Length Foot	*Thickneſs*		*Depth*
Joyſts to	10	3	and	7 Inches
Garret Floors	3			6

Scantlins of Timber for the other two Sorts of Houſes.

	Foot		*Breadth Foot*	*Inches*		*Depth Inches*		*Thickneſs Inches*	*Depth Inches*
Summers or Girders which bear in length from	10	to	15	11	and	8	Joyſts which bear 10 Foot	3	6
	15		18	13		9		3	7
	18		21	14		10		3	7
	21		24	16		12		3	8
	24		26	17		14		3	8

For the Floor.

	Inches		*Inches*
Principal Diſcharges upon Peers in the firſt Story in the Fronts	13	and	12
	15		13

	Thickneſs	*Inches*
Binding Joyſts with their Trimming Joyſts	5	depth equal to their own Floors

	Inches		*Inches*
Wall-plates, or Raiſing Pieces and Beams	10	and	6
	8		6
	7		5

		Inches		*Inches*
Lintels of Oak in the	1ſt. and 2d. Story	8	and	6
	3d. Story	5		4

Length

For the Roof:

	Length Foot	Foot		Inches	Thickness Inches
Principal Rafters from	15 to	18	at foot	9	7
			at top	7	
	18	21	at foot	10	8
			at top	8	
	21	24	at foot	12	8½
			at top	9	
	24	26	at foot	13	9
			at top	9	

	Length Foot	Foot	Inches	Inches
Purlins from	15 to	18	9	8
	18	21	12	9

		Foot	Inches	Inches
Single Rafters	not exceeding in length	9	5	4
	not exceeding in length	6	4	3½

Scantlins for Sawed Timber and Laths, usually brought out of the West Country, not less than

	Foot	Breadth Inches	Thickness Inches
Single Quarters in length	8	3½	1¾
Double Quart. in length	8	4	3½
Sawed Joysts in length	8	6	4
Laths in length	5 / 4	1¼	1 quarter and ½ Inch

Stone

Where Stone is used, to keep to these Scantlins-----

		Inches
First sort of Houses	Corner Peers	18 square
	Middle or Single Peers	14 and 12
	Double Peers between House and House	14 and 18
	Door-Jambs and Heads	12 and 8

		Foot	Inches
2d & 3d sorts	Corner Peers	2	6 square
	Middle or Single Peers		18 square
	Double Peers between House and House		24 and 18
	Door Jambs and Heads		14 and 10

	Foot	Thickness	
Scantlins for Sewers	3 wide	Side-walls-1 Brick ½	Bottom paved plain, and then 1 Brick on edge circular.
	5 high	Arch-1 Brick on end	

Gene-

General RULES.

IN every Foundation within the Ground add one Brick in thickneſs to the thickneſs of the Wall (as in the Scheme) next above the Foundation, to be ſet off in three Courſes equally on both ſides.

That no Timber be laid within twelve Inches of the fore-ſide of the Chimney Jambs : And that all Joyſts on the back of any Chimney be laid with a Trimmer at ſix Inches diſtance from the Back.

That no Timber be laid within the Tunnel of any Chimney, upon Penalty to the Workman for every Default ten Shillings, and ten Shillings every Week it contiuues un-reformed.

That no Joyſts or Rafters be laid at greater diſtances from one to the other, than twelve Inches; and no Quarters at greater diſtance than fourteen Inches.

That no Joyſts bear at longer length than ten Foot; and no ſingle Rafters at more in length than nine Foot.

That all Roofs, Window-frames, and Celler-floors be made of Oak.

The Tile-pins of Oak.

No Summers or Girders to lie over the Head of Doors and Windows.

No Summer or Girder to lie leſs than ten Inches into the Wall, no Joyſts than eight Inches, and to be laid in Lome.

But

But yet the *Carcaſs* is not compleated, till the *Quarters* and *Braces* between the *principal Poſts* and *Poſts* are fitted in; the *Window-frames* made and ſet up, and the *principal Rafters*, *Purlins*, *Gables*, &c. are alſo fram'd and ſet up. The manner of their Pitch and Scantlins you will ſee in *Plate* 11. And the Reaſons for ſeveral *Pitches* you may find among Books of *Architecture*. But the Names of every Member you will find in the *Alphabetical Table* at the latter end of theſe Exerciſes on *Carpentry*, referred unto by Letters and Arithmetical Figures in the Plate aforeſaid.

But now we will ſuppoſe the Carcaſs is thus finiſhed. The Bricklayer is then to bring up the Chimnies, and afterwards to *Tile* the Houſe. And then the next Work the Carpenter has to do, is to bring up the *Stairs*, and *Stair-caſes*, and afterwards to *Floor* the Rooms, and *Hang* the *Doors*, &c. For ſhould he either bring up the Stairs and Stair-caſes, or Floor the Rooms before the Houſe is Tiled, or otherwiſe covered, if wet Weather ſhould happen it might injure the Stairs, Flooring, &c.

A, *The Ground-plate, or Ground-ſell.*
BB, BB, *The Principal Poſts.*
C C, *The Binding Intertiſes, or indeed, more properly Interduces, Breſſummers, Girders.*
D, *Beam of the Roof, Breſſummer, or Girder to the Garret Floor.*
E E, *Principal Rafters.* F F, *Breſſummers.*
G, *Plate or Raiſing-piece, alſo a Beam.*
a a, Jaums or Door-poſts. *b b, Braces.* *c c, Jaums.*
d, Top-rail of the Balcony.
e e, Bottom-rail of the Balcony.
f f f, Poſts of the Balcony.
g g g, Baniſters.
h h, Breſſummers for the Shop-windows.

H, *King-*

H, *King-piece or Joggle-piece.*
i i, *Struts.*
k k, *Top-beam, Coller-beam, Wind-beam, Strut-beam.*
l l l, *Door-head.*
I I, *The Feet of the principal Rafters.*
K, *The Top of the Rafters.*
I I K, *The Gable-end.*
L L, *Knees of the principal Rafters, to be made all of one piece with the principal Rafters.*
M, *The Fust of the House.*
N N, *Purlins.*
O O, *Shop-windows.*
P P, *Flaps or Falls.*
m m m, *Quarters.*
n n, *Jaums of the Window.*
o o, *Back and Head of the Window.*
p p, *Transums.*
q q, *Munnions.*
r r, *Furrings, or Shreadings.*
V, *Single light Windows or Luteons.*
s s s, *Rafters.*

§ 16. *Of* Window-Frames.

IN Brick Buildings the *Window-Frames* are so framed, that the Tennants of the Head-sell, Ground-sell, and Transum, run though the outer *Jaums* about four Inches beyond them: And so they are set in a Lay of Morter upon the Brick-wall before the *Peers* on either side is brought up, at about three Inches within the Front; So that the Brick-work over the Head and about the Jaums defend it from the Weather. Then the *Bricklayer* brings up the *Peers* on both sides, so that the four Ends or Tennants that project through the outer Jaums being buried and trimmed into the Brick-work become a Fastning to the *Window-Frame.*

But

But if the Window-Frame ſtands on a Timber-houſe, the Head and Ground-ſell are ſometimes Tennanted into Poſts of the Carcaſs; and then the Poſts do the Office of the outer Jaums of the Window-Frame; and the Head and Ground-ſell are then called *Entertiſes*, and therefore both Head and Ground-ſell, and Poſts or Jaums, are rabbetted about half an Inch on the outſide of the Front, to receive the Pane of Glaſs that is fitted to it. And thus (as I ſaid) the Poſts become part of the Window-Frame.

But the better way is to frame a Window as the Brick-work Window, and to project it an Inch and a half beyond the ſide of the Building, and to Plaiſter againſt its ſides, for the better ſecuring the reſt of the Carcaſs from the Weather.

The Window-Frame hath every one of its Lights Rabbetted on its outſide about half an Inch into the Frame, and all theſe Rabbets, but that on the Ground-ſell, are grooved ſquare, but the Rabbets on the Ground-ſell is bevell'd downwards, that Rain or Snow, *&c.* may the freelier fall off it. Into theſe Rabbets the ſeveral Panes of Glaſs-work is ſet, and faſtned by the Glaſier.

The ſquare Corners of the Frame next the Glaſs is Bevell'd away both on the out and inſide of the Building, that the Light may the freelier play upon the Glaſs. And upon that Bevel is commonly Stuck a Molding (for Ornament ſake) according to the Fancy of the Workman, but more generally according to the various Mode of the Times.

Of

§ 17. *Of* Stairs, *and* Stair-Cases.

SEveral Writers of *Architecture* have delivered different Rules for the Height and Breadth of *Steps*, and that according to the ſeveral Capacities of the *Stair-Caſes*. They forbid more than ſix, and leſs than four Inches for the Heighth of each Step, and more than ſixteen, and leſs than twelve, for the Breadth of each Step. But here we muſt underſtand they mean theſe Meaſures ſhould be obſerved in large and ſumptuous Buildings: But we have here propoſed an ordinary private Houſe, which will admit of no ſuch Meaſures, for want of room. Therefore to our preſent purpoſe.

The firſt and ſecond Pair of Stairs the Steps ſhall be about $7\frac{1}{3}$ Inches high, and 10 Inches broad. The third Pair of Stairs each Step may be about $6\frac{1}{2}$ Inches high, and $9\frac{1}{2}$ Inches broad. And for the fourth Pair of Stairs, each Step may be about 6 Inches high, and 9 Inches broad. But this Rule they do, or ſhould follow, *viz.* to make all the Steps belonging to the ſame pair of Stairs of an equal height; which to do, they firſt conſider the heighth of the Room in Feet and odd Inches, if any odd be, and multiply the Feet by 12, whoſe Product, with the number of odd Inches, gives the ſum of the whole Heighth in Inches; which ſum they divide by the number of Steps they intend to have in that Heighth, and the Quotient ſhall be the number of Inches and parts that each Step ſhall be high. Or, if they firſt deſign the Heighth of each Step in Inches, they try by Arithmetick how many times the Heighth of a Step they can have out of the whole Heighth of the Story, and ſo know the number of Steps.

MECHA-

Page.145

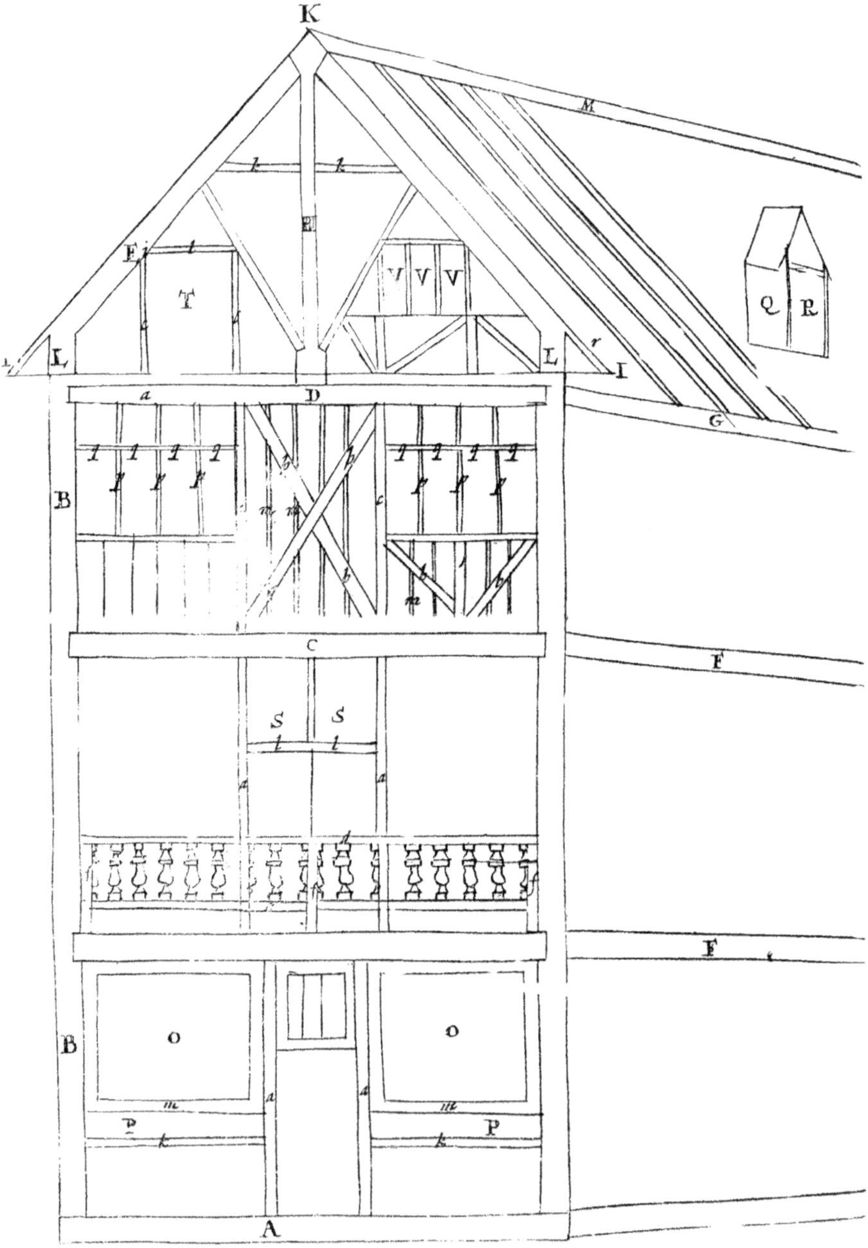

MECHANICK EXERCISES:

O R,

The Doctrine of *Handy-Works.*

Continued in the ART of *House-Carpentry.*

STAIRS are either made about a *Solid Newel*, or an *Open Newel*, and sometimes mixt, *viz.* with a Solid Newel for some few Steps; then a straight or Foreright Ascent, with *Flyers* upon the side of the square Open Newel, and afterwards a Solid Newel again. Than reiterate, *&c.*

The last, *viz.* the *Mixt Newel'd Stairs*, are commonly made in our *Party-walled Houses* in *London*, where no Light can be placed in the Stair-Case, because of the Party-walls; so that there is a necessity to let in a *Sky-light* through the Hollow Newel: But this sort of Stair-Cases take up more room than those with a single solid Newel; because the Stairs of a solid Newel spread only upon one small Newel, as the several Foulds of the Fans Woman use spread about their Center: But these because they sometimes wind, and sometimes fly off from that winding, take therefore the more room up in the Stair-Case.

The manner of projecting them, is copiously taught in many Books of *Architecture*, whether I referr you: Yet not to leave you wholly in the dark,

dark, I ſhall give you a ſmall light into it. And firſt of the *Solid Nowel.*

Winding Stairs are projected on a round *Profile*, whoſe Diameter is equal to the Baſe the Stair-Caſe is to ſtand on, ſuppoſe ſix foot ſquare. This *Profile* hath its Circumference divided into 16 equal parts. The Semi-diameter of the *Profile* is divided into four equal parts, and one of them uſed for the Newel, and the reſt for the length of the Steps: If you draw Lines from the Center through every one of the equal parts into the Circumference, the ſpace between every two Lines will be the true Figure of a *Winding-Step.* And if they were all cut out and placed one above another, over the true place on the Profile round about the Newel, whoſe Diameter is one quarter the length of a Step, you would by ſupporting each Step with a *Raiſer* have the modle of a true pair of *Winding-Stairs.* See Plate 10. Fig. 2.

Hollow Newel'd Stairs are made about a ſquare Hollow Newel. We will ſuppoſe the *Well-hole* to be eleven foot long, and ſix foot wide; and we would bring up a pair of Stairs from the firſt *Floor* eleven Foot high; it being intended that a Skie-light ſhall fall through the Hollow Newel upon the Stairs: We muſt therefore conſider the width and breadth of the Hollow Newel; and in this example admit it to be two foot and a half wide, and two foot broad: By the width I mean the ſides that range with the Front and Rear of the Building, and by the breadth I mean the ſides that range with the Party-walls.

I find (by the Rule aforeſaid) that if I aſſign 18 Steps up, each Step will be ſeven Inches and one third of an Inch high.

You

You muſt Note, that the flying off, or elſe winding of theſe Steps will vary their places according as you deſign the firſt Aſcent. For if you make the firſt Aſcent as you come ſtraight out of the Street (as in Plate 10.) on the *South-ſide*, you will firſt aſcend upon a Pitch of *Flyers*, which Pitch (making an Angle of 38 deg. with the Floor) with ten Steps raiſe you ſix Foot high above the Floor, and bring you eight Foot towards the *North*-end of the *Well-hole*, by making each Step ten Inches broad.

But now you muſt leave *Flyers*, and make four Winding Steps. Theſe Winding Steps are made about a ſolid *Newel* (as hath been taught) and this *Newel* ſerves alſo for a *Poſt* to *Trim* the *Stair-Caſe* too. This Poſt ſtands upon the Floor, and is prolonged upwards ſo high, that Morteſſes made in it may receive the Tennants of the *Top* and *Bottom Rails* of the whole Stair-caſe for that Floor: Theſe four Winding ſteps aforeſaid, rounding one quarter about the Newel, turns your Face in your Aſcent now towards the *Eaſt*; theſe four ſteps are raiſed 2 foot, $5\frac{1}{3}$ Inches above the Flyers, ſo that (in all) your Stairs are now raiſed 8 foot $6\frac{2}{3}$ Inches. Here remains now only 2 foot $5\frac{1}{2}$ Inches to the *Landing place*, and theſe take up juſt four Flyers, which muſt be made as was taught before.

But now in your ſecond pair of Stairs, it will be proper to begin your Aſcent with your Face towards the *Weſt*: For landing by the firſt pair of Stairs with your Face towards the *Eaſt*, you turn by the ſide of the Rail on the ſecond Floor from the *Eaſt* towards the *North*, and at the further end of that Rail, you turn your Face again from the *North* towards the *Weſt*, and begin your Aſcent on the ſecond pair of Stairs.

Between the Skie-light and the Aſcent is a Poſt ſet upright to faſten Rails into: (to bound the Stair-caſe) from the bottom of which, *viz.* on the ſecond Floor you trim up three Flyers, and then turn off a quarter of a Circle, with Winding Steps: Then again, Flyers to your deſigned pitch: And then again another quarter of a Circle with Winding Steps, *&c.*

The Rail theſe Steps are built upon, being at the beginning or bottom of the Aſcent framed or otherwiſe faſtned to the firſt upright Poſt, muſt at its higher end be framed into the next Poſt alſo, with a Bevel Tennant, as you were taught to frame *Quarters* into one another, *Numb.* 5. § 17. Only with this difference, that there you were taught to frame Square; but here you muſt frame upon the *Bevel*, as you were taught, *Numb* 5. § 19. This Poſt aforeſaid bears upon the Floor, to make its Bearing the ſtronger; and this Poſt muſt be continued to ſuch an heighth, as it may alſo ſerve to receive the Tennanted end of an upper and lower Rail framed into it. And between theſe *Bevelling Rails*, *Banniſters* make good the outſide of the *Stair-Caſe.*

Though I have here deſcribed this Contrivance of a pair of Stairs, yet do I not deliver it as the beſt Patern for this Building, or for theſe ſorts of Stairs, nor matters it to our purpoſe whether it be or no; for (as I told you before) my undertaking is the *Doctrine of Handy-works*, not *Architecture*; but it's *Architecture* conſiders the beſt forming of all Members in a Building for the capacity of the Ground-Plot, and the Convenience of the intended Inhabitant; but Carpenters (as Carpenters) only work by directions preſcribed by the Architect.

Theſe therefore are the common Rules that theſe ſorts of Stairs, and indeed all others with

carving

carving according to the Profile or Ground-plot of the Stairs are made by. But thoſe that will ſee many Inventions may conſult Books of *Architecture*, &c.

§ 18. *Of* Flooring *of* Rooms.

THough Carpenters never Floor the Rooms till the Carcaſs is ſet up, and alſo incloſed by the Plaiſterer, leſt weather ſhould wrong the Flooring; yet they generally *Rough-plane* their *Boards* for Flooring before they begin any thing elſe about the Building, that they may ſet them by to ſeaſon: Which thus they do, they lean them one by one on end aſlant with the edge of the Board againſt a Bauk, ſomewhat above the height of half the length of the Board, and ſet another Board in the ſame poſture on the other ſide the Bauk, ſo that above the Bauk they croſs one another: Then on the firſt ſide they ſet another Board in that poſture, and on the ſecond ſide another, till the whole number of Boards are ſet an end: Being ſet in this poſture, there remains the thickneſs of a Board between every Board all the length, but juſt where they croſs one another, for the Air to paſs through to dry and ſhrink them, againſt they have occaſion to uſe them: But they ſet them under ſome covered Shed, that the Rain or Sun comes not at them; for if the Rain wet them, inſtead of ſhrinking them, it will ſmell them; or if the Sun ſhine fiercely upon them, it will dry them ſo faſt, that the Boards will *Tear* or *Shake*, which is in vulgar Engliſh, *Split* or *Crack*.

They have another way to dry and ſeaſon them, by laying them flat upon three or four Bauks, each Board about the breadth of a Board aſunder, the whole length of the Bauks. Then they lay another Lay of Boards athwart upon them, each Board alſo the breadth of a Board aſunder; then another Lay athwart the laſt, till all are thus laid: So that in this poſition they alſo lye hollow for the Air to play between them.

Thus then, the Boards being Rough-plain'd and Seaſon'd. They try one ſide flat, as by *Numb. 6.* § 31. and both the edges ſtraight, as if they were to ſhoot a Joint; as by *Numb.* 4. § 4. and cut the Boards to an exact length, becauſe if the Boards are not long enough to reach athwart the whole Room, the ends may all lye in a ſtraight Line, that the ſtraight ends of other Boards laid againſt them may make the truer Joint, and this they call a *Beaking Joint.* But before they lay them upon the Floor, they try with the *Level* (deſcribed § 7.) the flatneſs of the whole Frame of Flooring again, leſt any part of it ſhould be *Caſt* ſince it was firſt framed together; and if any part of the Floor lye too high, they with the *Adz* (if the eminency be large) take it off, as was ſhewed § 2. Or if it be ſmall, with the *Jack-Plain* in *Numb.* 4 § 2. till it lye level with the reſt of the Floor. But if any part of the Floor prove hollow, they lay a Chip, or ſome ſuch thing, upon that hollow place, to bare up the Board, before they nail it down.

All this being done, they chuſe a Board of the commoneſt thickneſs of the whole Pile for the firſt Board, and lay it cloſe again one ſide of the Room athwart the Joyſts, and ſo nail it firmly down with two Brads into every Joyſt it croſſes, each Brad about an Inch, or an Inch and a half within the edge of the Board.

If they ſhould lay more than an ordinary thick or thin Board at the firſt, they would have a greater number of Boards to work to a Level

than

than they need, becauſe all the reſt of the Boards muſt be equalized in thickneſs to the firſt.

Then they lay a ſecond Board cloſe to the firſt. But before they nail it down they again try how its ſides agrees with the ſide of the firſt, and alſo how its thickneſs agrees with the firſt Board. If any part of its edge lye hollow off the edge of the firſt Board, they ſhoot off ſo much of the length of the Board from that hollowneſs towards either end, till it comply and make a cloſe Joint with the firſt. But if the edge ſwell in any place, they plain of that ſwelling till it comply as aforeſaid.

If the ſecond Board prove thicker than the firſt, then with the *Adz* (as aforeſaid) they hew away the under ſide of that Board (moſt commonly croſs the Grain, leſt with the Grain the edge of the *Adz* ſhould ſlip too deep into the Board) in every part of it that ſhall bare upon a Joyſt, and ſo ſink it to a flat ſuperficies to comply with the firſt Board. If the Board be too thin, they underlay that Board upon every Joyſt with a Cap, *&c.*

And as this ſecond Board is laid, ſo are the other Boards laid, if they be well aſſured the Boards are dry, and will not ſhrink; but if they doubt the drineſs of the Boards, they (ſometimes do, or ſhould) take a little more pains; for after they have nailed down the firſt Board, they will meaſure the breadth of two other Boards, laying them by the ſide of the firſt. But yet they will not allow them their full Room to lye in, but after there edges are true ſhot in a ſtraight line, they will pinch them off about half a quarter of an Inch room more or leſs, according as they gueſs at the well-ſeaſonedneſs of the Boards; by nailing down the fourth Board nearer to the firſt Board by half a quarter of an Inch (more or leſs) then the breadth of both Boards are. And though it be afterwards ſomewhat hard to get theſe two Boards into that narrow room, *viz.* between the firſt and fourth Board, yet they help themſelves thus: The under-edge of theſe Boards that are to join to each other, they Bevel ſomewhat away, and then the firſt and fourth Board being faſt nailed down (as aforeſaid) they ſet the outer edges of theſe two Boards again the two nailed Boards, letting the inner edges of the two looſe Boards meet, and make an Angle perpendicular to the Floor. Then with two or three Men jumping all at once upon that Angle, theſe two Boards with this force and reiterated jumps by degrees preſs flat down into the ſuperficies of the Floor, or elſe with forcing Pins and Wedges, force them together: And then with Brads they nail them down, as they did the firſt Board. Thus afterwards they nail down a ſeventh Board, as they did the fourth, and then fit in the fifth and ſixth Boards, as they did the ſecond and third Boards. And ſo on, nailing down every third Board, and forcing two others between it and the laſt nailed Board, till the whole Floor be boarded.

But if theſe Boards are not long enough (as I hinted before) to reach through the whole Room, they examine how true the ends lye in a ſtraight line with one another, by applying the edge of the Two-foot Rule to the ends, and where the ends of any Boards keep of the edge of the Two-foot Rule from complying with the whole range of ends, they with the *Chiſſel* and *Mallet* cut off that irregularity, holding and guiding the Chiſſel, ſo that it may rather cut away more of the bottom then top of the Board, that ſo the Boards joined to the ends of the firſt

laid

laid Boards, may make on the Superficies of the Floor the finer and truer Joint.

Having thus Boarded the whole Room, notwithstanding they used their best diligence to do it exactly, yet may the edges of some Boards lye somewhat higher than the Board it lies next to; therefore they peruse the whole Floor, and where they find any irregularities they plane them off with the Plane, *&c.*

§ 19. *The* Hanging *of* Doors, Windows, *&c.*

THe Floors being Boarded, the next work is to *Hang* the *Doors*, in which tho' there be little difficulty, yet is there much care to be taking, that the *Door* open and shut well.

If the *Door* have a *Door-Case* (as Chamber-Doors, and Closet-Doors commonly have) the *Jaums* of the Door-Case must stand exactly perpendicular, which you must try by the Plumb-line, as by § 8. and the Head of the *Door-Case* or Entertise must be fitted exactly square to the *Jaums*, as you where taught *Numb.* 3. § 17, 18, 19. and the Angles of the *Door* must be made exactly square, and the *Rabbets* of the *Door* to fit axactly into the *Rabbets* of the *Door-Case.* But yet they commonly make the *Door* about one quarter of an Inch shorter than the insides of the *Jaums* of the *Door-Case*, least if the Boards of the Floor chance to swell within the sweep of the *Door*, the bottom of the *Door* should drag upon the *Floor.*

They consider what sort of *Hindges* are properest for the *Door* they are to *Hang.* When they have a *Street-door* (which commonly is to take off and lift on) they use *Hooks* and *Hindges.* In a *Battend-door*, *Back-door*, or other *Battend-door*, or *Shop-windows*, they use *Cross-Garnets.* If a *Framed Door*, *Side Hindges:* And for *Cup-*

board

boards Doors, and ſuch like, *Duf-tails.* (See the deſcription of theſe Hindges in *Numb.* 1. *Fig.* 1. 5, 6.) But what ſort of Hindges ſoever they uſe, they have care to provide them of a ſtrength proportionable to the ſize and weight of the *Door* they hang with them. Well-made Hindges I have deſcribed *Numb.* 1. *fol.* 20. whither to avoid repetition I refer you.

If they hang a *Street-door* (which is commonly about ſix *foot* high) they firſt drive the *Hooks* into the *Door-poſt*, by entring the Poſt firſt with an *Augure:* But the *Bit* of the *Augure*, muſt be leſs than the Shank of the *Hook*, and the hole boared not ſo long, becauſe the Shank of the *Hook*, muſt be ſtrongly forced into the Augure-hole, and ſhould the Augure-hole be too wide, the Shank would be looſe in it, and not ſtick ſtrong enough in it. Therefore if the Shank be an Inch ſquare, an half Inch-Augure is big enough to bore that hole with, becauſe it will then endure the heavier blows of an Hammer, to drive it ſo far as it muſt go; and the ſtronger it is forced in, the faſter the *Hook* ſticks; but yet they are careful not to ſplit the *Door-poſt.*

Theſe *Hooks* are commonly drove in about Fifteen Inches and an half above the *Ground-ſell*, and as much below the top of the *Door.* It is, or ſhould be, their care to chuſe the Pin of the lower *Hook* about a quarter of an Inch longer than that they uſe for the upper *Hook* (or elſe to make it ſo) becauſe theſe *Doors* are commonly unweildy to lift off and on, eſpecially to lift both the Hindges on both the *Hooks* at once. Therefore when the lower Hindge is lifted on the lower *Hook*, if the *Door* be then lifted perpendicularly upright, ſo high as the under ſide of the upper Hindge may juſt reach the top of of the upper *Hook*, you may the eaſier ſlip the Eye of the upper Hindge upon the *Hook*; whereas, if the lower *Hook* be either ſhorter, or juſt no longer than the other, inſtead of lifting it readily upon the upper *Hook*, you may lift it off the lower *Hook*, and ſo begin the labour again.

Having drove in the *Hooks*, they ſet the *Rabbets* of the *Door* within the *Rabbets* of the *Door-poſt*, and underlay the bottom of the *Door*, with a Chip or two about half a quarter of an Inch thick, to raiſe the *Door* that it drag not. Then they put the Eyes of the Hindges over the Pins of the *Hooks*, and placing the Tail piece of the Hindges parallel to the bottom and top of the *Door*, they ſo nail them upon.

This is the Rule they generally obſerve for Hanging *Doors*, *Shop-windows*, &c. Only, ſometimes inſtead of Nailing the Hindges upon the Door, they *Rivet* them on, for more ſtrength. And then, after they have fitted the Door, or Window, into its Rabbets, and laid the Hindges in there proper place and poſition (as aforeſaid) they make marks in the Nail-holes of the Hindge with the point of their Compaſſes upon the *Door*, and at thoſe marks they Pierce holes, with a *Piercer-Bit*, that fits the ſhank of the *Rivet*; then they put the ſhank of the *Rivet* thro' the holes made in the *Door*; yet ſo that the Head of the Rivet be on the outſide of the *Door*; and they alſo put the end of the Shank into the Nail-hole of the Hinge, and ſo whilſt another Man holds the head of the Hatchet againſt the Head of the Rivet, they with the *Pen* of their *Hammer* batter and ſpread the flat end of the Shank over the Hole, as was ſhewn *Numb.* 2. *fol.* 24. 25.

The

The Titles of ſome Books of Architecture.

SEbaſtion Seirleo, in Folio.

Hans Bloom's Five Collumns, Folio.

Vignola, in Folio.

Vignola, Or the *Compleat Architect*, in Octvo.

Scamotzi, Quarto.

Palladio, Quarto.

Sir *Henry Wotton*'s Elements of Architecture, Quarto.

Theſe *Books* are all Printed in Engliſh: But there are many others extant in ſeveral other Languages, of which *Vitruvius* is the chief: For from his *Book* the reſt are generally derived; as *Philip Le Orm*, *Ditterlin*, *Marlois*, and many others, which being difficult to be had among *Book-ſellers*, and theſe ſufficient for information, I ſhall omit till another opportunity.

An Explanation of *Terms* uſed in *Carpentry*.

A

ADz, Plate 8. B § 2.

Arch, Any work wrought Circular, as the top part of ſome Window-frames, the top of ſome great Gates, the Roof of Vaults, *&c.*

Architrave, See Numb. 6. Plate 6. 1. and Plate 6. A. § 1.

Ax, Numb. 7. Plate 8. A.

B

BAck or *Hip-molding*. The backward Hips or *Valley-Rafters* in the way of an Angle for the back part of a Building.

Banniſter, Numb. 8. Plate 11. *ggg*.

Baſe, is commonly the Bottom of a Cullumn. See Numb. 6. Plate 6. *h*. and Plate 7. B.

Bate.

Batement, To abate or waſte a piece of Stuff, by forming of it to a deſigned purpoſe. Thus inſtead of asking how much was cut off ſuch a piece of Stuff, Carpenters ask what *Batement* that piece of Stuff had.

Batter, The ſide, or part of the ſide of a Wall, or any Timber that bulges from its bottom or Foundation, is ſaid to *Batter*, or *hang over* the Foundation.

Battlement, A flat Roof or Platform to walk on. But Battlements are more properly Walls built about the Platform to incloſe it, as is ſeen upon Towers for defence; part of the Battlement being Breaſt high that Muſquetiers may ſhoot over it, the other part Man high, to ſecure Men from the ſhot of their Enemies.

Bauk, A piece of Fir unſlit, from four to ten Inches ſquare, and of many lengths.

Bear, Timber is ſaid to *Bear* at its whole length, when neither a Brick-wall, or Poſts, &c, ſtand between the ends of it. But if either a Brick-wall or Poſts, &c. be Trimmed up to that Timber, than it is ſaid to Bear only at the diſtance between the Brick-wall or Poſt, and either end of the Timber. Thus Carpenters ask what

Bearing ſuch a piece of Timber has? The anſwer is 10, 12, 15, &c. Foot, according to the length of the whole Timber, or elſe according to the diſtance between either end of the Timber, and a

Bearer, *viz.* a Poſt or Brick-wall that is Trimmed up between the two ends of a piece of Timber, to ſhorten its *Bearing*.

Bond, When Workmen ſay make good Bond, they mean faſten the two or more pieces of Timber well together, either with Tennanting and Morteſſing, or Duff-tailing, &c.

Binding

Binding Joysts, See Trimmers, or Plate 10. *b b b.*

Brace, See Plate 11. *bbb.*

Brad, is a Nail to *Floor Rooms* with, they are about the ſize of a Ten-penny Nail, but have not their heads made with a ſhoulder over their ſhank, as other Nails, but are made pretty thick towards the upper end, that the very top of it may be driven into, and buried in the Board they nail down, ſo that the tops of theſe Brads will not catch (as the Heads of Nails would) the Thrums of the Mops when the *Floor* is waſhing. You may ſee them at moſt Ironmongers.

Break in, Carpenters with their Ripping Chiſſel do often *Break in* to Brick-walls; that is, they cut holes, but indeed more properly break the Bricks by force, and make their hole to their ſize and form.

Breſſummer, See Plate 11. CC, D, FF, *b b.*

Bring up, A Term moſt uſed amongſt Carpenters, when they diſcourſe *Bricklayers*; and then they ſay, *Bring up* the Foundation ſo high, *Bring up* ſuch a Wall, *Bring up* the Chimnies, *&c.* which is as much as to ſay, Build the Foundation ſo high, Build the Wall, Build the Chimnies, *&c.*

Butment, The piece of Ground in the Yard marked G, in Plate 10. is a *Butment* from the reſt of the Ground-plot.

Buttreſs, That ſtands on the outſide a Wall to ſupport it.

C.

C*Amber*, A piece of Timber cut Arching, ſo as when a weight conſiderable, ſhall be ſet upon it, it may in length of time be reduced to a ſtraight.

Cantilevers, Pieces of Wood framed into the Front or other ſides of an Houſe to ſuſtain the Molding and Eaves over it.

Carcaſs, is (as it were) the Skelleton of an Houſe, before it is Lath'd and Plaſtered.

Cartouſes. Ornamented *Corbels.*

Cleer Story Window, Windows that have no Tranſum in them.

Commander, See Numb. 7. Plate 8. K. and § 10.

Coping over, is a ſort of hanging over, but not ſquare to its upright, but Bevelling on its under ſide, till it end in an edge.

Corbel, A piece of Timber ſet under another piece of Timber, to diſcharge its Bearing.

Crab, The Engine deſcribed Plate 9. E. and BCD ſeveral of its Appurtenances, *viz.* BCC *Snatch Blocks.* D *Levers.* Its Office is to draw heavy Timber to a conſiderable height.

Crow, See Plate 8. L. its Office is to remove heavy Timber, and therefore for ſtrength is made of Iron.

Crown Poſt, See Plate 11. H. Alſo the *King-Piece*, or *Joggle-Piece.*

D

D*Iſcharge*, A Brick-wall or a Poſt trim'd up to a piece of Timber over charg'd for its Bearing, is a Diſcharge to that Bearing.

Dormer, Plate 11. Q R.

Double Quarters, See *Quarter.*

Draft, The Picture of an intended Building diſcribed on Paper, whereon is laid down the deviſed Diviſions and Partitions of every *Room* in its due proportion to the whole Building, See Numb. 7. § 13.

Drag, A *Door* is ſaid to *Drag* when either by its ill Hanging on its Hinges, or by the ill boarding of the *Room*, the bottom edge of the *Door*

rides

rides (in its ſweep) upon the *Floor*. See § 19.

Dragon-beams, are two ſtrong Braces or Struts that ſtands under a Breſſummer, meeting in a an angle upon the ſhoulder of the *King-piece*. In Plate 11, *i i* are *Dragon beams*.

Draw knife, deſcribed Plate 8. E and § 5.

Draw Pins, deſcribed Plate 8. F and § 6.

Drug, deſcribed Plate 9. E and § 12.

E

ENter, When Tennants are put into Morteſſes, they are ſaid to Enter the Morteſſes.

Enterduce, or *Entertiſe*, deſcribed Plate 11. CC.

F.

FEather-edge, Boards, or Planks, that have one edge thinner than another are called *Feather-edge* ſtuff.

Fir-Pole, A ſort of ſtuff cut off of the Fir-tree, ſmall and long, commonly from 10 to 16 Foot. They are ſometimes uſed in ſlight Buildings, to ſerve inſtead of Bauks and Quarters.

Flyers, are Stairs made of an Oblong ſquare Figure, whoſe fore and backſides are parallel to each other, and ſo are their ends; the ſecond of theſe *Flyers* ſtands parallel behind the firſt, the third behind the ſecond, and ſo are ſaid to fly off from one another.

Floor, in *Carpentry*, it is as well taken for the Fram'd work of Timber, as the Boarding over it.

Foot-pace, is a part of a pair of Stairs, whereon after four or ſix ſteps you arrive to a broad place, where you make two or three paces before you aſcend another ſtep; thereby to eaſe the legs in aſcending the reſt of the ſteps.

Furrings, The making good of the Rafters Feet in the Cornice.

Gable,

G

G*Able*, or *Gable-end*, in Plate 11. IIK.

Gain, The bevelling ſhoulder of a Joyſt, or other Stuff: It is uſed for the Lapping of the end of a Joyſt, *&c.* upon a Trimmer or Girder, and then the thickneſs of the ſhoulder is cut into the Trimmer alſo Bevilling upwards, that it may juſt receive that *Gain*, and ſo the Joyſt and Timber lye even and level upon their ſuperficies. This way of working is uſed in a Floor or Hearth.

Girder, deſcribed Plate 10 QQ.

Ground Plate, deſcribed Plate 11 A.

Ground Plate, The piece of Ground a Building is to be erected upon.

H.

H*Ang over*, See *Batter*.

Hips, deſcribed Plate 11. EE, They are alſo called *Principal Rafters*, and *Sleepers*.

Hook-pin, deſcribed Plate 8. F.

I.

J*Ack*, deſcribed Plate 8. M. An Engine uſed for the removing and commodious placing of great Timber.

Jack-Plane, called ſo by Carpenters, but is indeed the ſame that Joyners call the *Fore-Plane*, See Numb. 4. § 2. and Plate 4. B. 1.

Jaums, Door Poſts are ſo called: So are the upright outer Poſts of a Window frame, See Plate 11. *aaaa*, *cc*, *nn*.

Joggle-piece, See Plate 11. H.

Joyſts, See Plate 10. *aaaa*.

Juffers, Stuff, about 4 or 5 inches ſquare, and of ſeveral Lengths.

K.

KIng-piece, See *Joggle-piece.*

Kerf, See *Explanation of Terms* in Numb. 6.

Knee, A piece of Timber growing angularly, or crooked, that is, a great Branch ſhooting out near the top of the Trunk of the Tree, and is ſo cut that the Trunk and the Branch make an angle; as in Plate 11. EL, being made out of one piece of ſtuff: It is called a *Knee-piece*, or *Knee-rafter*.

L.

LAnding-place, is the uppermoſt Step of a pair of Stairs, *viz.* The Floor of the Room you aſcend upon.

Skirts, Projecting of the Eaves.

Level, See Plate 8. G and § 7.

Lever, See Plate 9. D.

Lintel, In Brick-buildings Carpenters lay a long piece of Timber over the Peers, to Trim with the Window-Frame; as well to bear the thickneſs of the Brick-wall above it, as to make Bond with the ſides of the Walls.

Long-plane, The ſame that Joyners call a *Joynter.* See Numb. 4. B. 2. § 4.

Luthern, See *Dormer.*

M.

MOdillon, See *Cantelever.*

Molding, Moldings are ſtuck upon the edges of ſtuff to Ornament it: As on Chimney-pieces, the inner edges of Window-frames, Shelves, &c. See *Numb.* 4. §. 9.

Munnion,

Munnion, the upright Poſt that divide the ſeveral Lights in a Window-frame, are called *Munnions*, See Plate 11. *qqq*.

N.

NEwel, the upright poſt that a pair of Winding-ſtairs are turned about.

P.

PItch, The Angle a Gable-end is ſet to, is called the *Pitch* of the Gable-end.

Planchier, An Ornament to which the Cornice is faſtned.

Plate. A piece of Timber upon which ſome conſiderable weight is framed, is called a Plate. Hence *Ground-Plate*, Plate 11. A. *Window-plate*, &c.

Plumb-line, deſcribed Plate 8. H § 8.

Poſts, See *Principal-Poſts*.

Prick-Poſts, Poſts that are framed into *Breſſummers*, between Principal-Poſts, for the ſtrengthning of the Carcaſs.

Principal-Poſts, The corner Poſts of a Carcaſs, See Plate 11. B. B.

Profile, The ſame with *Ground-Plot*.

Projecture, is a jetting over the upright of a Building: Thus *Balconies* project into the Street.

Puncheons, Short pieces of Timber placed under ſome conſiderable weight to ſupport it.

Pudlaies, Pieces of Stuff to do the Office of Hand-Spikes.

Purlins, See Plate 11. NN.

Q.

QUarters are *ſingle* and *double*. *Single Quarters* are Sawen ſtuff, two Inches thick, and four Inches broad. The *Double Quarters* are ſawen to Four Inches ſquare.

Quartering, In the Front of the third Story in Plate 11. All the Work, except the Principal Posts, Jaums, and Window-frames, *viz.* the upright Triming, and the Braces is called *Quartering.*

Quirk, A piece taken out of any regular Ground-plot, or Floor: For example, the whole Ground-plot A B C D. in Plate 10. is a regular Ground-plot. But if the piece K be taking out of it, K shall be a *Quirk*.

R.

R*After*, See Plate 11. *cccc.*

Rail, Rails stand over and under Bannisters of *Balconies*, Stair-Cases, &c.

Raiser, is a Board set on edge under the Foreside of a step.

Raising-piece, Pieces that lye under the Beams upon Brick or Timber by the side of the House.

Rellish, See *Projecture.*

Return, Either of the adjoining sides of the Front of an House, or Ground-plot, is called a *Return-side*, as in Plate 10. the Front is A B, the *Return-sides* to this Front is A C and B D.

Ridge, the meeting of the Rafters on both sides the House is called the *Ridge*.

Ripping-Chissel, See Plate 8. D § 4.

Roof, The Covering of a House: But the word is used in Carpentery for the Triming work of the Covering.

S.

S*Cribe*, See Number 6. in *Explanation of Terms.*

Shake, Such stuff as is crackt either with the heat of the Sun, or the droughth of the wind, is called *Shaken Stuff*.

Shingles,

Shingles, Small pieces of Wood uſed to cover Houſes with, inſtead of Tiles or Slates.

Shreadings, See Plate 11. the lower end of the Principal Rafters markt *r r* are called *Shreadings*, or *Furrings*.

Sleepers, The ſame with *Purlins*.

Snatch-blocks, See Plate 9. B C C.

Socket-Chiſſel, Deſcribed Plate 8. and § 3.

Soils, or *Sells*, are either *Ground-Sells* deſcribed Plate 11. A. or *Window Sells*, which are the bottom Pieces of Window Frames.

Stair-Caſe, The incloſure of a pair of Stairs, whether it be with Walls, or with Walls and Railes and Banniſters, *&c.*

Stancheons, See *Puncheons*.

Strut, See *Dragon-beam*.

Summer, In Plate 10. P P is a *Summer*, where into the Girders are Tennanted.

T.

TEn-*Foot-Rod*, See § 13.

Tranſom, The Piece that is fram'd a-croſs a double Light-window. See Plare 11. P P.

Trim, When workmen fit a piece into other Work, they ſay they *Trim* in a piece.

Trimmers, See Plate 10. *b b b b*.

Truſs, See *King-piece*, or *Joggle-piece*.

Tusk, A Bevel ſhoulder, made to ſtrengthen the Tennant of Joyſt, which is let into the Girder.

V.

V*Alley Rafter*, See *Back*, or *Hip-molding*.

W.

W*Ell-hole*, See Plate 10. I.
Wall-Plate, In Plate 10. A C, B D and N O are *Wall-Plates*.

Thus much of *Carpentry*. The next *Exercises* will (God willing) be upon the Art of *Turning*, *Soft Wood*, *Hard Wood*, *Ivory*, *Brass*, *Iron*, &c. With several Inventions of *Oval-work*, *Rose-work*, *Rake-work*, *Angular-work*, &c.

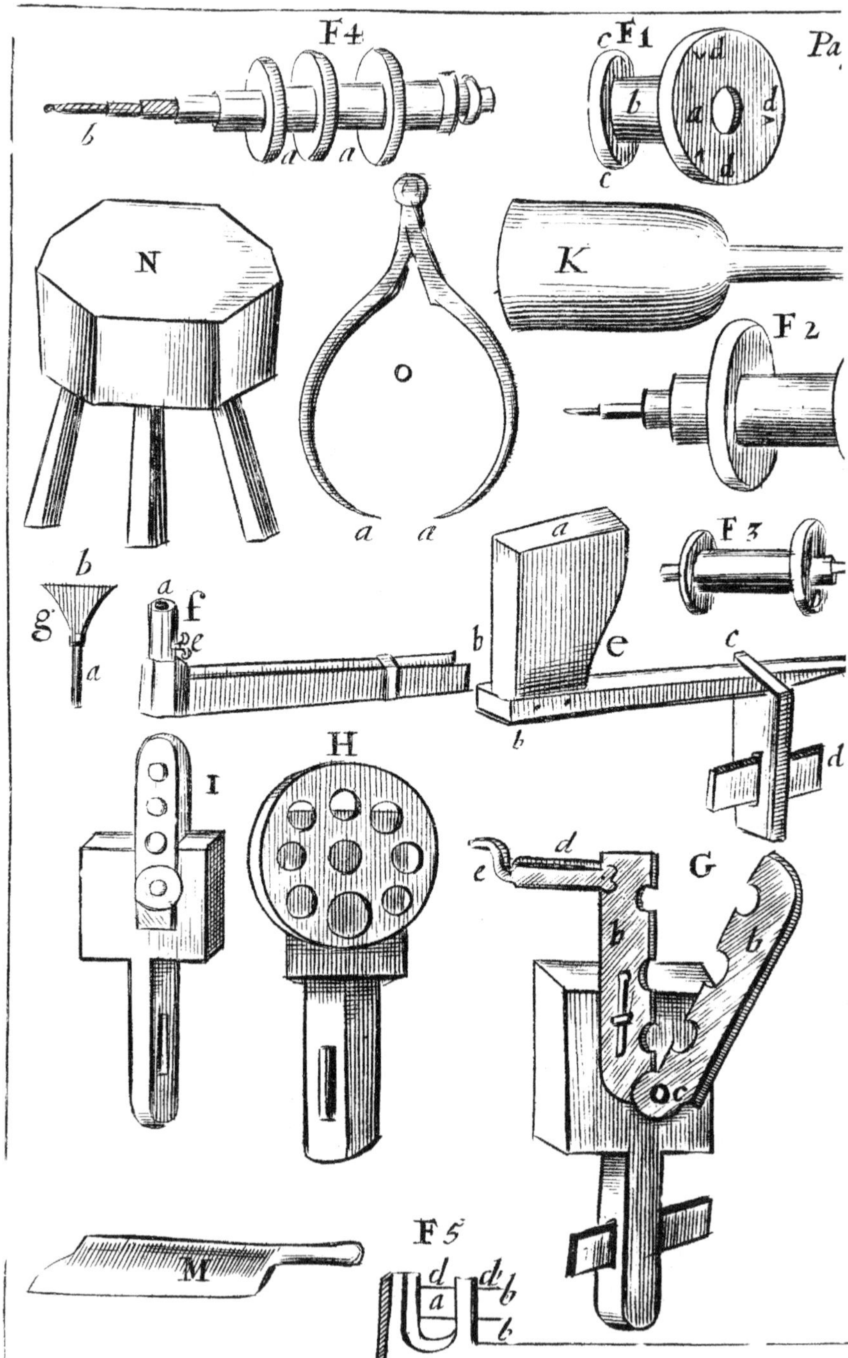
F4
F1
Pa
N
K
F2
F3
I
H
G
M
F5

MECHANICK EXERCISES:

OR,

The Doctrine of *Handy-Works.*

Applied to the ART of *TURNING.*

Of Turning.

AS by placing one Foot of a pair of Compaſſes on a Plane, and moving about the other Foot or point, deſcribes on that Plane a Circle with the moving point; ſo any Subſtance, be it *Wood*, *Ivory*, *Braſs*, &c. pitcht ſteddy upon two points (as on an *Axis*) and moved about on that *Axis*, alſo deſcribes a Circle Concentrick to the *Axis*: And an Edge-Tool ſet ſteddy to that part of the outſide of the aforeſaid Subſtance that is neareſt the *Axis*, will in a Circumvolution of that Subſtance, cut off all the parts of Subſtance that lies farther off the *Axis*, and make the outſide of that Subſtance alſo Concentrick to the *Axis*. This is a brief Collection, and indeed the whole Sum of *Turning.*

Now, as there is different Matter, or Subſtance, to be *Turned*, ſo there is alſo different Ways, and different Tools to be uſed in *Turning* each different Matter.

The different Matters are *Soft Wood*, *Hard Wood*, *Ivory*, *Brass*, *Iron*, &c. each of which (when I have described the Turners Tools for soft Wood) I shall discourse upon. But,

§ I. *Of the* Lathe.

THe *Lathe* is described in *Plate* 12. A. This Machine is so vulgarly known, that tho' it cannot be described in Draft, so as all its parts shall appear at one single View, yet enough of it to give you the Names of its several Members, and their Uses are represented, *viz.*

a a a a The *Legs* or *Stiles.*
b b The *Cheeks* or *Sides.*
c c The *Puppets.*
d The *Screw.*
d The *Pike.*
e The *Rest.*
f The Handle of the *Screw.*
g The Tennants of the *Puppets.*
h The *Wedge.*
i The *Treddle.*
k The *Cross-Treddle.*
l The *Pole.*
m The *String.*
n The *Horn.*

¶ 1. *Of the* Legs, *or* Stiles.

THe *Legs*, or *Stiles*, are commonly about two Foot and ten Inches high, and are set perpendicularly upright; having each of them a Tennant on its upperend, of the thickness the two *Cheeks* are to stand assunder: And on either side the Shoulder of these two *Tennants*, is laid one of the *Cheeks* close to the sides of the *Tennants*, and so pinned close to the *Tennant*, as was

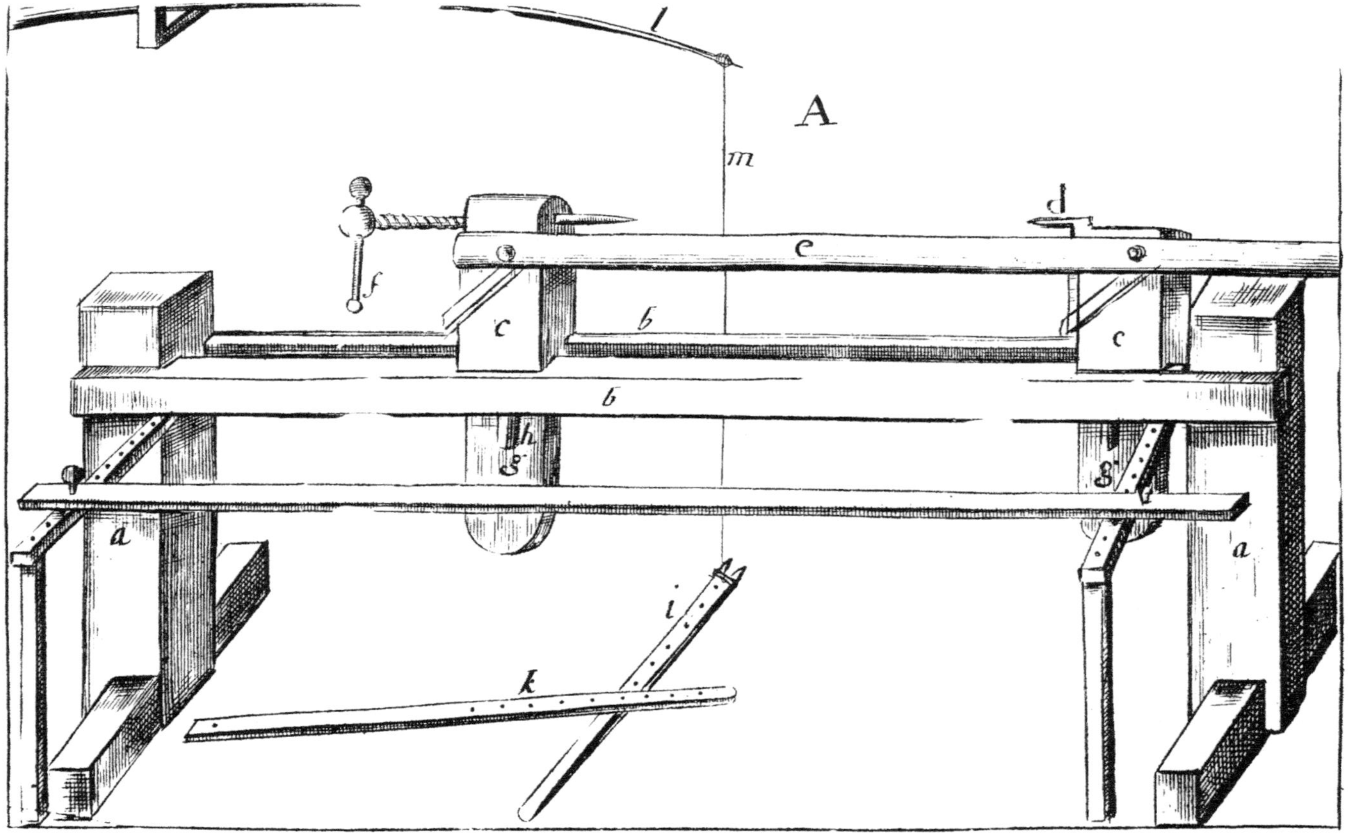
A
l
m
a
b
c
d
e
f
g
h
i
k

was taught *Numb.* 5. § 17. But a ſteddier and more ſecure way, is to have a ſtrong Iron Screw made with a ſquare Shank near the Head, that when it enters into a ſquare hole made fit to it in the hithermoſt *Cheek*, it may not twiſt about, but by the Turning about of an Iron Nut, upon the fore-end of the Screw, the Nut ſhall draw the two Cheeks cloſe to the two ſides of the *Tennants*, or the upper ends of the *Legs*.

¶ 2. *Of the* Cheeks.

AS I told you, the Legs are to be ſet up directly perpendicular, ſo the *Cheeks* are to be faſtned directly Horizontally upon them: And the *Legs* and *Cheeks* are to be faſtned with *Braces* to the Floor, and other parts of the Room the *Lathe* ſtands in, according to the convenience of the Room for faſtning, that the whole *Lathe* may ſtand as ſteedy and ſolid as may be. For if with *Turning* large Work the ſtrength of the Tread ſhould make the *Lathe* tremble, you will not be able to make true and neat Work; but the Tool will job into ſofter parts of the Stuff, and fly off where a Knot or other harder parts of the Stuff comes to the Tool.

¶ 3. *Of the* Puppets.

THe *Puppets* are ſquare pieces of Wood, of a Subſtance convenient to the light or heavy work they intend to *Turn*: And *Turnners* will rather have their *Puppets* too ſtrong than too weak; becauſe, though the *Puppets* be very ſtrong, yet they can turn light work with them; whereas if they be weak they cannot turn Heavy work with them: For the weight of heavy unequal tempered Stuff running about, will be apt both to ſhake the *Puppets*, aud looſen the

ſmall

ſmall hole of the *Wedge* in the *Tennant*; by either of which Inconveniences the Work in the *Lathe* may tremble, as aforeſaid.

And though no ſize for the height of the *Puppets* can be well aſſerted, becauſe of the ſeveral Diameters of Work to be *Turned*, yet Workmen generally covet to have their *Puppets* as ſhort as they well can, to bear their Work off the *Cheeks* of the *Lathe*, becauſe theſe *Puppets* ſtand in the firmer, and are leſs ſubject to looſen. But then, if the Diameters of the work be large, the *Puppets* may be too ſhort to *Turn* that work in: For the *Pikes* of the *Puppets* muſt ſtand ſomewhat more than half the Diameter of the Work above the ſuperficies of the *Cheeks*. Therefore *Turners* have commonly two or three pair of *Puppets* to fit one *Lathe*, and always ſtrive to uſe the ſhorteſt they can to ſerve their Work, unleſs the ſhortneſs of the *Legs* of the *Lathe*, makes the work fall too low for the pitch of the Workman that is to work at the *Lathe*. Therefore in the making of the *Lathe*, the height of the *Legs* with relation to the intended Work, and height of the Work-man, are to be well conſidered.

At the lower end of theſe *Puppets* are made two *Tennants*, of ſuch a thickneſs, that they may eaſily ſlide in the *Grove* between the two *Cheeks*, and ſo long, that a *Morteſs* through it of the length of the *Cheeks* depth, and a ſufficient ſtrength of Wood below it may be contained. Into this *Morteſs* is fitted a Tapering-*Wedge*, ſomewhat leſs at the fore end, and bigger at the hinder end than the *Morteſs*, that as it is forced into the *Morteſs* with a *Mallet*, or a *Maul*, it may draw the bottom Shoulder of the *Puppet* cloſe and firmly down upon the *Cheeks*, that they may neither joggle or tremble in working.

¶ 4. *Of*

¶ 4. *Of the Horn.*

UPon the Right Hand *Puppet* on the out ſide near the top of it, is hung the Tip-end of an *Horn* with its Tip downwards, to hold Oyl in, and ought to have a Wooden round *Cover* to fit into it, that neither Chips or Dirt get in to ſpoil the Oyl; and in the handle of the *Cover* ſhould be fitted a wooden *Butten*, which may ſerve for an *Handle* to the *Cover*: And through this *Butten* ſhould be faſtned an Iron Wyer, to reach almoſt to the bottom of the *Horn*: This Wyer ſtands always in the Oyl, that ſo oft as the Workman has occaſion to oyl the Centers of the Work, to make his Work ſlip about the eaſier, he takes the wooden *Cover* by the *Button*, Wyer and all, and with the end of the Wyer, oyls his Center-holes, and pops his Wyer and *Cover* again into the *Horn* againſt he has occaſion to uſe it the next time.

¶ 5. *Of the* Pikes *and* Screw.

NEar the upper end of one of theſe *Puppets* is faſtned a ſtrong Iron *Pike*, but its point is made of tempered Steel: And near the upper end of the other *Puppet* is fitted an Iron *Screw* quite through a *Nut* in the *Puppet*, whoſe point is alſo made of Temper'd Steel. This Iron *Pike* in one *Puppet*, and the *Screw* in the other *Puppet* are ſo fitted into the *Puppets*, that their Shanks lye in a ſtraight Line with one another, and both their points lie alſo in that ſtraight Line pointing to one another: And in the Head of the Iron *Screw* is a Hole where into is fitted an Iron *Handle* about ſeven or eight Inches long, with a round *Knob* at each end of it that it ſlip

not

not through the hole in the Head. This Iron *Handle* is to turn about the *Screw* forward or backward as your purpose shall require.

Upon the points of this *Screw* and *Pike* the Centers of the Work are pitcht, and afterwards screwed with the *Screw* hard, and so far into the Stuff, that it may not slip off the points in working, especially if it be soft Wood, and the work large and heavy.

Also, near the upper end of these *Puppets*, upon that side the Workman stands when he works, the Wood of the *Puppets* is wrought away to square flat shoulders somewhat below the *Pikes*, that the *Rest* may (if occasion be) lye near the *Pikes*, and bear steddy upon the *Shoulders*.

¶ 6. *Of the* Rest.

THe *Rest* is a square piece of Stuff about an Inch, or an Inch and half thick, and two Inches, or two and an half broad, and somewhat longer than the distance between the *Puppets*. Its Office is to rest the Tool upon, that it may lie in a steddy position while the Workman uses it.

¶ 7. *Of the* Side-Rest.

BUt besides this *Rest*, *Turnners* have another *Rest*, called the *Side-rest*. This they use when they *Turn* the flat sides of Boards; because the flat sides of Boards standing athwart the *Pikes*, and this *Rest* standing also athwart the *Pikes*, they can the more conveniently rest their Tool upon it. It is marked *e* in plate 13. and is in the *Plate* disjunct from the *Lathe*; as well because it and the Common *Rest* cannot both together be exprest in Picture, as also because it is made to take off and put on as occasion requires. The

The *Rest* is marked *a*, and is a piece of an Oaken plank, or Elm plank, about two Inches think, and ſtands ſo high above the *Cheeks* of the *Lathe* as the *points* of the *Pikes* do, or ſometimes a little higher: Its Breadth is about a Foot, or more, or leſs, as the Work requires, or the Workman fancies. The Bottom of it is firmly nailed to one ſide of a Quarter of Oak, or Elm, of about three Inches ſquare, and two Foot, or two Foot and an half long, cloſe to one end, as you ſee in the Figure at *b*, ſo as the *Rest* ſtand upright to the piece of Quarter. This piece of Quarter is as a *Tennant* to ſlide into a ſquare Iron Collar marked *e*; this ſquare Iron Collar is made ſo long as to reach through the depth of the *Cheeks* of the *Lathe*, and to receive the Quarter or Tennant thruſt through it above the *Cheeks*, and a *Wedge* under the *Cheeks* marked *d*, which *Wedge* (when ſtiff knock'd up) draws the *Tennant* ſtrong and firmly down to the *Cheeks*, and conſequently keeps the *Side-rest* ſteddy on any part of the *Cheeks*, according as you ſlide the *Collar* forwards or backwards towards either *Pike*, or as you thruſt the *Rest* nearer or farther to and from the *Pikes*.

Some *Turnners* for ſome Work, inſtead of a plank for this *Rest*, faſten to one end of the Quarter or *Tennant*, a long Iron with a round Cilindrick *Socket* in it, as at the Figure marked *f* in Plate 13, *a* is the *Socket* of about an Inch, or an Inch and an half Diameter, to reach within two or three Inches as high as the *Pikes*, and into this *Socket* they put a long round Iron *Shank*, as in Figure *g* of the ſame *Plate*, *a* is the *Shank*, and at the top of this *Shank* is made the *Rest*, marked *b*. This *Shank* (I ſay) ſlips eaſily into the *Socket*, that it may be raiſed, or let down, as occaſion requires, and by the

help

help of a *Screw* through the *Socket* at *e*, may be faſtned at that length.

The *Reſt*, (by reaſon of its Round *Shank*) may be alſo turned with its upper edge more or leſs oblique or athwart the Work, or elſe parallel to the Work, according as the purpoſe may require.

Near one end of the *Reſt* is fitted and faſtned a piece of Wood about an Inch ſquare, and ten or twelve Inches long: This piece of wood is fitted ſtiff into a ſquare Hole or Morteſs made in the *Puppet*, a little above the *Shoulder* for the *Reſt*, to ſet the *Reſt* to any diſtance from the *Pikes*, which, with the ends of wooden *Screws* entred into wooden *Nuts* on the further ſide of the *Puppet*, and coming through againſt the *Reſt*, keeps the *Reſt* from being thruſt nearer to the work when the Workman is working.

¶ 8. *Of the* Treddle *and* Croſs-Treddle.

ABout the middle between the ends, is placed a wooden *Treddle* about two Inches and an half broad, an Inch thick, and three Foot long, and ſometimes three and an half, to four Foot long. The hinder end of it is faſtned to the Floor, with a piece of Leather (ſometimes a piece of the Upper-leather of an old Shoe, which piece of Leather is nailed to the under-ſide of the hinder end of the *Treddle*, ſo as to leave Leather enough beyond the end of the *Treddle* to nail down upon the Floor; which *Treddle* being thus nailed down, will move upwards, as the Spring of the *Pole* draws up the *String*; the *String* being alſo faſtned to the fore-end of the *Treddle*.

The

The hinder end of the *Treddle* is nailed down about a foot, or a Foot and an half behind the *Lathe*, and about the middle between both the *Legs*, ſo that the fore-end of the *Treddle* reaches beyond the fore-ſide of the *Lathe*, about a Foot and an half, or two Foot. And Note, that the farther the Fore-end of the *Treddle* reaches out beyond the Fore-ſide of the *Lathe*, the greater will the ſweep of the Fore-end of the *Treddle* be, and conſequently it will draw the more *String* down; and the more *String* comes down at one *Tread*, the more Revolutions of the Work is made at one *Tread*, and therefore it makes the greater riddance of the Work.

But then again, if the Fore-end of the *Treddle* reach too far before the Fore-ſide of the *Lathe*, it may draw the end of the *Pole* ſo low as to brake it: And it will alſo be the harder to *Tread* down, becauſe the power commanding (which is the weight of the *Tread*) lies ſo far from the weight to be commanded, which is the ſtrength of the *Pole*, augmented by the diſtance that the end of the *Treddle* hath from the Work in the *Lathe*; ſo that you may ſee, that the nearer the Fore-end of the *Treddle* lies to the Perpendicular of the Work in the *Lathe*, the eaſier the *Tread* will be: And ſome *Turners* that *Turn* altogether ſmall Work, have the Fore-end of the *Treddle* placed juſt under their work; ſo that their *String* works between the *Cheeks* of the *Lathe*: But then the Sweep of the *Treddle* being ſo ſmall, the *Pole* draws up but a ſmall length of *String*, and conſequently makes the fewer Revolutions of the Work in one *Tread*, which hinders the riddance of the Work; unleſs with every Spring of the *Pole*, they ſhould lift their Treading Leg ſo high, as to tire it

quickly

quickly with bringing it down again, after it is raiſed to ſo uncommodious a poſition.

This *Treddle* hath a ſquare Notch in the middle of the further end, about an Inch and an half wide, and two Inches long, that the end of the *String* may be wound either off or on the Wood on either ſide the Notch, to lengthen or ſhorten the *String*, as the different Diameters of the Work ſhall require.

About the midde of the *Treddle* is fixed a round Iron *Pin* about half an Inch in Diameter; ſo as to ſtand upright about an Inch and an half, or two Inches long above the *Treddle*. And under the *Cheeks* is alſo fixed down the *Croſs-Treddle*, which is ſuch another piece of Wood as the *Treddle* is, but longer or ſhorter, according to the length of the *Lathe*: And in the middle of the Breadth of the *Croſs-Treddle*, is made ſeveral holes all a-row to receive the Iron *Pin* ſet upright in the *Treddle*. Theſe holes are commonly boared about two or three Inches aſſunder, that the *Pin* or the *Treddle* may be put into any one of them, according as the *String* is to be placed nearer to or further off either end of the *Lathe*.

---

§ 9. Of

¶ 9. *Of the* Pole.

THe *Pole* is commonly made of a *Fir-pole*, and is longer or ſhorter, or bigger or ſmaller, according to the weight of the Work the Workman deſigns to *Turn*: For the thicker the *Pole* is, the harder muſt the *Tread* be to bring it down; and for this reaſon, if the *Pole* prove too ſtrong for their common or continued Work, they will weaken it by cutting away (with a Draw-knife, deſcribed *Numb.* 7. Plate 8. E, and § 5.) part of the ſubſtance off the upper and under ſides of the Pole.

The thick end of this *Pole* is nailed (or indeed rather pinned) up to ſome Girder, or other Timber in the Ceiling of the Room, with one ſingle Nail or a Pin, that the *Pole* may move upon that Nail, or Pin, as on a Center, and its thin end paſs from one *Puppet* to the other, as the Work may require. And at about a diſtance or more, is alſo nailed up to ſome Joyſts, or other Timbers of the Ceiling, two *Cheeks* of a convenient ſtrength, and at the lower end of theſe two *Cheeks* is nailed a Quarter or Batten to bear the *Pole*, though the weight of a *Tread* be added to it, as you may ſee at *n n* in Plate 12.

¶ 10. *Of the* Side-Reſt.

BUt it ſometimes happens that the Ceiling of the Work-room is not high enough for the *Pole* to play upwards and downwards; therefore in ſuch caſe, they place the thin end of the *Pole* at ſome conſiderable diſtance off the *Lathe*, either before or behind it, and ſo make the Spring of the *Pole* Horizantal towards the *Lathe*, conveying and guiding the *String* from the *Pole* to the Work by throwing it over a

Rowler, moving on two Iron *Center-pins* faſtned at both ends, and placed parallel to the *Cheeks* of the *Lathe*, above the Work as high as they can; and thus every *Tread* draws the *Rowler* about: But ſhould the *Rowler* not move about upon theſe Irons Pins, the *String* every *Tread* would both cut a Groove in the *Ruler*, and fret it ſelf more or leſs upon the *Rowler*.

¶ 11. *Of the* Bow.

SOme *Turners* that work light Work, ſuch as *Cane-heads*, *Ink-horns*, &c. for which they need ſcarce remove the *Puppets* off their *Lathe*, uſe a common *Bow*, ſuch as Archers uſe. The middle of this *Bow* they faſten over Head, with its *String* Horizontally downwards, and in the middle of that *String* they faſten another *String* perpendicularly downwards, whoſe other end they faſten to the *Treddle*, and the *String* wound round their Work brings it about.

¶ 12. *Of the* Great Wheel.

BUt when *Turners* work heavy Work, ſuch as the Pole and *Tread* will not Command, they uſe the *Great Wheel*. This Wheel is ſo commonly known, that I ſhall need give you no other Deſcription of it than the Figure it ſelf, which you may ſee in *Plate* 14. a. It is turned about with one, and ſometimes with two Iron *Handles*, according as the weight of the Work may require.

Its *String* hath both its ends ſtrong and neatly faſtned together, not with a Knot, but lapt over one another about three Inches in length, and ſo is firmly whipt about with ſmall Gut, that it may the eaſier paſs over the narrow *Groove* in the edge of the *Rowler*. This *String* is laid in the *Groove* made on the edge of the Wheel,

Wheel, and alſo in the *Groove* of the Work. But before it is laid upon both, one part of the *String* is lapt over and croſſes the other, and the *String* receives the Form of a Figure of Eight (only one of its Bows or Circles becomes no bigger than the *Groove* in the Work, and the other as big as the *Groove* in the *Wheel.*)

Then the whole Frame wherein the *Wheel* is fixed is removed farther off the *Lathe*, that the *String* may draw tight upon the Work.

The reaſon why the *String* thus croſſes it ſelf, is, becauſe it will touch and gird more upon the *Groove* of the Work, and conſequently (as was ſaid before ¶ 14.) will the better command the Work about.

The manner of Turning this *Wheel*, is as the manner of Turning other *Wheels* with *Handles.*

Beſides the commanding heavy Work about, the Wheel rids Work faſter off than the Pole can do; becauſe the ſpringing up of the Pole makes an intermiſſion in the running about of the Work, but with the *Wheel* the Work runs always the ſame way; ſo that the Tool need never be off it, unleſs it be to examine the work as it is doing.

When the Wheel is uſed, its Edge ſtands athwart the *Cheeks* of the *Lathe.*

¶ 13. *Of the* Treddle-Wheel.

THis is a *Wheel* made of a round Board of about two Foot and an half Diameter, conveniently to ſtand under the *Cheeks* of the *Lathe*. It alſo hath a *Groove* on its Edge for the *String* to run in; it hath an Iron *Axis* with a *Crook* or *Crank* at one end: And on this *Crook* is ſlipt the Nooſe of a *Leather Thong*, which having its other end faſtned to a *Treddle*, does, by keeping exact time in *Treads*, carry it swiftly about without intermission.

But the length of the *Thong* must be so fitted, that when the *Wheel* stands still, and the *Crook* at the end of the *Axis* hangs downwards, the end of the *Treddle* to which the *Thong* is fastned may hang about two or three Inches off the Ground: For then, giving the *Wheel* a small turn with the Hand, till the *Crook* rises to the highest, and passes a little beyond it; if just then (I say) the Workman gives a quick *Tread* upon the *Treddle* to bring the *Crook* down again with a jerk, that *Tread* will set it in a motion for several revolutions; and then if he observes to make his next *Tread* just when the *Crook* comes about again to the same position, it will continue the motion, and cause of the motion, and keep the *Wheel* always running the same way, if he punctually times his *Treads*.

The *Treddel Wheel* is used for small work only, as not having strength enough to carry heavy Work about, such as *Cane-heads*, *Small Boxes*, &c. and it is fitted below the *Cheeks* between the *Puppets*, as the *Bow* is above.

Besides these Inventions to carry about the Work in the *Lathe*, there are many more; as with a great *Iron Wheel*, having Teeth on its edge, which Teeth are to fall into an Iron *Nut* upon an Iron *Axis*, pitcht upon the *Pikes* of the *Puppets* of the *Lathe*, or fitted into *Collars*, &c.

Also, for very heavy Work, as Guns, great Mortars, *&c.* *Wheels* turn'd with *Wind*, *Water*, or *Horses*, to carry the Work about. Of which more in their proper places.

§ 14. *Of the* String.

UPon the thin end of the *Pole* is wound a considerable Bundle of *String*, that as a *Mandrel* requires to be bigger than ordinary, or the Work heavier, they may unwind ſo much of the *String* as will compaſs the *Mandrel* twice, or (if the Work be heavy) thrice; the eaſier to carry it about.

This *String* is made of the Guts of Beaſts (moſt commonly of Sheep, and ſpun round of ſeveral thickneſſes, of which the Workman chuſes ſuch ſizes as are apteſt for his Work; for large and heavy Work, very thick, but for ſmall and light work, thin: And there are ſeveral reaſons for his Choice; for a thin *String* will be too weak for heavy Work; but if it were not too weak for heavy work, it would be apt to mark ſoft wood more than a thick *String* would, when they are forc'd to ſhift the *String*, and let it run upon the Work. Beſides, a thin *String* (though it were ſtrong enough) would not ſo well bring heavy Work about; becauſe being ſmall, but little of the *String* touches the wood to command it, unleſs they wind it the oftner about the Work, which both takes up time, and hazards the breaking of the *String*, by the fretting of the ſeveral twiſts againſt one another.

Now a thick *String* is uncommodious for ſmall work; becauſe having a ſtrength and ſtubbornneſs proportionable to its ſize, it will not comply cloſely to a piece of Work of ſmall Diameter, but will be apt to ſlip about it, unleſs both *Pole* and *Tread* be very ſtrong; and then, if the Center-holes be not very deep, and the *Pikes* fill them not very tight, and the *Puppets* alſo not very well fixt, the ſtrength of the

String will alter the Center-holes; especially, when the work is upon soft Wood, or else it will endanger the breaking the work in its weakest place.

¶ 15. *Of the* Seat.

PArallel to the *Cheeks* on the inside the *Lathe* is fitted a Seat, about two and an half Inches square, and the whole length of the *Lathe*; having an Iron Pin fastned on either end the underside of it: It lies upon two *Bearers* of Wood, that are fastned athwart the outer sides the *Legs*, (or else to set it higher) the outer ends of the *Cheeks*, according to the height of the person that works at the *Lathe*. These Bearers reach in length so far inwards, as that they may be capable to bear the Seat so far off from the *Lathe*, as in the Diameter of the *Work* they intend to *Turn* in the *Lathe*, and also the bulk of the Workman that stands between the *Lathe* and it, may be contained.

It is not called a Seat, because it is so; but because the *Workman* places the upper part of his *Buttocks* against it, that he may stand the steddier to his *Work*, and consequently guide his Foot the firmer and exacter.

The two *Bearers* have several Holes made in them, from within sixteen Inches off the *Lathe*, to the ends of them, that the Iron Pins fastned in the ends of the *Seat*, may be removed nearer or farther off the *Lathe*, according to the greatness or smallness of the Diameter of their Work.

Having thus described the parts of a Common *Lathe*, I shall now follow with their other Tools also.

§ II. Of

§ II. *Of* Gouges.

GOuges are marked B B in *Plate* 15. They do the Office of *Fore-plains* in *Joynery*, and the *Jack-plains* in *Carpentry*, and ſerve only to take off the Irregularities the *Hatchet*, or ſometimes the *Draw-knife* leaves, after the work is hewed or drawn pretty near a Round with either of them: And therefore as the *Fore-plain* is made with a Corner-edge, only to take off the Irregularities of a Board, ſo the *Gouge* that it may alſo take off the Irregularities or Extuberancies that lye fartheſt from the *Axis* of the Work, and alſo frame pretty near the hollow Moldings required in the *Work*, precede the *Smoothing-Chiſſels*. And that the *Gouge* may the more commodiouſly and effectually do it, the Blade of this Tool is formed about half round to an edge, and the two extream ends of this half round a little ſloped off towards the middle of it, that a ſmall part about the middle may the eaſier cut off the prominencies that are not concentrick to the *Axis*, and ſo bring the *Work* into a Method of Formation.

The hollow edge is ground upon the Corner of a *Grind-ſtone*, which in ſhort time wears the outſide of that Corner to comply and form with the hollow of the *Gouge*. It is afterwards ſet upon a round *Whet-ſtone*, that fits the hollow of the edge, or is ſomewhat leſs. But they do not ſet their *Gouges* or *Chiſſels* as (I told you in *Numb.* 4. § 10.) the Joyners do; for *Turners* Tools being ſomewhat unweldy, by reaſon of their ſize, and long Handles, they lay the *Blade* of the *Gouge* with its convex ſide upon the *Reſt* of the *Lathe*; and ſo with the *Whet-ſtone* in their right hand they rub upon the *Baſil* the *Grind-ſtone* made, and as they rub, they often turn another part of the hollow of the edge to bear upon the round of the *Whet-ſtone*, till they have with the *Whet-ſtone* taken off the roughneſs of the *Grind-ſtone*.

Of theſe *Gouges* there are ſeveral ſizes, *viz.* from a quarter of an Inch, to an whole Inch, and ſometimes for very large *Work*, two Inches over.

The *Handles* to theſe *Gouges* (and indeed to all other *Turning Tools*) are not made as the *Handles* of *Joyners* or *Carpenters Tools* are, but tapering towards the end, and ſo long that the *Handle* may reach (when they uſe it) under the Arm-pit of the *Work-man*, that he may have more ſtay and ſteddy management of the Tool.

Page. 185

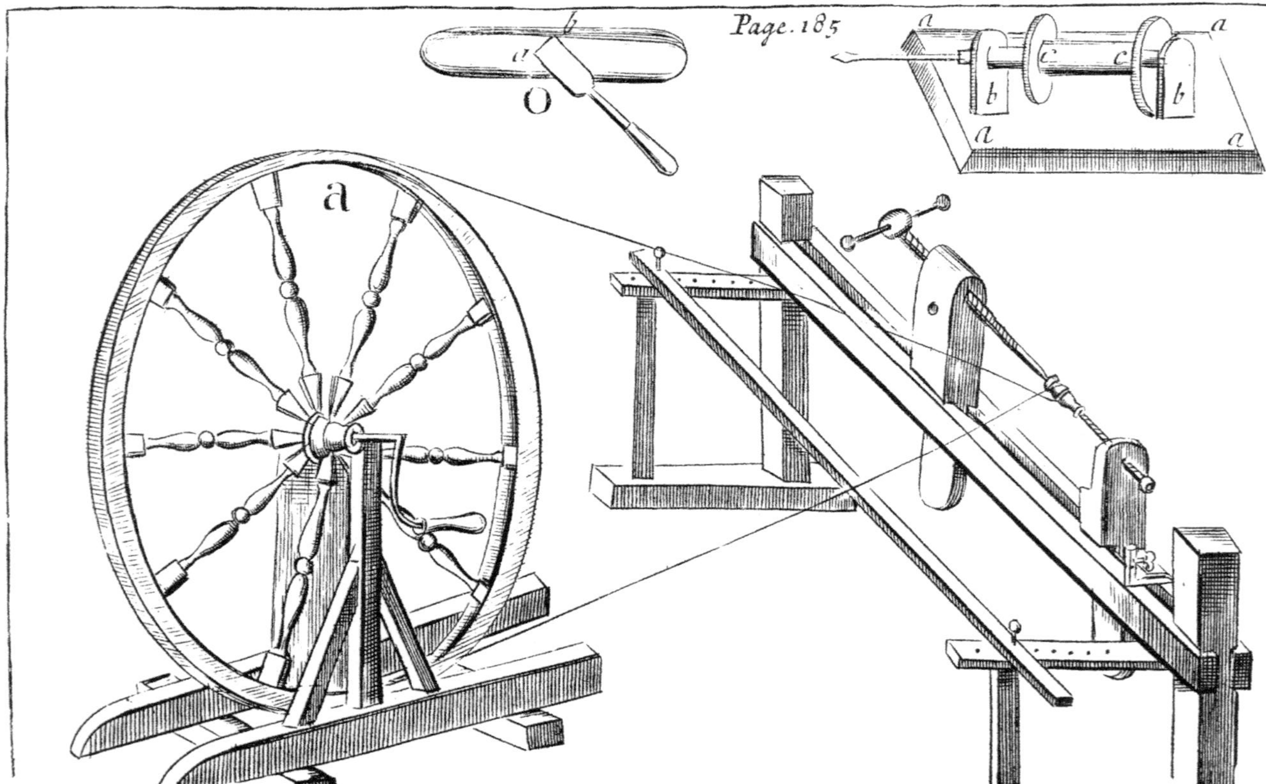

MECHANICK EXERCISES:

OR,

The Doctrine of *Handy-Works*.

Applied to the ART of TURNING.

§ III. *Of Flat Chissels.*

THE *Flat Chissels* are marked CC in *Plate* 15. These do the Office of *Smoothing Plains* in *Joyning* and *Carpentry*; for coming after the *Gouges* they cut off the prominent Risings that the *Gouges* leaves above the hollow.

The edges of these *Flat Chissels* are not ground to such a *Basil* as the *Joyners Chissels* are, which are made on one of the Flat sides of the *Chissels*, but are *Basil'd* away on both the flat sides; so that the edge lyes between both the sides in the middle of the *Tool*: And therefore either sides of the *Tool* may indifferently be applied to the Work; which could not well be, should the edge lye on one of the sides of the *Tool*: Because, if they should apply the *Basil* side of the *Tool* to the Work, the thickness of the *Basil* would bear the edge of the *Tool* off: And should they apply that side of the *Tool* the edge lyes on to the *Work*, the swift coming about of the *Work* would (where a small irregularity of Stuff

Stuff ſhould happen) draw or jobb the ſuddain edge into the Stuff, and ſo dawk it; which if the Stuff be already ſmall enough, would now be too ſmall, becauſe in *Turnings*, all Irregularities muſt be wrought ſmooth down.

Of thoſe *Flat Chiſſels* there are ſeveral ſizes, *viz.* from a quarter of an Inch, one Inch, two Inches, to three Inches broad, according to the largneſs of the *Work*.

Theſe are Set with the *Whet-ſtone* as the *Gouges* are, only they often turn the *Gouges* upon the round ſide, becauſe they would ſmoothen all the hollow edge; but theſe are laid flat upon the Reſt, and with a flat *Whet-ſtone* rubbed on the *Baſil*, as the *Gouge* was with the Round.

§ IV. *Of* Hooks.

THe *Hook* is marked D in *Plate* 15. As the *Gouge* is uſed when the Work lyes before the *Workman*, viz. parallel to its *Axis*, and cuts right forwards, ſo the *Hook* is uſed when the *Work* ſtands on the right or left ſide the *Workman*, as the flat ſides of Boards to be Turned do; and therefore this *Work* may be ſaid to lye athwart its *Axis*. And the *Hook* is made ſo as to cut on the right or left ſide a Board, and to take off the extuberances from the plain of the Board. But though this *Tool* does the Office of a *Gouge*, yet it is more difficult for a *Workman* to uſe than a *Gouge*, becauſe it is made thinner and ſlenderer than a *Gouge*, that its edge cutting at a greater Bearing from the *Reſt*, may the eaſier come at the Stuff it works upon, and the farther the edge that cuts lyes from the *Reſt*, the more difficult it is for a *Workman* to guide it, becauſe it is then more ſubject to tremble; eſpecially ſince (as aforeſaid) the edge of the *Hook* is and muſt be thinner than the edge of the *Gouge*.

Theſe

These *Tools*, as also the *Gouges*, and *Flat-Chissels*, are all about ten or twelve Inches long without the Handles.

The *Hooks* when they want sharpening cannot be *ground* as the *Gouges* and *Chissels* are; but they must be first softned in the Fire and turned straight, and then brought to an edge, and by heating again red hot turned into its form: Then must it be hardned and tempered as you were taught, *Numb.* 3. *fol.* 57, 58. Yet do not *Workmen* proceed thus with their *Hook* every time it grows bluntish, but only when the edge is either by long use, or bad Temper, grown so thick, that this following way will not help them: For they *Whet* the outer edge with a *Whet-stone* as they do other *Tools*. But because they cannot come at the inner edge of the *Hook* with a *Whet-stone*, unless the *Hook* be very wide, and the *Whet-stone* very thin, they make use of a piece of Temper'd Steel, as sometimes the thin side of a *Chissel*, or the back of a *Knife*, and so with the edge of the Square, scrape along the hollow edge of the *Hook*, and force the edge as much to the outside of the *Hook* as they can. Thus *Butchers* wear at their Girdles small round Rods of Steel well tempered and polisht, that they may with quick dispatch whet their *Knives* upon it, by forcing the edge forwards upon the Blade, or pressing down the Shoulder that hinders the edge Entrance; for their Steels being so well polisht, cannot properly be said to wear away any part of the Shoulder that should hinder the edge from doing its Office.

§ V. Of

§ V. *Of* Grooving Hooks, *and* Grooving Tools.

THe *Grooving Hook* is marked E in *Plate* 15, and hath its Tooth of different forms, according to the Fashion of the *Groove* to be made on the Plain of the Board; for sometime its Tooth hath a flat Edge, sometimes a round Edge, sometimes a point only, and sometimes two points, or other Forms as aforesaid.

Its whole Blade is made much stronger than the *Gouge* and *Chissels*, and hath the sides of its Edge more obtuse to make it the stronger.

The *Flat Tools* work the Boards Flat either to the Plain of the Board, or to a Flat Groove in the Board.

The *Round Edge* cuts an half-round hollow in the Board.

The Point cuts a fine Hollow Circle or Swage in the Flat of the Board; and being made Triangular, hath three Edges each, of which cuts the Ridges smooth down that the *Hook* left upon the Board.

The *Two-point Grooving-Hook* cuts two fine hollow Circles or Swages on the Plain of the Board.

The *Grooving-Hooks* do not work as the *Hooks* do, for the Hooks cut the Wood; but these do but indeed scrape off the Extuberancies, or fret into the Wood, and therefore they are very seldom used to soft Wood, because its being loose, will not endure scraping without leaving a roughness upon the Work; but hard Wood, or Ivory (for the Reason converted) will.

§ VI. *Of* Mandrels. *And* ¶ 1. *Of* Flat Mandrels.

MAndrels are marked F 1. F 2. F 3. F 4. in *Plate* 15. There are different ſorts of *Mandrels*, and the ſizes of them alſo different, according to the ſizes of the Work.

1. *Broad Flat Mandrels* marked F 1. in *Plate* 15. with three or more little Iron *Pegs*, or *Points* near the Verge of its Flat: And theſe are uſed for the *Turning* Flat Boards upon. For the backſide of a Board placed Flat upon it, will when ſcrewed up tight between the *Pikes*, by help of the Irong *Pegs*, remain in its place and poſition, whilſt the Flat ſide of the Work is working upon.

Behind the Backſide of this *Mandrel* (and indeed all other *Mandrels*) is fitted a long *Shank*, or *Rowler*, for the *String* to be wound about while the Work is *Turning*. This *Rowler* muſt be ſo large in Diameter, that the *String* wound about it may command the *Work* about. If the *Work* be large and heavy, the *Rowler* muſt be bigger than if the *Work* be light; for elſe the *String* will not command it about: But if the Diameter of the *Rowler* be ſmaller, the work comes ſo much ſwifter about. The *Rowler* muſt alſo be ſo long between its *Shoulders*, that it may conveniently contain ſo many Diameters of the *String* as ſhall be neceſſary to wind about it.

This whole *Mandrel* is marked F 1. in *Plate* 15. *a.* The *Round Flat*, or *Face*, of the *Mandrel*. *b.* The *Rowler*. *c c* The *Shoulders* of the *Rowler*. *d d d* The *Pegs*.

¶ 2. *Of* Pin-Mandrels.

2. MAndrels are made with a long *Wooden Shank*, to fit ſtiff into a round hole that is made in the Work that is to be *Turned*. This *Mandrel*

Mandrel is called a *Shank*, or *Pin-Mandrel*, and is marked F 2. in Plate 15. And if the hole the *Shank* is to fit into be very ſmall, and the Work to be faſtned on it pretty heavy, then *Turners* faſten a round Iron *Shank*, or *Pin*, of the ſize of the Hole it is to be fitted into, and faſten their Work upon it. Theſe *Mandrels* with Iron *Shanks* are uſed by *Turnners* that *Turn* Bobbins, or ſuch like Work: Becauſe a *Wooden Shank* to fit the ſmall Hole though the work would not be ſtrong enough to carry the work about.

¶ 3. *Of* Hollow-Mandrels.

3. THere is another ſort of *Mandrels* called *Hollow Mandrels*, deſcribed F 3. Plate 15. It is both a *Hollow-Mandrel*, and alſo uſed to *Turn* hollow *Work* in it. This *Mandrel* hath but one Center-hole belonging to it, *viz.* at the *Rowler* end or Neck; but it hath a *Shank*, which ſupplies the Office of another Center-hole, *a* the hollow, *b* the *Shank*, or *Neck*. The *Hollow* is made ſo wide, that the *Work* intended to be *Turned* hollow in it may fit very ſtiff into it, and ſo deep that it may contain the intended *Work*.

When it is uſed, it is pitcht upon the Center at the farther end of the *Rowler*, and hath its *Shank* put into one of the Holes of the *Joint-Coller* deſcribed in Plate 13. *fig. G.* that will beſt fit it; which Hole ſtanding directly againſt the *Pike* in the hinder *Puppet*, and receiving the *Shank* into it, guides the *Mandrel* about, as if it were pitcht upon two Centers: And the *Work* being forced ſtiff into the Hollow of this *Mandrel*, will be carried about with it, expoſing the Fore-ſide of the work bare and free from the *Joynt-Coller*, and not impeded by *Spikes* from coming at the *work*; ſo that with the *Hook*, *Grooving-*

Grooving-Hook, *Gouge*, or *Flat-Chiſſel*, according as your *work* requires, you may come at it to *Turn* your intended Form.

Hollow Mandrels are alſo uſed in *Collers* that open not with a *Joynt*; but then the *Spindle* is made of Iron, and hath a *Screw* juſt at its end, upon which is ſcrewed a Block with an hollow, in it, made fit to receive the *work* ſtiff into it.

¶ 4. *Of the* Screw-Mandrel.

4. ANother ſort of *Mandrel* is called the *Screw-Mandrel*, and is marked F 4. in Plate 15. *a* the *Rowler* of the *Mandrel*, *b.* the *Shank*, or *Screw*, is made of Iron, having its two ends Round, and in the middle between the Round ends a Square the length of the *Rowler*, and this Square is fitted ſtiff into a Square-hole made through the middle of the *Rowler* that it turn not about in the Square-hole. In each Flat-end of this Iron *Shank*, or *Spindle*, is made a Center-hole, wherein the *Pikes* of the *Puppets* are pitcht when this *Mandrel* is uſed. This Iron *Shank*, or *Axis*, muſt be made very ſtraight, and ought to be turned upon the two Center-holes for exactneſs; becauſe on one of the round ends, or ſometimes on both, a Screw, or indeed ſeveral Screws of ſeveral Diameters is made. That Screw next the end of the *Shank* is the ſmalleſt, *viz.* about three quarters of an Inch over, and takes up in length towards the middle of the *Shank*, about an Inch, or an Inch and an half; and ſo far from the end of the *Shank* it is of an equal Diameter all the way; and on this portion of the *Shank* is made a *Male-ſcrew* of the fineſt Thread. The next Inch and half (wrought as before) hath another *Male-ſcrew*; but about half a quarter of an Inch more in Diameter than the former, and hath its Threads courſer. Another

ther Inch and half hath its Diameter ſtill greater, and its Threads yet courſer. And thus you may make the *Shank* as long as you will, that you may have the more variety of ſizes for *Screws*.

Theſe ſorts of *Mandrels* are made for the making of *Screws* to *Boxes*, and their *Lids*, as ſhall be ſhewed in the next Paragraph.

¶ *Of* Sockets, *or* Chocks, *belonging to the* Screw-Mandrel.

TO this *Screw-Mandrel* belongs ſo many *Sockets* as there are ſeveral ſizes of *Screws* on the *Shank*. They are marked F 5. in *Plate* 15. *a* the *Socket* or *Chock*: *b b*, the Wooden *Pin*, *c* the *Stay*, *d d* the *Notch* to ſlip over the *Male-ſcrew*.

Theſe *Hollow Sockets* have *Female-Screws* in them, made before the Notch to ſlip over the *Male-ſcrew* of the *Screw-Mandrel* is cut. The manner of making *Female-ſcrews* is taught *Numb.* 2. *fol.* 29, 30, 31. only inſtead of a *Tap* (uſed there) you uſe the ſeveral and different ſizes of *Screws* made on the *Screws-Mandrel* to do the Office of a *Tap* into each reſpective *Socket*; which *Sockets* being only made of hard Wood, it will eaſily perform, though the *Shank*, or *Axis* be but Iron.

Therefore (as aforeſaid) to each of the *Male-ſcrews* on the *Screw-Mandrel* is fitted ſuch a *Socket*, that you may chuſe a *Thread* Courſer or Finer as you pleaſe; but this *Female-ſcrew* is open, or hath a *Notch* on one ſide of it, that it may ſlip over the *Male-ſcrew*, and the Threads of each other fit into each others *Grooves*; and when they are thus fitted to one another, the further or open ſide of the *Male-ſcrew* is gaged in, or pin'd on the *Female-ſcrew* with a wooden *Pin* thruſt through two oppoſite Holes, made

for

for that purpoſe in the *Cheeks* of the wooden Sockets, that it ſhake not.

When the *Treddle* comes down in working, and the *Socket* is fitted on its proper *Screw*, and pinn'd ſtiff upon it, and the Stay held down to the *Reſt* of the *Lathe*, then will the *Socket*, and conſequently the *Stay* ſlide farwards upon the *Male-ſcrews*; ſo that a Tool held ſteddy on any part of the *Stay*, and applied to the out or inſide of your *Work*, that Tools point will deſcribe and cut a Screw, whoſe Thread ſhall be of the ſame fineneſs that the Screw and the Shank is of.

§ VII. *Of* Collers.

THere are ſeveral faſhion'd *Collers*; As the *Joynt-Coller* marked G, the *Round-Coller* marked H, and the *Coller* marked I, in Plate 13.

The *Joynt-Coller* is made of two Iron *Cheeks* marked *b b*, which moving upon a Joint *c* at the Bottom, may be ſet cloſe together, or elſe opened as the two inſides of the *Joynt-Rule* Carpenters uſe to do. On the inner Edge of each *Cheek* is formed as many half-round holes or Semi-circles as you pleaſe, or the length of the *Cheeks* will conveniently admit: Theſe Semicircles are made of different Diameters, that they may fit the *Shanks* or *Necks*, of different ſiz'd *Mandrels*: And theſe Semi-circles muſt be made ſo exactly againſt each other on the edges of the *Cheeks*, that when the two *Cheeks* moving upon their *Joynt* are clapt cloſe together, the Semicircles on both the *Cheeks* ſhall become a perfect round hole, or circumference.

Near the top of one of theſe *Cheeks* is faſtned with a *Center-pin*, a ſquare Iron Coller marked *d*, with a ſmall *Handle* to it marked *e*. This ſquare Coller is made to contain the breadth of both the *Cheeks* when they are ſhut together, and to hold them ſo faſt together, that they ſhall not ſtart aſſunder; and yet is made ſo fit, that it may ſlip off and on both the *Cheeks*.

This *Joynt-Coller* may ſerve to do the Office of the other two *Collers*, and its one particular Office too: Yet to ſave the Charge of the price of this Tool, *Turners* ſeldom uſe them, but make ſhift with either of the other, or ſometimes with a hole made in a Board only: But its particular Office is to hold a *Mandrel*, whoſe Neck is fitted to one of its Holes, and the work they are to *Turn* is required to ſtand out free from the outer Flat of the *Cheeks* of the *Coller*, the better to come at it with the *Tool*; ſuch as are deep Boxes, or deep Cups, &c.

MECHANICK EXERCISES:

OR,

The Doctrine of *Handy-Works*.

Applied to the ART of *TURNING*.

§ VIII. *Of the* Mawl.

THE *Mawl* is marked K in Plate 13. The Figure of it there is Deſcription ſufficient: Its Office is to knock and unknock the Wedge in the *Puppets*; and to knock upon the back of the *Cleaving Knife*, when they ſplit their Wood for their Work. The *Joyner's Mallet* would ſupply the Office of this Tool; but uſe has made the *Mawl* more handy for them: Beſides when one is batter'd to ſhivers, they can quickly, of a Chump of Wood, accommodate themſelves with another.

§ IX. *Of the* Hatchet, Draw-knife *and* Cleaving-knife.

THe *Hatchet* is marked L in Plate 4. It is of the ſame ſort that *Joyners* uſe; which I deſcribed *Numb.* 5. § 25. and therefore refer you thither. And the *Draw-knife* is deſcribed in *Numb.* 7. § 5. Plate 8. marked E. The *Cleaving-knife* marked M in Plate 13. needs no other Deſcription than that Figure.

§ X. *Of the* Chopping-Block.

THe *Chopping-Block* is marked N in Plate 13. It is made of a piece of *Elm-Tree* placed with its Grain upwards and downwards as it grew. It hath three Leges in it, that ſtand ſtradling out from the underſide of the *Block* to the Floor, and of ſuch an height, as the Workman may have moſt Command of the Work. See the Figure. Sometimes *Turnners* uſe inſtead of it, a piece of the Trunk of a Tree, of about a Foot and an half, or two Foot, in length from the Ground, or more or leſs.

§ XI. *Of the* Callippers.

THe *Callippers* is marked O in *Plate* 13. As common Compaſſes (deſcribed *Numb.* 6. § 32.) are for meaſuring Diſtances upon a plain Superficies; ſo *Callippers* meaſure the diſtance of any round *Cilindrick* Conical Body, either in their Extremity, or any part leſs than the Extream: So that when Workmen uſe them, they open the two points *a a* to their deſcribed width, and *Turn* ſo much ſtuff off the intended place, till the two points of the *Callippers* fit juſt over their Work; ſo ſhall their Work have juſt the Diameter in that place, as is the diſtance between the two points of the *Callippers*, be it either Feet or Inches, *&c.*

§ XII. *Of the* Drill-Bench.

THere is yet another Tool, or rather a *Machine* uſed by ſome *Turnners*, called a *Drill-Bench.* It is deſcribed in Plate 14. *a a a a* a thick Board, about three Inches thick, five Inches broad, and eighteen Inches long, *b b* two Stiles placed towards either end, and faſtned upright. In the hithermoſt Stile is a *Coller* deſcribed § 7. and Plate

Plate 13. H. or any of the other *Collers*: And in the further *Stile* is fitted a ſquare flat tempered piece of Steel having a Center-hole in the middle of it, and is placed juſt againſt the Center or middle point of the Hole of the *Coller*, *c c* the *Rowler*, whoſe hither end is *Turned* away, ſo as it juſt fit into the *Coller*, and at the further end of it, it hath a temper'd *Steel Pin*, to be placed in the Center-hole: And in the middle of the hither end of it, it hath a *Piercer-Bit* faſtned ſtraight in, ſo that it lie in a true ſtraight Line, with the *Axis* of the *Rowler*. Of theſe *Rowlers* they have ſeveral, and *Bits* of different ſizes fitted into them, that upon all occaſions they may chuſe one to fit their purpoſe.

On the under-ſide, about the middle of the *Bench*, is fitted and faſtned athwart it a ſquare Iron *Coller*, deep enough to reach through the *Cheeks* of the *Lathe*, and ſo much deeper as it may receive a Wooden *Wedge*, ſuch a one as belongs to one of the *Puppets*: And by the force and ſtrength of the *Wedge*, the whole *Drill-bench* is drawn down and faſtned athwart the *Cheeks* of the *Lathe*.

When it is uſed, it ſtands athwart the *Cheeks* of the *Lathe* (as aforeſaid) with the point or end of the *Bit* towards you; and then the *String* being turned twice or thrice about the *Rowler*, will (with *Treading* on the *Treddle*) turn the *Rowler* and its *Bit* forcibly about, and cauſe it to enter ſwiftly into a piece of Wood that ſhall be preſt forwards upon the *Bit*.

When they uſe it, they hold the piece of Wood they intend to *Drill*, or *Pierce*, faſt in both their Hands, right before them, and preſs it forwards upon the *Piercer-Bit*; ſo that by its running about, it cuts a ſtraight round hole into the Wood, of what length they pleaſe.

 But

But while the *Pole* is rising after every *Tread*, they preſs not againſt the *Piercer-Bit*, ſo that it is diſ-ingaged from doing its Office in the Wood; but in that while, they nimbly give the Wood a turn in their hands, of about one third part of its Circumference; which makes the *Bit* very ſucceſſive *Tread*, go the ſtraighter through the middle of the Wood: And thus they reiterate *Treads*, and keep the Wood turning in their Hands, till the *Bit* is enter'd deep enough.

Thus much of the *Tools* uſed in common *Turning*: I ſhall proceed to the Working a Pattern or two in ſoft Wood; which being well underſtood, may render a Practicer capable of moſt common Work.

§ XIII. *Of* Turning *a* Cilinder *in ſoft Wood.*

THe ſoft Wood *Turners* Uſe is commonly either *Maple*, *Alder*, *Birch*, *Beech*, *Elm*, *Oak*, *Fir*, &c. and for ſome particular purpoſes each of theſe ſorts are beſt.

The firſt Pattern we purpoſe ſhall be a *Cilinder* two Inches over, and eight Inches long: Therefore you muſt chuſe a piece of Wood at leſt two Inches and a quarter over, leſt you want Stuff to work upon: Nay, if your Stuff prove ſhaken, or otherwiſe unſound, or your Center be not very exactly pitcht, you may want yet more Stuff; and that according as it proves more or leſs faulty, or as the Centers are more unequally pitcht. But ſuppoſing the Stuff good, you may take a piece of two Inches and a quarter over, as I ſaid before, and about ten or eleven Inches long. For though the length of the *Cilinder* be but eight Inches, yet you muſt cut your Stuff long enough to make a Groove at one end of it beſides, for the *String* to run in. If your Stuff be ſomewhat too big for your

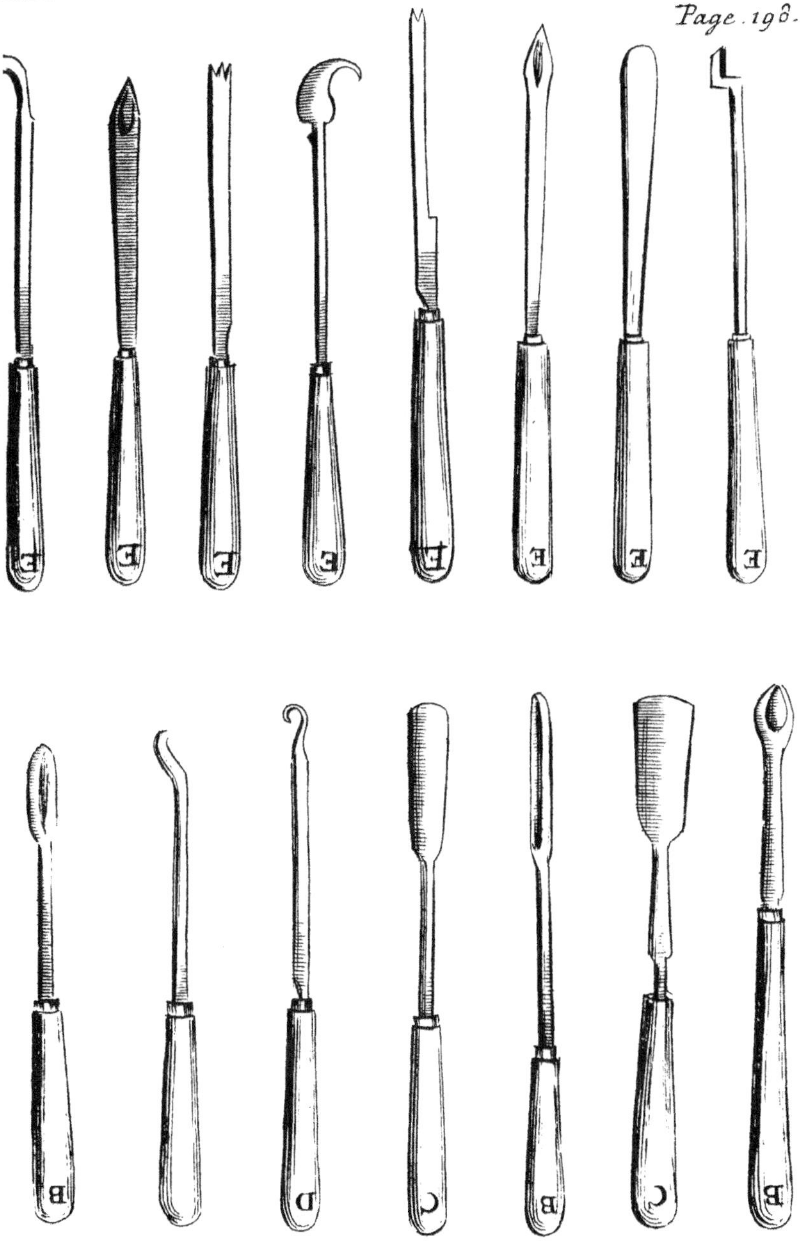

Plate 15.

Scantlin, and not round enough to go into the *Lathe*, you muſt *Hew* it pretty near with the *Hatchet* to make it ſizable, and afterwards ſmoothen it nearer with a *Draw-knife*, as you were taught, *Numb.* 7. § 5.

But if you have not Stuff at hand near your ſize, then you muſt Saw off your length from a Billet, or ſome other piece of Stuff, and with the *Cleaving-knife* and the *Mawl*, ſplit it into a ſquare piece near the ſize, and with the *Draw-knife* round off the Edges to make it fit for the *Lathe.*

Then ſet your *Puppets*, and wedge them right up, ſo as the *Points* of your *Spikes* ſtand pretty near the length of your Work aſſunder, and move the *Pole*, ſo as the end of it may hang over between the *Pikes*, and alſo fit the Iron *Pin* in the *Treddle* into a proper *Hole* in the *Croſs-Treddle*, ſo as the end of the *Treddle* may draw the *String* below the Work into pretty near a ſtraight Line with the ſtring above the Work: And take the Work in your Right Hand, and put it beyond the *String* before you, and with your Left Hand wind the *String* below the Work, but once about the Work, leſt it ſhould be too ſtrong for your ſhallow Centers, as you ſhall underſtand by and by, and then with a pretty ſtrength preſs the middle of one end of your Work over the Point of one of the *Pikes*, and ſo make a hole in your Work for one of the Center holes: Then ſcrew your Pike wider or cloſer, according as the length of your Work requires, and pitch the other end of your Work upon the other Pike alſo, and ſcrew your Work a little lightly up: Then try how the Centers are pitcht, by Treading the *Treddle* lightly down; and if you find the Centers are well pitcht, you may without more ado ſcrew up your Work tight;

But if your Centers, or either of them be not well pitcht, you muſt alter them. You may know when they are well pitcht, by treading ſoftly upon your *Treddle*, and holding your Finger ſteddy on the *Reſt*, direct the point of it pretty cloſe to the Work: For if in a Revolution of your Work, its Out-ſide keeps it an equal diſtance from the end of your Finger, you may conclude your Work is well pitcht. But if you find one ſide of your Work comes nearer your Finger than the other ſide, you muſt with your *Flat Chiſſel*, or *Gouge*, (or what is neareſt at hand) knock ſoftly, or hard, upon that ſide that comes neareſt to your Finger, till you have forc'd the *Pikes* into the true Centers at the end of your Work; and then you may boldly ſcrew it hard up: But you muſt be ſure to ſcrew it hard up; becauſe it is ſoft Wood you purpoſe to work upon, and the ſtrength of the *Pole* may endanger the drawing or removing the Centers, if the *Pikes* have not good hold of them.

Having found your Centers, take your Work again off the *Pikes*, and wind the *String* once or twice more about your Work, that your *String* (as I ſaid in *Numb.* 10. § 1. when I wrote of the *String*) may the better command it, and then wind off or no more *String* at the end of your *Pole*, or end of your *Treddle*, or both, if your Work require it, till the *Pole* draws the *Treddle* up a little above half the length of the *Legs* of the *Lathe*. For about the height your Leg may without ſudden trying, command the *Pole* down again.

But before you begin to work upon the Stuff, I ſhall inform you how to *Tread* the *Treddle*, in which you may obſerve this General Rule; That the nearer the Fore-end of the *Treddle* you *Tread*, the eaſier you bring down the *Pole*; but then the

the *Pole* in its Spring raſes your Leg the higher, and may draw the upper ſide of the your Thigh againſt the underſide of the *Cheek* of the *Lathe*, and with reiterated Riſings Gawl, and alſo tire your Thigh.

Place therefore your Foot ſteddy upon the *Treddle*, ſo far forward as you can, to avoid the *Poles* riſing from drawing your Thigh againſt the underſide of the *Lathe*; and Tread the *Treadle* nimbly down, but not quite ſo low as to knock againſt the Floor: Then abate the weight of your Tread, and let the *Pole* draw the *Treddle* up, but ſtill keep your Foot ſteddy, and lightly Bearing upon the *Treddle:* For then your ſucceeding *Treads* will prove eaſier to your Leg and Thigh, and you will with your Foot the better and quicker command the *Treddle.* Then *Tread* again nimbly down as before, and keep this train of Treading till your Work be finiſh'd, or that you may have occaſion to ſtop and exaime how rightly you proceed.

In all ſmall Work the *Tread* is lightly and nimbly performed; but in large and heavy work the *Tread* comes ſlow and heavily down.

This being premiſed, you may begin with your *Gouge*; lay the round ſide of it upon the *Reſt*, and take the Handle of it in your Right Hand, and lay the Fore and Middle Fingers of your Left Hand upon the Hollow of the *Gouge* near the Work, mounting the Edge about a quarter of an Inch above the *Axis* of your Work, and ſinking your Right Hand a little; for in this poſition the *Gouge* cuts beſt: And thus cut down on your Work near one end, a *Groove* for your *String* to run in: The *Groove* may be about an Inch, or an Inch and an half long; but it matters not much what depth. Then ſlip your *String* into the *Groove*, and if you find the *String* will

will not ſlip eaſily, you may put your Foot under the *Treddle* and lift it a little up, that the *String* when no weight is hanged to it, may ſlide the eaſier into the *Groove.*

And by the way you may take notice, that the deeper you cut down the *Groove*, the oftner will your Work come about every Tread; becauſe the *String* that comes down every Tread, meaſure a ſmall Circumference oftener than it does a greater Circumference: But then the work is not ſo ſtrongly carried about; becauſe it hath a leſs portion of the *String* to command it. This I hint, not that in this our ſmall propoſed Pattern it is very conſiderable: For if you only cut the *Groove* down but ſo low as there may be a Shoulder at the end, and another againſt the Work, to keep the *String* from ſlipping out of the Groove, it will be ſufficient: But in heavy Work this *Groove* ought to be cut with diſcretion.

Now come to the Forming of your Work, and hold your *Gouge*, as you were taught before, but ſomewhat lightly againſt your Work, beginning at one end, and ſliding your *Gouge* gradually to the other, cutting with its Edge all the way you go, and bearing ſomewhat ſtiff againſt the Work every Tread you make on the *Treddle:* And withdrawing it again a little lightly from the *work* every Spring of the Pole. And thus by Uſe you muſt habituate your ſelf to let the edge of your *Tool* bear upon the Work when the Pole and *Treddle* comes down, and to draw it back juſt off the Work, as the Pole and *Treddle* goes up. And thus you muſt continue till you have rough-wrought all your work from end to end.

If you have not at firſt brought your Work clean; that is, if you have not gone deep enough with your *Gouge* to take off all the Riſings

ſings of the Stuff the *Draw-knife* left, even with the ſmalleſt part of your Work, you muſt in like manner (as before) work it over again. But you muſt have a ſpecial Care you take not too much Stuff away on any part of the whole Work: For this propoſed Pattern being a *Cilinder*, if you take but a ſmall matter to much away from any part, and make it ſmaller than your given meaſure there, the whole Work will be ſpoiled, as being ſmaller than the propoſed Diameter; which to know, you may by opening the Points of your *Callippers* to two Inches on your *Rule* (the propoſed Diameter of your *Cilinder*) try if the Points at that diſtance will juſt ſlip over the deepeſt *Grooves* of your Work (for we will not ſuppoſe that the *Grooves* are of an equal depth with the Rough-working of the *Gouge*) without ſtraining the Joint, for then your Work is juſt ſizeable: If not, work over again as before, *&c.* But we will now ſuppoſe you have not taken too much away, but have made a due proceſs with your *Gouge.* Therefore now proceed, and uſe a *Flat Chiſſel*, about an Inch and an half broad, to take off the Irregularities the *Gouge* left.

Take the Handle of it in your Right Hand, as you did the *Gouge*, and claſpſing the *Blade* of it in your Left Hand, lean it ſteddy upon the *Reſt*, holding the Edge a little aſlant over the Work, ſo as a Corner of the thin ſide of the *Chiſſel* may bear upon the *Reſt*, and that the Flat ſide of the *Chiſſel* may make a ſmall Angle with the *Reſt*, and conſequently with the Work; (which is parallel to the *Reſt*) for ſhould you ſet the edge of the *Chiſſel* parallel to the Work, it might run too faſt into the Work, and dawk it. Therefore you muſt ſet the *Chiſſel* in ſuch a poſition, that the lower, Corner, or near the lower Corner of the

edge

edge, may cut lightly upon the Work: But this poſition is beſt deſcribed by a Figure, which to that purpoſe I have inſerted in *Plate* 14. at O, where you may perceive in, or near, what poſition the *Chiſſel* muſt be ſet to cut the Work; and how the edge of the *Chiſſel a b* lying aſlant the Work, and the further Corner of the edge of the *Chiſſel b* being ſomewhat mounted, as the Work comes about, the Bottom, or near the Bottom, of the edge of the *Chiſſel* is only capable to cut a narrow Shaving off the Work: And juſt in this manner you muſt keep the *Chiſſel* ſteddy bearing upon the Work, as the *Pole* comes down, and withdrawing it from the Work as the *Pole* Springs up (as you were taught to uſe the *Gouge*) and at the ſame time ſliding it forwards from one end of the Work to the other, till it be wrought down all the way to its true Diameter between the points of the *Callippers*: For then a ſtraight *Ruler* applied to your Work, the outſide of your purpoſes *Cilinder* will be formed.

Only the ends muſt be cut down ſquare to the length: Therefore open the points of your Compaſſes to the diſtance of eight Inches on your *Rule*, and prick that diſtance hard off upon your Work, that the points of your *Compaſſes* may leave viſible marks, by placing one point as near one end as you can, to leave Stuff enough to cut ſtraight down all the way; that is, to cut it ſquare down at right Angles with the outſide of the Work. Which to do, you muſt hold the Handle of the *Flat Chiſſel* in your Right Hand (as before) and claſp the Blade of it in your Left, and lay one of the thin ſides of it upon the *Reſt*, ſo that the edge may ſtand upright, or very near upright againſt the Work. Then ſink your Right Hand ſomewhat below the Level of the *Reſt*, that the lower Corner of the edge of the

the *Chiſſel* may mount, and being thruſt ſteddy againſt the Work, juſt in the mark one Point of the *Compaſſes* made, Tread the *Treddle*, and cut a pretty deep Circle into the Stuff. But you muſt have a care you do not direct the cutting Corner of the *Chiſſel* inwards, but rather outwards, leſt you make the end hollow inſtead of Flat: For if you do take off too little at firſt, you may by degrees cut it down to a Flat afterwards. As you cut deeper into the Stuff, you muſt turn the Flat of the *Chiſſel*, and with it cut down the Shoulder juſt at the end on the outſide the mark, for elſe that may hinder the Corner of the edge of the *Chiſſel* for coming at the Work.

Note, That if you hold not the edge of the *Chiſſel* truly before the Work, but direct it inwards, and if you hold it not very ſteddy, and have a good guidance of it, the quick coming about of the Work, may draw the edge of the *Chiſſel* into it inwards and run a dawk on *Cilinder*, like the Grooves of a *Screw*, and ſo ſpoil your Work: For being once wrought to the true ſize, you cannot afterwards take any more off to cleanſe it, *&c.*

The other end muſt be cut down as this.

§ 14. Of

§ 14. *Of* Turning Flat Boards.

IF your Board be thick enough, you may boar a round Hole in the middle of it; and turn a *Mandrel* with a *Pin* a very little Tapering, to fit hard and ſtiff into the round Hole: And if the *Hole* and *Pin* be proportionable in ſize to the weight of the Board, the *Pin* will carry it about. But you muſt be very careful the *Hole* be boarded exactly ſtraight through the middle, and not inclining on either ſide the Board, more to any part of the Verge than to another; but that the middle of the *Hole* be exactly the Center of the Board the whole thickneſs through. This *Pin-Mandrel* is deſcribed *Numb.* 11. § 6. and *Plate* 13.

If your Board be not thick enough to be faſtned upon a *Pin-Mandrel*, or that your Work will not admit of an Hole to be bored through the middle of it, you may uſe the *Flat-Mandrel* deſcribed *Plate* 13. F 2. And then you muſt with your *Compaſſes* find the Center on the backſide of the Round Board (with ſeveral proffers if need require) till you have found it, and prick there an Hole for a mark: Then open the points of your *Compaſſes* to about the thickneſs of a Shilling wider than the Semidiameter of the *Flat-Mandrel*; and with the points of your *Compaſſes* at that diſtance deſcribe a Circle on the backſide of the Board to be turned, by placing one Foot in the prick-mark, and turning about the other Foot. By this Circle you may pitch the Center of the Board exactly upon the Center of the *Flat-Mandrel*: For the points of the *Compaſſes* being opened about the thickneſs of a Shilling wider than the Semidiameter of the *Flat-Mandrel*: will

(when

(when you have pitcht the Center of the Board on the Center of the *Mandrel*) place the outer Verge of the *Mandrel* the thickneſs of a Shilling round about within the Circle deſcribed on the the backſide of the Board: And when it is thus pitcht, you may, by laying the Board flat down, knock upon the *Rowler* end of the *Mandrel*, and drive the *Pegs* in the flat of the *Mandrel* into the Board, and ſo hold it ſteddy upon the *Mandrel*: Then find the Center on the Foreſide of the Board alſo, as you were taught to find the Center on the backſide, and put your Board and *Mandrel* upon the *Pikes* of the *Puppets*, and ſcrew them hard up, as you have been taught before.

Sometimes *Turners* uſe this *Flat-Mandrel* without *Pegs*, and then they chalk the Flat ſide of it very well, and clap the backſide of the Board to it, which will (if the Board to be *Turned* be not too heavy, but be well ſcrewed up between the *Pikes*) keep the Board ſteddy from ſlipping from its ſet-poſition, till you work it.

If in going about of your Work you find it *Wabble*, that is, that one ſide of the Flat incline either to the Right or Left Hand, you muſt with ſoft Blows of an Hammer, or other Tool at hand, ſet it to right, and then again ſcrew it hard up: For ſo often as you thus ſtrike upon the Verge to ſet the Board true, you force the Steel point of the *Pike* more or leſs (according to the ſoftneſs of the Wood) towards that ſide of the Verge you ſtrike upon; and therefore you may perceive a reaſon for ſcrewing up the *Pike* ſo oft as you knock upon the outer Verge of the Board.

But we will now ſuppoſe the Board well pitcht and faſtned on the *Mandrel* and Center; therefore take the *Side-Reſt* deſcribed in § 1. *Numb.*

10. ¶ 7. and *Plate* 82. at the Figure e, and f g, and fit it ſo into the *Lathe*, as the upper edge of it may ſtand range, or parallel to the ſide of the Board you are to work upon, and ſo wedge it hard up.

Now you muſt come to uſe the *Hook*, deſcribed *Numb.* 12. § 5. and *Plate* 15. For this Tool is moſt commodious to ſerve you inſtead of the *Gouge*, when the Work ſtands athwart the *Pikes*; becauſe the end of the Blade of this Tool being on its Flat ſide turned into a Circular Figure, and that Circular Figure turned a little backwards, one of the Edges of this Circular Figure will conveniently (though the Tool be not held ſtraight before the Work) come at any part of the Flat of the Board, and ſo by the Circulation of the Board againſt the Edge of the *Hook*, cut off its irregular Extuberances.

In the uſing of this Tool, you muſt place the end of the *Handle* under your Arm-pit, and hold your Left Hand on the upper ſide of the Blade of the Tool cloſe to the *Reſt*, and your Right Hand cloſe beſides your Left Hand under the Tool, and with both your hands claſp the Tool hard, and preſs it ſteddy upon the *Reſt*, and at the ſame time hold it alſo ſteddy, and yet lightly bearing againſt the Work, that by the ſwift coming about of the Work it draw not the Edge of the thin and tender Blade of the *Hook* into it.

You muſt not hold the Blade of this Tool perpendicularly before the Work, *viz.* parallel to the *Pikes*, but aſlant, ſo as ſomewhat above the middle of the Convex of the *Hook* may touch againſt the Work. You may begin at the Verge, and ſo lay ſeveral Grooves cloſe by one another

till

till you come to the Center: But you must observe (as was said before in the *Cilinder*) that you lay all your *Grooves* of an equal depth into the Board: For if you lay one deeper than the rest, and an Hollow may not properly be in that place, you must again go over your work with your *Hook*, to work that dawk out: And then perhaps your Board may be made too thin for its intended purpose. But this Craft of the Hand must be acquired with some continued Use and Practice, which will better inform your Judgment what Errours you may be subject to commit, than many words (though significant) upon this Doctrine. And this I'm sure I found, when I first practised upon *Turning*.

Having thus with the *Hook* rough-plain'd the Board (for this *Hook* does in *Turning* the Office of a *Fore-plain* in *Joynery*) you must use the *Triangular Grooving Tool*, described in Turning § 5. *Plate* 15. and with one of its Edges smoothen down the ridges the *Hook* left on the Board.

But if your Work require any Molding near the Verge, or any other part of it, you must work that Molding as near as you can with the *Hook*, especially where Hollows are required; for that cuts faster and smoother than any other Tool, and most artificially forms an Hollow.

If a Flat be to be laid in the Board, you must first use the *Triangular Point Tool*, and with it strike so many Threds as the breadth of the Flat requires, and lay each Thred almost so deep into the Board as you intend the Flat shall be: And afterwards to smoothen it down, you must use the *Flat Grooving Tool*, or a *Flat Chissel*, and with either of them finish the Flat to its intended Depth and Breadth. And where a fine Thred, or Circle, is to be laid in the Board, you muſt uſe the *Triangular Point Tool.* And thus as you ſee occaſion, you muſt accommodate your ſelf with a Tool apt and proper for your purpoſe, *viz.* ſuch a Tool as will moſt conveniently come at, and from the intended Work.

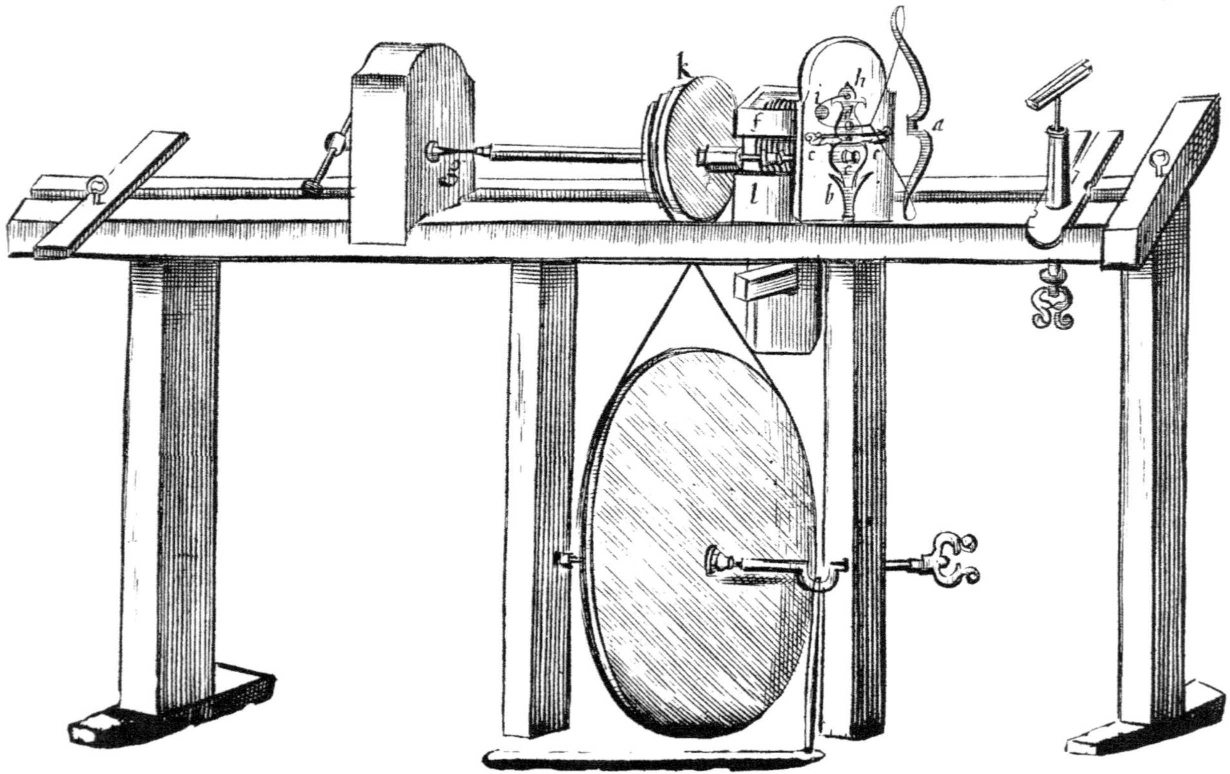
k
h
i
f
a
c
c
b
l
g

MECHANICK EXERCISES:

O R,

The Doctrine of *Handy-Works.*

Applied to the ART of TURNING.

§ XV. *Of Turning* Hard Wood, *and* Ivory.

IF the Wood be very hard, as *Ebony*, *Lignum Vitæ*; or if it be *Ivory*, *Bone*, or *Horn* they are to Turn; they neither uſe the ſame Tools they do for ſoft Wood; becauſe their edge is to tender: Nor do they uſe their other Tools as they do ſoft Wood. For the Tools made for Hard Wood are made with a ſtronger Point, Edge, &c. than they are for ſoft, as was ſaid in Turning § 5. And they uſe them differently, becauſe for Turning Soft Wood, they hold the Edge of the *Gouge* and *Flat Chiſſel*, at ſome conſiderable Diſtance from the *Reſt*, mounting the Edge at ſuch an Angle as will beſt cut off from the Work, as a great Chip as they can, or deſire. And as they Turn the Work ſmaller, they guide the *Chiſſel* to follow the Work: But for Hard Wood, they raiſe the *Reſt* near the Horizontal Plain of the *Axis* of the Work, ſetting it as cloſe as conveniently they can to their Work, and lay their Tool flat and ſteddy upon the *Reſt*; which being hard held in this poſition, does by the comming about of the Work, cut or tear off all the Extuberances the Tool touches in the ſweep of the Work. So that (as I ſaid before) as in *Turning* ſoft Wood the Tool does ſomewhat follow the Work; in *Turning* hard Wood the Work comes to the *Tool:* And therefore you may perceive a great reaſon they have to keep the *Tool* ſteddy: For ſhould it in one ſweep of the Work be thruſt nearer the *Axis* in any place, it would there take off more than it ſhould.

Having prepared the Work fit for the *Lathe*, either with Hewing, or as ſome Hard Woods and Ivory may require, with Raſping, they pitch it between the *Pikes*, as before has been ſhewn, or ſuch Work as it may be, as Boxes, and generally all Hollow Work, they fit into *Collers*, either by ſcrewing the *Mandrel* on an Iron *Axis*; or fitting it with ſome other of the *Mandrels* deſcribed in Turning § 6. as is proper for it: As ſometimes they fit the Work tight into an *Hollow Mandrel*, and the tight fitting in holds it whilſt it is working upon: And ſometimes, if the Work be very thin, they fix it on a *Flat Mandrel* with Cement; But they are always either to chuſe one of the *Mandrels* deſcribed already in Turning § 6. or elſe contrive (as they often do) ſome other *Mandrel* convenient to the opportunity that accidentally their Buſineſs may require. For the Work (whether it be pitcht on the *Pikes*, or fitted into *Hollow Mandrels*, or otherwiſe) muſt run very ſteddy and tight.

But having thus fitted it into the *Lathe*, they begin to work with the *Sharp-pointed Grooving Tool*, or elſe with the *Triangular Grooving Tool*, and

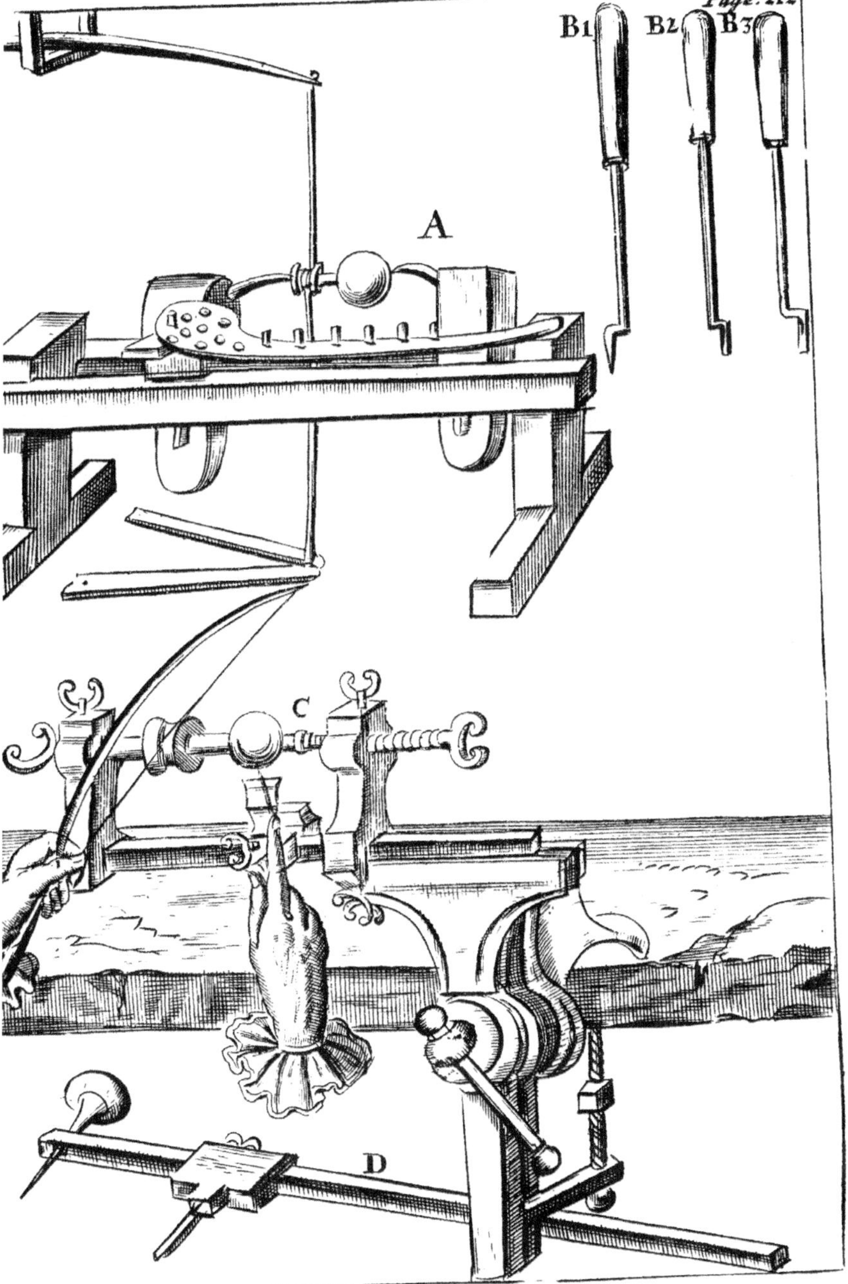
B1
B2
B3
A
C
D

and with the point of either of theſe *Tools* break the Grain of the Wood, by laying ſmall Grooves upon its Surface, till they have pretty well wrought away Extuberances, and brought the Work tollerably near an intended ſhape, by ſtreightning, hollowing, and leaving Riſings in their ſeveral proper places.

Afterwards with edg'd *Grooving Tools* of a proper Breadth, they cut down and ſmoothen away the Extuberances left by the *Sharp-pointed Grooving Tool*, or the *Triangular Grooving Tool*, and bring the Work into a perfect ſhape. Which done, they ſmoothen the work with the Edge of a piece of a Blade of a broken Knife, baſil'd away, by following the Work with it: That is, holding the baſil'd Edge of the Knife cloſe againſt the Work while it comes about: For then its ſharp Edge ſcrapes or ſhaves off the little roughneſs the groſſer *Tools* left upon the Work.

Laſtly, they hold either a piece of Seal-skin or *Dutch* Reeds (whoſe outer Skin or Filme ſomewhat finely cuts) pretty hard againſt the Work, and ſo make it ſmooth enough to poliſh.

Hard Wood they poliſh with *Bees-wax*, *viz.* by holding *Bees-wax* againſt it, till it have ſufficiently toucht it all over; and preſs it hard into it by holding hard the edge of a Flat piece of hard Wood made ſizable and ſuitable to the Work they work upon, as the Work is going about. Then they ſet a Gloſs on it with a very dry Woollen Rag, lightly ſmear'd with *Sallad Oyl.*

But *Ivory* they poliſh with Chalk and Water, and afterwards dry it with a Woollen Rag, and a light touch of *Sallad Oyl*; which at laſt they rub off again with a dry Woollen Rag, and ſo ſet a Gloſs on it.

If there be a Screw to be made upon the thin Edge of an *Ivory*, or *Hard Wood*, or *Braſs Box*, they uſe the *Screw-Mandrel*, and its *Socket*, deſcribed in Turning § 6. ¶ 4. and 5. as is ſhewn at the latter end of that Section.

§ XVI. *Of* Turning *long and ſlender Work of* Ivory.

SOme *Turners* to ſhew their Dexterity in *Turning*, and make others that know not the way how it is done admire their Skill, *Turn* long and ſlender Sprigs of *Ivory*, as ſmall as an Hay-ſtalk, and perhaps a Foot or more long: Which perform they cut a piece of *Ivory* to its intended length, but ſtrong enough to bear working till they bring it to as ſmall a *Cilinder* as they can; which being thus forwarded, they place a *Joint Coller* (as is deſcribed in Turning § 7.) made ſmall and fit for their purpoſe, juſt in the middle of their Work: Only that their Work may *Bear* at a ſmaller length, and conſequently be ſtronger for being thus ſupported while it is *Turned* yet ſmaller. Then they place other *Collers* between the *Pikes*, and the middle *Coller*, and *Turn* the whole *Cilinder* ſlender yet. And thus by placing *Collers* where ever they find the Work buckle, they (as aforeſaid) with *Sharp Tools*, tender touches, ſomewhat a looſe and fine *String*, weak Bow, and great care and diligence work the whole *Cilinder* down as ſmall as they liſt, either with Moldings, or other Work upon it, as beſt likes them.

The propereſt *Lathe* to *Turn* this ſlender Work in, is the *Turn-Bench* deſcribed § 18. *Plate* 16.

§ XVII. Of

§ XVII. *Of the* Brasiers Lathe *and* Turning Tools; *and their manner of using them.*

B*Rrasiers* that *Turn* Andirons, Pots, Kettles, *&c.* have their *Lathe* made different from the Common *Turners Lathe*, as you may see in *Plate* 16. at A, where the *Cheeks*, *Puppets* and *Rests*, &c. are much stronger and the *Pikes* stronger and longer than those the common *Turners* use. Their *Edge Tools* which they call *Hooks*, are also of a different shape, as the Figures of them described at B 1, B 2, B 3. in the said *Plate* shew, as being bent backwards and forwards towards the cutting end, somewhat like an z. And as the common *Turners* work with a round *String* made of Gut, as hath been described in Turning § 1. ¶ 14. The *Brasiers* work with a *Flat Leather Thong*, which wrapping close and tight about the *Rowler* of their *Mandrel*, commands it the easier and more forciably about. Their *Thong* runs between the *Cheeks* of the *Lathe*.

The whole *Lathe*, and its parts, are made so strong, because the Matter they *Turn* being Metal, is much heavier than Wood, and consequently with forciable coming about, would (if the *Lathe* were slight) make it tremble, and so spoil the Work; as hath been said before.

The reason why the *Hook* is so turned backwards, and again forwards, towards the end, is, that they may the better direct the Edge of it as much below the Horizontal Plain of the *Pikes* as they list, the better (in many cases) to come at the Work: For contrary to Soft Wood, Hard Wood and Ivory *Turners*, they always dip the end of their *Hook* below the *Rest*, that so the *Hook* resting very steddy upon the *Rest*, and also against one of the Iron *Pins* standing upright in

P 4 the

the *Reſt*, and held very ſteddy forwards to the Work, the ſtrong coming about of the Work againſt the ſtrong Edge of the *Hook*, ſcrapes off the extuberant Mettle lying in that Sweep.

I need no further deſcribe the *Lathe*, and other *Tools* that belong to *Braſiers* Turning; or more of the manner of uſing them; becauſe, by the whole proceeding Diſcourſe, theſe Arguments are largely and ſufficiently handled; eſpecially conſidering I have given you the Figures of them in *Plate* 16. as aforeſaid.

Only, their way of *Whetting* their *Tools* being different from the *Whetting* of other Turning *Tools*, I ſhall ſay ſomewhat to: For they *Whet* their *Hooks* upon a broad Flat Slate, holding the *Hook* almoſt perpendicular, that the *Baſil* of its Edge may comply with the Flat of the *Slate*; with claſping the upper end of the *Handle* in their left hand to ſo lean the heavier on it, and clutching the *Shank* of the *Blade* near the *Hook-end* in the right hand, to guide it: And thus with Spittle, or Water, rub forwards and backwards on the Slate, till they have ſharpned the Edge of the *Hook*. But if it be a round end *Hook* they whet, they chuſe a *Groove* in the *Slate* fit to comply with the round edge of the *Hook* (for they have different ſized *Grooves* in the Slate for that purpoſe) and ſo in it rub forwards and backwards as aforeſaid.

§ XVIII. *Of* Turning *Small Work of* Braſs, *or other* Mettle.

SMall Work in *Mettal* is *Turned* in an *Iron Lathe* called a *Turn-bench*. The Figure of it is deſcribed in *Plate* 16. at C. when they uſe it they ſcrew it in the *Chaps* of a *Vice*, and having fitted their Work upon a ſmall *Iron Axis*, with a *Drill-Barrel* fitted upon a ſquare Shank at the end of the

the *Axis* next the left hand, they with a *Drill-bow* and *Drill-ſtring* carry it about, as was ſhewn in Smithing *fol. 6.* with this difference, that when a Hole is drill'd in a piece of Mettal, they hold the *Drill-bow* in their Right Hand; but when they *Turn* Small Work, they hold the *Drill-bow* in their Left Hand, and with their Right Hand uſe the *Tool*, which is commonly a *Graver*, or ſometimes a *Sculpter*, fit to ſuch Moldings as are to be made on the *Mettal.*

They begin to work firſt with the ſharp point of a *Graver*, laying the Blade of it firm upon the *Reſt*, and directing the point to the Work, and lay Circles upon it cloſe to one another, till they have wrought it pretty true: Then with one of the broad Edges of the *Graver* they ſmoothen down what the Point left, and afterwards with *Sculpters*, *Round* or *Flat*, or great or ſmall, they work their intended Moldings.

The Circumſtances and Conſiderations in the choice of a *Drill-bow* and *Drill-ſtring* for *Turning*, are the ſame with what you find in Smithing *fol.* 6, 7. for Drilling.

§ XIX. *Of laying* Moldings *either upon* Mettal, *or* Wood, *without fitting the Work in a* Lathe.

I Had, ſoon after the Fire of *London*, occaſion to lay Moldings upon the Verges of ſeveral round and weighty flat pieces of *Braſs*: And being at that time, by reaſon of the ſaid Fire, unaccommodated of a *Lathe* of my own, I intended to put them out to be *Turned*: But then *Turners* were all full of Employment, which made them ſo unreaſonable in their Prizes, that I was forc'd to contrive this following way to lay Moldings on their Verges.

I provided a ſtrong Iron *Bar* for the *Beam* of a *Sweep*: (For the whole *Tool* marked in *Plate* 16,

is

is by Mathematical *Inſtrument-makers* called a *Sweep.*) To this *Tool* is filed a *Tooth* of Steel with ſuch *Roundings* and *Hollows* in the bottom of it, as I intended to have *Hollows* and *Roundings* upon my Work: For an Hollow on the *Tooth*, makes a *Round* upon the Work; and a *Round* upon the *Tooth*, makes an *Hollow* on the Work; even as they do in the *Molding-plains Joyners* uſe. Then I placed the *Center-point* of the *Sweep* in a Center-hole made in a ſquare *Stud* of *Mettal*, and fixed in the *Center* of the Plain of the Work; and removed the *Socket* that rides on the *Beam* of the *Sweep*, till the *Tooth* ſtood juſt upon its intended place on the Verge of the Work, and there ſcrew'd the *Socket* faſt to the *Beam.*

To work it out, I employ'd a Labourer, directing him in his Left Hand to hold the Head of the *Center-pin*, and with his Right Hand to draw about the *Beam* and *Tooth*, which (according to the ſtrength) he us'd, cut and tore away great Flakes of the *Mettal*, till it receiv'd the whole and perfect Form the *Tooth* would make; which was as compleat a Molding as any Skillful *Turner* could have laid upon it.

Having ſuch good Succeſs upon *Braſs*, I improv'd the invention ſo, as to make it ſerve for Wood alſo. And make a *Plain-Stock* with my intended Molding on the *Sole* of it, and fitted an *Iron* to that *Stock* with the ſame Molding the *Sole* had.

Through the ſides of this *Stock* I fitted an Iron *Beam*, to do the Office of the *Beam* I uſed for the *Sweep*, viz. to keep the Plain always at what poſition I liſted from the Center (for thus the Iron in the Plain wrought about the Center, even as the Tooth in the *Sweep* (before rehearſed) and to that purpoſe I made a round Hole of about half

half an Inch Diameter near the end of the Iron: Then in the Center of the Work I fixed a round Iron *Pin*, exactly to fit the ſaid round Hole, putting the round Hole over the *Pin*, and fitting the *Iron* into the *Stock* commodious to work with. I uſed this Plain with both Hands, even as *Joyners* do other *Plains*: For the *Iron Pin* in the Hole of the *Beam* kept it to its due diſtance from the Center; ſo that neither hand was ingaged to guide it.

But note, The *Stock* of this *Plain* was not ſtraight (as the Stocks of other Plains are) but by Hand cut Circular pretty near the ſize of the Diameter of the intended Molding: And yet was made to ſlide upon the *Beam*, farther from or nearer to the Center, as different Diameters of Verges might require.

§ XX. *To Turn ſeveral* Globes *or* Balls *of* Ivory *within one another, with a* Solid Ball *in the middle.*

YOu muſt firſt Turn your *Ivory Ball* or *Globe* truly round, of your intended Diameter: Then deſcribe a Circle exactly through the middle, or Equinoctial of the *Globe*: Divide that Circle into four equal parts, and pitch one point of a pair of Compaſſes in one of thoſe Diviſions, and extend the other point to either of the next Diviſions, and deſcribe with it a Circle round about the *Globe*. Then remove the ſtanding point of the Compaſſes to either of the next Diviſions in the Equinoctial, and in like manner deſcribe another Circle round about the *Globe*.

But Note, That the moving point of your Compaſſes muſt be ſomewhat bended inwards; for elſe its point will not deſcribe a Circle on the greateſt Extuberances of the *Globe*, but will ſlide off it.

Thus

Thus ſhall the Ball or Globe be divided into eight Spherical Quadrants: Deſcribe as great a Circle as you can in each of theſe Quadrants, and each two Centers of every two oppoſite Circles ſhall have an imaginary *Axix* paſs between them: And if the *Globe* be ſucceſſively pitcht upon all the reſt of the Centers, ſo as the imagined *Axis* paſſing between it and its oppoſite Center, lye in a ſtraight line with the *Pike* and the Center of the *Coller* it is *Turned* in, the working out of all the *Hollows* on the *Ball* will be but common *Turners* Work, as you will find hereafter. This is in brief the Theory: But to the Practice.

You muſt uſe an *Hollow-Mandrel*, made fit ſtifly to receive the convexity of the *Globe* in its concavity, ſo as it may ſtick firmly in the *Mandrel*, in its poſition: And you muſt take care that in pitching the *Globe* into the *Mandrel*, that the imaginary *Axis* of the *Globe* (which is the Line paſſing between the two Centers of the two oppoſite Circles as aforeſaid) lye in a ſtraight Line with the *Axis* of the *Mandrel*; which you may know by examining whether the Circle deſcribed with your *Compaſſes* (as aforeſaid) on the Center (aforeſaid) wabble not in a whole Revolution of the *Globe*, from the point of a Tool applied ſteddy to it.

Having thus pitcht the *Globe* true, and fixt it faſt into the *Mandrel*, you muſt begin to work with the *Triangular Grooving Point* (deſcribed in Turning § 5. and *Plate* 15.) placing the point of it pretty near the Center of the Circle, and work into the *Ball* with the *Grooving Point*, and ſo by degrees make a Hollow in the *Ball* ſo deep, and ſo wide, as you think convenient, I mean ſo deep from the Superficies of the *Globe* towards the Center of the *Globe*, and ſo wide from the Center of the Circle deſcribed on the Superficies of the *Globe*

Globe towards that Circle, as it may have a convenient Subſtance between this Hole, and the next intended to be *Turned.*

Thus muſt every one of the eight Circles deſcribed on the *Globe*, be ſucceſſively by the ſame Rule, and after the ſame manner be pitcht outwards, and fixt into the *Mandrel*, and then Hollowed out as the firſt was. Where Note, That every Hollow is to be *Turned* to the ſame depth and width exactly as the firſt was: Which to do, you muſt uſe a *Gage* made of a thin Plate of Iron or Braſs, as is deſcribed in *Plate* 17. *Fig.* D. whoſe two ſides from *a* the Bottom of the *Gage*, to *b* the *Shoulder* are the depth of the *Hollow* from the Superficies of the *Globe* towards the Center: *b b*. is the width of the *Hollow* at the Superficies of the *Globe*; and *a a* is the bottom width of the *Hollow*; and the concave Arch between *a a* is an Arch that the Convexity of the little ſolid *Ball* to be *Turned* within all the *Spheres* muſt comply with. So that when each *Hollow* is *Turned*, the *Gage* muſt be put into it to try how the ſides of the *Hollow* complies with the ſides of the *Gage*, and alſo how the Arch in the bottom of the *Gage*, complies with the ſurface of the Solid *Ball* in the middle.

Having thus *Turned* all the *Hallows* in the *Globe*, you muſt provide ſeveral thin and narrow Arching *Grooving Tools*, whoſe convex and concave Arches comply both with the Convexity and Concavity of each *Globe*, or *Sphere*, to be *Turned* within the outermoſt: So that begining at the bottom of the Hollow, you Turn juſt half way of the Solid *Ball* looſe from the Sphere it is contained in, *viz.* as far as the Equinoctial of the *Globe*; and in thus Turning it, you muſt take great care, that the Solid Ball on its Convexity and the Concavity of the Sphere it is contained in, be both at the ſame time Turned exactly Spherical. Thus

Thus one half of the Solid *Ball* being *Turned* looſe, you may in like manner *Turn* the next Sphere it is included in half looſe alſo: And ſo ſucceſſively as many Spheres as you liſt.

Having thus *Turned* one half of all the *Spheres* looſe, you muſt take the whole *Globe* out of the *Hollow-Mandrel*, and pitcht and fix the *Globe* again into the *Mandrel*, ſo as the imagined *Axis* of the *Hollow* oppoſite to the laſt looſned *Hollow* lye in a ſtraight line (as before was taught) with the *Pike* and *Center* of the *Coller* the *Mandrel* runs in, and then *Turn* the other half of the Solid *Ball* and *Spheres* alſo looſe, as the firſt half was *Turned*.

§ XXI. *To* Turn *a* Globe *with ſeveral looſe* Spheres *in it, and a* Solid Cube, *or* Dy, *in the middle of it.*

THis is *Turned* after the ſame manner the former *Ball* was *Turned*; only inſtead of dividing the Equinoctial of that *Globe* into four equal parts, the Equinoctial of this muſt be divided but into three equal parts, and their Semi-Circle draw through the diviſions into either Pole of the *Globe*: So ſhall the *Globe* be divided into ſix equal parts, or Segments; in each of which parts muſt be deſcribed a Circle, as was deſcribed before in the *Globes* of eight equal parts; and in theſe ſix Circles muſt be made ſix Hollows, as before there was eight: But inſtead of working the Bottom of each hollow Spherical, now the Bottom muſt be wrought Flat: So ſhall the *Cube* when theſe ſix Hollows are thus made, be formed: And the Hollows being exactly of the ſame depth, and flat in the Bottom, the *Cube* or *Dy* will looſen, and each of the ſix Flats in the Bottom will become the ſix ſides or Faces of the *Cube*;

The

The manner of loosning all the other inward *Spheres*, is as the Former: Only, that was loosned with twice pitching the *Ball* in the *Mandrel*, because the Centers of the *Hollows* lay opposite to one another; but to loosen this *Ball* will require three Pitchings into the *Mandrel*; because the Centers lye not opposite to one another.

§ XXII. *To* Turn *a* Cube, *or* Dy, *in an Hollow* Globe, *that shall have but one Hole on the outside to work at.*

THe Outside of this *Globe* must be Turned Round, *viz.* Spherical, as the former, and fixed in an Hollow *Socket* (as before hath been taught.) Then must an Hole be Turned in the *Globe* so deep and so wide as you please, as in the former *Globes*, and the Bottom of that Hole Turned flat, for one side, or Face of the *Cube*, or *Dy*: Then with a Semi-circular Tool loosen the whole Core, or middle of the Ball, and pitch the Core with the point opposite to the Center of the already flatted face of the *Dy*, outwards against the Hole in the *Globe*, and so fasten it in this position, by powring in some melted hard Wax, or other Cement; and then with a flat Tool Turn the foreside, (*viz.* the side opposite to the first side) flat also: Which done, loosen it out of the Wax, and successively pitch the other sides to be Turned flat carefully against the Hole, so as all the sides have right Angles to each other, and fastning them with Wax, or Cement (as before) Turn them by the same Rule flat also.

Now

Now to make this Thing more admirable to the ignorant Spectator, you may make the *Dy* as big as you can, and the Hole you Turn it at as little as you can; that it may the more puzzle the Wit of the Enquirer to find how so great a *Dy* should have Entrance at a small Hole, unless the hollow Ball were turned in two Halves, *&c.*

MECHANICK EXERCISES:

OR,

The Doctrine of *Handy-Works*.

Applied to the ART of TURNING.

§ XXIII. *Of Turning* Oval Work.

THIS Work may be perform'd in the Common *Lathe* that goes either with the *Treddle-Wheel*, or the great Wheel; because the Work must run always one way, if the *Puppet* be made to it with the Machination described in *Plate* 17. and an Iron *Axis* be made to carry the Work about, and to its end be fitted and fastned a *Brass Coller*, with a Female Screw in it, to screw on the *Mandrel* that the Work you intend to Turn is fixt upon.

To the Foreside of this *Puppet* is fastned at *b*, as on a Center-pin, a strong Iron *Coller* marked *b b*, and this Coller is called the *Moving Coller*; because it moves between the Iron *Shackle c c*, and the Foreside of the *Puppet*. Into this *Moving Coller* is fitted the *Hollow Axis* marked *c*, so as to turn round in it as if it were in any of the other *Collors* formerly described; but the *Moving Coller* moving between the *Shackles*, and the Foreside of the *Puppet*, carries the *Hollow Axis* with it athwart the *Puppet*, even so far as is the width of the *Hollow* between the *Shackle*, and the Foreſide of the *Puppet*. And thus by the moving of the *Hollow Axis* backwards and forwards the Work ſcrewed in it, having an *Edg'd*, or a *Pointed-Tool* applied to it, receives that *Oval* Form which is made upon the *Guide*.

But to make it move thus to and from you, there are required ſeveral Machinal Helps: For there is a ſtrong *Steel Bow* as at *a*, faſtned about its middle part to the further ſide of the *Puppet*, which ſtands about an Inch forwarder than the Foreſide of the *Puppet* with its hollow ſide to the Workman. And to the ends of this *Steel Bow* is faſtned a ſtrong *String* of Gut, and to the middle of that *String* in a Noos is faſtned another ſtrong *Gut-ſtring*, with a Noos at its end. This laſt mentioned *String* is made exactly of that length, that when the neareſt ſide of the *Guide*, viz. its leaſt Diameter is ſet into the *Groove* of the *Guide-pulley*, and the *Bow* is ſtrained, and this *String* laid in the *Groove* of the *String-pulley*, the Noos at the end of it may be put over the Iron *Button* fixed in the top of the *Moving-Coller*. For then as the *Treddle-Wheel* carries the *Axis* about, the *Guide* being firmly faſtned upon the *Axis*, comes alſo about; and having the *Groove* of the *Guide-pulley* ſet againſt the outer edge of the *Guide*, as the great Diameter of the *Guide* is turned againſt the *Guide-pulley*, the *Moving-Coller* being drawn by the ſtrength of the *Bow*, draws the *Hollow Axis* along with it, as alſo the Work ſcrewed in the *Hollow Axis*: And thus as the ſmall Diameter of the *Guide* comes to the *Guide-pulley*, the ſmall Diameter of the Work is Formed; and as the great Diameter of the *Guide* comes to the *Guide-pulley*, the great Diameter of the Work is formed.

This is the ſum of *Oval Turning*.

But

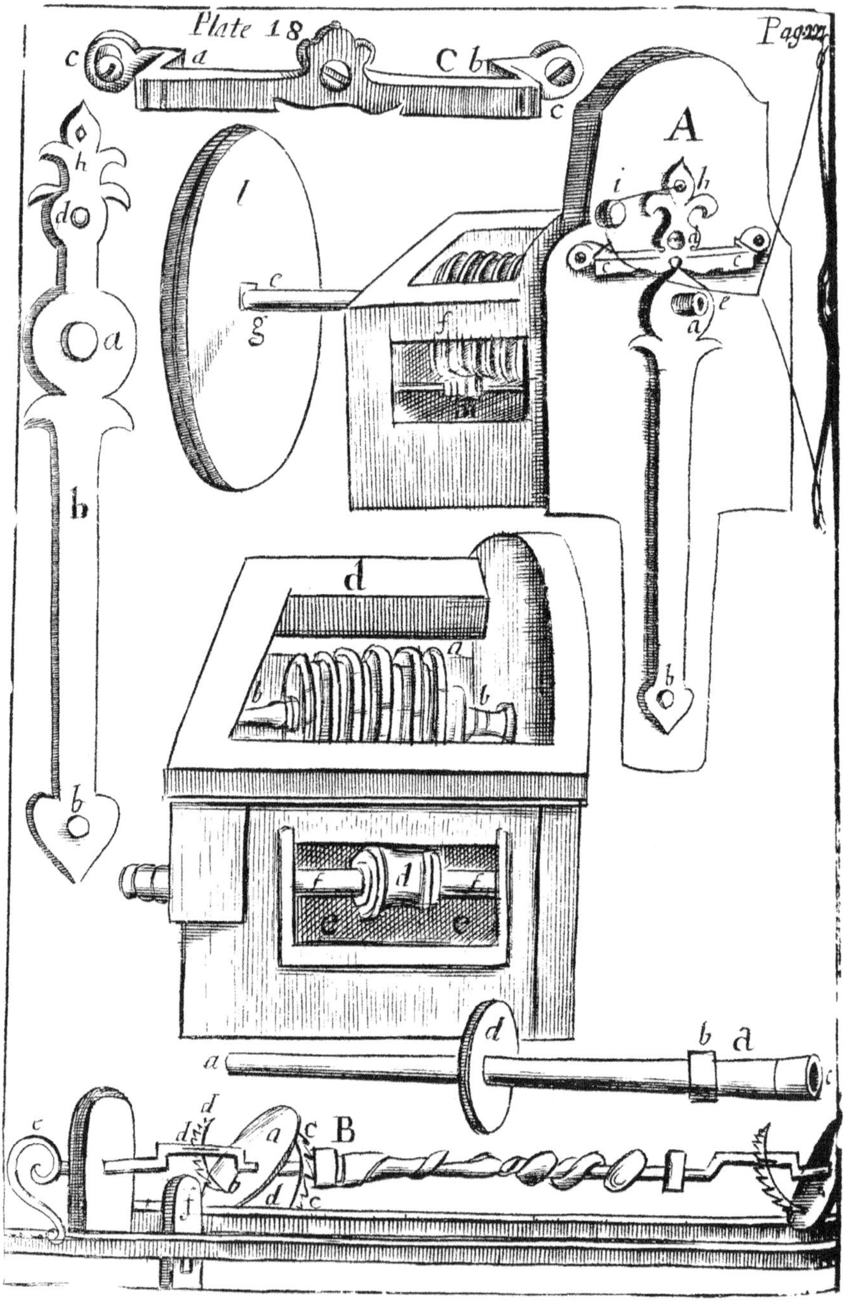
Plate 18
Pag 227
A
B
C

But that the whole Machine may be yet better underſtood, I ſhall more particularly give you the names of all its parts, together with a Deſcription upon its moſt material parts, where the *Fore-puppet* is more largely delineated in *Plate* 18. at A, where alſo ſome of the Members moſt difficult to be deſcribed, are drawn more at large by themſelves.

a The *Bow*.
b The *Moving Coller*.
c c The *Socket* in which the *Coller* is moved.
d The *Stop-ſcrew*, to take out when the *Hollow Axis* moves in the *Moving-Coller*.
e The *Hollow Axis*.
f The *Head*, in which is contained the ſeveral *Guides*.
g The *Center Head*.
h The *Button*.
i The *String-pulley*.
k The *Wheel-pulley*.
l The *Guide-pulley*.

¶ 1. *Of the* Hollow Axis, *and its* Shank, *marked* a *in* Plate 18.

THE *Shank* is a Bar of Iron about an Inch thick, and two Foot long, having in its further end a Center-hole to pitch upon the *Pike* in the further *Puppet*; but its hither end is made ſquare to fit tight into a ſquare *Socket*, in the Braſs *Hollow Axis*: And when it is thus fitted into the hither end of the Braſs, it is Turned true Cilindrically round, ſo as to fit into the round Hole in the *Moving Coller*. The Diameter of the Round is about two Inches, and the length about two Inches ſtraight; but then a Shoulder is Turned to the Braſs Cilinder, to ſtop it from ſlipping thro' the *Moving Center*. In the Fore-end of this *Hollow Axis* (*viz.* in the Braſs Cilinder) is Turned a wide Hole about an Inch and a quarter Diameter, and an Inch deep: And in this wide Hole is Turned a Female Screw with a courſe Thred, to receive a Male Screw made behind the *Mandrel* that the Work is fixed upon.

About the middle of this Iron *Shank* is placed a *Pulley* made of Wainſcot Board, about eight Inches Diameter, and an Inch thick, with a *Groove* on its outer edge about half an Inch wide, and half an Inch deep, for the *String* of the *Treddle Wheel* that carries the *Axis* about to run in: And between this *Pulley* you may (if you will) have ſeveral lengths of ſuch *Male-ſcrews* as was deſcribed in Turning § 6. ¶ 4. and *Plate* 15. to make Screws with, if you pleaſe.

See the Figure *a d c b*, disjunct from the reſt of the Work.

a The hinder end.

d The Pulley of the *Axis*, or *Wheel-pulley*.

c The Hollow, or Hole in the Fore-end of the *Hollow Axis*.

b The *Shoulder* of the *Hollow Axis*.

¶ 2. *Of the* Moving Coller marked b, in *Plate* 18.

THis whole Member is called the *Moving Coller*, tho' the *Coller* ſtrictly is only the round Hole at *a*, into which the *Hollow Axis* is fitted. It is made of Iron to reach from its top at *b* (the *Button*) down to the bottom of the *Cheeks* of the *Lathe*, as at *b*; upon which Pin (as on a Center) the whole *Moving Coller* moves backwards and forwards; its extream Breadth is about three Inches, and its thickneſs above a quarter of an Inch. Its Neck at *c* is claſped, but not fixed down to the Foreſide of the *Puppet*; for this *Neck* is only gaged in the *Shackle* marcked *c*, ſo as the *Neck*, (and conſequently the whole *Moving Coller*)

ler) may ſlide from end to end of the *Shackle* forwards and backwards. *d* A ſmall *Female Screw*, into which through a Hole in the *Shackle* is fitted a *Male Screw* to hold the *Moving Coller* and the *Shackle* together, that the *Moving Coller* may not move when only round Work is Turned in the *Coller*.

¶ 3. *Of the Foreſide of the* Puppet, *and the* Shackle *marked* c.

UNder this *Shackle* (viz. between it and the Foreſide of the *Puppet*) moves the *Neck* of the *Sliding-Coller* from *a* to *b*, when the ends at *c c* are fixed down to the Foreſide of the *Puppet* with two Iron Screws.

¶ 4. *Of the* Hollow *in the* Puppet *marked* d.

IN the middle of the *Puppet* is hollowed out a Hole about three Inches between the Fore and Back-ſide of the *Puppet*, and four Inches athwart the *Cheeks* in the *Puppet*, and four Inches deep: So that about an Inch of Subſtance remains on each of the four upright ſides. But the Top is quite open, (as at *a*) through the middle of this ſquare *Hole* runs the Iron *Axis* marked *b b*, on which is fixed the ſeveral *Guides* that are to be uſed in this ſort of Working.

It is open at the Top, that Light may be let in to ſet the *Guide-pulley* to which *Guide* you pleaſe, and it is open on the hither ſide as at *e e*, about an Inch and an half above and below the *Axis*, that the *Guide-pulley* may be ſlid on its *Axis* to any of the *Guides*.

The *Guide-pulley* marked *d*, is a braſs Pulley of about an Inch Diameter, and a little above a quarter of an Inch thick, having a *Groove* in the Edge of it to receive the Edge of the *Guide*. It hath in its middle a round Hole about half an

Inch Diameter, which round Hole ſlips over a round Iron *Pin* of the ſame Diameter, marked *f f*, ſo as it may ſlide from one end of the ſaid Iron *Pin* to the other, according as the *Guides* may be fixed towards either end.

When it is uſed, the Groove in the Edge of this *Guide-pulley* is ſet againſt the Edge of the *Guide*, and being fitted tight on the round Iron *Pin* aforeſaid, and the two ends of the Iron Pin faſt fixed into the Wood of the *Puppet*, the *Guide-pulley* may indeed move round on the Iron *Pin*; but the ſtrength of the Iron *Pin*, and *Guide-pulley* will reſiſt the extuberick parts of the Edge of the *Guide*; and ſo with the aſſiſtance of the ſtrength of the *Steel Bow* force the *Guide* and *Hollow Axis* to move backwards; and then an Edge-Tool held to the Work in the *Mandrel* ſcrewed in the *Hollow Axis*, will deſcribe the ſame Figure on the Work, as is on the out Edge of the *Guide*.

Note, that when you are at Work, you muſt keep the Hole in the middle of the *Guide-pulley* well oyl'd, as alſo the round Iron *Pin* it ſlides and turns round upon; becauſe this *Guide-pulley* ought to run round: For then the *Axis* will have and eaſier and ſwifter motion, tho' it may indeed perform the Work if it run not round upon the Iron Pin.

§ XXIV. *Of* Roſe-work, *&c.*

R*Oſe-Work* Turning, or Works of any other Figure, are performed by the ſame Rule, and after the ſame manner as *Oval Work* is made; only by changing the *Guides*, and uſing one whoſe outer Edge is made with the Figure, or ſeveral Figures you intend to have on your Work.

§ XXV.

§ XXV. *Of Turning* Swash-Work.

TO the Turning of *Swash-work* you must have two such *Puppets*, as the *Fore-puppet* described in § 22. And also a round *Swash-board*, about ten Inches Diameter, and an Inch and an half thick, as is *a* in Fig. B. *Plate* 18. Upon both the flat sides of this *Swash-board*, in a diametrical Line, is fastned upright an Arch of a Quadrant made of a Steel Plate, about half a quarter of an Inch thick, and an Inch and a quarter broad, as at *b b*, *c c*. The Convex edges of these Quadrants are cut into Notches, like the Teeth of an Hand-saw; that according as you may have occasion to set the *Swash-board* more or less a-slope, you may be accommodated with a Notch or Tooth to set it at. This *Swash-board* hath an Hole made about its Center, to slip over the *Iron Axis*, and being thus slipt over the *Iron Axis*, you set it to that Slope you intend the *Swash* on your Work shall have. And to fix it fast in this position, you must put the Blades of the Quadrants into two *Slits*, made in the *Iron Axis* as at *d d*, and fit the two opposite Teeth against the two outer Shoulders of the *Slits*.

You must moreover make two strong Steel *Springs* as at *c c*, to reach from the bottom of the outer sides of the *Puppets*, being strong nailed, or rather screwed down there, which must reach up so high as the *Axis*. And in the inner sides of these *Springs* must be made two Center holes for the points of the *Axis* to be fitted in: For the *Oval-Guide* being fitted to one end of the *Axis*, and a Low-Puppet, as at *f*, wedged close to one side of the *Swash-board*, when the *Swash-board* stands in its greatest declirity; then in a Revolution of the *Axis*, as the farther part of the

the circumference of the *Swash-board* comes to the *Low-Puppet*, one *Spring* will be forced backwards, and the other will spring forwards; and an Edg'd-Tool held against the Work fixed on the *Axis*, will make on the Work the Form of a *Swash*, &c.

These *Oval-Engines*, *Swash-Engines*, and all other *Engines*, are excellently well made by Mr. *Thomas Oldfield*, at the sign of the *Flower-de-luce*, near the *Savoy* in the *Strand*, *London*.

An Explanation of Terms used in these Exercises of Turning, *Alphabetically digested.*

A.

AXis. The imagined ſtraight Line that paſſes through the two Center-points that Turned Work is Turned upon. Thus the imagined Line that paſſes between the two Pikes through the Work in the Lathe is the Axis.

B.

BOw. The Bow that common Turners uſe is deſcribed § 1. ¶ 11. And the Bow that Oval Turners uſe is deſcribed § 23. and Plate 17, 18. at *a*.

Button. The Button is deſcribed § 23. and Plate 17. at *b*.

C.

C*Allippers*. Compaſſes with bowed ſhanks to meaſure the Diameter of any round Body. See § 11. and Plate 14. at O.

Center-head, See § 23. and Plate 17. at *g*.

Cheeks. See § 1. ¶ 2. and Plate 12. *b b*.

Chock. See § 6. ¶ 5. and Plate 13. at F. 5. *a*.

Cleaving-knife. See § 9. and Plate 13. at M.

Crank. The end of an Iron Axis turned Square down, and again turned Square to the firſt turning down, ſo that on the laſt turning down a Leather Thong is ſlipt, to Tread the Treddle-wheel about.

Coller. See § 7. and Plate 13. at G H I.

Crook. See *Crank*.

Croſs-Treddle. See § 1. ¶ 8. and Plate 12. at *k*.

Drill-

D.

DRill-Barrel. See Smithing Fol. 6. Plate 1. and Fig. 8. at C.

Drill-Bench. See § 12. Plate 14. at *a a a a.*

Drill-Bow. See Smithing Fol. 6, 7.

F

FEmale Screw. The Screw made in the round Hole of a Nut.

Flat-Chissel. See § 3. and Plate 15. at C C.

Flat-Mandrel. See § 6. and Plate 13. at F 1.

G

GOuge. See § 2. ¶ 1. and Plate 15. at B. B.

Great Wheel. See § 1. ¶ 12. and Plate 14. at a.

Grooving Hooks. See § 5. and Plate 15. at E.

Grooving Tools. See *Grooving Hooks.*

Guide. See § 23. ¶ 4. and Plate 18.

Guide-Pulley. See § 23. ¶ 4. and *Plate* 18. at *d.*

H.

HEad. See § 23. and Plate 17.

Hook. See § 17. and Plate 16. at B. 1. B 2. B 3.

Hollow Axis. See § 17. and Plate 17. at *e.*

Hollow Mandrels. See § 6. ¶ 3. and Plate 13. at F 3.

I.

JOynt Collar. See § 7. and *Plate* 13. at G.

L.

LAthe. See § 1. and Plate 12.

Legs. See § 1. and Plate 12. at *a a a a.*

Man-

M.

M*Andrel.* See § 6. ¶. 1. and Plate 13. at F 1. F 2. F 3. F 4.

Mawl. See § 8. and Plate 13. at K.

Male-Screw. The Screw made upon a Shank, or Pin.

Moving-Collar. See § 23. ¶ 2. and Plate 18. at *b.*

N.

N*Ut.* A piece of Iron that a Female Screw is made in.

P.

P*Ike.* See § 1. ¶ 5. and Plate 12.

Pin Mandrel See § 6. ¶ 2. and Plate 13. at F 2.

Pole. See § 1. ¶ 9. and Plate 12 at *l.*

Puppet. See § 1. ¶ 3. and Plate 12. at *c e.*

R.

R*Eſt.* See § 1. ¶ 6. and Plate 12. at *e.*

Rowler. See § 6. and Plate 13. F 1. at *b.*

S.

S*Crew-Mandrel.* See § 6. ¶ 4. and Plate 13. at F 4.

Seat. See § 1. ¶ 15.

Shackles. See § 23. ¶ 2. and Plate 18. V at *c c.*

Side-Reſt. See § 1. ¶ 7. and Plate 13. at *e.*

Socket. See *Chock.*

Steel-bow. See § 23. and Plate 18. at *a.*

Stop-Screw. See § 23. and Plate 17. at *d.*

String. See § 1. and Plate 12. at *m.*

String-Pulley. See § 23. and Plate 17. at *i.*

Swaſh. A *Swaſh* is a Figure whoſe Circumference is not Round but Oval; and whoſe Moldings lye

lye not at Right Angles, but Oblique to the *Axis* of the Work. See § 25. and Plate 18. at Fig. B.

Swash-Board. See § 25. and Plate 18. at *a* in Fig. B.

Sweep. See § 19. and Plate 16. at D.

T.

T*Read.* See § 13. Fol. 209.

Treddle. See § 1. and Plate 12. at *i.*

Treddle Wheel. See § 1. ¶ 13.

Turn-Bench. See § 18. and Plate 16. at C.

W.

W*Abble.* When a piece of Work is not pitcht true upon its Centers, it will in a Revolution incline more on one ſide of its Circumference than on its oppoſite ſide. See § 23. and Plate 17. at *k.*

There are ſeveral other Terms uſed in theſe *Exerciſes* of *Turning*, not explain'd here: But becauſe they are uſed in ſome of the former *Exerciſes*, and there explain'd, I ſhall referr you to them.

Page. 23

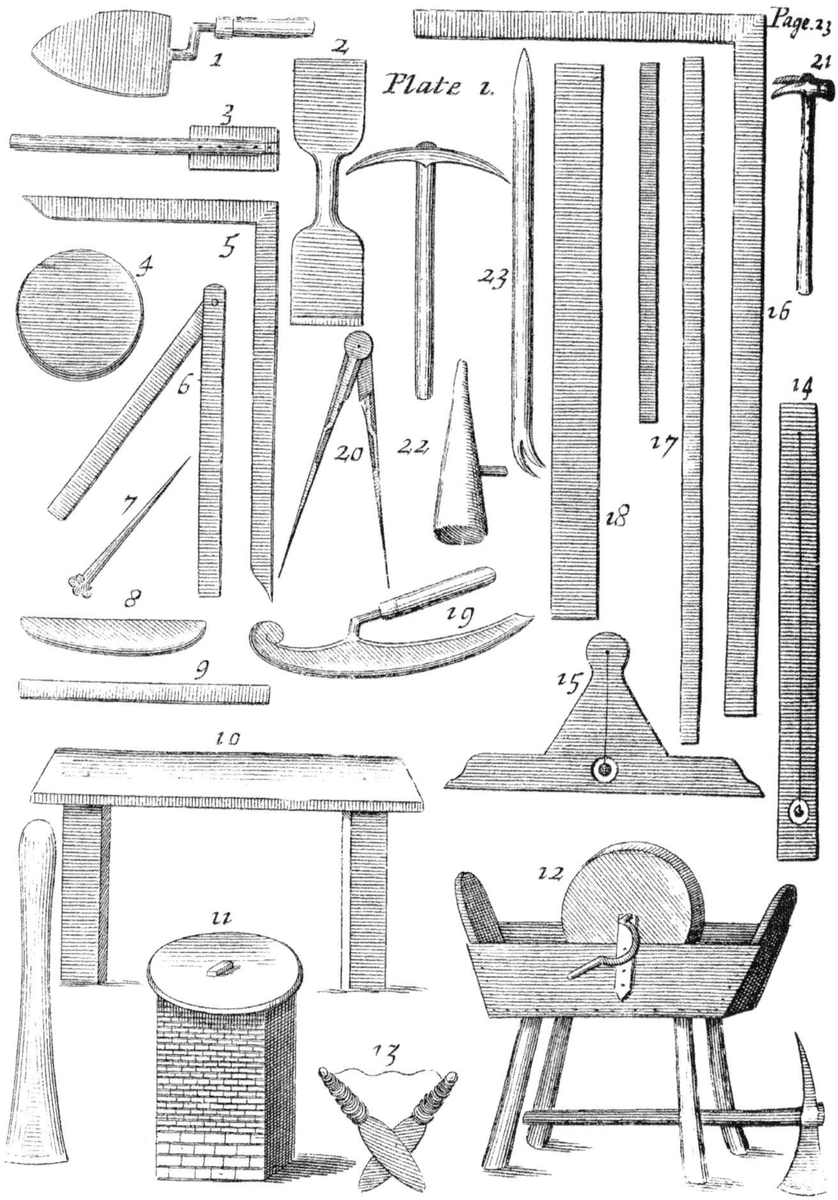

Plate 1.

Plate 2. Page. 237

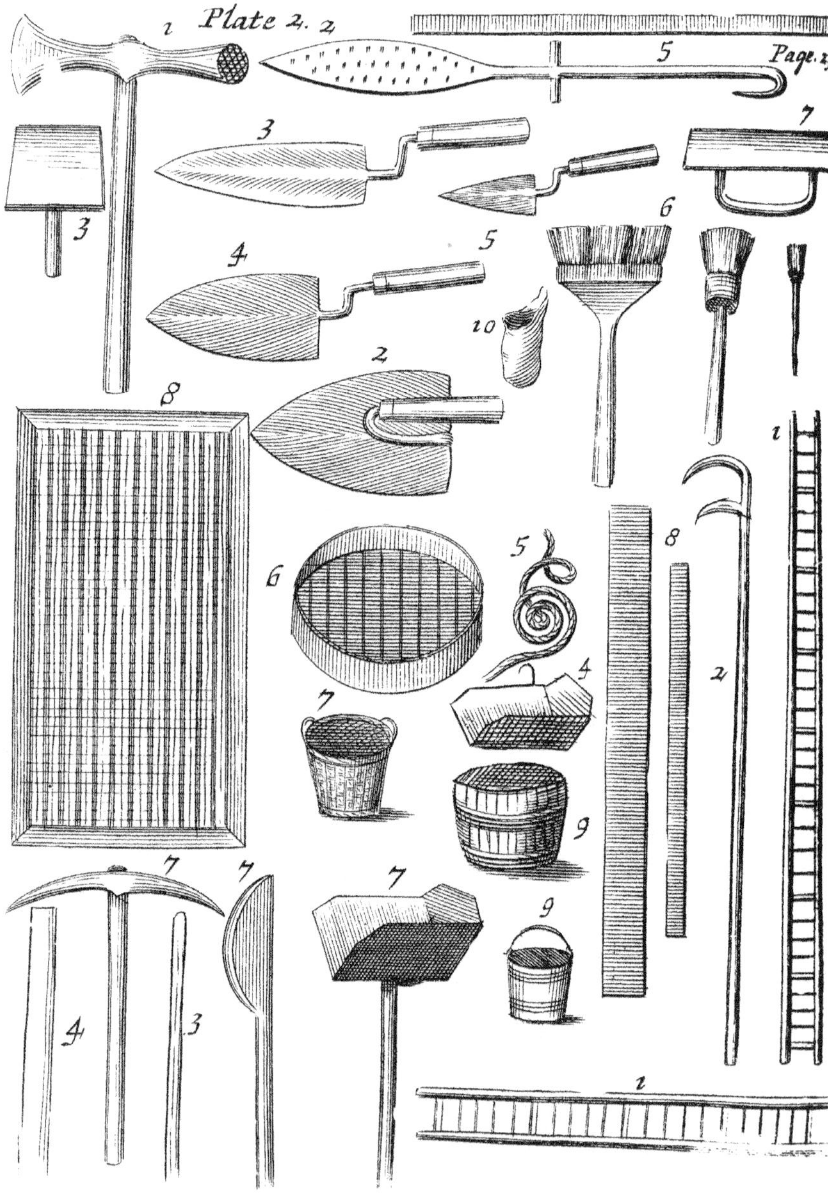

MECHANICK EXERCISES:

O R,

The Doctrine of *Handy-Works.*

Applied to the ART of *Bricklayers Work.*

Definition.

B*Ricklayers-Work is an Art Manual, which Joins ſeveral Bodies ſo together, that they adhere like one entire Body.*

Whether the *White Maſon*, which is the Hewer of Stone, or the *Red Maſon*, which is the Hewer of Brick, be the moſt Ancient, I know not: but in Holy Writ, we read of making of Bricks, before we read of Digging or Hewing of Stones; therefore we may ſuppoſe the *Red Maſon* (or *Bricklayer*) to be the moſt Ancient.

The method that I ſhall uſe in Treating of this Art ſhall be this.

Firſt, I will ſhew what Materials they uſe, and their Compoſition.

Secondly, I will treat of their Tools, and deſcribe their Names and Uſes.

Thirdly, I will declare their Method of Working, both in *Bricks*, *Tiles*, &c.

And first of Materials.

WHich are comprised under six Heads, *viz.* 1. *Bricks*, 2. *Tiles*, 3. *Morter*, 4. *Laths*, 5. *Nailes*, 6. *Tile-pins.*

Of Bricks.

THey are made of Earth, of which the white-ish Chalky sort of Earth, and the Redish are the best.

At *Lunenburg* in *Saxony*, they make them of a fat Earth full of *Allom.* Also there are good *Bricks* made at *Pitane* in *Asia*, of a Pumice sort of Earth, which being dryed, will swim in Water and not Sink.

Likewise the Antients made them of Earth which was Sandy.

But here in *England* they are made for the most part of a yellowish coloured fat Earth somewhat Redish.

And they are made of several sorts and sizes.

IN *Holland* they make small ones, being about six Inches long, three Inches broad, and one Inch in thickness.

Which sort of Bricks, is commonly used here in *England*, to pave Yards or Stables withal; and they make a good Pavement, and are very Durable, and being laid edge-ways looks handsomly, especially if laid Herring-bone fashion.

They are also used in Soap-boilers Fats, and in making of Cisterns.

THe common Bricks that are made here in *England*, are nine Inches in length, four Inches and $\frac{1}{4}$ in Breadth, and two and an half in thickness; and sometimes three Inches thick.

Most

Most Counties in England *afford Earth for the making of* Bricks.

BUt the best Earth that we have in *England* for *making* of *Bricks*, is in the County of *Kent*, from whence we have most of the *Bricks* which are Rubbed and Hewed for the Ornaments of the chief Fronts in the City of *London*: The Ornamental part of which Fronts, are done with the reddest Bricks they can pick from among them; and the Rough or Plain Work, is done with the *Grey Kentish Bricks*; also those *Gray Kentish Bricks* are used in making of Cisterns to hold Water, and Horse-Ponds, and also Fats for Soap-Boilers; and I am of the Opinion, that no time will impair or decay those *Grey Kentish Bricks*: But, as *Pliny* says, (speaking of *Bricks*,) that they will last to Eternity.

There are also in most Counties of *England*, Bricks made for the Paving of *Floors* of *Rooms*, *Cellers*, *Dary-houses*, &c. which are made of a stronger sort of Earth, than the common *Bricks* for Building, the *Earth* being a kind of *Clay*, and in some Countries are called *Clay Bricks*, which are dearer than the *Ordinary Bricks* by about six Shillings in a Thousand.

Likewise in several Counties, but chiefly in *Surrey*, are made Paving *Tiles* of three several Magnitudes; the largest sort being twelve Inches long, and twelve broad, and one Inch and an half in Thickness.

The second sort are ten Inches long, and ten Inches broad, and one Inch and a quarter thick.

The third sort are eight Inches long, eight broad, and one Inch thick.

Either of which sorts being Polished or rubbed with sharp Sand on the Surface, and the joints made exactly square, and the sides equal, by hewing

hewing them with a *Brick Ax*, and rubbing them on a rubbing Stone with ſharp Sand, makes an excellent Pavement and pleaſing to the Eye, eſpecially when laid *Arris ways*.

Having thus deſcribed the ſeveral ſorts of *Bricks*, and alſo paving Tiles, we come in the next place to treat of *Tiles*, made and uſed in the Covering of *Roofs* of *Houſes*, both Publick and Particular, of which are four ſorts or kinds.

The firſt ſort are called *Plains Tiles*, being made of a ſtrong ſort of Earth like *Clay*; and are, or ſhould be ten Inches and an half in length, in breadth ſix Inches and a Quarter, and in thickneſs three quarters of an Inch.

The ſecond ſort are *Gutter* or *Hip Tiles*, which are uſed ſometimes for *Vallies* and *Hips* of *Rooffs*, altho' here at *London*, the *Vallies* are commonly tiled with *Plain Tiles*, and the *Hips* with *Ridge*, or (as ſome call them) *Roof Toiles*: Theſe *Gutter Tiles* are in length ten Inches and an half, with convenient breadth and thickneſs accordingly, and are made Circular or hollow, and wider at one end than at the other.

The third ſort are *Ridge* or *Roof Tiles*, being in length thirteen Inches, and made Circular breadthways like an half Cylinder, whoſe Diameter is about ten Inches, or more, and about half an Inch and half a quarter in thickneſs: Theſe are laid upon the upper parr, or ridge of the Roof, and alſo on the Hips.

The fourth ſort are *Pan-Tiles*, being about thirteen Inches long, with a Nob or Button to hang on the Laths, and are made hollow or circular breadthways, being eight Inches in breadth, and about half an Inch in thickneſs, or ſomewhat more. The beſt ſort of theſe are brought from *Holland* into *England*, and are called *Flemmiſh Pan-Tiles*, we having ſuch Tiles made here

in

in *England*, but not ſo good: Which *Flemmiſh Tiles* are ſometimes glazed, and are of a Lead, or Blewiſh colour, and being glazed they are very durable and handſom.

Having done with the Deſcription of *Tiles*, for the Covering of Roofs, we come in the next place to treat of *Morter*, and firſt of *Lime*, being the chief Material of which the *Mortar* is made, for the Cementing or joining of *Tiles*, as well as *Bricks* together, we will Treat of it in the firſt place.

Of Lime.

THere are two ſorts, one made of Stone, which is the ſtrongeſt, and the other of Chalk, both ſorts being burnt in a *Kilne*..

The Lime that is made of ſoft Stone or Chalk is uſeful for Plaſtering of Seelings and Walls within Doors, or on the inſides of Houſes; and that made of hard Stone, is fit for Structures or Buildings, and Plaſtering without Doors, or on the out ſide of Buildings that lies in the Weather; and that which is made of greaſy clammy Stone, is ſtronger than that made of lean poor Stone; and that which is made of ſpongy Stone, is lighter than that made of firm and cloſe ſtone; that is again more Commodious for Plaſtering, this for Building.

Alſo very good *Lime* may be made of *Mill-ſtone*, not courſe and Sandy, but fine and Greaſy.

Likewiſe of all kinds of Flints (but they are hard to burn except in a *Reverbratory Kilne*) except thoſe that are roled in the Water, becauſe a great part of its increaſe goes away by a kind of Glaſs.

But the ſhells of Fiſh, as of Cockles, Oyſters, &c. are good to burn for *Lime*.

And the Fire in *Lime* burnt, Affwages not, but lies hid, fo that it appears to be cold, but Water excites it again, whereby it Slacks and crumbles into fine Powder.

Lime alfo is ufeful in divers things, for 'tis ufeful in Oyles and Wines, and good to Manure Land with; fome feafon new Wine with it, mitigating the unpleafantnefs of the Wine therewith.

Moreover *quick Lime* being caft into an arched Vault, and Water thrown upon it, confumes dead Bodies put therein.

Alfo *Diers* and *Tanners*, and likewife *Phyficians* ufe it, but they choofe the neweft, to wit, that which is newly drawn out of the *Kiln*, and not flack'd with Water or Air.

It will burn fo vehemently, that it makes crufts, and will fire Boards or Timber againft which it lies; but being flackt for fometime, it burns no more, yet it warms and dries, and diffolves Flefh; and being wafhed three or four times, it Bites or Eats not, but dries quickly.

Lime mixt with Sand is much ufed in Buildings; and *Vitruvius* fays, That you may put three parts of Sand that is digged (or pit Sand) and one part of *Lime* to make *Morter*; but if the Sand be taken out of a *River*, or out of the *Sea*, then two parts thereof, and one of *Lime*; as alfo to *River* to *Sea*-Sand, if you put a third part of Powder of *Tiles* or *Bricks*, (to wit, *Tile*, or *Brick* duft) it works the better.

But *Vitruvius* his Proportion of Sand feems too much, altho' he fhould mean the *Lime* before it is flacked; for one Bufhel of *Lime* before it is flack'd, will be five Pecks after 'tis flack'd.

Here at *London*, where for the moft part our *Lime* is made of *Chalk*, we put about thirty fix Bufhels of Pit-Sand, to twenty five Bufhels of Quick-

Quick-Lime, that is about one Bushel and half of Sand, to one Bushel of *Lime*.

And *Lime* mixt with *Sand*, and made into *Morter*, if it lye in an heap two or three Years before 'tis used, it will be the stronger and better, and the reason of so many insufficient Buildings, is the using of the *Morter*, as soon as 'tis made, as *Agricola* saith.

Moreover there is other *Morter* used in making of Water-courses, Cisterns, Fish-ponds, *&c.* which is very hard and durable, as may be seen at *Rome*, at this day, which is called *Maltha*, from a kind of *Bitumen* Dug there; for as they build most firm Walls thereof naturally, so they use it in making of Cisterns to hold Water, and all manner of Water-works; and also in finishing or Plastering of Fronts to represent Stone.

And I find two kinds of Artifices used by the Antients, both of which is compounded of *Lime* and *Hogs-grease*, but to one is added the Juice of Figs, and to the other *Liquid Pitch*; and the Lumps of *Lime* are first wet or slack'd with Wine, then pounded or beat with *Hogs-grease*, and juice of *Figs*, or with the same *Pitch*; that which hath *Pitch* in it, is blacker and easily distinguished from the other by its Colour, and that which is Plastered with this *Tarrace*, is done over with *Linseed* Oil.

Metalists use a kind of *Tarrace* in their Vessels for fining of *Mettals*, that the melted Mettle run not out; for as the Moderns restrain *Water*, and contain it, so the Antients, this liquid Mettal, and 'tis compounded or made of *Quick-Lime* and *Ox Blood*, the *Lime* being beat to Powder and sifted, and then mixt with the *Blood* and beat with a *Beater*.

But their *Cement* differs from both the *Malthas* in Composition and use, for 'tis made of Dust or Powder of *Marble*, and *Glew* made of *Bull* or *Ox* Leather, and with this they glew pieces of Marble or Stones together.

In latter times, two kinds of *Cement* are in uſe, in both which they uſe the Powder of *Marble*, or other *Stone*, to one is added the Whites of Eggs, to the other is added *Pitch*; to theſe ſome add other things, as the Gravers of *Gems*, they make it of *Tile Duſt* and *Pitch*.

Another Material which *Bricklayers* uſe are *Laths*, which are made of heart of *Oak*, for out ſide Work, as *Tiling* and *Plaſtering*; and of *Fir* for inſide *Plaſtering* and *Pantile Lathing*; their uſual lengths being 5 Foot, and 4 Foot, and ſometimes longer or ſhorter; their Breadth ſometimes 2 Inches, and one Inch and an half, the thickneſs about ¼ of an Inch or thicker: But for *Pantiling*, the *Laths*, are about ten Foot long, one Inch and half Broad, and half an Inch or more thick.

Another Material is *Nails*, of which they uſe three ſorts, one is called, *Reparatian* or *Lath Nails*, which are uſed for plain *Tile Lathing*, and outſide and inſide *Lathing* for Plaſtring; another ſort are four Penny, and ſix Penny Nails, uſed for *Pantile Lathing*; and a third ſort are great Nails for Scaffolding.

Moreover they uſe *Tile-Pins*, which are ſometimes made of *Oak*, and ſometimes of *Fir*, which they drive into holes that are made in the *Plain Tiles* to hang them upon their *Lathing*.

They alſo put *Ox* or *Cow* Hair into the *Mortar* which they uſe for *Plaſtering*, being called *Lime* and *Hair*, which Hair keeps the *Mortar* from Cracking or Chaping, and makes it hold or bind together.

And whereas they make uſe of the ſharpeſt Sand they can get (that being beſt) for *Morter*, to to lay *Bricks* and *Tiles* in; ſo they choſe a fat *Loamy* or Greaſy Sand for inſide Plaſterning, by reaſon it ſticks together, and is not ſo ſubject to fall aſſunder when they lay it on Seelings or Walls.

Having given you an account of the ſeveral Materials that are uſed in *Bricklayers Work*, we ſhall in the next place Treat of their Tools and their uſes, which are as follows.

Tools uſed in Brick Work.

1. A *Brick Trowel* to take up the Morter with, and to ſpread it on the *Bricks*, with which alſo they cut the *Bricks* to ſuch lengths as they have occaſion, and alſo ſtop the joints.

2. A *Brick Ax*, with which they cut *Bricks* to what ſhape they pleaſe, as ſome for Arches both ſtreight and Circular, others for the mouldings of Architecture, as Archytrave Friez and Cornice.

3. A *Saw* made of Tinn, to ſaw the Bricks which they cut.

4. A *Rub-ſtone*, which is round, and is about fourteen Inches Diameter, and ſometimes more or leſs at pleaſure, on which they rub the Bricks which they cut into ſeveral ſhapes, and alſo others which they cut not, being call'd *Rubbed Returns*, and *Rubbed Headers* and *Stretchers*.

5. A *Square*, to try the bed of the Brick, (*viz.* that ſide which lies in the Morter) with the ſuperficies or face of the Brick, to make the Brick ſquare, or at Rect-angles one ſide with the other, which is done by rubing it on the Rub-ſtone till it exactly anſwers, or fits to the Square.

6. A *Bevel*, by which they cut the underſides of the Bricks, of Arches ſtreight or circular, to ſuch oblique Angles as the Arches require, and alſo for other Uſes.

7. *A small Trannel of Iron*, or a large Nail ground'd to a sharp point, with which they mark the Brick, either from a Square or Bevel, or a Mould made of thin Wainscot, or Pastboard to direct them in the cutting thereof.

8. Some use a *Float Stone*, with which they rub the moulding of the Brick, after they have cut it with the *Ax*, pretty near to the Pattern described on the Brick, by the *Trannel* from the Wainscot, or Pastboard Mould, that so they may make the Brick exactly to answer to the Pattern or Mould. Others use no Stone at all, but cut the Brick exactly to the Pattern with their Brick-Ax, leaving the Ax stroaks to be seen on the Brick, which, if they be streight and parallel one to another, look very prettily, and is the truest way of Working; but then they must take care, to Ax the Brick off, with an Ax that is exactly streight on the edge, that the moulding in the Brick be neither round nor hollow, from side to side of a Header, or from end to end of a Stretcher.

9. *A Little Ruler*, about 12 Inches in length, and 1 Inch and ½ broad, which they lay on the Brick to draw streight Lines by, with the *Trannel* or *Nail.*

10. A *Banker*, to cut the Bricks upon, which is a piece of Timber about six foot long, or more, according to the number of those who are to work at it, and 9 or 10 Inches square, which must be laid on two Piers of Brick, or fixt on Bearers of Timber about three foot high from the Floor, on which they stand to work.

11. They work up a Pier of Brick-work, about the same height to lay their *Rubbing-Stone* upon, which must be laid in Morter that it may lye fast.

12. A *Grinding-ſtone*, to ſharpen their Axes, Hammers, Trowels, *&c.* upon.

13. A *Pair of Line Pins of Iron*, with a length of Line on them about ſixty feet in length, to lay each Row, or Courſe of *Bricks*, level on the Bed, and ſtreight on the Surface by, a Line ſeldom holding to ſtrein, or draw ſtreight in length, above 50 or 60 feet.

14. A *Plumb Rule* about 4 foot long, with a Line and Plummet of Lead, to carry their Work upright, or perpendicular withal.

15. A *Level*, about 10 or 12 foot long, to ſet out their Foundations level, or parallel to the Horizon, and alſo to try whether the Walls of the Building, or Jambs of Chimneys, be carried level, as they raiſe the Work, that ſo they may bring up all their *Brick-work* to an exact horizontal height, at the laying on of ever floor of Carpentry.

16. A *Large Square*, to ſet their Walls at rectangles, which may alſo be done without a *Square*, by ſetting 6 foot from the angle one way, and 8 foot the other way, then if the Diagonal line, or Hypotenuſe, be exactly 10 feet, the angle is a rectangle: If not, you muſt ſet the Wall that is to be at rectangles to the other, either this or that way, till the two meaſures of 6 and 8 feet anſwer exactly to 10 feet.

17. A *Ten Foot* and a *Five Foot Rod*, as alſo a *Two Foot Rule*, to take and lay down Lengths, and Breadths, and Heights.

18. A *Jointing Rule*, about 10 foot long, and about 4 Inches broad, whereby to run the long Joints of the *Brick-work*.

19. A *Jointer of Iron*, with which, and the foreſaid Rule, they joint the long *Joints*, and alſo the *Croſs Joints*, theſe being done with the *Jointer* without the *Rule*.

20. *Compasses*, to describe the several Mouldings on Wainscot or Pastboard.

21. A *Hammer*, to cut Holes in *Brick-work*, and drive Nails for Scarfolding.

22. A *Rammer*, to Ram the Foundations.

23. A *Crow of Iron*, to dig through a Wall, and also a *Pick-Ax*.

The *Manner* and *Shapes* of the aforesaid *Tools*, you may see in Plate 1. and the Name of each *Tool* in the Page next the Plate wherein they are delineated.

The Names and Uses of Tools *relating to* Tyling.

1. A *Lathing Hammer*, to nail on the Laths withal, with two *Gauge Stroaks* (for Lathing for *Tyling*) cut upon the handle of it, one at 7 Inches from the head, and the other at 7 Inches and an half; some indeed Lath at 8 Inches, but that is too wide, occasioning Rainings in.

2. A *Lathing Staff of Iron*, in the form of a Cross, to stay the cross Laths while they are nailed to the long Laths, and also to clinch the Nails.

3. A *Tyling Trowel*, to take up the Morter and lay it on the Tiles, it being longer and narrower than a *Brick-Trowel*, altho' for a shift many times they use a *Brick-Trowel* to Tyle withal, when they have not a *Tyling-Trowel*.

4. A *Bosse*, made of Wood, with an Iron Hook, to hang on the Laths, or on a Ladder, in which the Labourer puts the Morter which the Tyler uses.

5. A *Striker*, which is only a piece of Lath about 10 Inches long, with which they strike, or cut off the Morter at the britches of the Tiles.

6. A *Broome*, to sweep the Tyling after 'tis strooke.

Of

Of the Names and Uſes of Tools *relating to Plaſtering.*

1. A *Lathing Hammer* being the ſame as before in Tyling, with which the Laths are nailed on with its head, and with its Edge they cut them to any length, and likewiſe cut off any part of a Qurter, or Joyſt, that ſticks further out than the reſt.

2. A *Laying Trowel*, to lay the Lime and Hair withall upon the Laths, it being larger than a *Brick Trowel*, and faſtned its handle in a different manner from the *Brick Trowel.*

3. A *Hawke*, made of Wood about the bigneſs of a ſquare Trencher, with a handle to hold it by, whereon the Lime and Hair being put, they take from it more or leſs as they pleaſe.

4. A *Setting Trowel*, being leſs than the *Laying Trowel*, with which they finiſh the Plaſtering when it is almoſt dry, either by Trowelling and briſhing it over with fair Water, or elſe by laying a thin Coat of fine ſtuff made of clean Lime, and mixt with Hair without any Sand, and ſetting it, that is to ſay, Trowelling and briſhing it.

5. A ſmall *Pointing Trowel*, to go into ſharp Angles.

6. *Briſhes*, of three ſorts, *viz.* A *Stock Briſh*, a *Round Briſh*, and a *Pencil.* With theſe *Briſhes*, they wet old Walls before they mend them, and alſo briſh over their new Plaſtering when they ſet, or finiſh it, and moreover white and ſize their Plaſtering with them. The *Pencil*, or *Drawing Tool*, is uſed in blacking the bottoms, or lower ports of Rooms, *&c.*

7. *Floats*, made of Wood, with handles to them, which they ſometimes uſe to float Seelings or Walls with, when they are minded to make their Plaſtering very ſtreight and even, theſe

theſe *Floats* being ſome larger, and ſome leſſer, than the *Laying Trowels*: Likewiſe they uſe *Floats* made to fit to Mouldings, for the finiſhing of ſeveral ſorts of Mouldings with finiſhing Morter to repreſent Stone, ſuch as *Cornices*, *Facias*, *Archytraves*, &c.

The finiſhing Morter to repreſent Stone, ſhould be made of the ſtrongeſt Lime, and the ſharpeſt Sand you can get, which Sand muſt be waſhed in a large Tub, very well, till no Scum or Filth ariſe in the Water, when you ſtir it about, which ſometimes will require to have Water 5 or 6 times, when the Sand is ſomewhat foul; and it requires a greater Proportion of Sand than the ordinary Morter, becauſe it muſt be extreamly beaten, which will break all the knots of *Lime*, and by that means it will require more Sand.

8. *Streight Rules* of ſeveral lengths, to lay Quines ſtreight by, and alſo to try whether the Plaſtering be laid true and ſtreight, by applying the Rules to their Work.

9. A *Pale*, to hold *Water* or *Whitewaſh*, or *White* and *Size*.

10. Some uſe a *Budget* or *Pocket* to hang by their ſides, to put their *Nails* in when they *Lath*, and others Tuck and tye up their *Aprons*, and put the *Nails* therein.

Having given you a Deſcription of the ſeveral *Tools* and uſes, there are ſome things yet remaining, which tho' they cannot be properly called *Tools*, yet they are *Utenſils*, without which they cannot well perform their Work.

And

And they are.

1. LAdders, of ſeveral lengths, as *Standard-Ladders*, two Story, and one Story *Ladders*, &c.

2. *Fir Poles*, of ſeveral lengths for *Standards* and *Ledgers* for *Scaffolding.*

3. *Putlogs*, which are pieces of Timber, or ſhort Poles, about 7 Foot long, which lies from the *Leggers* into their *Brickwork*, to bear the boards they ſtand on to Work, and to lay *Bricks* and *Morter* upon.

4. *Fir Boards*, about 10 Foot long, and any Breadth, but commonly about a Foot broad, becauſe for the moſt part, four of them in breadth, makes the breadth of the Scaffold : Which boards ought to be one Inch and or two Inches in thickneſs, altho' commonly they make uſe of ſome, which are not above one Inch thick, which are ſometimes ſubject to break, eſpecially when the *Putlogs* lye far aſunder from one another.

5. *Chords*, which ſhould be well Pitched to preſerve them from the Weather, and rotting, with which they faſten the *Ledgers* to the *Standards*, or upright *Poles.*

6. *Sieves*, of ſeveral ſorts, ſome larger, others leſſer, ſome finer, others courſer, to ſift the *Lime* and *Sand* withal, before they wet it into *Morter* or *Lime* and *Hair.*

7. A *Loame-hook*, *Beater*, *Shovel*, *Pick-Ax*, *Basket* and *Hod*, which commonly belong to *Bricklayers*, *Labourers*, and may be called the *Labourers* Tools.

8. A *Skreen* made of Boards and Wyer, which performs the Office of a *Sieve*, and with which one Man will Skreen as much *Lime*, mixt with *Sand* or *Rubiſh*, as two Men can with a *Sieve.*

9. *Boards*

9. *Boards* or *Tubs*, to put the *Morter* in.

And except my memory fails me, theſe are all, or the moſt uſual Tools and Utenſils, which they make uſe of.

Having now given you an account of their ſeveral Materials, together with their neceſſary Tools and Utenſils; we ſhall proceed in the next place to treat of the Method of working, which is various, ſome working after a better Method, and more conciſely than others.

And firſt of Foundations.

T'Is uſual, and alſo very convenient, for any perſon before he begins to Erect a Building, to have Deſigns or Draughts drawn upon Paper or Vellum, and alſo if it be a large Building, to have a Model of it made in Wainſcot; in which Deſigns and Model, the Ground Plat or Ichnography of each Floor or Story, is delineated and repreſented: As alſo the faſhion and form of each Front, together with the Windows, Doors, and Ornaments, if they intend any, to wit, *Facias*, *Ruſtick Quines*, *Architraves*, *Friezes* and *Cornices*, are to be ſhewn in the Draughts or Deſigns of the Uprights or *Orthographyes.*

If more Fronts than one be ſhewn *Perſpectively* in one Draught, then 'tis called *Scenography*, which is not eaſily underſtood, except by thoſe who underſtand the Rules of *Perſpective.*

Therefore it will be more Intelligible to the ſeveral Workmen, to have a Draught of each Front in a Paper by it ſelf, and alſo to have a Draught of the Ground-Plat or *Ichnography* of every ſtory, in a Paper by it ſelf; becauſe many times the Conveniences, or Contrivances in one Story, differs from thoſe in another, either in bigneſs of Chimneys, or diviſion of the Rooms, ſome being larger in one Story than another, and ſome-

ſometimes having more Chimnies in one Story than in another, *&c.*

All which things being well conſidered, and drawn on Papers, or a Model made thereof, before the Building is begun, there will be no need of Alterations, or Tearing and pulling the Building to pieces after it is begun; for beſides the hindrance of the Procedure of the Work, it makes the Building lame and Deficient, nothing being ſo well done, when 'tis put up, and pulled down, and ſet up again, as if it were well done at firſt.

Beſides it makes the Workmen uneaſy, to ſee their Work, in which they have taken a great deal of pains, and uſed a great deal of Art, to be pull'd to pieces.

The drawing of Draughts is moſt commonly the work of a Surveyor, although there be many Maſter Workmen that will contrive a Building, and draw the Deſigns thereof, as well, and as curiouſly, as moſt Surveyors: Yea, ſome of them will do it better than ſome Surveyors; eſpecially thoſe Workmen who underſtand the Theorick part of Building, as well as the Practick.

MECHANICK EXERCISES:

O R,

The Doctrine of *Handy-Works.*

And now concerning the Foundations.

AFter the Cellars are dug, if there are to be any, or if none, after the Trenches are dug, in which the Walls are to ſtand; the Maſter-Bricklayer, or elſe his Foreman (which ought to be an ingenious Workman) muſt in the firſt place try all the Foundations, in ſeveral places, with an Iron Croe, and Rammer, or, indeed, with a Borer (ſuch as Well-Diggers uſe, to try what Ground they have to produce Water) to ſee whether the *Foundations* are all ſound, and fit to bear the Weight which is to be ſet upon them. If he find any part of the *Foundations* defective, he ought to dig it deeper till he comes to firm ground; or if it proves to be looſe, or made Ground to a great depth, then he muſt take care to make it good and ſufficient to carry its Weight by Art, which may be done ſeveral ways.

Firſt, If the *Foundation* be not very loſe, and inſufficient, it may be made good, by ramming in in great Stones with a heavy Rammer, the Stones being placed cloſe together, and about a foot wider on each ſide of the Trench than the width of the Wall is to be; becauſe all Walls ought to have a Baſis, or Footing, at leaſt 4 Inches on a ſide broader than the thickneſs of the Wall; which Stones being well rammed, and the Baſis being 8 Inches more in breadth than the thickneſs of the Wall, and this 8 Inches being ſet off, about one Inch, or one Inch and an half at a time on both ſides (that ſo the middle of the Wall may ſtand on the middle of the Baſis) may make the Foundation good, and able to bear its Burden.

But if the *Foundation* be ſomewhat worſe than as aforeſaid, then he muſt get good pieces of Oak, whoſe length muſt be the breadth of the Trench, or about two foot longer than the breadth of the Wall, which muſt be laid croſs the *Foundation* about foot aſunder, and being well rammed down, lay long Planks upon them, which planking need not be the length of the croſs pieces, but only 4 Inches of a ſide wider than the Baſis, or footing of the Wall is to be, and pin'd or ſpiked down to the pieces of Oak on which they lye.

But if the *Foundations* be ſo bad that this will not do, then he muſt provide good Piles made of Heart of Oak, of ſuch a length as will reach ground, whoſe Diameter muſt be about $\frac{1}{12}$ part of their length, which muſt be drove or forced down with a Commander, or an Engin for that purpoſe, and then lay long Planks upon them, and ſpike or pin the Planks to them, and the cloſer together that theſe Piles are drove the better it will be.

More-

Moreover, if the *Foundation* be faulty but in here and there a place, and there be good Ground in the other parts of it, you may turn Arches over thoſe inſufficient places, which will diſcharge and take off the weight from the looſe places.

And when you make theſe Arches to ſhun the difficulty of the Earth, and to ſave the charge of Expence, they muſt be made of Bricks and Morter that are very good, and be well wrought, that they do neither ſettle nor give way.

You may obſerve for the greater ſtrength of theſe Arches, or Diſcharges, to make them higher than a Semicircle, or half round, if the Work will admit of it, and to make the ſame, of Portions of Arches: As in *Plate* 3. *Fig*. 4. you may ſee, they are deſcribed from an Equilateral Triangle; that is to ſay, ſuppoſing the breadth of the Arch between the Piers to be *A B*; with this width, and from the points *A* and *B*, make the two Portions of the Arches *A C* and *B C*; this riſing ſo high, adds great ſtrength to the Arches to reſiſt, or carry the Weight which they are to bear.

The ancient Architect *Leon Baptiſta Albert* adviſes, when the Earth on which we would make Pillars or Piers is of equal reſiſtance, that is to ſay, not good, to turn Arches inverſed, or upſide down, and ſays, by this means one Pillar ſhall bear no more weight than another, when the Earth that is underneath is not ſo ſtrong, or that it bears more than another part; which he doth thus.

Having wrought up the Pillars, or Piers, as high as is neceſſary from the *Foundation*, make from theſe Piers inverſe Arches, as *A B C* in *Plate* 3. *Fig*. 5. whoſe Joints tend to the Center *D*.

By

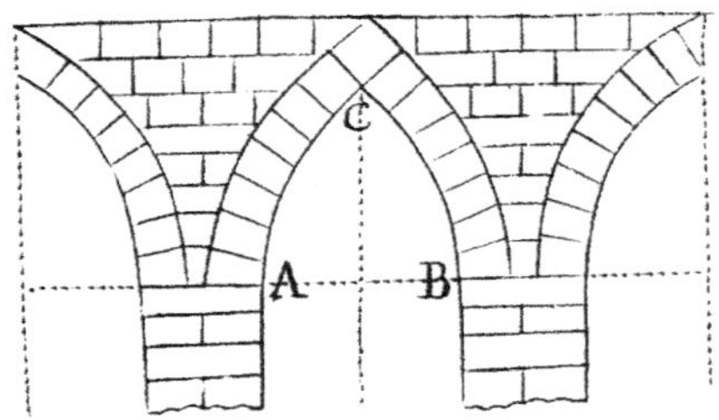

Fig. 4.

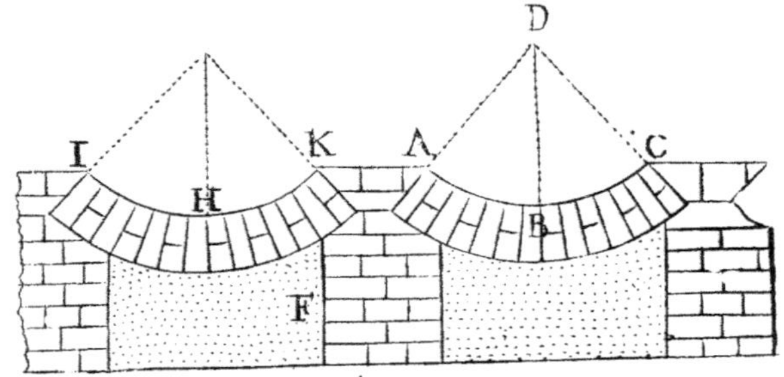

Fig. 5.

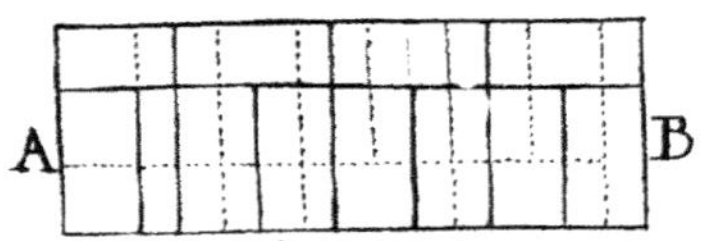

Fig. 2.

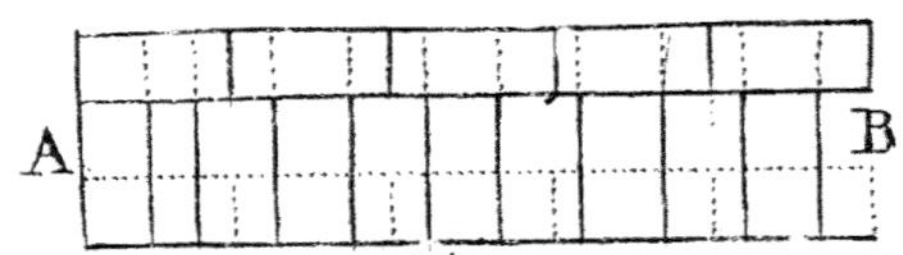

Fig. 1.

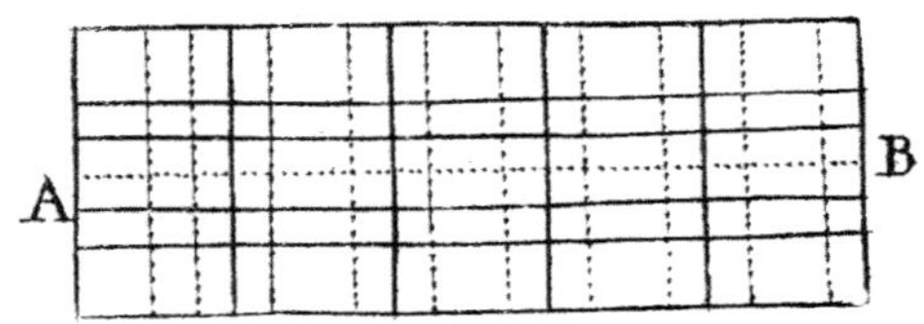

Fig. 3.

By this conſtruction he pretends for Example, that if the Pier *F* hath a worſe *Foundation*, or hath a greater Weight, that is to ſay, is more charged than the other Piers, this charge, or weight, will be ſtopped, or ſtayed by the Inverſe Arches *ABC*, *IHK*, becauſe the Earth which is under theſe Arches keeps the Piers in the ſame height, that is to ſay, that they ſhall not ſink.

But he muſt alſo ſuppoſe that this Earth is as firm as that of the *Foundation* of the Piers, or at leaſt it muſt be made ſo.

The Ingenious Surveyor Mr. *Hook*, made uſe of this Artifice, as I am informed, in building the Lord *Montague*'s brave Houſe in *Bloomsbury*, in the County of *Middleſex*, and where he was then Surveyor.

The *Foundation* being all made firm, and levelled, the Maſter-Bricklayer, or his Foreman, muſt take care to ſee all the *Foundations* ſet truly out, according to the deſign of the Ground-plat, or Cellar-floor, and that all his Walls be made of the ſame thickneſs as they are in the Deſign; which is very difficult to do, to wit, to take the true thickneſs of the Walls from a Deſign that is drawn to a ſmall Scale, becauſe the breadth of the Points of the Compaſſes will vary ſomewhat; therefore 'tis adviſable for him that draws the Draught, to ſet the Dimenſions in Figures to each Wall, Chimney, Window, *&c.* and then the Workman cannot ſo eaſily make a Miſtake.

And becauſe the well-working and bonding of Brick-walls conduces very much to their ſtrength, I will here add ſome ſome neceſſary Rules to be obſerved in the laying of Bricks, to make the Walls and ſtrong and durable.

First. That the Morter be made of well burnt good Lime, and ſharp Sand, and that it have a due proportion of Sand, that is to ſay, if it be very ſharp, a Load of Sand, being about 36 Buſhels, is ſufficient for an Hundred of Lime, being 25 Buſhels, or an hundred Pecks, (for I imagine that the word *Hundred of Lime* is uſed, becauſe it contains an Hundred Pecks, and that in Old Time they uſed to ſell it by the Peck, but now by the Buſhel) to wit, to one Buſhel of Quick Lime, a Buſhel and half of Sand.

But if the Sand be not very ſharp, then you may put a greater quantity of Sand, for Morter which hath its due proportion of Sand, is ſtronger than that which hath leſs Sand in it, altho' ſome think otherwiſe.

Secondly, When you ſlack the Lime, take care to wet it every where a little, but do not overwet it, and cover with Sand every laying, or bed of Lime, being about a Buſhel at a time as you ſlack it up, that ſo the Stream, or Spirit of the Lime, may be kept in, and not flee away, but mix it ſelf with the Sand, which will make the Morter much ſtronger, than if you ſlack all your Lime firſt, and throw on your Sand altogether at laſt, as ſome uſe to do.

Thirdly, That you beat all your Morter with a Beater three or four times over before you uſe it, for thereby you break all the Knots of Lime that go through the Sieve, and incorporate the Sand and Lime well together, and the Air which the Beater forces into the Morter at every ſtroak, conduces very much to the ſtrength thereof.

If I might advise any one that is minded to build well, or use strong Morter for Repairs, I would have them beat the Morter well, and let it lie 2 or 3 Days, and then beat it well again when 'tis to be used.

Fourthly, If you lay bricks in hot dry Weather, and be it some small piece of Work that you would have very strong, dip every Brick you lay, all over in a Pale of Water, which will make the Wall much stronger than if the Bricks were laid dry: The reason why I mention a small piece of Work is, because 'tis a great deal of trouble to wet them for much Work, or a whole Building, and besides it makes the Workmen's Fingers sore; to prevent which, they may throw Pales of Water on the Wall after the Bricks are lay'd, as was done at the building of *Physicians College* in *Warwick-Lane*, by order of the Surveyor, which was the aforesaid Ingenious Mr. *Hook*, if I mistake not.

Fifthly, Cover all your Walls in the Summer-time to keep them from drying too hastily, for the Morter doth not Cement so strongly to the Bricks when it dries hastily, as when slowly.

Sixthly, Be sure to cover them very well in the Winter-time, to preserve them from Rain, Snow and Frost, which last is a great Enemy to all kinds of Morter, especially to that which hath taken wet just before the Frost.

Seventhly, In working up the Walls of a Building, do not work any Wall above 3 foot high before you work up the next adjoining Wall, that so you may join them together, and make good Bond in the Work: For 'tis an ill Cuſtom among ſome *Bricklayers*, to carry, or work up a whole Story of the Party-walls, before they work up the Fronts, or other Work adjoining, that ſhould be bonded or worked up together with them, which occaſions Cracks and Setlings in the Walls.

Eightly, Take care that you do not lay Joint on Joint, in the middle of the Walls as ſeldom as may be, but make bond there as well as on the outſides; for I have ſeen ſome, who in working of a Brick and half Wall, have laid the Header on one ſide of the Wall, upright upon the Header on the other ſide of the Wall, and ſo all along through the whole courſe, which indeed neceſſarily follows from the inconſiderate ſetting up of the Quine at a Toothing; for 'tis common to Tooth in the ſtretching courſe two Inches with the Stretcher only, and the Header on the other ſide, to be ſet upright upon the Header on this ſide, which cauſes the Headers to lye Joint in Joint in the middle of the Wall, as in *Plate* 3. *Fig.* 1. you may ſee.

Whereas if the Header of one ſide of the Wall, toothed as much as the Stretcher on the other ſide, it would be a ſtronger Toothing, and the Joints of the Headers of one ſide, would be in the middle of the Headers of the courſe they lye upon of the other ſide, as in *Plate* 3. *Fig.* 2.

All that can be ſaid for this ill Cuſtom of working, is this, that the Header will not well hang two Inches over the Bricks underneath it; I grant it will not, but then it may be made, by having a piece of Fir, or any other Wood of the thickneſs of a Courſe of Bricks, and two Inches

Inches broad, and lay it on the laſt Toothing Courſe to bear it; or a *Bat*, put upon the laſt Toothing, will bear it till the next *Quine* is ſet upon it, and then the *Bat* may be taken away.

Ninthly, The ſame Inconveniency happens at an upright *Quine* in a *Brick* and half Wall, where 'tis uſual to lay a Cloſier next the Header on both ſides of the Wall, and in ſo doing 'tis Joint in Joint all the length of the Wall, except by chance a three quartern Bat happen to be laid.

To prevent which Inconveniency, and to make the Wall much ſtronger, lay a Cloſure on one ſide, and none on the other; but lay a three quarter Bat at the Quine in the ſtretching courſe, and in the Heading courſe adjoin an Header next to the Header at the Quine, as you may ſee it done in Plate 3. *Fig.* 1. and 2.

Where A and B in both Figures or Diagrams, repreſents a Brick and half Wall, having an upright Quine at A, and a Toothing at B, and the Prick Lines repreſents the Courſe of Bricks laid upon the other courſe; ſo in *Fig.* 1. the black Lines next you are an heading courſe, and the Prick-lines next you, ſhew a Stretching courſe: And on the further ſide from you, the black Lines ſhew a ſtretching courſe, and the Prick-Lines an Heading courſe.

In which *Fig.* 1. is ſhewn the uſual way of bad Working, but in *Fig.* 2. is ſhewn the true way it ſhould be wrought, to be made firm and ſtrong.

Alſo in working a two Brick Wall, I would adviſe in the Stretching courſes, wherein you lay ſtretching on both ſides the Wall next the Line, ſo alſo to lay ſtretching in the middle of the Wall, and Cloſiers next to each ſtretching Courſe that lies next the Line, as in *Fig.* 3. of *Plate* 3. you may ſee.

Where the Diagram or Fig. A B, signifies a two Brick Wall, A being an upright Quine, and B the Toothing, in which, the black lines represent the stretching course, and the Prickt Lines the Heading course, that lies upon the stretching course: In a two Brick Wall if you lay a closier next the upright Quine on both sides of the Wall, it makes good Bond.

Tenthly, In Summer time use your Morter as soft as you can, but in the Winter time pretty stiff or hard.

Eleventhly, If you build in the City of *London*, you must make all your Walls of such thicknesses as the Act of Parliament for rebuilding of the said City enjoyns, but in other places you may use your Discretion.

And because the Act of Parliament may not be in every Builders hands, I will therefore Incert so much of it as relates to *Bricklayers* Work, to wit, the Heights and number of Stories, and the Thickness of Walls of the four several sorts of Buildings, which is as follows.

And be it further Enacted, That the said Houses of the First and least sort of Building Fronting by Streets or Lanes, as aforesaid, shall be of two Stories high, besides Cellars and Garrats; That the Cellars thereof 6 Foot and an half high, if the Springs of Water hinder not; and the First Story be 9 Foot high from the Floor to the Seeling; and the second Story 9 Foot high from the Floor to the Seeling; that all Walls in Front and Reer as high as the first Story, be of the full thickness of the length of two Bricks, and thence upwards to the Garrats of the thickness

neſs of one Brick and an half; and that the thickneſs of the Garrat Walls on the back part, be left to the Diſcretion of the Builder, ſo that the ſame be not leſs than the length of one Brick; and alſo that the thickneſs of the party Walls between theſe Houſes of the Firſt and leſſer ſort of Building, be one Brick and ½ as high as the ſaid Garrats, and that the thickneſs of the party Wall in the Garrat, be of the thickneſs of the length of one Brick at the leaſt.

And be further Enacted, That the Houſes of the ſecond ſort of Building fronting Streets and Lanes of Note, and the River of *Thames*, ſhall conſiſt of three Stories high, beſides Cellars and Garrats as aforeſaid; that the Cellars thereof be 6 Foot and ½ high, (if the Springs hinder not) that the firſt Story contain full 10 Foot in height from the Floor to the Seeling: The ſecond full 10 Foot, the third 9 Foot; that all the ſaid Walls in Front and Reer, as high as the firſt Story, be two Bricks and ½ thick, and from thence upwards to the Garrat Floor, of one Brink and ½ thick; and the thickneſs of the Garrat Walls on the back part be left to the diſcreation of the Builder, ſo that the ſame be not leſs than one Brick thick: And alſo that the thickneſs of the party-walls between every Houſe of this ſecond, and larger ſort of Building, be two Bricks thick as high as the firſt Story, and thence upwards to the Garrats, of the thickneſs of one Brick and ½.

Alſo, that the Houſes of the thirl ſort of *Buildings*, fronting the high and principle Streets, ſhall conſiſt of 4 Stories high, beſides Cellars and Garrats as aforeſaid: That the firſt Story contain full 10 foot in height from the Floor to the Seeling; the ſecond 10 foot and ½; the third

9 foot; the fourth 8 foot and ½: That all the ſaid Walls in Front and Reer, as high as the firſt Story, be of two Bricks and ½ in thickneſs, and from thence upwards to the Garrat Floor, of the thickneſs of one Brick ½: That the thickneſs of the Garrat Walls on the back part be left to the diſcretion of the Builder, ſo as the ſame be not leſs than one Brick: And alſo that the Party-walls between every Houſe, of this third and larger ſort of Building, be two Bricks thick as high as the firſt Floor, and thence upwards to Garrat Floor, the 1 ½ Brick in thickneſs.

And, *Be it further Enacted, That all Houſes of the fourth ſort of Building, being Manſion Houſes, and of the greateſt bigneſs, not fronting upon any of the Streets or Lanes as aforeſaid; the number of Stories, and the Height thereof, ſhall be left to the diſcretion of the Builder, ſo as he exceeds not four Stories.*

Alſo, the ſame Act enjoins, That no Timber be laid within 12 Inches of the foreſide of the Chimny Jambs; and that all Joyſts on the back of any Chimny be laid with a Trimmer, at ſix Inches diſtant from the back: Alſo, that no Timber be laid within the Tunnel of any Chimny, upon penalty to the Workman for every Default ten Shillings, and ten Shillings every week it continues unreform'd.

Twelfthly, When you lay any Timber on Brick-work, as Torſels for Mantle-Trees to lye on, or Lintols over Windows, or Templets under Girders, or any other Timbers, lay them in Loam, which is a great preſerver of Timber, for Morter eats and corrodes the Timber: Likewiſe the Joyſt ends, and Girders which lye in the Walls, muſt be Loamed all over, to preſerve them from the

Plate 4

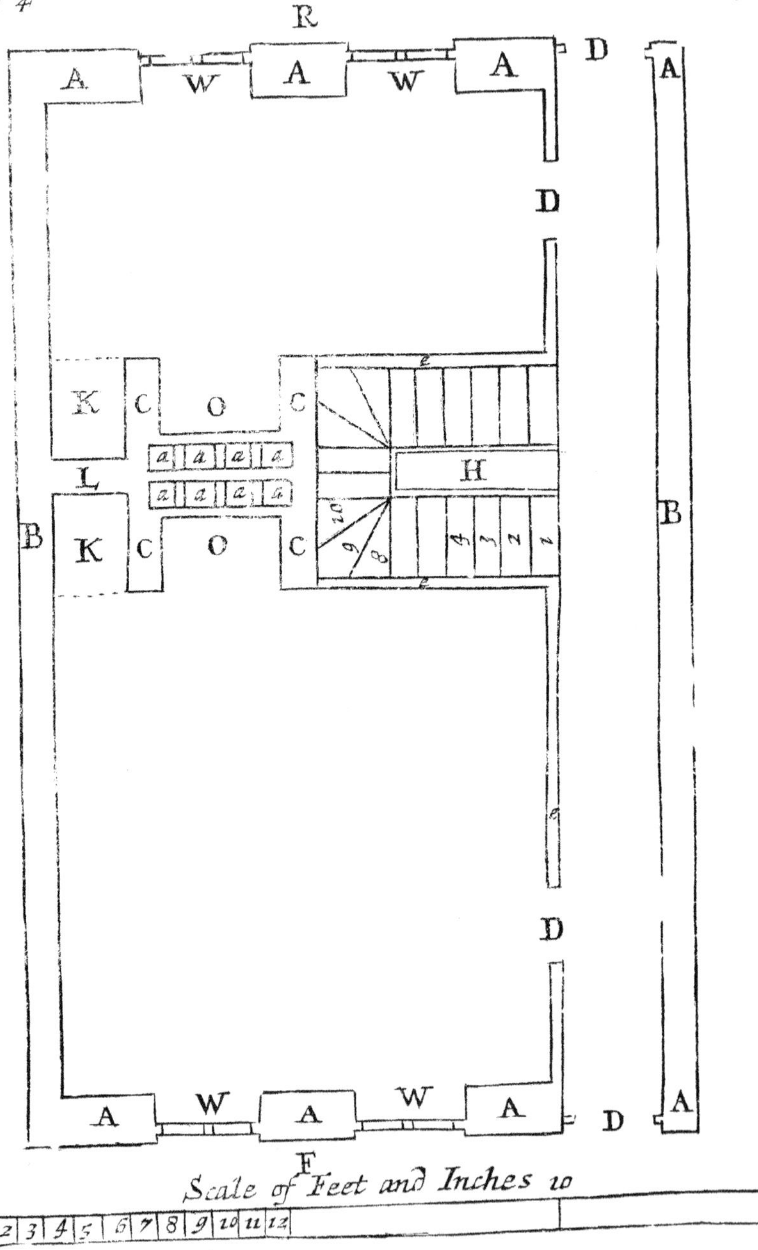
R
A W A W A
D
D
K C O C
a a a a
L
a a a a
H
B K C O C B
1 2 3 4 8 9 10
D
A W A W A
D
F
Scale of Feet and Inches 10
1 2 3 4 5 6 7 8 9 10 11 12

the corroding of the Morter. Some Workmen pitch the ends of the Timber that lye in the Walls to preſerve them from the Morter.

In the next place you ſhall have the Ground Plat of a Building, and its Explanation.

IN Plate 4, you have the Draught of a Ground Plat of a Building, which is 25 Feet, both in the Front and Reer Front; and 40 Feet in the Flank or Depth: The Front and Reer Front Walls, are 2 Bricks and ½ in thickneſs; the Flank Walls are 2 Bricks in thickneſs, as you may prove by the Scale of Feet and Inches annext to the Deſign.

You may imagine this Deſign to be the Ground Floor, having no Cellar beneath it: And the height of the Story between the Floor and the Seeling to be 10 Foot; and becauſe we do ſuppoſe this Building to have Houſes adjoining it on each ſide, therefore we have drawn the Stair-caſe with an open Nuel to give light to the Stairs; but if the Houſe had ſtood by it ſelf, without other Houſes adjoyning, then we might have had light to the Stairs from the Flank Wall.

Explanation of the Deſign.

F. The Front.
R. Reer Front.
B. Flank Walls.
A. Piers of Brick.
W. Windows of Timber.
D. Door-caſes of Timber.
O. Chimneys.
C. Jambs of Chimneys.

H. Open

H. Open Nuel to give light to the Stairs.
K. Cloſſets.
L. A Brick and half Wall between the Cloſſets.
a. Funnels or Tunnels of Chimneys.
1. 2. 3. 4, *&c.* Steps of Stairs called Fliers.
8. 9. 10, *&c.* Steps of Stairs called Winders.
e. Timber Partitions.

The Scale contains 32 Feet, with a Diagonal Line to ſhew the Inches in a Foot: For Example, if you would take of 8 Inches, take the Interval from 8 in the Horizontal Line to the Diagonal Line, and that is 8 Inches: From 3 in the Horizontal Line to the Diagonal Line, is 3 Inches, and ſo of the reſt.

In the next *Plate* you have the Orthography, or upright of this Ground Plat, and this the Explanation thereof, with a Scale of Feet and Inches annext thereto,

Explanation of Plate 5.

A. The Water-Table.
B. Firſt Faſcia.
C. Second Faſcia.
D. Three plain Courſes of Bricks over the Arches.
E. Cornice.
F. Chimnies.
G. Gable-end.
H. Streight Arches.
W. Shas Frames.
S. Shas lights.
K. Door-caſe.
L. Window-Lighte over the Door.

The

Plate 5

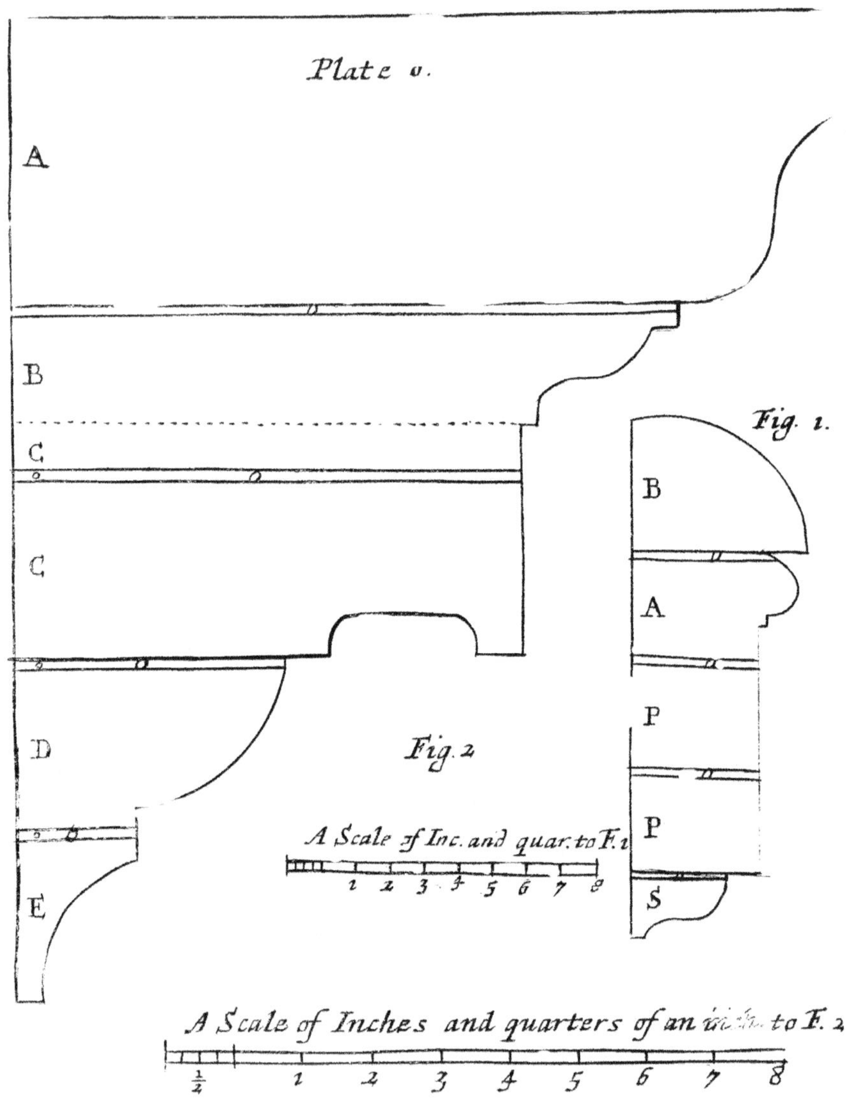

Plate 0.
A
B
C
C
D
E
Fig. 2
Fig. 1.
B
A
P
P
S
A Scale of Inc. and quar. to F. 1
1 2 3 4 5 6 7 8
A Scale of Inches and quarters of an
to F. 2
½ 1 2 3 4 5 6 7 8

The Scale of Feet and Inches being the ſame, as in the Ground Plat of *Plate* 4. I need not ſay any thing concerning it, becauſe I have there ſhewn the uſe of it.

And although I have in this Deſign, drawn the Faſcias plain without any Mouldings, yet ſometimes they are made with Mouldings, which ſhew very neat and handſome, I have therefore in *Plate* 6. given you a Deſign of a Brick Faſcia, wrought with Mouldings, in which Deſign

S. Is Scima reverſa.
O. Joints of Morter.
P. Plain Courſes.
A. Aſtragal.
B. Ovolo, or Boltel, reverſed.

In the ſame *Plate*, you have the deſign of a Brick Cornice, and the Names of the Mouldings, are

A. Scima recta, or Ogee;
O. Joint of Morter.
B. Scima reverſa, or Scimatium.
C. Corona, or Plancheer.
D. Ovolo, or Boltel.
E. Cavetto, or Caſement.

In which Cornice, the Corona, or Plancheer, ought (according to the Rules of Architecture) to Sail over, or project more; but the length of a Brick being but about 8 Inches when its head is rubbed for hewing, it will not hang, if it ſail over, more than is ſhewn in the Draught, which is about 3 Inches and an half. But if you would make it to project more, then you muſt Cement pieces to the ends of your bricks for tail-
ing

ing, or to make them longer: Of which Cement there is two ſorts, one is called cold Cement, and the other is hot, the making and uſe whereof, we will ſhew towards the latter end.

To deſcribe Mouldings on Wainſcot, or Paſtboard, for Patterns, to cut Bricks by.

There are two ways to deſcribe the Hollows, and rounds of Moulding in Faſcias, or Cornices; one from the *oxi*, or *oxigonium*, the other from the *half round*, or *Semicircle*, that makes the Moulding flatter, this more circular; I will ſhew both ways, and then you may make uſe of which you pleaſe.

Firſt, We will deſcribe a Cavetto, or Caſement, both ways.

In *Plate* 7. the *Fig.* 1. is deſcribed from the *oxi*, in this manner, having allowed the projecture of the Moulding at the bottom, and the Fillet at top, draw the Line *a b*, then with the Compaſſes taking the interval *a b*, place one point of the Compaſſes in *a*, and with the other deſcribe the Arch *d d*; then with one Foot in *b*, with the other deſcribe the Arch *c c*, and where theſe two Arches interſect each other, there is the Center to deſcribe the Cavetto; then fixing one Foot in the Center, extend the other to *a* or *b*, and deſcribe the Arch *a g b*.

You may deſcribe it from a Semicircle thus: In *Fig.* 2. having allowed the Projecture at bottom, and the Fillet at top, as before, draw the Line *a b*, biſect, or middle it, as at *c*, then upon *c* as a center, with the Interval *c a*, or *c b*, deſcribe the Semicircle *a d b*, and biſect it in *d*, which is the Center to deſcribe the Cavetto, or Caſement by; then fixing one point of the Compaſſes

Plate 7

Pag. 263.

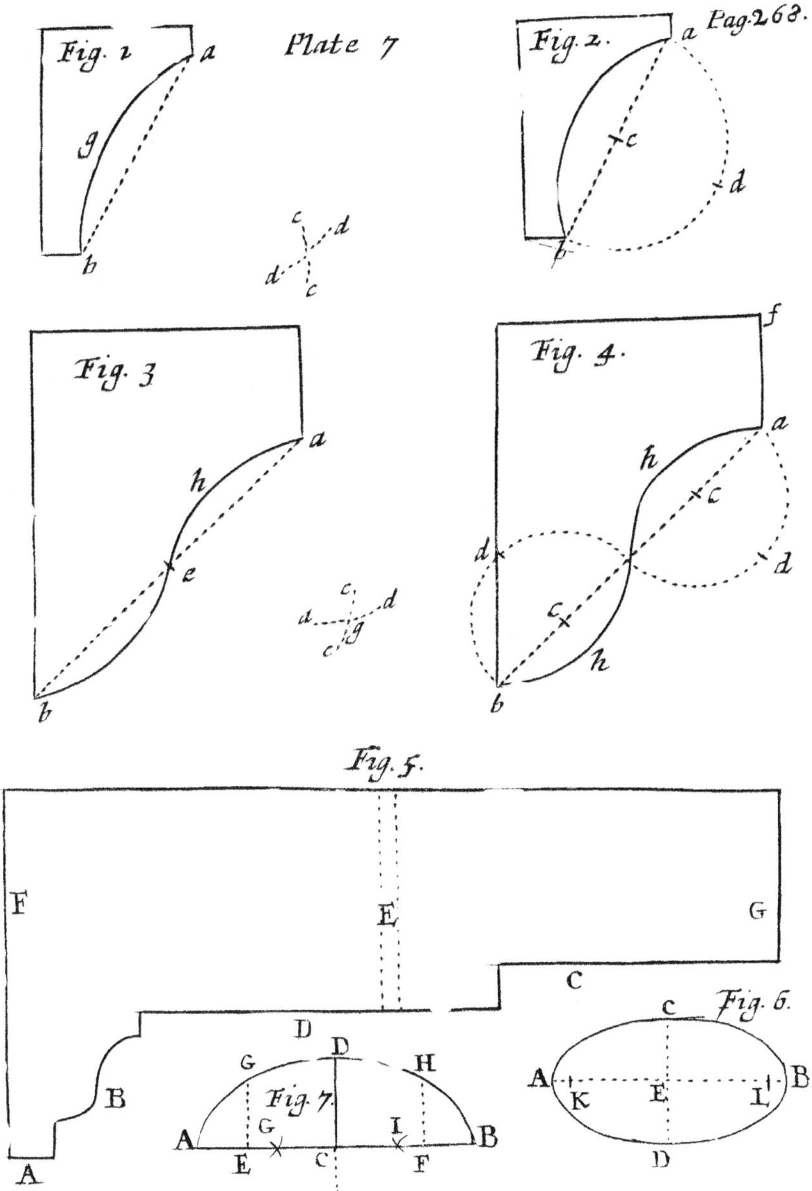

passes in *d*, extend the other to *a* or *b*, and describe the Arch *a g b*.

To describe the Scima Recta, *or* Ogee, *both ways.*

Fig. 3. is described by the *Oxi* in this manner; having allowed the Fillet at top *a f*, draw the Line *a b*, and bisect it, that is, part it in the middle in *e*; then with your Compasses take the Interval *e b*, and fixing one point in *e*, with the other describe the Arch *c c*, then with the same Interval, or distance, fixing one point in *b*, with the other, describe the Arch *d d*, and where these two Arches Intersect, or cut each other, there is the Center to discribe the round, or lower part of the *Ogee*, to wit, *e h b*: Then fixing one point of the Compasses on the Intersection by *d*, extend the other to *b*, or *e*, and describe the Arch *e h b*: Then to describe the Hollow, or upper part of the *Ogee*, take with your Compasses the Distance, or Interval *e a*, and fixing one point in *e*, with the other describe the Arch *c c*, then keeping the Compasses, at the same distance, fix one foot in *a*, and with the other describe the Arch *d d*, intersecting the other Arch in *g*: Then fixing one Foot in *g*, extend the other to *e* or *a*, and describe the Arch *e b a*, which compleats the *Scima recta*, or Ogee.

To

To describe the same Ogee *by a Semicircle.* Fig. 4.

1. After you have allowed the Fillet *a f*, draw the Line *a b*.

2. Bisect the Line in *s*.

3. Bisect *e b* and *s a*, as at *c c*.

4. On the Center *c*. with the Interval *c a*, describe the Semicircle *s d a*.

5. Middle it, as at *d*.

6. Fixing one point in *d*. extend the other to *a* or *s*, and describe the Arch *a h s*.

7. On the Center *c*, with the distance *c b*, describe the Semicircle *b d s*.

8. Middle it, as at *d*.

9. Fix one Foot in *d*, and extend the other to *b* or *s*.

10. Describe the Arch *b h s*, which compleats the *Scima Recta*, or *Ogee*; and after either of these ways, which you like best, you may describe any other Moulding.

And because many times *Bricklayers* make Archytrave Jambs and Arches, about Windows and Door-cases in a Front, I will therefore delineat an Archytrave to be cut in the length of a Brick; which is most usual, although you may make your Archytrave larger, and cut it in the length of one Brick and an half.

In *Plate* 7. *Fig.* 5. you have Delineated the Ground Plat of an Archytrave Jamb, to be cut in the length of a Brick, which suppose to be F G, and also Imagine F E G to be a Stretcher, or a Stretching Archytrave: Also you may understand the design to be divided in the middle by the two Prick Lines on each side E, which represents a Joint of Morter, and imagining it

to

Plate. 8. Pag. 271.

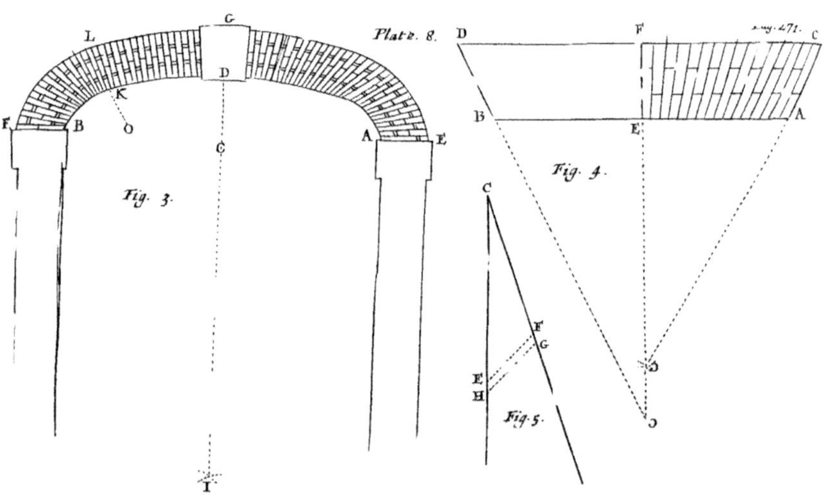

to be thus divided; then E F is called a Header; or a heading Archytrave, and E G is called a Jak.

Here follows the Names of the ſeveral parts of the Archytrave.

A. Fillet.
B. Scima.
C. Upper Faſcia.
D. Lower Faſcia.

I did intend here to have added ſomething about the Arching of Vaults, but intending, God willing, to treat largely of the Deſcription of all manner of Arches, and making of Moulds, or Patterns, to cut them by, when I come to exerciſe in *Maſonry*, which will ſucceed this: I ſhall therefore omit ſpeaking of Vaults in this Exerciſe.

I ſhall now in the next place ſhew how to deſcribe any Ellipſis Arch in Brick; and make the Moulds, as alſo to deſcribe ſtreight Arches, and make the Moulds for the ſame.

To deſcribe an Oval *to any Length and Breadth given.*

An *Ellipſis Arch* is an half Oval: Therefore in *Plate* 8. *Fig.* 1. let the length given be A B, and the Breadth C D.

Apply the two given Lines together, ſo that they may cut each other into two equal parts, and at right angles in the point E, then take half the line A B, between your Compaſſes, and ſetting one point of the Compaſſes in C, extend the other till it touch the line A B, in K and L, which

which two points are called the *Focasses*, or burning points, in which points drive two Nails, if you describe it on Boards, but upon Paper, as here two Pins will do; the Pins being stuck fast in the points K and L, stick also another Pin in the Point C, then take a Thread, and Encompass these 3 Pins in form of a Triangle, pulling the Thread tight, tye the two ends of the Thread together, by a knot at C, then taking out the Pin at C, take a Pencil of Black-Lead, holding it close to the inside of the Thread, and carrying the Pencil round upon the Paper, about the Pins, with the Thread always streight, the *Ellipsis* or *Oval* ACBD, will be thereby described.

Another way to describe the same.

Here I shall only describe a Semi-Oval, *being an Ellipsis Arch.*

In *Fig.* 2. let the length given be A B, and the Semidiameter or height of the Arch C D; Divide A B into seven equal parts, then upon one seventh part from A as at E, raise a Perpendicular from the Line A B, (viz. E G.) also at one seventh part from B, as at F, raise another Perpendicular F H; then divide the Semidiameter given C D, into 15 equal Parts, and take Eleven of those Parts, and set upon the Perpendicular from E to G, and likewise from F to H; then taking the space between A and G, setting one point of the Compasses in A, describe the Arch G *i*, keeping the Compasses at the same distance, set one point in G, and describe another Arch, which will cut the former in the point by *i*; from which point, with the Radius A *i*, us A *i*, deſcribe the *Hanſe* A G; this being done, take between your Compaſſes the ſpace B H, and ſetting one point in B, deſcribe the arch I *i*, then remove your Compaſſes to H, and interſect that Arch in the point by *i*, then ſetting your Compaſſes on the point *i*, with the ſame diſtance, deſcribe a part of the *Ellipſis* B H, which is called the *Hanſe*: The other part to be deſcribed from G to H, is called the *Scheam*, which to deſcribe, continue or draw longer the Semidiameter D C, and in that line find a Center, whereon ſetting one point of the Compaſſes, the other point may touch the three points G D H, as on the Center I; whereby deſcribe the *Scheam* G D H, which was to be done.

Theſe *Ellipſis*, or *Semi-Oval* Arches, being neatly wrought in Brick, ſhew very pleaſant, and are ſometimes made over Gate-ways, and alſo over Kitchin-Chimnies, inſtead of Mantle-trees.

We will ſuppoſe an Ellipſis Arch to be made over a Chimny, whoſe Diameter between the Jambs is eight feet, and the under ſide of the Arch at the Key to riſe in height 18 Inches from the level of the place, whence you begin to ſpring the Arch; the height or depth of the Arch we will ſuppoſe to be made of the length of two Bricks, which when they are cut to the ſweep of the Arch, will not contain above 14 Inches, and perhaps you muſt Cement pieces to many of the Courſes in the Hanſe to make them long enough to contain, or hold 14 Inches, eſpecially if you intend to make the Courſes of the Hanſe, and the Courſes of the Scheam to ſeem alike in greatneſs, on the under ſide of the Arch; For if you make the Hanſe to come to a true Sommering for the Scheam, by that time that you have ended the Hanſe, and are ready to ſet the firſt Courſes of the Scheam: The Mould, and ſo likewiſe each Courſe in the Hanſe, will be much leſs at the lower part, or under ſide of the Arch, than the Mould, or Courſes of the Scheam, as you may perceive by the Hanſe B K, in the 3d. *Fig.* which way of working theſe kind of Arches is ſtronger, than to make the Courſes ſeem alike in bigneſs in Hanſe and Scheam, although it be not ſo pleaſing to the eye. In the 3d. *Fig.* I will ſhew how to make one half of the Arch this way, and in the other half ſhew how to make the Courſes in Hanſe and Scheam of a bigneſs.

Firſt, Deſcribe the under ſide of the Arch, (*viz.* the Ellipſis A D B, whoſe Diameter A B is eight feet, and the height C D 18 Inches) upon ſome ſmooth Floor, or ſtreight plaiſtered Wall, or ſuch like; then continue (*viz.* draw longer) both the lines A B, C D, cutting each other at right Angles, then from A to E, alſo from B to F, likewiſe from D to G, ſet 14 Inches, the intended height of your Arch. Then deſcribe another Ellipſis to that length and height, after this manner; lay a ſtreight Ruler on the Centre by I, and on the joining of the Hanſe, and the Scheam together, as at K, and draw the line K L, then ſet one point of your Compaſſes in the centre of the Hanſe at M, and open the other point of the Compaſſes to F, and deſcribe the upper Hanſe F L, likewiſe ſetting one point of the Compaſſes in the centre by I, with the other extended to G, deſcribe the Scheam G L, (although I ſpeak here of Compaſſes, yet when you deſcribe an Arch to its full bigneſs, you muſt make uſe of centre Lines or

Rues;

Rules; the laſt are beſt, becauſe Lines are ſubject to ſtretch) then taking between your Compaſſes the thickneſs of a Brick, abating ſome ſmall matter which will be rub'd off from both beds of the Brick; with the Compaſſes at this diſtance divide the upper Hanſe from L to F into equal parts, and if they happen not to divide it into equal parts, then open them a ſmall matter wider, or ſhut them a ſmall matter cloſer, till it doth divide it into equal parts, and look how many equal parts you divide the upper Hanſe into, ſo many equal parts you muſt divide the lower Hanſe from K to B into likewiſewiſe (or you may divide the upper Hanſe from the centre O, making a right Angle from each ſommering Line to the Ellipſis, as is ſhewn in deſcribing the ſtreight Arches following; and from the centre O, and the Diviſions in the upper Hanſe being thus divided, you may draw the ſtreight Lines to the lower Hanſe, and not divide it with the Compaſſes) through each of which diviſions with a Rule, and Pencil, draw ſtreight lines, then get a piece of thin Wainſcot, and make it to fit between two of theſe Lines, allowing what thickneſs for Morter you intend, this will be the Sommering Mould for the Hanſe; then divide the upper Scheam likewiſe, with the Compaſſes at the ſame diſtance into equal parts, and laying a Ruler on the centre I, from each Diviſion in the Scheam G L, draw ſtreight Lines to the lower Scheam D K, then make another Sommering Mould to fit between two of theſe Lines, abating ſo much as you intend the thickneſs of your Joints of Morter to be, which if you ſet very cloſe Morters, the breadth of the Line will be enough to allow; then laying the inner Edge of a Bevil ſtreight on the line K L, bring the Tongue to touch the under ſide of the firſt Courſe of the Scheam, then take up the Bevil, and ſet that Bevil line upon the Sommering Mould of the Scheam; which Bevil line ſerves for each Courſe in the Scheam; but you muſt take the Bevil of each Courſe in the Hanſe, and ſet them upon your Sommering Mould by themſelves, and Number them with 1, 2, 3, 4, *&c.* becauſe each Courſe varies.

Thus having made your Sommering Moulds, in the next place you muſt make the Moulds for the length of your Stretchers, and for the breadth of the Headers and the Cloſiers; a piece of Wainſcot ſeven Inches long, and three Inches and an half broad will ſerve for the length of the Stretchers, and the breadth of the Headers, the Cloſiers will be 1 Inch and ¾. broad. So the Cloſier will be half the breadth of the Header, and the Header half the length of the Stretcher, which will look well.

It remains now to ſpeak ſomething to the other part of the Arch, to wit, A D, whoſe Courſes both in *Hanſe* and *Scheam*, run alike upon the *Ellipſis* Lines, and ſeem of one bigneſs, although perhaps there may be ſome ſmall matter of difference, by reaſon I have not divided the Courſes to this Figure, from a right Angle, but every Courſe from the Angle, which it makes with the *Ellipſis*, which I choſe rather to do, that ſo the *Bevil* of one Courſe, might not ſeem to run more upon the *Ellipſis* than the *Bevil* of another, and the difference of the thickneſſes being ſo inconſiderate, is not diſcerned.

Having

Having deſcribed both the *Ellipſis* lines A D, E G, divide each of them into a like number of equal parts, always remembring to make each Diviſion on the upper *Ellipſis* line, no greater than the thickneſs of the Brick will contain, when it is wrought; then through each Diviſion in both the *Ellipſes* draw ſtreight lines; continuing them four or five Inches above the upper *Ellipſis* Line, and as much below the lower *Ellipſis* Line; then having provided ſome thin Sheets of fine Paſtboard about 20 Inches ſquare, cutting one edge ſtreight, take one ſheet and lay the ſtreight edge even upon the line A E, ſo that it may cover both the Ellipſis lines, and being cut to advantage, it may cover eight courſes (or nine of the ſtreight Lines) having laid it thus upon the figure of the Arch, ſtick a Pin, or two, through it, to keep it in its place; then lay a Ruler upon the Paſt-board true to the 7, 8, or 9th. ſtreight Line of the Arch, according as the Paſt-board is in bigneſs to cover them, and take a ſharp Pen-knife, laying the Ruler upon the Paſt-board true to the ſtreight Line (whoſe ends being continued longer than the Arch is deep, as I directed before, will be ſeen beyond the Paſt-board) and cut the Paſt-board true to the Line, then take another ſheet, and join to it, and cut it as you did the firſt, ſo continue till you have covered the Arch from A E, juſt to the line D G, ſticking Pins in each Sheet to keep them in the places where you lay them: Then deſcribe both the Ellipſis Lines upon the Paſt-board, from the ſame Centres and Radii that you deſcribed the Ellipſis's under the Paſt-board, and either divide the Ellipſis Lines with the Compaſſes on the Paſt-board, or elſe draw lines upon the Past-board from or by the streight lines underneath them whose ends you see; but the surer way is to divide the Ellipsis's on the Past-board, and draw Lines through those Divisions, as you did beneath the Past-board; then set seven Inches, being the length of each Stretcher, from A towards E, and from D towards G, and describe from the former Centres, the Ellipsis *o o* through each other course on the Past-board, as you may see in the *Fig.* also set three Inches and an half, being the breadth of the Header, from A towards E, and and likewise from D towards G: Also set the same three Inches and an half from E towards A, and from G towards D, and describe these two Ellipsis lines from the same Centres thro' each Course, which the Ellipsis line of the Stretchers miss'd; likewise draw in the same Courses, two other Ellipsis lines, one Inch and $\frac{3}{4}$ from each of those two Lines you drew last, which is the breadth of the Closiers; thus one Course of the Arch will be divided into two Stretchers, and the next to it into three Headers and two Closiers through the whole Arch; this being done, cut the Past-board according to the lines into several Courses, and each other Course into two Stretchers, and the Heading-courses into three Headers, and two Closiers, exactly according to the Sweep of the Black-lead lines, and mark each Course with Figures, marking the first Course of the Hanse with 1, the next with 2, the third with 3, and so continue till you have marked all the Courses to the Key, or middle, for every Course differs; you were best to mark the lower Closier in each course with a Cipher on the left hand of its own number, that you may know it readily from the

upper

upper Closier, and make no mistakes when you come to set them; also the middle Headers in each Course should be marked besides its own number; the thickness of the upper Header being easily discerned from the lower Header needs no marking besides its own number; the cross Joints, and likewise the under side and upper side of each 'Course must be cut circular, as the Past-boards which are your Moulds direct you.

If you will add a Keystone, and Chaptrels to the Arch, as in the *Figure*, let the breadth of the upper part of the Keystone be the height of the Arch, *viz.* 14 Inches, and Sommer, from the Centre at I, then make your Chaptrels the same thickness that your lower part of the Keystone is, and let the Keystone break without the Arch, so much as you project or Sale over the Jaums with the Chaptrels.

Other kind of *Circular Arches*, as half Rounds and Scheams, being described from one Centre, are so plain and easy, that I need say nothing concerning them: But since *Streight Arches* are much used, and many Workmen know not the true way of describing them, I shall write something briefly concerning them. *Streight Arches* are used generally over Windows and Doors, according to the breadth of the Piers between the Windows, so ought the Skew-back or Sommering of the Arch to be; for if the Piers be of a good breadth, as three or four Bricks in length, then the *Streight Arch* may be described (as its vulgarly said) from the *Oxi*, which being but part of a Word, is taken from the word *Oxigonium*, signifying an Equilateral Triangle, with three ſharp Angles; but if the Piers are ſmall, as ſometimes they are but the length of two Bricks, and ſometimes but one Brick and an half, then the breadth of the Window, or more, may be ſet down upon the middle Line for the Centre, which will give a leſs Skew-back, or Sommering, than the centre from an *Oxi*. I will ſhew how to deſcribe them both ways, and firſt from the *Oxi*.

Suppoſe a *Streight Arch*, one Brick and an half in height, to be made over a Window, 4 feet in width. [See *Fig*. 4.] wherein one half of the Arch is deſcribed from the *Oxi*, and the other half from the width of the Window, let the width of the Window be A B, taking the width between the Compaſſes, from A and B as two Centres, deſcribe the two Arches, interſecting each other at P, (though I ſpeak here of Compaſſes, yet when you deſcribe the Arch to its full bigneſs, you muſt uſe a Ruler, or a Line, ſcarce any Compaſſes being to be got large enough.) Then draw another Line above the line A B, as the line C D, being parallel to it, at ſuch a height as you intend your Arch to be, as in this *Fig*. at 12 Inches; but moſt commonly theſe ſort of Arches are but 11 Inches in the height, or thereabouts, which anſwers to four Courſes of Bricks, but you may make them more or leſs in height according as occaſion requires; then laying a Ruler on the centre P, and on the end of the line A, draw the line A C, which is vulgarly called the *Skew-back* for the Arch.

The next thing to be done, is to divide thoſe two lines A B and C D into ſo many Courſes as as the Arch will contain; the thickneſs of a Brick being one of them, which ſome do by dividing the upper line into ſo many equal parts, and from thoſe parts, and from the Centre P, draw the Sommering Lines or Courſes; others divide both the upper and lower line into ſo many equal parts, and make no uſe of a Centre, but draw the Courſes by a Ruler, being laid from the Diviſions on the upper line, to the Diviſions on the lower line, both which ways are falſe and erroneous; [but this by way of caution.]

Having drawn the *Skew-back* A C, take between your Compaſſes the thickneſs that a Brick will contain, which I ſuppoſe to be two Inches when it is rub'd, and ſetting one point of the Compaſſes on the line C D. So that when you turn the other Point about, it may juſt touch the line A C in one place, and there make a Prick in the line C D, but do not draw the Sommering lines until you have gone over half the Arch, to ſee how you come to the Key, or middle; and if you happen to come juſt to the middle line, or want an Inch of it, then you may draw the lines, but if not, then you muſt open, or ſhut the Compaſſes a little till you do.

Then keeping one end of the Rule cloſe to the Centre at P. (the ſureſt way is to ſtrike a ſmall Nail in the Centre P. and keep the Rule cloſe to the Nail) lay the other end of the Rule cloſe to the Prick that you made on the line C D, keeping the Compaſſes at the ſame width (*viz.* two Inches) ſet one point of the Compaſſes on the line C D, as before, ſo that the

the other Point being turned about, may juſt paſs by the Rule; and as it were touch it in one place; (you muſt remove the point of the Compaſſes upon the line C D, farther or nearer to the Rule, until it juſt touch the Rule in one place,) and ſo continue with the Rule and Compaſſes, until you come to the middle line, and if it happen, that your laſt ſpace want an Inch of the middle, then the middle of the Key-courſe will be the middle of the Arch, and the number of the Courſes in the whole Arch will be odd, but if the laſt ſpace happen to fall juſt upon the middle line E F, as it doth in the *Fig.* then the Joint is the middle of the Arch, (but if it ſhould happen neither to come even to the line, nor want an Inch of it, then you muſt open or ſhut the Compaſſes a ſmall matter, and begin again till it doth come right) and the number of the Courſes in the whole Arch, is an even Number.

Note, When the number of all the Courſes in the Arch, is an even Number, then you muſt begin the two ſides contrary, *viz.* A Header to be the lower Brick of the firſt Courſe on one ſide (or half) of the Arch, and a Stretcher the lower Brick of the firſt Courſe on the other ſide (or half) of the Arch: And contrariwiſe, if it happen that the Number of the Courſes be an odd Number, as 25 or 27, or ſuch like, then the firſt Courſes of each half of the Arch, muſt be alike, that is, either both Headers, or both Stretchers, at the bottom.

Thus having deſcribed the Arch, the next thing to be done, is to make the Sommering Mould, which to do, get a piece of thin Wainſcot (being ſtreight on one edge, and having one ſide plained ſmooth, to ſet the Bevil ſtrokes upon) about 14 Inches long, and any breadth above two Inches, then laying your Ruler, one end at the Centre P, and the other end even in the Skew-back line, clap the ſtreight edge of the Wainſcot cloſe to the Rule, ſo that the lower end of the Wainſcot may lye a little below the line A B, then take away the Centre Rule, but ſtir not the Wainſcot; and laying a Ruler upon the Wainſcot juſt over the line C D, ſtrike a line upon the Wainſcot, then ſet one Point of the Compaſſes being at the width of a Courſe (*viz.* two Inches) upon that line, ſo that the other Point being turned about, may juſt touch the ſtreight edge of the Wainſcot; (as you did before in dividing the Courſes) then make a Prick on the line on the Wainſcot, and laying your Centre Rule upon it, and on the Centre P, draw a line upon the Wainſcot by the Ruler, with a Pencil, or the Point of a Compaſs, and cut the Wainſcot to that line, and make it ſtreight by ſhooting it with a Plain, then your Wainſcot will fit exactly between any two lines of the Arch; you may let it want the thickneſs of one of the lines, or ſome ſmall matter more, which is enough for the thickneſs of a Mortar; the length of your Stretcher in this Arch, may be 8 Inches and $\frac{1}{4}$, and the Header 3 Inches and $\frac{3}{4}$, but if your Arch be but 11 Inches in height, then make your Stretcher 7 Inches and $\frac{1}{2}$ long, and the Header 3 Inches $\frac{1}{2}$; one piece of Wainſcot will ſerve both for the length of the Stretcher, and the length of the Header, making it like a long ſquare or Oblong, whoſe ſides are 8 Inches $\frac{1}{4}$, and 3 Inches and $\frac{3}{4}$. Then take a Bevil, and laying

ing the inner edge of it ſtreight with the line A B, and the Angle of the Bevil juſt over the Angle at A, take off the Angle that the Skew-back line A C makes with the line A B, and ſet it upon the ſmoothed ſide of your Sommering Mould, for the Bevil ſtroke of your firſt Courſe; then drawing your Bevil towards E, ſtreight in the line, until the Angle of the Bevil be juſt over the Angle, that the ſecond Sommering line makes with the line A B; when it is ſo, draw the Tongue of the Bevil to lye even upon the ſecond Sommering line; (in brief, cauſe the Bevil to lye exactly on the line A B, and on the ſecond Sommering line) then take up your Bevil and lay it on the Mould; and ſtrike that Bevil line on the Mould, with the Point of the Compaſſes, about half a quarter of an Inch diſtant from the firſt, and that is the Bevil of the underſide of the ſecond Courſe; proceed thus until you come to the middle line E F, but after you have ſet three Bevil lines upon your Sommering Mould, leave about $\frac{1}{4}$ of an Inch between the third and the fourth, and ſo likewiſe between the 6th and 7th, and the 9th, and 10th, which will be a great help to you, in knowing the Number of each line on the Mould.

The Moulds for the other half of the Arch, namely E B, are made after the ſame manner, but but the Arch is deſcribed from a Centre beneath P, as Q which cauſeth a leſs Skew-back (*viz.* B. D.)

The diminiſhing of the Sommering Mould to any Skew-back may be found by the Rule of Three, by dividing a foot into 10 equal parts, and

and each of these into 10 parts, so that the whole foot may contain 100 parts, then proceed thus. The upper line C F, will be 309, that is three Feet and almost one Inch, and the lower line A E will be 252, that is two Feet and an half an $\frac{2}{100}$, and the upper part of the Sommering Mould will be 17 almost, that is, two Inches of such whereof there are 12 in a foot line measure; having these three Numbers (viz. 309, 252, 17.) work according to the Rule of Three, and you will find 13 and $\frac{6}{1}$ of 100 parts, that is almost 14 (such parts whereof there are 100 in a Foot line measure) for the breadth of the lower part of the Mould.

You may likewise find it Geometrically thus.

HAving drawn the upper line and under line of the Arch, as C F, and A E, and drawn any Skew-back, as suppose A C in [*Fig.* 4.] make at discretion the Angle G C H in [*Fig.*5.] then take the upper line C F, and set it from C. to F; also take the lower line A E, and set it from C to E, and draw the line E F; then take the thickness of your Brick, which suppose to be two Inches, and set it from F to G, and draw G H, parallel to F E, I say F G is the breadth of the upper part of the Sommering Mould, and E H the breadth of the lower part: Then make your Sommering Mould true to those two lines, and beginning in the middle line F E, describe the streight lines by the Mould from the Key F E, until you come to the Skew-back A C, and then take of the Bevil lines, and set them on your Sommering Mould.

I shall

I ſhall conclude this Exerciſe with the Art of making two ſorts of Cements, for the Cementing Bricks.

THere are two ſorts of Cement, which ſome Bricklayers uſe in Cementing of Bricks for ſome kind of Mouldings, or in Cementing a block of Bricks, as they call it, for the Carving of Scroles or Capitals or ſuch like, &c. One is called cold Cement, the other is called hot Cement, becauſe the former is made and uſed without Fire, but the latter is both made and uſed with Fire; the cold Cement being accounted a Secret, is known but to few Bricklayers, but the hot Cement is common.

To make the cold Cement.

TAke ½ a Pound of Old Cheſhire-Cheeſe, pair of the Rine, and throw it away, cut or grate the Cheeſe very ſmall, and put it into a Pot, put to it about a Pint of Cows-milk, let it ſtand all Night, the next Morning get the Whites of 12 or 14 Eggs, then take ½ a Pound of the beſt Unſlackt or Quick Lime that you can get, and beat it to Powder in a Morter, then ſift it through a fine Hair Sieve into a Tray or Bole of Wood, or into an Earthen Diſh, to which put the Cheeſe and Milk, and ſtir them well together with a Trowel, or ſuch like thing, breaking the Knots of Cheeſe, if there be any, then add the Whites of the Eggs, and Temper all well together, and ſo uſe it; this Cement will be a White Colour, but if you would have it of the Colour of the Brick, put into it either ſome very fine Brick-Duſt, or Almegram, not too much, but only juſt to colour it.

To

To make the hot Cement.

TAke one Pound of Rozin, one Quarter of a Pound of Bees-Wax, half an Ounce of fine Brick-Duſt, half an Ounce of Chalk-Duſt, or Powder of Chalk, ſift both the Brick-Duſt and Chalk-Duſt through a fine Hair Sieve, (you may beat the Brick and the Chalk in a Morter, before you ſift it) boil altogether in a Pipkin, or other Veſſel, about a quarter of an hour, ſtirring it all the while with an Iron or a piece of Lath or ſuch like, then take it of, and let it ſtand 4 or 5 Minutes, and 'tis fit for uſe.

Note, That the Bricks that are to be Cemented with this kind of Cement, muſt be made hot by the Fire before you ſpread the Cement on them, and then rub them to and fro on one another, as Joiners do, when they Glew two Boards together.

F I N I S.

Mechanick Dyalling:

TEACHING

Any Man, tho' of an Ordinary Capacity and unlearned in the Mathematicks,

To Draw a True

SUN-DYAL

ON ANY

GIVEN PLANE,

However Scituated:

Only with the help of a ſtraight *Rule* and a pair of *Compaſſes*; and without any Arithmetical Calculation.

The Fourth Edition.

By JOSEPH MOXON, *Fellow of the Royal Society, and Hydrographer to the late King* Charles.

LONDON:

Printed for *Tho. Leigh* and *Dan. Midwinter*, at the *Roſe and Crown* in St. *Paul's-Church-Yard.* 1703.

Mechanick Dyalling.

Description of Dyalling.

DYalling originally is a *Mathematical Science*, attained by the Philosophical contemplation of the Motion of the Sun, the Motion of the Shadow, the Constitution of the Sphere, the Scituation of Planes, and the Consideration of Lines.

Explanation.

THE Motion of the Sun is reguler, it moving in equal Space in equal Time; But the Moon of the Shadow irregular, in all parts of the Earth, unless under the two Poles, and that more or less according to the Constitution of the *Sphere* and Scituation of the *Plane*. And therefore Scientifick Dyalists by the Geometrick Considerations of Lines, have found out Rules, to mark out the irregular Motion of the *Shadow* in all *Latitudes*, and on all *Planes*, to Comply with the regular Motion of the Sun. And these Rules of adjusting the Motion of the Shadow to the Motion of the Sun, may be called *Scientifick Dyalling*.

But though we may justly account *Dyalling* originally a *Science*, yet such have been the Generosity of many of its studious Contemplators, that they have communicated their acquired Rules; whereby it is now become to many of the Ingenious no more difficult than an *Art*, and by many late Authors ſo Intituled: Nay more, by this ſmall Treatiſe it will ſcarce be accounted more than a *Manual Operation*; for, though (hitherto) all the Authors I have met with ſeem to pre-ſuppoſe their Reader to underſtand *Geomeſtry*, and the *Projecting of the Sphere* already, or elſe endeavour in their Works to make him underſtand them, as if they were abſolutely neceſſary to be known by every one that would make a Dyal, when as in truth, (the Contemplative pains of others aforeſaid of conſidered) they are not; but indeed are only uſeful to thoſe that would know the reaſon of *Dyalling*. Thus they do not only diſcourage young beginners, but alſo diſappoint many Gentlemen and others, that would willingly either make them themſelves, or ſet their Workmen about them, if they knew how to make them.

This little Piece I have therefore compoſed for the help of thoſe who underſtand neither the *Projection of the Sphere*, or *Geometrical Operations*: Only, if they know how to draw a ſtraight Line between two points by the ſide of a Ruler, deſcribe a Circle with a pair of Compaſſes, erect a Perpendicular and draw one Line parallel to another, they may know how to draw a *Dyal* for any given *Plane*, however ſcituated in any Latitude.

But perhaps theſe two laſt little Tricks are not known to all new beginners, therefore I ſhall ſhew them. Firſt,

How to erect a Perpendicular. For Example, in Fig. 1.

Upon the Line A B, you would erect a Perpendicular to the Point C: Place one Foot of your Compaſſes upon the point C, and open the other to what diſtance you pleaſe: For *Example*, to the point A, make there a mark; then keeping the firſt Foot ſtill in C, turn the other Foot towards B, and make there another mark; then open your

Com-

Compaſſes wider, ſuppoſe to the length A B, and placing one Foot in the point A, with the other Foot deſcribe a ſmall Arch over the point C, and removing the Foot of your Compaſſes to the point B, with the other Foot deſcribe another ſmall Arch, to cut the firſt Arch, as at D. Then lay your ſtraight Ruler to the point where the two ſmall Arches cut each other, and upon the point C, and by the ſide of the Ruler draw the Line C D, which ſhall be a Perpendicular to the Line A B.

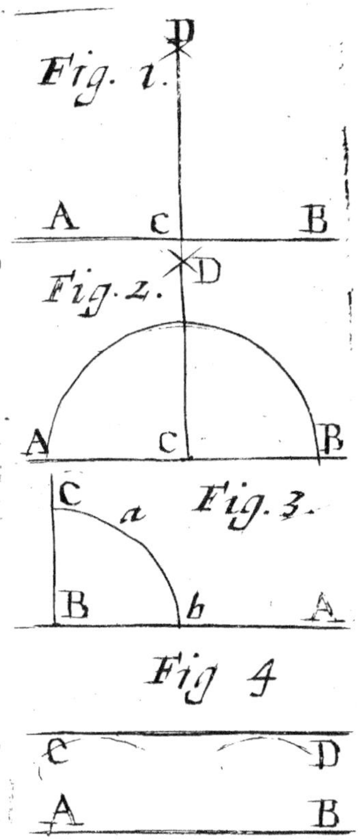

Another way with once opening the Compaſſes, as by Fig. 2.

Draw the Line A B, and place one Foot of your Compaſſes upon the point you would have the Perpendicular erected, as at the Point C, and with the other Foot deſcribe the Semi-circle A *a b* B, then placing one foot in B, extend the other foot to *b*, in the Semi-circle; and keeping that Foot in *b*, extend the other Foot to D, and make there a ſmall Arch: Then remove one Foot of your Compaſſes to A, and extend the other Foot to *a* in the Semi-circle, and keeping that Foot in *a*, extend the other to D, and make there another ſmall Arch, to cut the firſt ſmall Arch; and laying a ſtraight Ruler to the point where theſe two ſmall Arches cut each other, and upon the point C, draw by the ſide of the Ruler the Line C D, which ſhall be perpendicular to the Line A B.

To erect a Perpendicular upon the end of a Line, as by Fig. 3.

On the point B, at one end of the Line A B, place one Foot of your Compaſſes in the point B, and extend the other on the Line towards A, as to *b*, and with it deſcribe the Arch *b a* C; then placing one Foot in *b*, extend the other to *a* in the Arch, and make there a mark; Divide with your Compaſſes the Arch *b a* into two equal parts, and keeping the Feet of your Compaſſes at that diſtance, meaſure in the Arch from *a* to C, then draw a ſtraight Line from the point C to the end of the Line B, and that ſtraight Line ſhall be Perpendicular to the end of the Line A B.

To draw a Line Parallel to another Line, as by Fig. 4.

Example. If you would draw a Line parallel to the Line A B, open your Compaſſes to the diſtance you intend the Lines ſhall ſtand off each other, and placing one Foot ſucceſſively near each end, deſcribe with other Foot the ſmall Arches C D; lay a ſtraight Ruler to the top of theſe Arches, and draw a Line by the ſide of it, and that Line ſhall be parallel to the Line A B.

Definitions.

A *Dyal Plane* is that Flat whereon a *Dyal* is intended to be projected.

Of *Dyal Planes* ſome be *Direct*, others *Decliners*, others *Oblique*.

Of *Direct Planes* there are five ſorts.

1. The *Horizontal* whoſe Plane lies flat, and is parallel to the *Horizon*, beholding the *Zenith*.

2. The *South Erect*, whoſe Plane ſtands upright, and directly beholds the *South*.

3. The

3. The *North Erect*, whoſe Plane ſtands upright, and directly beholds the *North*.

4. The *Eaſt Erect*, whoſe Plane ſtands upright, and directly beholds the *Eaſt*.

5. The *Weſt Erect*, whoſe Plane ſtands upright and directly beholds the *Weſt*.

Of *Decliners* there are infinite; and yet may be reduced into theſe two *Kinds*.

1. The *South Erect* Plane, declining more or leſs towards the *Eaſt* or *Weſt*.

2. The *North Erect* Plane, declining more or leſs towards the *Eaſt* or *Weſt*.

Of *Obliqae Planes* ſome are *Direct* other *Declining*; and are of four ſorts.

1. *Direct Inclining* Planes, which lean towards you, and lie directly in the *Eaſt*, *Weſt*, *North*, or *South* quarters of Heaven.

2. *Direct Reclinig* Planes, which lean from you, and lie directly in the *Eaſt*, *Weſt*, *North* or *Sonth* quarters of Heaven.

3. *Inclining Declining* Planes, which lean towards you, but lie not directly in the *Eaſt*, *Weſt*, *North*, or *South* quarters of Heaven; But decline more or leſs from the *North* or *South*, towards the *Eaſt* or *Weſt*.

4. *Reclining Declining* Planes, which lean from you, but lie not directly in the *Eaſt*, *Weſt*, *North* or *South* quarters of Heaven; But Decline more or leſs from the *North* or *South*, towards the *Eaſt* or *Weſt*.

If the Scituation of the *Plane* be not given, you muſt ſeek it: For, there are ſeveral ways how to know theſe ſeveral kinds of *Planes* uſed among Artiſts; But the readieſt and eaſieſt is by an Inſtument called a *Declinatory*, fitted to the variation of your Place: And if it be truly made, you may as ſafely rely upon it as any other.

OPERARTIONI I.

The Description of the Clinatory.

THE Clinatory is made of a ſquare Board, ABCD, of a good thickneſs, and the larger the better; between two of the ſides is deſcribed on the Center A, a *Quadrant* as EF divided into 90 equal parts or degrees, which are figured with 10, 20, 30 to 90; and then back again with the Complements of the ſame Numbers to 90: Between the Limb and the two Semi-diameters is made a round Box, into which a Magnetical Needle is fitted; and a Card of the Nautical Compaſs, divided into four nineties, beginning their Numbers at the *East West North* and *South* points of the Compaſs, from which points the oppoſite ſides of the Clinatory receives their Names of *East*, *West*, *North* and *South*.

But *Note*, That the North point of the Card muſt be placed ſo many degrees towards the *East* or *West* ſides of the Clinatory, as the Needle varies from the true *North* point of the World, in the place where you make your Dyal; which your Workman that makes your Clinatory will know how to fit.

Upon the Center A, whereon the Quadrant was deſcribed, is faſtned a Plumb-line, having a Plummet of Lead or Braſs faſtned to the end of it, which Plumb-line is of ſuch length that the Plummet may fall juſt into the Groove G H, below the Quadrant, which is for that purpoſe made of ſuch a depth, that the Plummet may ride freely within it, without ſtopping at the ſides of it, *See the Figure annexed.*

With

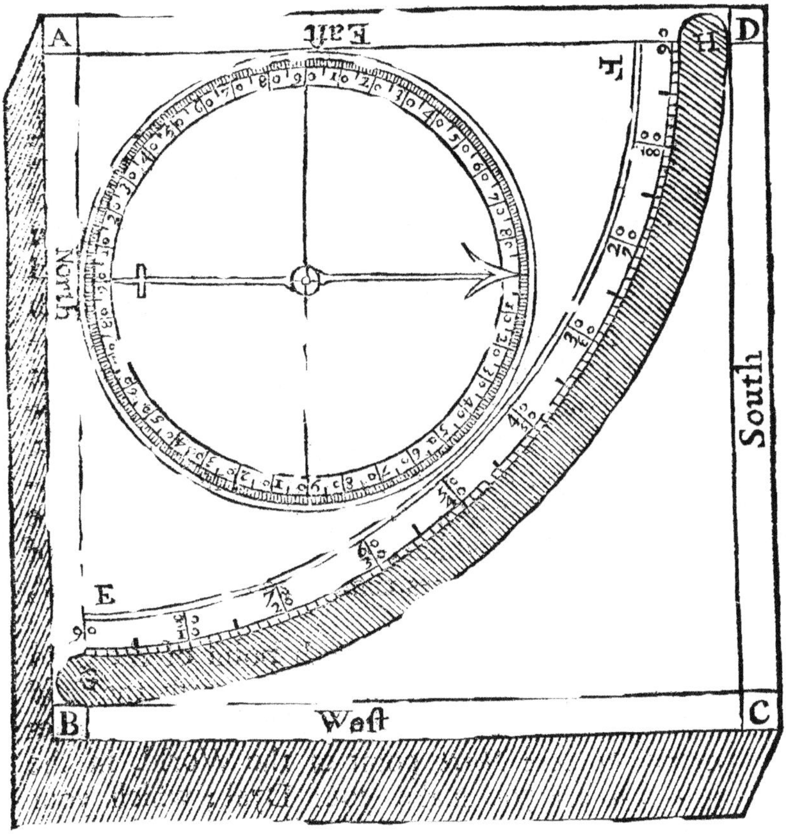

With this Clinatory you may examine the ſcituation of Planes. As if your Plane be Horizontal, it is direct: and then for the true ſcituating your Dyal, you have only the true North and South Line to find: which is done only by ſetting the Clinatory flat down upon the Plane, and turning it towards the right or left hand, till you can bring the North point of the Needle to hang juſt over the Flower-de-luce; for then if you draw a Line by either of the ſides parallel to the Needle, that Line ſhall be a North and South Line.

If your Plane either Recline or Incline, apply one of the ſides of your Clinatory parallel to one of of the Semi-diameters of the Quadrant to the Plane, in ſuch ſort that the Plumb-line hanging at liberty, may fall upon the Circumference of the Quadrant, for then the number of degrees of the Quadrant comprehended between the ſide of the Quadrant parallel to the Plane, and the Plumb-line ſhall be the number of degrees for Reclination, if the Center of the Quadrant points upwards; or Inclination, if the Center points downwards.

If your Reclining or Inclining Plane decline, draw upon it a Line parallel to the Horizon, which you may do by applying the Back-ſide of the Clinatory, and raiſing or depreſſing the Center of the Quadrant, till the Plumb-line hang juſt upon one of the Semi-diameters, for then you may by the upper-ſide of the Clinatory draw an Horizontal Line if the Plane Incline, or by the under-ſide, if it Recline. If it neither Incline or Recline, you may draw a Horizontal Line both by the upper and under ſides of the Clinatory. Having drawn the Horizontal Line, apply the North ſide of the Clinatory to it, and if the North end of the Needle points directly towards the Plane, it is then a South Plane. If the North point of the Needle points directly from the Plane, it is a *North* Plane: But if it points towards the *Eaſt*, it is an *Eaſt* Plane: If towards the *Weſt*, a *Weſt* Plane. If it do not point directly either Eaſt, Weſt, North, or South, then ſo many degrees as the Needle declines from any of theſe four points to any of the other of theſe four points, ſo many degrees is the Declination of the Plane.

You may find a Meridian Line another way; thus, If the Sun ſhine juſt at Noon, hold up a Plumb-line ſo as the ſhadow of it may fall upon your Plane, and that ſhadow ſhall be a *Meridian Line*.

OPE-

OPERAT. II.

To describe a Dyal upon a Horizontal Plane.

First draw a North and South Line (which is called a *Meridian Line*) through the middle of the Plane; Thus. Set your *Declinatory* flat upon the Plane, and turn it too and fro till the Needle hang precisely over the *Meridian Line* of the *Declinatory*; then by the side of the *Declinatory* parallel to its *Meridian Line*, draw a straight Line on the Plane, and if that straight Line be in the middle of the Plane, it shall be the *Meridian Line*, whithout more ado: But if it be not in the middle of the Plane, you must draw a Line parallel to it, through the middle of the Plane for the *Meridian Line*, or twelve a Clock Line: And it shall be the *Meridian Line*, and also be the *Substilar Line*; then draw another straight Line through the middle of this Line, to cut it at right Angles for the VI a Clock Lines; and where these two Lines cut one another make your Center, whereon you describe a Circle on your *Plane* as large as you can, which by the *Meridian Line*, and the Line drawn at right Angles with it will be divided into four *Quadrants*; one of the *Quadrants* divide into 90 degrees thus, keeping your Compasses at the same width they were at when you described the *Quadrant*, place one Foot in the twelve a Clock Line, and extend the other in the *Quadrant*, and make in the *Quadrant* a mark with it, so shall you have the sixtieth degree marked out: Then place one Foot of your Compasses in the six a Clock Line, and extend the other in the *Quadrant*, and make in the *Quadrant* another mark with it; so shall that *Quadrant* be divided into three equal parts, each of these three equal parts contains 30 Degrees: Then with your Compasses divide one of these three equal

equal parts into three parts, and transfer that diſtance to the other two third parts of the *Quadrant*, ſo ſhall the whole *Quadrant* be divided into nine equal parts. Then divide one of theſe nine equal parts into two equal parts, and transfer that diſtance to the other eight equal parts, ſo ſhall the *Quadrant* be divided into Eighteen equal parts. Then divide one of theſe Eighteen equal parts into five equal parts, and transfer that diſtance to the other Seventeen equal parts, ſo ſhall the whole *Quadrant* be divided into 90 equal parts, Each of theſe 90 equal parts are called Degrees.

Note, That you may in ſmall *Quadrants* divide truer and with leſs trouble with Steel Dividers, (which open or cloſe with a Screw for that purpoſe,) then you can with Compaſſes.

In this *Quadrant* (thus divided) count from the *Subſtilar* or *Meridian Line* the Elevation of the *Pole*, that is, the number of Degrees that the *Pole* of the World is elevated above the *Horizon* of your Place, and draw a Line from the Center through that number of Degrees for the *Stilar Line*. Then on the *Subſtilar Line* choſe a point (where you pleaſe) and through that point draw a Line at right Angles to the *Subſtilar Line* as long as you can, for the Line of *Contingence*, and from that point in the *Subſtilar Line* meaſure the neareſt diſtance any part of the *Stilar Line* hath to that point; and keeping one Foot of your Compaſſes ſtill in that point, ſet of that diſtance in the *Subſtilar Line*, and at that diſtance deſcribe againſt the *Line* of *Contingence* a Semi-circle, which divide from either ſide the *Meridian* or *Subſtilar Line* into ſix equal parts thus; Draw a line through the Center of this Semi-circle parallel to the *Line* of *Contingence*, which ſhall be the *Diametral Line*, and ſhall devide this Semi-circle into two *Quadrants*; one on one ſide the *Subſtiler Line*, and the

Qua-

Quadrant on the other side the *Substiler Line*: then keeping your Compasses at the same distance they were at when you described the Semi-circle, place one Foot first on one side the *Diametral Line* at the Intersection of it and the Semi-circle, and then on the other side, at the Intersection of it and the Semi-circle, and extend the other in the Semi-circle, and make marks in the Semi-circle on either side the *Substilar Line*; then place one Foot of your Compasses at the Intersection of the Semi-circle and the *Substilar Line*, and turn the other Foot about on either side the Semi-circle and make marks in the Semi-circle, so shall the Semi-circle be divided into six equal parts; Divide one of these equal parts into two equal parts, and transfer that distance to the other five equal parts, so shall the whole Semi-circle be divided into twelve equal parts. These twelve Divisions are to describe the twelve Hours of the Day, between six a Clock in the Morning, and six a Clock at Night.

If you will have half Hours, you may divide each of these twelve into two equal parts, as before: If you will have Quarters you may divide each of these twenty four into two equal parts more, as before.

For thus proportioning the Divisions in the Semi-circle, you may proportion the Divisions and Sub-divi-sions of Hours upon the *Dyal Plane*; for a straight Ruler laid upon each of these Divisions, and on the Center of this Semi-circle, shall shew on the *Line of Contingence* the several Distances of all the Hours and parts of Hours on the *Dyal Plane*. And straight Lines drawn from the Center of the *Dyal Plane*, through the several Divisions on the *Line of Contingence* shall be the several Hour Lines and parts on the *Dyal Plane*.

But

But an *Horizontal Dyal* in our Latitude will admit of four Hours more, *viz.* V, IV, in the Morning, and VII, VIII, in the Evening. Therefore in the Circle deſcribed on the Center of the *Dyal Plane* transfer the diſtance between VI and V, and VI and IV, on the other ſide the ſix a Clock Line; and transfer the Diſtances between VI and VII, and VI and VIII on the other ſide the oppoſite ſix a Clock Hour Line, and from the Center of the *Dyal Plane* draw Lines through thoſe transferred Diſtances for the Hour Lines before and after VI.

Then mark your Hour Lines with their reſpective numbers. The *Subſtilar Line* in this Dyal (as aforeſaid) is XII, from thence towards the right hand mark every ſucceſſive Hour Line with I, II, III, *&c.* and from XII towards the left hand with XI, X, IX, *&c.*

The *Stile* muſt be erected perpendicularly over the *Subſtilar Line*, ſo as to make an Angle with the *Dyal Plane* equal to the *Elevatioa* of the *Pole* of your Place.

Example.

You would draw a Dyal upon a *Horizontal Plane* here at *London*; Firſt draw the *Meridian* (or North and South Line) as XII B, and croſs it in the middle with another Line at right Angles, as VI, VI, which is an Eaſt and Weſt Line; where theſe two Lines cut each other as at A, make the Center, whereon deſcribe the Semi-circle B, VI, VI; but one of the *Quadrants*, viz. the *Quadrant* from XII to VI, towards the right hand yon muſt divide into 90 equal parts (as you were taught in *Fol.* 12.) and at 51½ degrees (which is *Londons* Latitude) make a mark, and laying a ſtraight Ruler to the Center of the *Plane*, and to this mark draw a Line by the ſide of it for the Stilar Line. Then on the

Subſtilar

Subſtilar Line chuſe a point as at C, and thro' that point draw a Line as long as you can perpendicular to the Eaſt and Weſt Line VI, VI, as E F, (which is called the *Contingent Line*) where this *Contingent Line* cuts the *Subſtilar Line* place one Foot of your Compaſſes, and from thence meaſure the ſhorteſt Diſtance between the point C and the *Stilar Line.* And keeping one Foot of your Compaſſes ſtill in the point C, ſet off the ſhorteſt diſtance between the point C, and the *Stilar Line* on the *Subſtilar Line*, as at D; which point D ſhall be a Center, whereon with your Compaſſes at the ſame width you muſt deſcribe a Semi-circle to repreſent a Semi-circle of the *Equinoctial.* This Semi-circle divide into ſix equal parts (as you were taught *Fol.* 13.) to each of which equal parts, and to the Center the *Equinoctial* Semi-circle lay a ſtraight Ruler, and where the ſtraight Ruler cuts the *Line of Contingence* make marks in the *Line of Contingence.* Then lay the ſtraight Ruler to the Semi-circle of the *Dyal Plane*, and to each of the marks in the *Line of Contingence*, and by the ſide of it draw twelve ſtraight Lines for the twelve Fore and Afternoon Hour Lines, *viz.* from VI in the Morning to VI in the Evening. Then in the *Quadrant* VI B, meaſure the diſtance between the VI a Clock Hour Line, and the V a Clock Hour Line, and transfer the ſame diſtances from the VI a Clock Line to VII, and V on both ſides the VI a Clock Hour Lines, and through thoſe diſtances draw from the Center of the Plane the VII and V a Clock Hour Lines, and meaſure the diſtance between the VI a Clock Hour Line and the IV a Clock Hour Line, and tranfer the ſame diſtance from the VI a Clock Line to VIII and IV, and through thoſe diſtances draw from the Center of the Plane the VIII a Clock and IV a Clock Hour Lines.

If

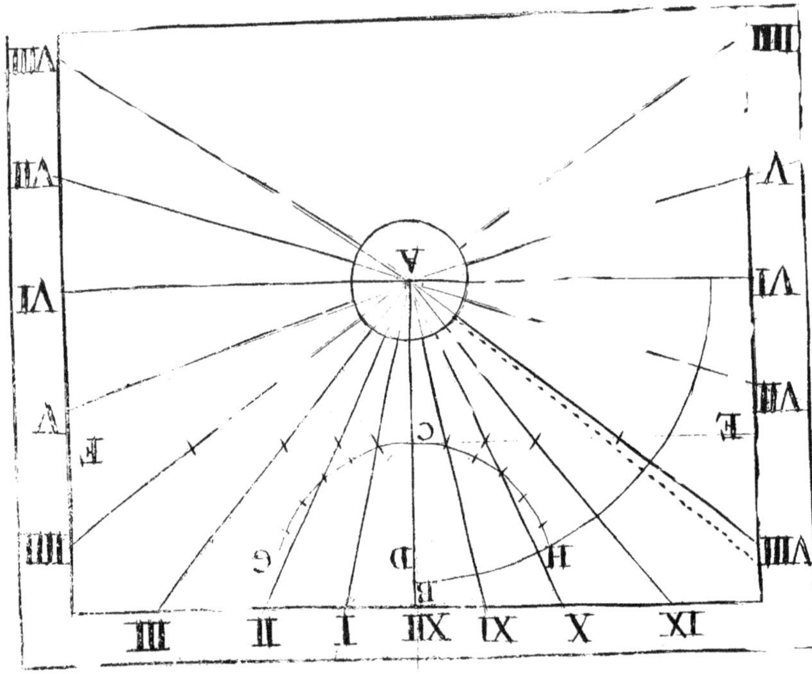

If you will have the half Hours and quarter Hours, or any other division of Hours, you must divide each six Divisions of the *Equinoctial* into so many parts as you intend, and by a straight Ruler laid to the Center of the *Equinoctial*, and those divisions in the *Equinoctial* Circle make marks in the *Line of Contingence*, as you did before for the whole Hour Lines: and Lines drawn from the Center of the Plane through those marks shall be the Sub-divisions of the Hours: But you must remember to make all Sub-divisions short Lines, and near the verge of the *Dyal Plane*, that you may the easier distinguish between the whole Hours and the parts of Hours; as you may see in the Figure.

Having drawn the Hour-Lines, set the Number of each Hour-Line under it, as you see in the Figure. Last of all fit a Triangular Iron, whose angular Point being laid to the Centre of the *Dyal* Plane

Plane, one side must agree with the *Substilar Line*, and its other side with the *Stilar Line*; so is the *Stile* made. And this *Stile* you must erect Perpendiculary over the *Substilar Line* on the *Dyal Plane*, and there fix it. Then is your *Dyal* finished.

OPERAT. III.

To describe an Erect Direct South-Dyal.

YOU may know an *Erect Direct South-Plane*, by applying the North-side of the *Declinatory* to it; For then, if the North-end of the Needle hang directly over the North-point of the Card in the bottom of the Box, it is a *South-Plane*; but if it hang not directly over the North-point of the Card it is not a *Direct South-Plane*, but *Declines* either East or West and that contrary to the Pointing of the Needle Easterly or Westerly, from the North-point of the Card: For, if the North-point of the Needle points Easterly, the *Plane Declines* from the South towards the West: if it point Westerly the *Plane Declines* from the South towards the East.

You may know, if the *Plane* be truly *Erect* or upright, by applying one of the sides A D or A B to it; for then by holding the Center A upwards, so as the Plumb-line play free in the Groove, if the Line falls upon o, or 90, the Plane is upright; but, if it hang upon any of the intermediate Degrees, it is not upright, but *Inclines* or *Reclines*.

If you find it incline, apply the side A B to it; and see what number of Degrees the Plumb-line falls on, for that number of Degrees, counted from the said A B, is the number of Degrees of *Inclination*.

If you find the *Plane Reclines*, apply the side A D to it, and see what number of Degrees the Plumb-line falls on, for that number of Degrees counted from the side A D, is the number of Degrees of *Reclination*.

These Rules being well underſtood, may ſerve you to find the ſcituation of all other ſort of *Planes*.

But for the making a *Dyal* on this *Plane*, you muſt firſt draw a *Meridian Line* through the middle of the *Plane*, by applying a Plumb-line to the middle of it, till the Plumbet hang quietly before it: for then, if the Plumb-line be blacked (for a white Ground, or chalked for a dark Ground) and ſtrained as Carpenters do their Lines, you may with one ſtroke of the ſtring on the *Plane*, deſcribe the *Meridian Line*, as A XII. This *Meridian* is alſo the *Subſtilar line*.

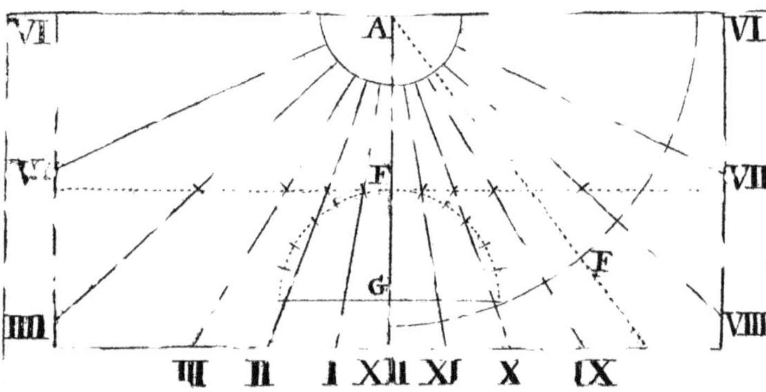

Then on the top of this *Meridian Line*, as at A draw another Line athwart it, to cut it at right Angles, as VI, VI. for an Eaſt and Weſt Line. At the meeting of theſe two Lines at the top, make your Center, whereon deſcribe a Semi-Circle on your *Plane*, as large as you can, which by the *Meridian Line* and the Eaſt and Weſt Line, will be divided into two *Quadrants*. One of theſe *Quadrants* divide into 90 Degrees (as you were taught *Fol.* 12.) and from the *Subſtilar Line* count the Complement of the *Poles Elevation*, which (here at *London* where the *Pole* is elevated 51 ½ Degrees, its Complement to 90) is 38 ½ Degrees, and make there

there a mark, as at E. Then on the *Subſtilar line* chuſe a point (where you pleaſe) as at F, for the *line of Contingence* to paſs through; which *Line of Contingence* draw as long as you can, ſo as it may cut the *Subſtilar Line* at right Angles, and from the point F in the *Subſtilar line*, meaſure the ſhorteſt diſtance between it and the *Stilar Line*, and keeping one Foot of your Compaſſes ſtill in the point F, transfer that diſtance into the *Subſtilar Line.* as at G; then on the point G deſcribe a Semi-Circle of the *Equinoctial* againſt the *Line of Contingence*, which Semi-Circle divide into twelve equal parts, (as you were taught by the *Example* in the *Horizontal Dyal*, Fol. 13.) and by a ſtraight Ruler laid to each of theſe Diviſions, and to the Center of the Semi-Circle make marks in the *Line of Contingence* by the ſide of the Ruler; For ſtraight Lines drawn from the Center of the *Dyal plane* through theſe marks in the *Contingent line* ſhall be the 12 Hour Lines before and after Noon.

Then mark your Hour Lines with their reſpective Numbers; the *Subſtilar* or *Meridian Line* is XII, from thence towards the right hand with I, II, III, *&c.* and from thence towards the left hand with a XI, X, IX, *&c.*

The *Stile* muſt be erected perpendicular over the *Subſtilar Line*, ſo as to make an Angle with the *Dyal Plane* equal to the Complement of the *Poles Elevation*, viz. 38 ½ Degrees.

OPERAT. IV.

To make an Erect Direct North Dyal.

THE *Erect Direct* North Dyal, Stile and all, is made by the ſame Rules, changing upwards for downwards, and the left ſide for the right, the *Erect Direct South Dyal* is made; for if the *Erect Direct South Dyal* be drawn on any tranſparent

 Plane,

Plane, as on Glaſs, Horn, or an oyled Paper, and the *Horizontal Line* VI, VI turned downwards, and the Line VII mark t with V, the Line VIII with IIII the Line V with VII, and the Line IIII with VIII, then have you of it a *North Erect Direct Dyal.*

All the other Hour Lines in this Dyal are uſeleſs, becauſe the Sun in our Latitude ſhines on a North Face the longeſt Day only before VI in the Morning, and after VI at Night.

OPERAT. V.

To deſcribe an Erect Direct Eaſt Dyal.

HAving a Plumb-line a little above the Place on the Wall where you intend to make your Dyal, and wait till it hang quietly before the wall: Then if the Line be rubbed with Chalk (like a Carpenters Line) you may by holding the Plumbet end cloſe to the wall, and ſtraining it pretty ſtiff, ſtrike with it a ſtraight Line, as Carpenters do: This Line ſhall be a perpendicular, as A B. Then chuſe a convenient point in this Perpendicular, as at C, for a Center, whereon deſcribe an occult Arch, as D E; This Arch muſt contain the number of Degrees of the *Elevation* of the *Equinoctial*, counted between D and E, which in our *Latitude* is 38½, or (which is all one) the Complement of the *Poles Elevation*. Therefore in a *Quadrant* of the ſame *Radius*, with the occult Arch meaſure 38½ Degrees, and ſet them off in the Plane from E to D: Then from D to the Center C in the Perpendicular, draw the prick't Line D C; this prick't Line ſhall repreſent the *Axis of the World*. Then croſs this Line at right Angles with the Line C F, and draw it from C to F, ſo long as poſſibly you can: This Line ſhall be the *Contingent Line*. Then chuſe a point in this *Contingent Line*, as at VI, draw a Line through that point at right Angles for the *Subſti-*

lar

lar Line, as G VI H for the *Subſtilar Line*; then open your Compaſſes to a convenient width, (as to VI G) and pitching one foot in the point G, with the other Foot deſcribe a Semi-Circle of the *Equinoctial* againſt the *Line of Contingence*, which Semi-Circle divide from VI both ways into ſix equal parts, as you were taught by the *Example* in the *Horizontal Dyal*; and laying a ſtraight Ruler on the Center of this Semi-Circle of the *Equinoctial*, and to each of thoſe equal parts mark on the *Contingent Line* where the Ruler cuts it, for thoſe marks ſhall be the ſeveral points from whence Lines drawn parallel to the Line CD ſhall be the reſpective Hour Lines.

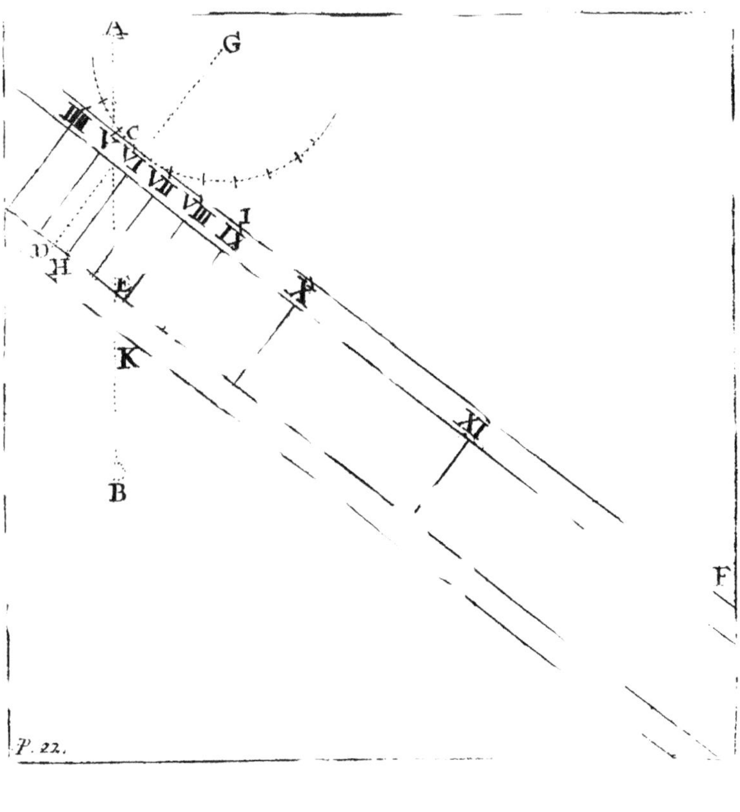

The reaſon why the *Contingent Line* is drawn from VI to F, ſo much longer than from VI to C is; becauſe the Hour Lines from VI towards XII are more in Number towards Noon, than they are from VI backwrd towards IIII, for this Dyal will only ſhew the Hours from a little before IV in the Morning to almoſt Noon. For juſt at Noon the Shadow goes off the Plane; as you may ſee, if you apply a ſtraight Ruler to the Center of the equinoctial Semi-Circle G, and lay it to the point 12 in the Semi-Circle; for the ſtraight Ruler will then never cut the *Line of Contingence*, becauſe the *Line of Contingence* is parallel to the line G XII on the Equinoctial Circle, and Lines parallel, though continued to never ſo great a length, never meet.

To theſe *Hour Lines*, ſet Figures as may be ſeen in the Scheme.

The *Stile* IK of this Dyal, as well as of all others, muſt ſtand parallel to the *Axis of the World*; and alſo parallel to the Face of the *Plane*, and parallel to all the *Hour lines*, and ſtand directly over the *Subſtilar* or VI a Clock *Hour line*, and that ſo high as is the diſtance of the Center of the Equinoctial Semi-Circle from the *Contingent Line*.

OPERAT. VI.

To deſcribe a Dyal *on an* Erect Direct Weſt Plane.

AN Erect Direct *Weſt-Dyal*, is the ſame in all reſpects with an Erect Direct Eaſt-Dyal; only as the Eaſt-Dyal ſhews the Forenoon Hours, ſo the Weſt ſhews the Afternoon Hours.

Thus, if you ſhould draw the *Eaſt-Dyal* on any tranſparent *Plane*, as on Glaſs, Horn, or oyled Paper, on the one ſide will appear an *Eaſt Dyal*, on the other ſide a *Weſt*; only the numbers to the *Hour Lines* (as was ſaid before in the *North-Dyal*,) muſt

be

be changed; for that which in the *East-Dyal* is XI, in the *West* must be I; that which in the *East-Dyal* is X, in the *West* must be II; that which in the *East-Dyal* is IX, in the *West* must be III, *&c.* The Stile is the same.

OPERAT. VII.

To Describe a Dyal on an Erect North, *or* Erect South Plane Declining *Eastwards or Westwards.*

THese four Dyals, viz. the *Erect North Declining Eastwards*, the *Erect North Declining Westwards*, the *Erect South Declining Eastwards*, and the *Erect South Declining Westwards*, are all projected by the same Rules; and therefore are in effect but one Dyal differently placed, as you shall see hereafter.

First draw on your *Plane* a straight Line to represent the *Horizon* of your place, and mark one end of it W for *West*, and the other end E for *East*. Chuse a point in this *Horizontal* Line for a Center, as at A, whereon you may describe a Circle to comprehend all these four *Dyals*: Draw a Line as MAM perpendicular to the *Horizontal Line* WE, through the Center A for a *Meridian Line* and on that Center describe a Circle, which by the two Lines WA E, and M A M will be divided into four *Quadrants*, which will comprehend the four *Dyals* aforesaid; for if it be a *North Declining West* you are to draw, the upper *Quadrant* to the left hand serves your purpose; If a *South declining West*, the same Lines continued through the Center A into the lower *Quadrant* to the right Hand serves your turn; if a *North Declining East*, the upper *Quadrant* to the right hand serves your turn; or if a *South declining East*, the same Lines continued through the Center A into the lower *Quadrant* to the left hand serves your turn; and you must draw the *Declination, Com-*

plement of the Poles Altitude; *Substile Stile* and *Hour Lines* in it; but the *Hour Lines* must be differently marked as you shall see hereafter. I shall only give you an Example of one of these Dyals, *viz.* A *South Declining East*.

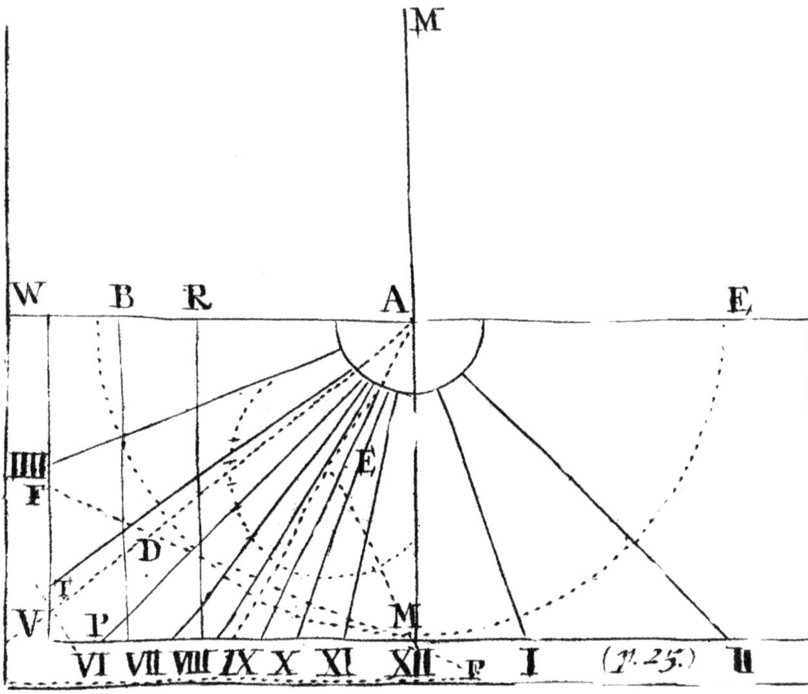

We will suppose you are to draw a Dyal that *declines* from the *South* 50 Degrees towards the *East*; here being but one *Dyal*, you need describe but one *Quadrant* of a Circle. Set off in the lower *Quadrant* W A M 50 degrees from the *Meridian Line* M towards W, and from the Center A draw a straight Line through that mark in the *Quadrant* as D A, which may be called the *Line of Declination*; then set off from the *Meridian Line* the *Complement* of the *Poles Elevation* which in our Latitude is 38 ½ degrees, and there draw another Line from the Center as A P, which we will call the *Polar Line*.

Then

Then take in the *Horizontal Line* a convenient portion of the *Quadrant*, as A B, and from the point B draw a Line parallel to the *Meridian Line* A M, and continue that Line till it interfect the *Polar Line*, as at P, from which Point P draw a Line parallel to W A, as P C: Then meaſure the diſtance of A B in the *Horizontal Line*, and ſet off that diſtance in the Line of *Declination*, as from A to D, and from that point of diſtance draw a Line parallel to the *Meridian* A M through the *Horizontal Line* at R, and through the Point D, and continue it through the Line P C, as at S; then laying a ſtraight Ruler to the Center A and the Interſection of the line P C, at S draw the Line A S for the *Subſtile*: Then upon the point S erect a Line perpendicularly as S T; Then meaſure the diſtance between R and D, and ſet that diſtance off from S to T, and from the Center to the point T draw the Line AT for the *Stile* or *Gnomon*; and the *Triangle* S AT made of Iron or Braſs, and erected perpendicularly over the *Subſtile* S A, ſhall by its upper ſide TA, caſt a ſhadow upon the Hour of the day. But you will ſay, the Hour Lines muſt be drawn firſt: It is true; Therefore to draw them you muſt chuſe a point in the *Subſtile Line* where you think good, and through it draw the Line F F as long as you can for the *Line of Contingence*; then with your Compaſſes take the diſtance between this point and the *Stile*, and transfer that diſtance below the *Line of Contingence* on the *Subſtile* as at Æ, and with your Compaſſes at that diſtance deſcribe on the Center Æ a Circle to repreſent the *Equinoctial*; then (as you were taught in the Example of the *Horizontal Dyal*) divide the Semi-Circle of the *Equinoctial* into twelve equal parts, beginning at the point in the *Equinoctial Circle*, where a ſtraight Line drawn from the Center of it to the Interſection of the Line of *Contingence* with the Meridian Line cuts the *Equinoctial*

noctial Line, as here at the Point G; then lay a ſtraight Ruler to the Center of the *Equinoctial Circle* and to every one of the Diviſions in the Semicle, and mark where the ſtraight Ruler cuts the *Contingent Line*; for ſtraight Lines drawn from the Center A of the Dyal to thoſe ſeveral marks on the *Contingent Line*, ſhall be the *Hour Lines*; and muſt be numbred from the Noon Line or *Meridian* A M backwards, as XII, XI, X, IX, *&c.* towards the left hand. So is your Dyal finiſhed.

This Dyal drawn on any tranſparent matter, as Horn, Glaſs, or an oyled Paper, ſhall on the other ſide the tranſparent matter become a *South Declining West* (*Stile* and all) but then the I a Clock Hour Line muſt be marked II. the XII, XII, the XI a Clock Hour Line, I, X, II, IX, III, *&c.*

If you project it a new, you muſt deſcribe the *Quadrant* M W on the other ſide the *Meridian Line*, on the Center A from M to E, and then count, (as before) the *Declination*, *Altitude* of the *Pole*, *Subſtile*, and *Stile* in the *Quadrant*, beginning at M towards E, and work in all reſpects as with the *South Declining East*; only number this *South Declining West* as in the foregoing Paragraph.

If you project a *North Declining East*, you muſt deſcribe the *Quadrant* above the *Horizontal Line* from M upwards, towards E on your right hand and count (as before) the *Declination*, *Altitude*, *Complement* of the *Pole*, *Subſtile* and *Stile* from the *meridian Line*, and work as with the *South Declining East*: It muſt be numbred from the *Meridian Line* M towards the right hand with XI, X, IX, VIII, *&c.*

If this Dyal were drawn on tranſparent matter, the other ſide would ſhew a *North Declining West*: Bnt if you will project it anew, you muſt deſcribe the *Quadrant* above the *Horizontal Line*, from M upwards towards W, and count from the *Meridian Line* A M the *Declination*, *Complement*, *Altitude* of the

the Pole, Subſtile and Stile, and work with them (in all reſpects) as with the *South Declining Eaſt*; bnt then the XI a Clock Hour Line muſt be marked I, the X, II; the IX, III, *&c.*

OPERAT. VIII.

To draw a Dyal on an Eaſt *or* Weſt Plane Reclining *or* Inclining.

DRaw a ſtraight Line parallel to the *Horizon*, to repreſent the *Meridian*, or XII a Clock Line and mark one end N, the other S; chuſe a point in this Line, as at A for a Center: Then if Your Plane be an *Eaſt*, or a *Weſt Incliner*, let fall a Perpendicular upon this Center, (that is, the Perpendicular muſt ſtand above the Meridian Line NS) as A E, and upon the Center A deſcribe a Semi-Circle above the Meridian Line N S; But if your Plane be an Eaſt Incliner, or a Weſt Recliner, let fall a Perpendicular from the Center A under the Meridian Line, and upon the Center A deſcribe a Semi-Circle under the *Meridian Line.* If your Plane be a *Weſt Incliner*; work (as ſhall be taught) in the *Quadrant* on the left hand above the *Meridian* Line. If an Eaſt Recliner, in the *Quadrant* on the right hand above the Meridian Line. If it be a Weſt Recliner, work in the *Quadrant* on the left hand under the *Meridian*. If an Eaſt Incliner, in the Quadrant under the Meridian Line the right hand.

For Example, *An Eaſt Dyal Reclining* 45 *Degrees.*

You would draw a *Dyal* on an *Eaſt Plane Reclining* 45 Degrees: Therefore in the *Quadrant* on the right hand above the *Meridian* Line, ſet off from the Perpendicular A E 45 Degrees on the *Quadrant* for the Reclination of the *Plane*; and ſet

off

off alſo in the *Quadrant* 38 ½ Degrees from the Perpendicular for the *Complement of the Poles Elevation*, and at theſe ſettings off make marks in the *Quadrant*; Then lay a ſtraight Ruler to the Center A, and to the marks in the *Quadrant*, and draw ſtraight Lines through them from the Center. Then chuſe in the *Meridian* Line N S a convenient point as at B, and through that point draw a Line parallel to the perpendicular A E, which will Interſect the Line drawn for the Complement of the *Poles Elevation* A P in P; from which point P, draw a Line parallel to the *Meridian* Line N S, to cut the Perpendicular A E in C. and alſo the Line of Obliquity A O in O. Then meaſure the length A O, and ſet off that length in the Perpendicular A C E from A to E, and draw the Line E G parallel to the *Meridian* Line N S which will cut the Line B P prolonged in G. Meaſure alſo the length of C O, and ſet that length off from A to Q on the Line of Obliquity A O, and draw the Line Q R parallel to the Perpendicular A C E. Then meaſure the diſtance of A R, and upon the Line G P B, ſet it off from G to S; and laying a ſtraight Ruler to the point S and the Center A, draw by the ſide of it the Line A S, for the *Subſtile* Line. Then meaſure the length of Q R, and from S raiſe a Perpendicular, and in that Perpendicular, ſet that length off from S to T; and laying a ſtraight Ruler to the Center A and the point T, draw the Line A T for the *Stilar* Line, which *Stilar* Line being Perpendicular erected over the *Subſtilar* Line A S, will ſtand parallel to the *Axis of the World*, and caſt its ſhadow on the Hour of the Day.

To

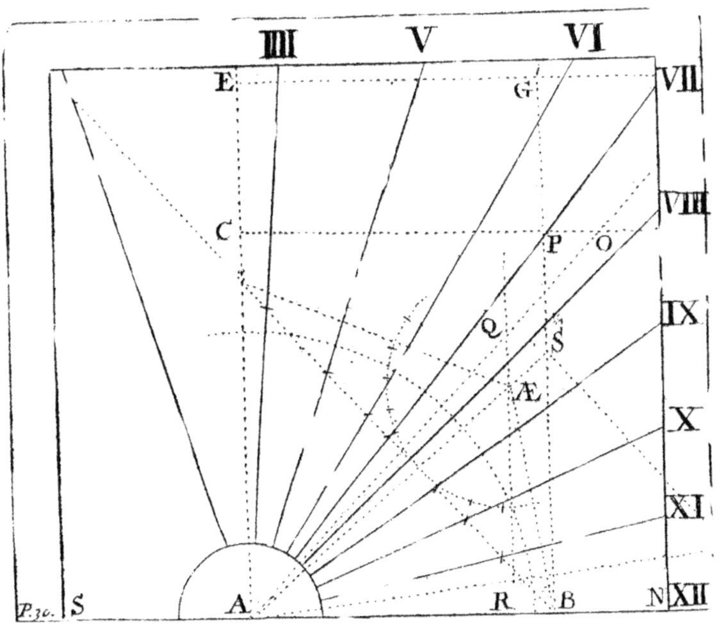

To draw the Hour Lines on this Plane, you must (as you have several times before been directed) chuse a point in the *Substilar* Line and through that point draw at right Angles with the *Substilar* Line, the Line of *Contingence* so long as you can: Then measure the shortest distance between that Point and the *Stilar* Line, and transfer that distance below the Line of *Contingence* in the *Substilar* Line, as at Æ, and with your Compasses at that distance, describe against the Line of Contingence the Equinoctial Circle; then divide the Semicircle of the *Equinoctial* next the Line of *Contingence* into twelve equal parts, as you have formerly been taught, beginning at the Point in the *Equinoctial Circle*, where a straight Line drawn from the Center of it to the Intersection of the Line of *Contingence* with

with the *Meridian* Line NS cuts the *Equinoctial Circle* as here at the point D; Then lay a ſtraight Ruler to the Center of the *Equinoctial* Circle, and to every one of the Diviſions in the *Equinoctial* Semi-Circle, and mark where the ſtraight Ruler cuts the *Contingent* Line; for ſtraight Lines drawn from the Center A of the Dyal, through theſe ſeveral marks in the *Contingent* Line ſhall be the Hour Lines and muſt be numbred from the *Meridian* or Noon-Line N S, which is the XII a Clock Line upwards, with XI, X, IX, VIII, *&c.* The Center of this Dyal muſt ſtand downward.

If this Dyal were turned with its Center upwards, it would ſhew a *Weſt Inclining* 45 degrees, only the numbers to the Hour Lines muſt be changed; for to XI you muſt ſet I, to X, II, to IX, III, *&c.* and the *Subſtile* over which the Stile muſt ſtand, muſt be placed in the Semi-circle (at firſt deſcribed) as much to the right hand the perpendicular A E, as it doth on the left hand.

If this Dyal were drawn on Glaſs, or Horn, or an oyled Paper, and you turn the *Meridian* Line N S upwards the back ſide ſhall be an *Eaſt Inclining* 45 degrees, and the Hour Lines muſt be numbred as they are on the *Eaſt Reclining*; But the Subſtile over which the Stile muſt ſtand muſt be placed in the Semi-circle (at firſt deſcribed) as much to the left hand the perpendiculer A E, as it is on the oyled Paper to the right hand.

If you turn the *Meridian* Line N S downwards, the backſide ſhall be a *Weſt Recliner* 45 Degrees, and the Hour Lines muſt be numbred from the XII a Clock line upwads, with I, II, III, *&c.*

You muſt Note that all the Hour-Lines of the Day will nor be deſcribed in this ſingle *Quadrant*, nor does the *Quadrant* at all relate to the Hour Lines; but is deſcribed only for ſetting off the *Complement* of the *Poles Elevation* and *Reclination* of the *Plane*, that

that by working (as hath been ſhewn) you may find the place of the Subſtilar Line, and the Angle the Stile makes with it; for having the Subſtilar Line, you know how to draw the Line of *Contingence*, and to deſcribe the *Equinoctial* Circle, by which all the Hours are deſcribed on the *Plane*.

To draw a Dyal *on a* Direct South *or* North Plane Inclining *or* Reclining.

Direct Reclining or *Inclining* Dyals are the ſame with Erect Direct Dyals that are made for the Latitude of ſome other Places; the Latitude of which Places are either more then the Latitude of your place, if the Plane *Recline*, or leſs, if it *Inclines*; and that in ſuch a proportion as the Arch of *Reclination* or *Inclination* is.

Thus a Direct South Dyal *Reclining* 10 degrees in *London*'s Latitude, (*viz.* 51 ½ degrees) is an Erect Direct South Dyal made for the Latitude of 61 ½ degrees. And a Direct South Dyal *Inclining* 10 in the Latitude of 51 ½ is an *Erect Direct South* Dyal in the Latitude of 41 ½ degrees, and is to be made according to the Direction given in *Operat.* III.

OPERAT. IX.

To draw a Dyal *on a* South *or* North Inclining Declining, *or* Reclining Declining Plane.

THeſe four ſorts of Dyals, *viz.* the South Inclining Declining, and South Reclining Declining, and North Inclining Declining, and South Reclining Declining, are all projected by the ſame Rules; and therefore are in effect but one Dyal differently placed, as you ſhall ſee hereafter.

First,

First, draw on your Plane a straight Line parallel to the *Horizon*, and mark one end W for *West*, and the other E for *East*. On South Incliners and Recliners, E on the right hand, and W on the left on North Incliners and Recliners E on the left and W on the right. Chuse a point in this *Horizontal* Line for a Center, as at A; through this point A draw a Line perpendicular to the *Horizon*, and on this point (as on a Center) describe a Semi-Circle, one *Quadrant* above, and another below the *Horizontal* Lines, (though for this Example I describe but one.) Then if the Plane respect the South, set off in the lower *Quadrant* from the perpendicular, the Declination, the Inclination, or the Reclination, and the Complement of the *Altitude* of the Pole; and thro' these several settings off in the *Quadrant*, draw straight Lines from the Center A, then take in the *Horizontal* line towards the Semi-circle, a convenient distance from the Center A, as B, and through the point B draw a straight Line parallel to the Perpendicular, and prolong it thro' the Polar line, as B P; thro' the point P; draw a Line parallel to the *Horizontal* line, as P C; this line will cut the Line of *Obliquity* in the point O, then measure the distance of A O, and set off that distance on the Perpendicular from A to F, and through the point F draw a straight line parallel to the *Horizontal* line, as F G, for the *Horizontal* Intersection. Then measure the distance of C O, and set off that distance on the Perpendicular from A to L; from the point L draw the line L D parallel to the *Horizontal* line, to cut the line of *Declination* in the point D. Then measure the distance of A B, and set off that distance in the Line of Declination from A to E; and from the point E, draw a straight line parallel to the *Horizontal* line W E, to cut the Perpendicular in the point K. Measure the distance of E K, and set off set off that distance on the other side the Perpendicular in the *Horizontal* Interfection, from F to H, and from the point H draw H N parallel to the Perpendicular to cut the *Horizontal* line in the point N.

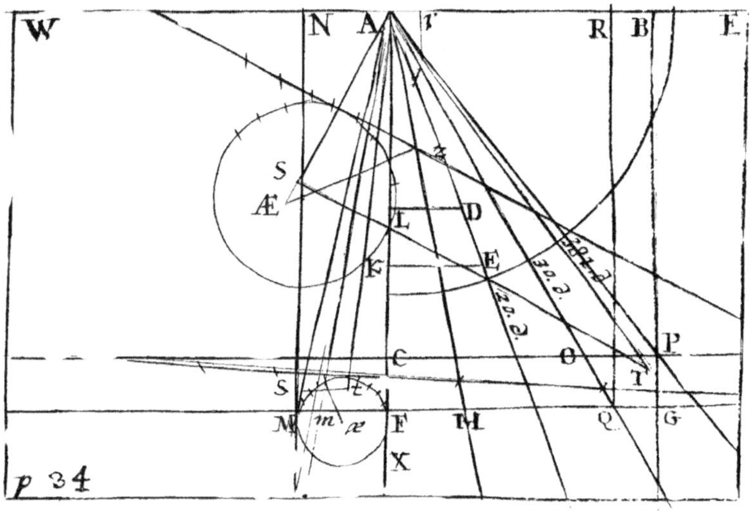

Then to find the *Meridian* line, *Substile* and *Stile*, do thus. If your *Plane* be a *Southern Incliner*, or a *Norhern Recliner*, measure the distance of L D, and and set off that distance in the *Horizontal* Intersection from F to M, and through the point M draw the line A M for the *Meridian* line. Then add the distance of A L to A K, thus: Measure the distance of A L, and place one Foot of your Compasses in the point K in the Perpendicular line, and extend the other to X, and measuring the distance of A X, set it off in the line of *Obliquity* from A to Q; and from the point Q draw the line Q R parallel to the Perpendicular, and cutting the *Horizontal* line in the point R. Then measure the distance of A R, and set off that distance from H in the *Horizontal* Intersection to S on the line H N, and to the point S draw the line A S for the *Substile.* Then measure the distance of Q R, and set off that distance perpendicularly from the point S to T; and lastly, from the point A draw the straight line A T for the *Stilar* line, which *Stilar* line being perpendicularly erected over the *Substilar* line A S, will stand parallel to the *Axis of the World*, and cast its shadow on the Hour of the Day.

But if the Plane be a *Southern Recliner*, or *Northern Incliner*, measure (as before) the distance of L D, and (as before you were directed) to set it off from F in the *Horizontal* Intersection on the right hand the perpendicular line: So now, set that distance from F to *m* in the Horizontal Intersection on the left hand in the Perpendicular line, and draw the line A *m* for the *Meridian* Line. Then as before you were directed, to add A L to A K; So now, substract the distance of A L from A K, and the remainder will be L K: Set therefore the distance of L K from A to *q* in the same line of *Obliquity*, and from the point *q* draw the line *q r* parallel to the perpendicular. Measure then the distance of A *r*, and set of that distance in the line H N, from H to *s* for the *Substilar* line; then erect on the point *s* a perpendicular, and on that Perpendicular set off from *s* to *t* the distance of *q r*: And lastly, from A draw the Line A *t* for the *Stilar Line.*

If K falls upon L the *Plane* is parallel to the *Axis of the World*, and the Dyal drawn upon it will have no Center; But *s* will fall upon H, and A H (or A *s*) will be the *Substile.*

I shall give you two Examples of these Rules: One of a Dyal with a Center, and the other of a Dyal without a Center. And first,

OPERAT. X.

How to draw a Dyal *with a Center,* Declining 20 *Degrees, and* Inclining 30 *Degrees.*

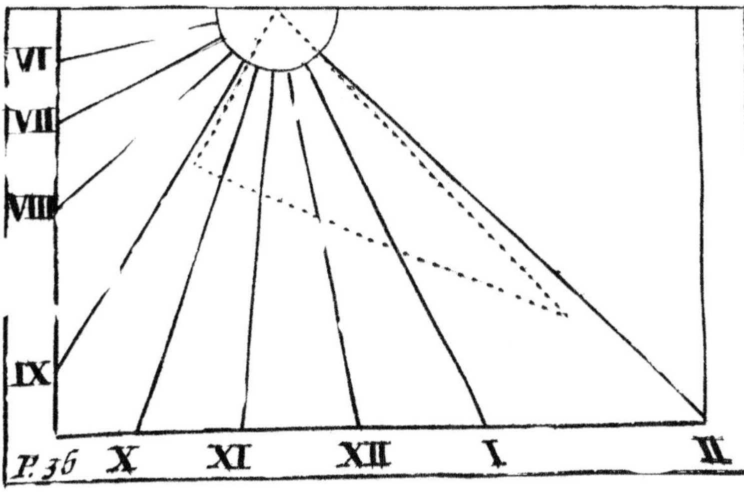

HAving by the foregoing Precepts of the last *Operat.* found the *Substile, Stile* and *Meridian*, you must (as you have often been directed) chuse a point in the *Substilar* line; through which, at right Angles to the *Substilar* line, draw the line of Contingence as long as you can; then measure the shortest distance between the point of Intersection and the *Stilar line*, and transfer that distance on one side of the *line* of *Contingence* upon the *Substilar line*, and so describe the *Equinoctial* Semicircle against the *line* of *Contingence*: Then lay a straight Ruler to the Center of the *Equinoctial Circle* as at Æ, and to the point where the *line* of *Contingence* cuts the *Meridian Line*, as at Z, and mark where the straight Ruler cuts the *Equinoctial Circle*, and from that mark begin to divide the *Semi-circle* into twelve equal parts, and by a ſtraight Ruler laid to thoſe diviſions and the Center of the *Equinoctial*, make marks in the *line* of *Contingence*. Then ſhall ſtraight *lines* drawn from the Center A of the Dyal, through every one of the marks in the *Contingent line* be the Hour lines of the Dyal, and muſt be numbred from the XII a Clock line towards the right Hand, with I, II, III, IV, *&c.* And the other way with XI, X, IX, *&c.*

OPERAT. XI.

How to draw a Dyal *without a* Center, *on a* South Plane; Declining Eaſt 30 *Degrees*, Recilning 34 *Degrees* 32 Minutes.

HAving by the Precepts of *Operat.* IX. found the *Subſtile*, you muſt find the *Meridian line* otherwiſe than you were there taught: For, having drawn the *lines* of *Latitude*, *Declination* and *Reclination*, and found the *Subſtile*, meaſure the diſtance of B P, and ſet it off on the *line* of *Declination* from A to K, and draw from the Perpendicular A F the line K Q parallel to A B: then meaſure the length of K Q, and ſet it off on the *Polar line* A P from A to V; then take the neareſt diſtance between the point V and the *line* A B, and ſet it off on the *line* Q K from Q to M; through which point M, draw a *line* from the Center A; then meaſure with your Compaſſes in the Semi-circle W N E (which in this Dyal may repreſent the Equinoctial) the diſtance of the Arch N *m*, and ſet off that diſtance from the Interſection of the *Subſtile* with the Semi-circle at S to T in the Semi-circle, which point T ſhall be the point in the *Equinoctial* that you muſt begin to divide the Hours at, for the finding their diſtances on the *line* of *Contingence*.

Then

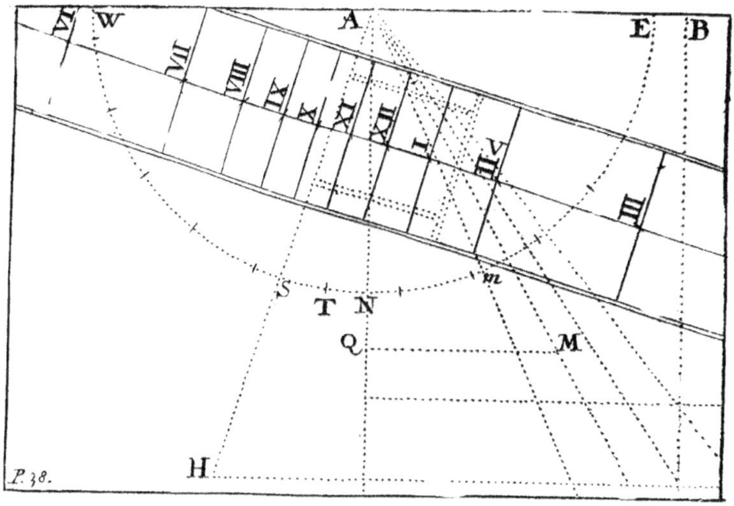

Then consider (according to the bigness of your Plane) what height your *Stile* shall stand above the *Substile*, and there make a mark in the *Substile*; for the distance between the Center A, and that mark must be the height of the *Stile* perpendicularly erected over the *Substile*, as at I. Draw through this point I a *line of Contingence*, as long as you can to cut the *Substile* at right *Angles*, and then laying a *Ruler* to the Center A, and successively to to each Division of the *Equinoctial* make marks in the *line of Contingence*, and through those marks draw straight *lines* parallel to the *Substile*, which shall be the *Hour lines*; and must be numbred from the left hand towards the right, beginning at the XII a *Clock line* with I, II, III, *&c.* and from the right hand towards the left on the XII a *Clock line* with XI, X, IX, *&c.*

The *Stile* to this Dyal may be either a straight Pin of the length of A I, or else a square of the same height, erected Perpendicularly upon the I, in the *Substilar-line*.

OPERAT. XII.

To make a Dyal *on the* Cieling *of a* Room, *where the* Direct Beams *of the* Sun *never come.*

FInd some convenient place in the Transum of a Window to place a small round piece of Looking-Glass about the bigness of a Groat or less, so as it may lie exactly Horizontal. The point in the middle of this Glass we will mark A, and for distinction-sake call it *Nodus*. Through this *Nodus* you must draw a *Meridian line* on the Floor, thus: Hang a plumb-line in the window exactly over *Nodus*, and the shadow that the plumb-line casts on the Floor just at Noon will be a *Meridian line*; or you may find a *Meridian line* otherwise by the Clinatory. Having drawn the *Meridian line* on the Cieling, thus: Hold a *Plumb-line* to the Cieling, over that end of the *Meridian line* nex the window; if the *Plumbet* hang not exactly on the *Meridian line* on the Floor, remove your hand on the *Cieling* one way or other, as you see cause till it do hang quietly just over it, and at the point where the *Plumb line* touches the *Cieling* make a mark, as at B; that mark B shall be directly over the *Meridian line* on the Floor: Then remove your *Plumb line* on the *Floor*, and find a point on the *Cieling* directly over it, as you did the former point, as at C, and through these two points B and C on the *Cieling*, strain and strike a *line* blackt with *Small-coal* or any other *Coluor* (as Carpenters do) and that *line* BC on the *Cieling* shall be the *Meridan line* as well as that on the Floor: Then fasten a string just on the *Nodus*, and remove that string, forwards or backwards, in the *Meridian line* on the *Cieling*, till it have the same Elevation in the *Quadrant* on the *Clinatory*

above

above the *Horizon* that the *Equinoctial* hath in your Habitation and through the point where the ſtring touches the *Meridian line* in the *Cieling*, ſhall a *line* be drawn at right *Angles* with the *Meridian*, to repreſent the *Equinoctial line*.

Thus in our Latitude the *Elevation* of the Equator being 38 ½ degrees ; I remove the ſtring faſtned to the *Nodus* forwards or backwards in the *Meridian line* of the *Cieling*, till the *Plumb-line* of the *Quadrant* on the *Clinatory*, when one of the ſides are applied to the ſtring, falls upon 38½ degrees, and then I find it touch the *Meridian line* at D in the *Cieling* ; therefore at D I make a mark, and through this mark ſtrike the *line* DE (as before I did in the *Meridian line*) to cut the *Meridian line* at right Angles: This *line* ſhall be the *Equinoctial line*, and ſerve to denote the Hour Diſtances, as the *Contingent* Lines does on other Dyals, as you have often ſeen.

Then I place the Center of the *Quadrant* on the *Clinatory* upon *Nodus*, ſo as the Arch of the *Quadrant* may be on the *Eaſt* ſide the *Meridian* Line, and underprop it ſo, that the flat ſide of the *Quadrant* may lie parallel to the ſtring, when it is ſtrained between the *Nodus* and the *Equinoctial*, and alſo ſo as the ſtring may lie on the Semi-diameter of the Quadrant, when it is held up to the Meridian Line on the Cieling. Then removing the ſtring the ſpace of 15 degrees in the Quadrant, and extending it to the *Equator* on the Cieling, where the ſtring touches the *Equator*, there ſhall be a point through which the I a Clock Hour-line ſhall be drawn : and removing the ſtring yet 15 degrees futher to the Eaſtwards in the Semi-Circle of Poſition, and extending it alſo to the *Equator*, where it touches the *Equator*, there ſhall be a point through which the II a Clock Hour-Line ſhall be drawn. Removing the ſtring yet 15 further to the Eaſtwards in the Semi-circle of Poſition, and extending it alſo to the *Equator*, where it touches the *Equator*, there ſhall be a point, through which the II a Clock Hour-line ſhall be drawn. Removing the ſtring yet 15 degrees further to the Eaſtwards in the Semi-circle of Poſition, and extending to the *Equator*; there ſhall be a point through which the III a Clock Hour-line ſhall be drawn: The like for all other Afternoon Hour lines. So oft as the ſtring is remov'd through 15 degrees on the Quadrant, ſo oft ſhall it point out the Afternoon diſtances in the Meridian line on the Cieling.

Having thus found out the points in the Equator through which the afternoon Hour-lines are to be drawn, I may find the Forenoon Hour-diſtances alſo the ſame way, *viz.* by removing the Arch of the Quadrant to the *Weſt*-ſide the Meridian, as before it was placed on the *Eaſt*, and bringing the ſtring to the ſeveral 15 degrees on the *Weſt*-ſide the Quadrant; or elſe I need only meaſure the diſtances of each Hours diſtance found in the Equator from the Meridian line on the Cieling; for the ſame number of the Hours from XII, have the ſame diſtance in the Equinoctial line on the other ſide the Meridian, both before and after-noon: The XI a Clock Hour diſtance is the ſame from the Meridian Line, with the I a Clock diſtance on the other ſide the Meridian; the X a Clock diſtance, the ſame with the II a Clock diſtance; the IX with the III, *&c.* And thus the diſtances of all the Hour lines are found out on the Equator.

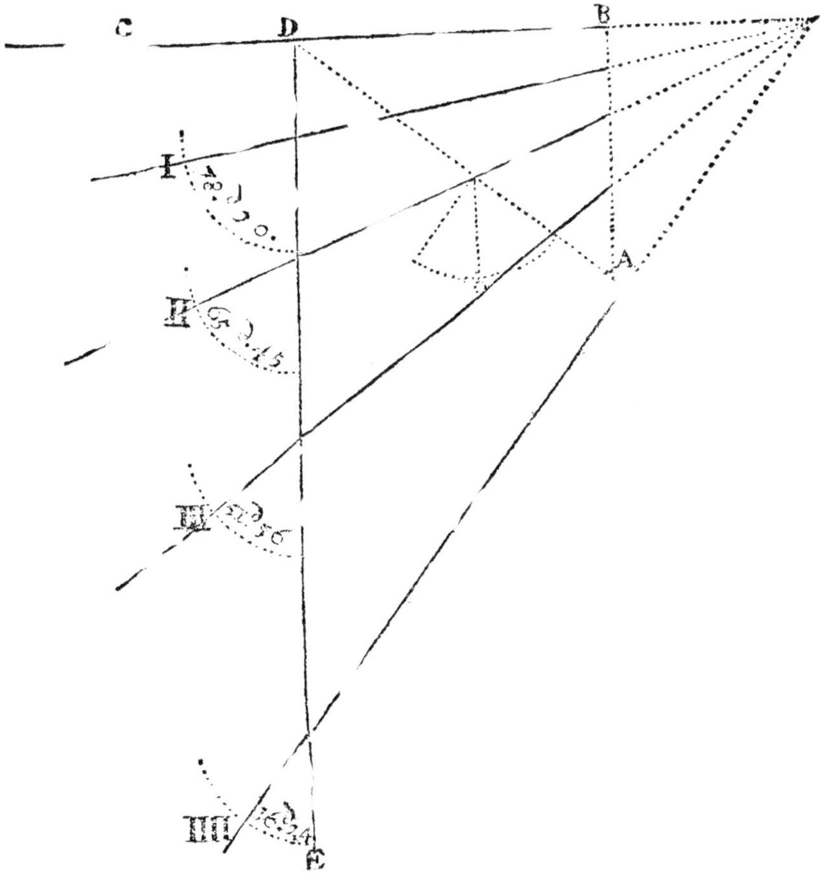

Now if the Center of this Dyal lay within doors, you might draw lines from the Center through these pricks in the Equator, and those lines should be the Hour lines, as in other Dyals: But the Center of this Dyal lies without doors in the Air, and therefore not convenient for this purpose: So that for drawing the Hour lines, you must consider what Angle every Hour line in a Horizontal Dyal makes with the Meridian; that is, at what distance in Degrees and Minutes the Hour lines of an Horizontal Dyal cut the Meridian; which you may examine, as by *Operat.* II. For

an

an Angle equal to the Complement of the ſame Angle, muſt each reſpective Hour line with the Equator on the Cieling have.

Thus upon the point markt for each Hours diſtance in the Equinoctial Line on the Cieling, I deſcribe the Arches I II, III, IV, as in the Figure, and finding the diſtance from the *Meridian* of the Hour Lines of an Horizontal Dyal to be according to *Operat.* II. Thus,

To	1	a Clock Hour-Line.	11.40	whoſe *Complement* to 90 is	78.20
	2		24.15		65.45
	3		38.14		51.56
	4		53 36		36.24

I meaſure in a Quadrant of the ſame Radius with thoſe Arches already drawn from the Equinoctial Line,

for the	1	a Clock Hour	78.30
	2		65.45
	3		51.56
	4		36.24

and transfer the diſtances to the Arches drawn on the Cieling: For then ſtraight lines drawn through the mark in the Arch, and through the mark in the Equator, and prolonged both ways to a convenient length, ſhall be the ſeveral Hours lines (aforeſaid ;) and when the Sun Shines upon the Glaſs at *Nodus* ; its Beames ſhall reflect upon the Hour of the Day.

Some Helps to a young Dyaliſt *for his more orderly and quick making of* Dyals.

IT may prove ſomewhat difficult to thoſe that are unpractiſed in Mathimatical projections, to divide

divide a Circle into 360 Degrees (or which is all one) a Semi-circle into 180 or a Quadrant into 90 Degrees; and though I have taught you in the projectioning the *Horizontal Dyal* the original way of doing this, yet you may do it a spedier way by a line of Cords, which if you will be curious in your Practise, you may make your self; or if you cacount it not worth your while, you may by it already made on Box or Brass of most Mathematical Instrument Makers. This Instrument is by them call a *Plain Scale* which does not only accommodate you with the divisions of a Quadrant, but also serves for a Ruler to draw straight lines with; the manner of making it is as follows.

Describe upon a smooth flat even grain'd Board a quarter of an whole Circle as BC, whose Radius A B or A C may be four Inches, if you intend to make large Dyals or two Inches, if small; but if you will you may have several lines of Chords on your *Scale* or *Rule*. Divide this Quadrant into 90 equal parts, as you were taught in the making the *Horizontal Dyal*

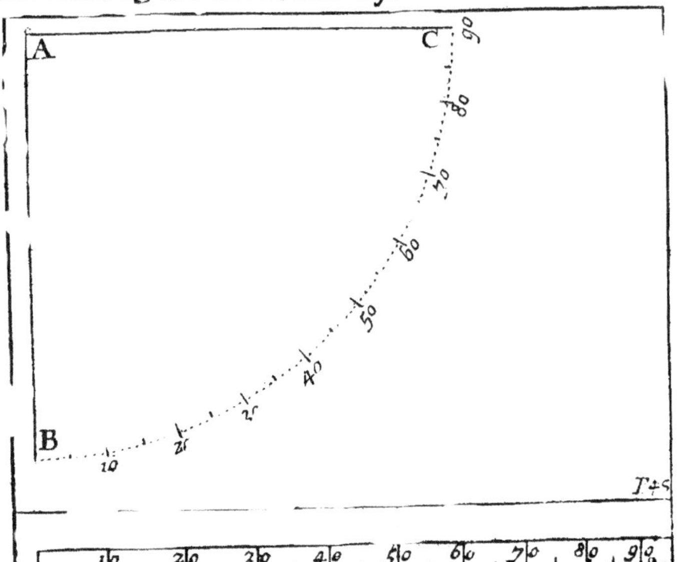

Then draw close by the edge of your straight Ruler a line parallel to the edge, and at about $\frac{1}{20}$ part of an Inch a second line parallel to that, and at about $\frac{1}{8}$ of an Inch a third line parallel to both. Then place one Foot of your Compasses at the beginning of the first degree on the Quadrant described on the Board, as at B, and open the other Foot to the end of the first degree, and transfer that distance upon your Rule, from B to the first mark or division, between the two first drawn lines. Then place one Foot of your Compasses again at the beginning of the first Degree on the Quadrant described on the Board, as at B, and open the other Foot to the end of the second Degree and transfer that distance upon your Rule from B to the second mark or division between the two first drawn Lines; and thus measure the distance of every Degree from the first Degree describe on the Quadrant, and transfer it to the Rule. But for distinction sake, you may draw every tenth division from the first line parallel to the edge of the third line, and mark them in succession from the beginning with 10, 20, 30, to 90. and the fifth Divisions you may draw half way between the second and the third parallel lines; the single Divisions only between the two first parallel lines. So is your lines of Chords made.

The use of the Line of Chords.

AS its use is very easie, so its convenience is very great; for placing one Foot of your Compasses at the first Division on the *Scale*, and opening the other to the 60th Degree, you may with the points of your Compasses (so extended) describe a Circle, and the several Divisions, on the *Scale* shall be the Degrees of the four Quadrants of of that Circle, as you may try by working backwards, to what you were just now taught in the making

making the *Scale*: For as before you meaſured the diſtance of the degrees of the Quadrant, and transfer'd them to the *Scale*, ſo now you only meaſure the Diviſions on the *Scale*, and transfer them to the Quadrant, Semi-circle, or whole Circle diſcribed on your Paper. For *Example*,

If you would meaſure 30 Degrees in your deſcribed Circle, place one Foot of your Compaſſes at the beginning of Diviſions on the *Scale*, as at A, and extend the other Foot to the Diviſions marked 30, and that diſtance transfer'd to the Circle, ſhall be the diſtance of 30 Degrees in that Circle. Do the like for any other number of Degrees.

You may draw your Dyal firſt on a large ſheet of Paper, if your Dyal Plane be ſo large; if it be not ſo large, draw it on a ſmaller piece of Paper; Then rub the back-ſide of your Paper Dyal with ſmall Coal, till it be well black't; and laying your Paper Dyal on your Dyal Plane, ſo that the Eaſt Weſt, North, or South lines of your Paper agree exactly with the Eaſt, Weſt, North or South ſcituation of your Dyal Plane; then with Wax or Pitch faſten the Corners of the Paper on the Plane, and laying a ſtraight Ruler on the Hour-lines of your Dyal, draw with the blunted point of a Needle by the ſide of the Ruler, and the Small-coal rub'd on the back ſide of the Paper will leave a mark of the lines on the Plane.

If you will have the lines drawn Red, you may rub the back ſide of your Paper with *Vermillion*; if blew with *Verditer*; if Yellow with *Orpiment*, &c. Then draw upon theſe marked Lines with Oyl Colours, as you pleaſe.

If your Dyal Decline far towards the East or West, the Hour Lines (unless projected to a very great lenght) will run very close to one another; therefore in this case you must project your Dyal

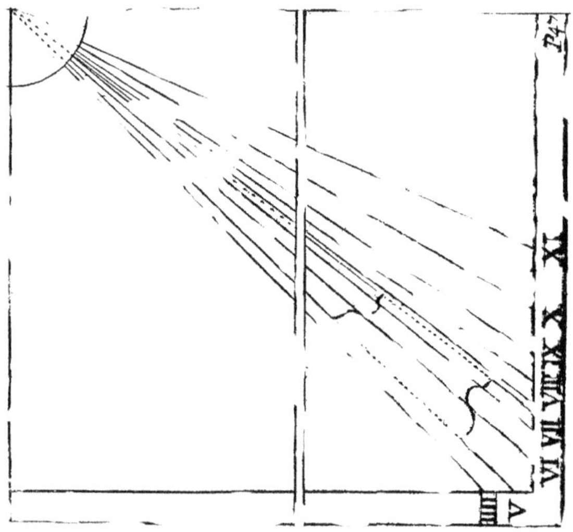

on a large Table, or sometimes on the Floor of a Room, and cut it off as far as you think good, from the Center; for the further from the Center, the larger the distance of the Hour-lines. *See the Figure.*

An Explanation of some Words of Art used in this.

A*Ngle.* The meeting or joyning of two Lines.

Arch. A part of a Circle.

Axis. The straight Line that runs through the Center of a Sphere, and both ways through the Circumference: though in *Dyalling* it is all one with the Diameter of a Circle.

Clinatory. See Fol. 8, 9, 10.

Chord. See Fol. 44, 45. 46.

Complement. The number that is wanting to make up another number 90 Degr. or 180 Degr. or 360 Degrees.

Con-

Contingent. A Line crossing the Substile at right Angles.

Degree. See Fol. 12.

Diameter. The longest straight Line that can be contained within a Circle, *viz.* the Line that passes through the Center to the Circumference both ways.

Dyal plane. See *Fol.* 7.

Elevation of the *Pole.* So many degrees as the *Pole* is elevated above the *Horizon.*

Equinoctial. The *Equinoctial* is a great Circle that runs evenly between the two *Poles* of the World. But when we name the *Equinoctial* in this Book, we mean a small Circle which represents it, and is the Circle or Arch of a Circle which is divided into equal parts, to find thereby the unequal parts on the *Line of Contingence.* In the *Horizontal Dyal* it is that Arch of a Circle marked GCH.

Horizon. Is a great Circle encompassing the place we stand upon; but in Dyalling it is represented by a straight Line, as in *Operat.* III. In the *South Dyal* the Line VI A VI is the *Horizontal Line.*

Latitude. The Latitude of a Place is the number of Degrees contained between the *Equinoctial* and the place inquired after.

Line of Contingence. See *Contingent.*

Magnetick Needle. The Needle touch'd with the *Loadstone,* to make it point to the North.

Meridian. Is a great Circle of Heaven passing thro' the North and South points of the *Horizon*; but in Dyalling it is represented by a straight *Line,* as in *Operat.* II. in the *Horizontal Dyal* the Line XII. A is a *Meridian line.*

Nadir. The point directly under our Feet.

Nautical Compass. Is the Compass used by *Navigators,* whereon is marked out all the 32 Winds or Points of the Compass.

Oblique

Oblique Plane. See *Fol.* 7.

Parallel. See *Fol.* 6.

Perpendiculer See *Fol.* 5.

Pole. The North or South Points on the Globe of the Earth, are called *North* or *South Pole.*

Quadrant. The fourth Part of a Circle.

Radius. Half the Diameter of a Circle.

Right Angle. A ſtraight *Line* that falls Perpendiculerly upon another ſtraight line, makes at the meeting of thoſe two *Lines* a Right Angle.

Semi-Circle. Half a Circle.

Semi-Diameter. The ſame *Radius* is.

Sphere. The higheſt Heaven with all its imagined Circle, is called the *Sphere.*

Stile. The *Gnomon* or Cock of a Dyal.

Subſtile. The line the Stile ſtands on upon a Dyal Plane.

Triangle. A Figure conſiſting of 3 Sides and 3 Angles.

Zenith. The point Directly over our Head.

FINIS.

Printed in Great Britain
by Amazon

11862884R00226